Inquiry in Music Education

Inquiry in Music Education provides an introduction to research and disciplined inquiry in music education. This textbook covers topic formulation, information literacy, reading and evaluating research studies, and planning and conducting original studies within accepted guidelines, based on research conventions in music, the other arts, education, and the humanities. Electronic search tools, hands-on assignments, supplementary teaching materials, and other resources are included on the companion website.

Skills in research and scholarship introduce students to the language and protocols by which to succeed in today's competitive market of grant writing, arts advocacy, and public outreach as a contributing member of the community of music educators.

Following the legacy begun by Rainbow and Froehlich in *Research in Music Education*, published in 1987, the objectives of this book are:

- To expand what is meant by music education and research;
- To help students find their niche in those definitions; and
- To teach tangible skills that are useful for music educators with diverse instructional goals and career aspirations.

Hildegard Froehlich is Professor Emeritus at the University of North Texas.

Carol Frierson-Campbell is Associate Professor at William Paterson University.

Inquiry in Music Education

Concepts and Methods for the Beginning Researcher

HILDEGARD FROEHLICH

CAROL FRIERSON-CAMPBELL

With contributions from
DEBBIE ROHWER
MARIE MCCARTHY
DARRYL COAN

Routledge
Taylor & Francis Group

NEW YORK AND LONDON

First published 2013
by Routledge
711 Third Avenue, New York, NY 10017

Simultaneously published in the UK
by Routledge
2 Park Square, Milton Park, Abingdon, Oxon OX14 4RN

Routledge is an imprint of the Taylor & Francis Group, an informa business

Library of Congress Cataloging in Publication Data
Froehlich, Hildegard C., author.
    Inquiry in music education : concepts and methods for the beginning researcher /
    Hildegard C. Froehlich, Carol Frierson-Campbell ; with contributions from Debbie Rohwer,
    Marie McCarthy, Darryl Coan. — New, revised edition.
       pages cm
    "New, revised edition of Rainbow, E.L., and Froehlich, H.C. (1987). Research in music education :
    an introduction to disciplined inquiry. Schirmer Books."—title page verso.
    Includes bibliographical references and index.
    1. Music—Instruction and study—Research. I. Frierson-Campbell, Carol, 1961– author.
    II. Rohwer, Debbie Ann, 1966– III. McCarthy, Marie, 1956– IV. Coan, Darryl A. V. Title.
    MT1.R26 2013
    780.71—dc23
    2012006926

ISBN: 978–0–415–89639–9 (hbk)
ISBN: 978–0–415–89640–5 (pbk)
ISBN: 978–0–203–80651–7 (ebk)

Typeset in Minion Pro
by Swales & Willis Ltd, Exeter, Devon

Printed and bound in the United States of America
by Edwards Brothers, Inc.

Hildegard Froehlich dedicates this book to Chuck Rainbow,
in memory of his father and her husband Ed Rainbow.

Carol Frierson-Campbell dedicates this book to ...
her students who taught her to teach,
her mother who taught her to sing,
and to Bob, who (still) makes her heart sing!

Contents

Unless noted otherwise, all chapters are jointly authored by Hildegard Froehlich and Carol Frierson-Campbell

Illustrations

Tables

Preface

Inquiry in Music Education: Concepts and Methods for the Beginning Researcher has its origins in a previous work; namely, *Research in Music Education: An Introduction to Disciplined Inquiry.* It was written by the same co-author Hildegard Froehlich along with Edward Rainbow and published in 1987 by Schirmer Books.

As excerpted from that Preface:

> This book is a reflection of our collective experiences in teaching research to both beginning and advanced graduate students. These experiences included introducing master's-level students to basic concepts of research, developing skills of critical analysis in doctoral students, and guiding doctoral candidates in dissertation work. In all these situations it appeared that the main problem in bringing research close to the students' minds was anchored in their diverse views of music education.
>
> For many, the content of music education consists of the methodologies and skills employed in teaching music to people from 5 to 18 years of age. For others, the content is found in the acquisition of knowledge about appropriate music and teaching literature. A third group tends to equate music education with any form of music teaching wherever it occurs—in schools, universities, church programs, camp activities, or private studies.

Because of the diverse goals most music education students have set for themselves, a research book in music education should have a two-fold aim: to train the future researcher and to make those who do not wish to conduct research comfortable with the role of disciplined thinking in music education. The book should be general and specific at the same time. (p. xiii)

Inquiry in Music Education attempts to follow the legacy begun by Rainbow and Froehlich, integrating the concept of research as disciplined inquiry into a description of the field of music education. The thought processes inherent in that inquiry are balanced with basic techniques for conducting research. In all instances, emphasis is placed on using specific questions to guide chosen methods and processes.

Purpose and Objectives

Since the publication of *Research in Music Education*, university requirements for research skills in music education have been re-shaped: Many master's degree programs have eliminated or cut back on thesis requirements, offering only a five-week summer research course to fulfill the requirements mandated for their degree. As a result, even some doctoral students enter degree programs without ever having undertaken an original research project.

In the *Coda* to the first edition, Rainbow and Froehlich (1987) stated: "Not all persons should be expected to become professional researchers any more than all music students should be expected to become professional musicians" (p. 281). We continue to subscribe to that statement, but also believe, as did Rainbow and Froehlich, that the field of music education needs critical readers with investigative skills that go beyond finding useful sources for writing term papers or completing required reading assignments.

Many graduate music students begin their respective degree programs questioning the usefulness of scholarly work in becoming better musicians and teachers. Skills in research and scholarship, however, should serve a larger purpose than simply commencing and completing one's master's or doctoral degree. They should introduce graduate students to the language and protocols by which to succeed in today's competitive market of grant writing, arts advocacy, and public outreach as a contributing member of the community of music educators. Mindful of this purpose, the objectives of *Inquiry in Music Education: Concepts and Methods for the Beginning Researcher* are fourfold:

1. Expand what we mean by music education and by research.
2. Help students find their niche in those definitions.
3. Teach tangible skills that are useful for music educators with diverse instructional goals and career aspirations.
4. Minimize the perception among most, if not all, music students that "research" is a foreign and possibly even unnecessary component in their career moves.

Approach

Accomplishing that task called for an even more student-centered approach than the previous work by Rainbow and Froehlich reflected. To accomplish that task we:

- use language and examples throughout the textbook that meet novice researchers at the place where they likely begin the process of doing research—in the classroom.
- utilize stories and examples from members of a fictitious introductory research class. Created from a combination of ethnographic research and informal experiences over many years of teaching research to music students in the United States, the stories are intended to illustrate the process of learning to do research from a variety of perspectives. Any resemblance to actual persons is unintentional.
- provide perspectives from a variety of experts in music education research; namely, our contributing authors Drs. Marie McCarthy (Chapter 6), Debbie Rohwer (Chapters 10–12), and Darryl Coan (web-based applications). We believe their voices bring additional depth to and expand the scope of the book beyond what two authors alone could have done. Their voices also demonstrate how form and content in various modes of inquiry might be reflected in a researcher's style, language, and tone of presentation.

Organization

The Introduction combined with Chapters 1–4, as well as the recommended reading and some written work, are intended to teach basic thought processes of research: Asking questions, accessing and reading appropriate literature, and examining such literature critically. Depending on the instructor's focus, these chapters could provide the major content of a quarter or semester course on an introduction to research in music education, followed by selected chapters about particular research methodologies (Chapter 5 for philosophical inquiries, Chapter 6 for historical work, Chapters 7 and 8 for qualitative research approaches, and Chapters 9–12 for quantitative designs). Chapter 13, dedicated to the use of research tools suitable in both quantitative and qualitative research approaches, is recommended for those students who want to "dig deeper." The same is true for Chapter 14: How to interpret and disseminate findings in the form of scholarly or general-interest papers and articles, grant proposals, and workshops.

To the Instructor

This book would be difficult to teach in its entirety in one course. The instructor, therefore, should make a judgment as to what to use. Some of the chapters are lengthy. In many instances, the subsections of a chapter were written in such a way that they would stand by themselves and allow for specific reading assignments of manageable proportions. The, at times, lengthy recommended reading lists at the end of each chapter should be viewed as an invitation to begin what should become the foundation of all research: Becoming familiar with important scholarship in the field. It is unreasonable for any or all of the recommendations to be assigned or made mandatory reading. Many of the sources are not only pertinent to the topic but also represent good examples of how to look at the usual in an unusual way.

It is customary for textbook writers to present a series of questions at the end of each chapter by which the material may be reviewed. We have found that these questions seldom meet the rules of a specific class since the students themselves usually generate better questions than the author. Second, the kind of questions being asked depends entirely on the focus the instructor has chosen for the overall course. Because the book seeks to be useful for a variety of teaching situations, we have listed a few topics from which questions might be developed. But even these topics are only suggestions. It is our opinion that the instructor should teach "around" the book, not "by" the book.

Acknowledgments

Indebted to our anonymous peers who critiqued the original manuscript and made constructive criticisms and contributions, we incorporated into the present version of the text many of their comments and suggestions. Any remaining errors and misrepresentations remain our responsibility. Some decisions had to be made to address the different needs of upper-level undergraduates, master's students, doctoral students, and possibly others. How comprehensive should the coverage be? How much in-depth? If we were to go further in-depth on certain topics, would it overwhelm those who would not use that information (and also inflate the price of the book)? If we omitted such concerns, would the book cease to be useful for more advanced instruction? Believing that research skills at every level develop on a continuum, we decided on a compromise between depth and breadth.

Special thanks are due to many colleagues and students—past and present—who used and critiqued preliminary drafts of the text, making many excellent points along the way. We also gratefully acknowledge Drs. Dale Bazan, Wayne Bowman, Richard Colwell, Susan Conkling, Terry Gates, Adria Hoffman, Kathryn Roulston, Craig Resta, and members of the William Paterson University Professional Writers Group for advice at various stages of the manuscript completion. A special acknowledgment is due to Brad Haefner for his expert assistance with all illustrations and to WPU student Malden Comanda for invaluable help with the final manuscript. We also recognize William Paterson University for granting Carol a sabbatical leave and Assigned Release Time. Routledge Senior Editor Constance Ditzel and Assistant Editor Denny Tek both deserve our most sincere thank you for their guidance and encouragement.

Research is an ongoing process and so is writing: This edition is not anymore "final" than one would consider the performance of a musical composition in recital to be the final product in one's career as a musician. As soon as one steps off the stage, thoughts about improving the next performance come up. So it is with this textbook: Plans for further work immediately arise.

Hildegard Froehlich and Carol Frierson-Campbell
January 2012

Introduction
Learning About the Book and Getting Involved

As its title suggests, the Introduction:

- States the book's objectives and its layout;
- Gets you started with the research process itself.

Involving yourself in the task of asking questions is unarguably one of the most important attributes of a good researcher. That task is aided by keenly observing what goes on around you and documenting those observations.

Purpose of the Book and Its Objectives

Conceptually derived from Rainbow and Froehlich's (1987) *Research in Music Education*, this textbook portrays scholarship in music education as an ongoing, inverted spiral of thinking, reading, observing, and publicly sharing the results of your efforts. Each activity is supported by the other. Similar to subsequent research books in music education (Phelps, Sadoff, Warburton & Ferrara, 2005; Phillips, 2007; Yarbrough, 2008), this book has two objectives:

1. Engaging music educators and other novice music education researchers in skills of:

   - Critical reading of research articles and books;

- Scholarly writing as a tool for professional communication;
- Basic skills for conducting research projects on the learning and teaching of music.

2. Responding to challenges not explicitly addressed by Rainbow and Froehlich:

- A variety of research approaches, methods, and designs that have emerged since the 1980s as accepted scholarship in educational and other disciplines.
- Technological advances through the Internet and e-publishing that have brought about an information explosion impacting all aspects of the research process.
- Increased expectations toward ongoing scholarly productivity among music education professionals at colleges and universities. Institutions like these now expect faculty in all disciplines to actively apply for external grants in order to fund institution-internal programs, student fellowships, and equipment, including musical instruments and electronic compositional devices.
- Basic skills in professional writing, research, and scholarship required far beyond the completion of the master's or doctoral degree. Research and scholarship in the arts have become important communicative tools by which to succeed in today's competitive market, and otherwise reach out to the public.
- Ethical concerns and laws for the protection of privacy that have made the application process for research grants and projects of any kind very stringent.

We retain Rainbow and Froehlich's description of the characteristics and skills that define a scholarly mindset:

- Having a basic inquisitiveness and intellectual curiosity about the learning and teaching processes wherever they occur.
- Turning basic curiosity into detailed questions, and addressing them in appropriate ways.
- Being aware of and open to creative thoughts and ideas in fields other than one's own.
- Thinking about and systematically planning approaches and perspectives by which to study an issue.
- Sharing (in the written word, in public speaking, or in both) newly discovered insights with members of the field.

The shorter version of those characteristics is: (1) asking questions; (2) turning any one of them into a finite research purpose; (3) applying specific methods of data gathering and analysis to your purpose; and (4) reporting the findings through speech and publication. These activities are what the spiral of inquiry portrays: think, read, observe, share, and think again—in any order. It is a short description for a lifelong process.

When registering for an introductory research class at the graduate level, many students tend to doubt that research is "for them." Far more pressing matters—practicing their instruments, playing in or conducting ensembles, and "having a life"—occupy their minds and time. Perhaps you feel similarly. But because of your general sense of curiosity and interest in your chosen career path, you likely will soon discover the excitement inherent in learning how researchers in the field of music, education, music education, and many other fields have addressed important questions about learning and teaching. Learning to do research connects you with those researchers as your future peers. This, at least, is the hope that guides the purpose of this book.

In this textbook, you will be led in a sequential and hands-on way through the entirety of several possible research approaches, progressing from formulating questions about your own professional ideas and experiences to the production of a research proposal (and perhaps even a study) in which you know how to choose appropriate tools for addressing a wide variety of research questions. The field of music education subsumes many different occupations and research perspectives and therefore offers also many choices for you to proceed as a future scholar.

Exploration: A Round Table Discussion

1. Why have you enrolled in this class?
2. How much do you know about research?
3. What are your plans after graduation?
4. What has been your greatest experience as a Musician? Teacher? Student?

An Excursion Into Cyberspace: Considering Perspective

Earthcam, an Internet "webcam" that overlooks New York City's Times Square, enables Internet viewers to zoom the lens in and out to get different real-time views of this famous setting. The camera can be accessed by going to http://www.earthcam.com and choosing the Times Square camera.

With the lens zoomed in, you see only one person or car but get a lot of detailed information about that one person or vehicle. It is a perspective that does not allow for easy comparisons. With the lens zoomed out, you give up detail for getting "the bigger picture," allowing you to see many more people and objects, thereby gaining in numbers but losing in detail.

The lesson to be learned from this example is this: Perspective impacts on what you see. When you take an overview, you miss details; when you zoom in on details, their place in the larger scheme of things gets lost. So it is with research: Taking a macro perspective of the learning and teaching of music can obscure the details of how individual learners learn or how particular teachers teach. The opposite is true as well: Being concerned with a micro view of the teaching–learning process in music can prevent you from seeing how your own actions or that of a few colleagues fit into the bigger picture of music education as it is practiced in the country or even the world.

Now imagine that you decided to devote an entire semester to a study of Times Square. What would it take to expand the webcam observations into an extended project that would interest a music educator? The best and fastest way to start any observation project would be to ask "who, what, where, when, why, and how." Given your interest in music performance and teaching, focus first on music-related questions:

- *Who* are the musicians that work in Times Square?
- *How* do they find employment?
- *What* music do they play?
- *Where* do Times Square musicians get their training?
- *When* did Times Square become an icon of U.S. popular culture?
- *How* has the music performed in Times Square changed over time?
- *How well* does Times Square music represent the music across the United States?
- *Why* is Times Square so famous?
- *Why* is Times Square so commercial?

Any one of these questions catapults you into a myriad further questions by which to try to answer the first one. To illustrate, let us take the question about Times Square seemingly being so commercial. Before seeking answers to that question, however, consider why you might ask the question in the first place? Two possibilities come to mind. One, as a classically trained performer, you find the commercialism of Times Square unnerving and view the glamour associated with it as a cultural centerpiece overstated. Your intent is to document this point of view by identifying what you consider to be the most flagrantly commercial characteristics of Times Square. Two, as a budding entrepreneur, you are interested in making Times Square a model for other cities. You look to replicate in your home town what you consider the main reasons for Times Square's success as a tourist attraction: Its buzzing commercialism.

What would you need to do to take either of these two scenarios and derive questions from them that instigate the need for research? In both cases, you would need to clearly define the term "commercial" as it relates to your questions. Only once that is accomplished can you look for and catalogue the characteristics mentioned in any definition of "commercialism." Such cataloguing however triggers new questions:

- When would the observations take place?
- Do all observations address the criteria of the term "commercial" as originally formulated? Are there some that do not? If so, what needs to be done to account for those things that confound the issue—things that are not readily observable but likely present?
- How could you set up the observations to assure agreement among several observers? Where might disagreement occur, and why might it exist?

After all observations are collected, catalogued, and analyzed, equating the music lover's findings to those compiled by the entrepreneur would be like comparing apples and oranges. Therefore, good scholarship mandates that perspectives chosen and actions taken be articulated, justified, and documented. This means to (1) state reasons for asking specific questions before making particular observations, (2) define key terms in a question, and (3) document each and every step taken in zooming in on certain details, thereby zooming out of others.

Exploration: A Writing Exercise

For the purpose of comparing what you and your classmates saw when engaging in the webcam exercise, select *one* of the three tasks as your first writing exercise:

1. Put into words what you see with the lens zoomed in. Make your description as detailed as possible and document the time of day when you made this observation. Write your observations down and share them with your classmates.
2. Look for and discuss agreements and disagreements between your descriptions and those of your classmates.
3. Given who you are and what you do, create your own questions for a *Times Square Observation Study* or a comparable study in your own neighborhood. Then carry this one step forward and apply it to what you do professionally or as a student.

Viewing Music Education from a Personal Angle

Earthcam allowed you to zoom in and out of a geographical location to obtain either a bird's eye view of its overall character or obtain details about specific buildings, roads, street corners. A similar process can be applied to examining yourself with the above "who, what, where, when, why and how" questions: How have you become who you believe you are? What events, persons, and experiences have contributed to where you stand on an issue at any given time? When and where did those events shape your own private and professional self the most?

Comparing your answers and life story to that of others around you, it probably comes as no surprise that each biography is unique. Variances in life styles, acquired knowledge and skills, upbringing, age, race, nationality, gender, and other factors too many to list here contribute to how you see the world and yourself in it. Call it your worldview—the source for and reason why answers to "who, what, where, when, why, and how" questions differ from person to person and groups to groups. A good researcher becomes aware of those differences and accounts for them in the way answers to any given questions come about. To illustrate, we begin with you and other students (un)like you.

Other Students (Un)Like You

Who you are impacts not only the topics you are interested in but also on *how* you approach their study. Take, for instance, *Carlos, Chi-Hui, Christy, Dale, Greg, Jeannette, Juan, Keisha, Liam, Marguerite, Michelle,* and *Muna,* students in a research class (RC 533) like the one you are enrolled in. Their instructor was Professor Edwards (known to most students as Prof. E.), an experienced college teacher and researcher with ten years of public school and seven years of college teaching experience.

Prof. E allowed his students the freedom to explore many different topics before settling in on any one project. Responding to the fact that each adult learner brings to the class unique life experiences, varying personal and professional histories, motivations, and aspirations, Prof. E.'s instructional plans included a high degree of individualization of class assignments and projects.

Carlos pursued an MME degree during the summers. Teaching band and choir in a small rural high school in the Midwest, he looked for particular hi-tech aids for teaching general musicianship skills, such as composing and music analysis/theory, to his ensembles. He expected to find those tools while taking the research class.

Chi-Hui, a last semester Senior in music education, received special permission to enroll in the research class because of her intention of continuing with her master's degree at the same university. She was already certified as an elementary music teacher in Taiwan, with two years of teaching experience to her credit. Fearing that what she learned in the U.S. might not be applicable to what was going on back home, she occasionally expressed that concern to her peers. She pursued the U.S. degree believing it would open doors for her at home.

Christy pursued a Ph.D. in performance with music education as a related field. She was an experienced private studio violin teacher who freelanced at night. She came back to school because she felt her life to be in a rut. Always a challenge seeker, she wanted to get excited about research but was hesitant about thinking about teaching in new ways.

Dale, a Ph.D. student in music education with a background as a teacher of jazz, rock 'n' roll and concert band ensembles, also played the guitar and composed music for his home band. His master's thesis, completed a year earlier, involved a survey of all of his band students and their parents about their views concerning scheduling, trips, uniforms, and instructional content. Valuing the expertise gained by doing that study, he now was motivated to expand that knowledge. But he was a bit impatient about the "hoops" of the degree program that at times seem unrelated to his own interests.

Greg was in the early stage of the Ph.D. program in music education after nearly 15 years of teaching strings in the Midwest and after a divorce had upset his life goals. He came back to school to get away from his "former life." Still somewhat unclear as to the purpose of the degree in his career plans, the idea of teaching at college level appealed to him. He was concerned, however, about the cut in pay he would likely face as a beginning college instructor.

Jeannette, a Ph.D. student in music education with a minor in education administration, was also a seasoned choir director who continued to conduct a very successful church choir in her own community. She also had some teaching awards to her credit and was highly motivated to do her doctoral research. Because of her teaching experience, she had developed a particular interest in the education of minority students and has learned in her education classes about the construct of cultural mistrust. She actively tried to direct each and every assignment in any of her courses toward that interest.

Juan, pursuing a Master of Music (MM) with conducting as his major field, was a high school band director with three years of teaching experience. His primary objective for his degree was to improve his performance and conducting skills. Although he found the courses for the degree valuable, he sometimes felt that they did not really tell him what it took to become a better-applied teacher–conductor. A good student academically, he mostly focused on finding conducting opportunities and on score study in the listening library.

Keisha, an MM student with aspirations of getting a Ph.D. later, was an elementary general music teacher with 10 years of experience and on leave from her school. She was interested in issues concerning child development with special emphasis on early childhood. Holding endorsements by Kodaly, Gordon, and Orff Associations, she was married and had two small children.

Liam, an MM jazz studies major who worked on the side as a jingle singer in a recording studio, was interested in scat singing and liked to listen to such artists as Louis Armstrong, Ella Fitzgerald, Sara Vaughn, and Billie Holiday. Liam was especially intrigued by what he considered Armstrong's invention of scat singing and was excited about the research class because he planned to document Armstrong's leadership role in the development of scat singing.

Marguerite came to the field of music education later in her life. With a master's degree in music education and a bachelor's in English to her credit, she had developed an interest in philosophy and the arts in general and wanted to pursue a Ph.D. with emphasis in those areas. A quiet, yet inquisitive person, she preferred writing to talking. She thought a great deal about music making and learning outside of the confines of school and had already started seeking reading sources on that subject prior to taking the research class.

Michelle pursued a Master of Music Education degree (MME). With more than 20 years of experience teaching music in the inner city, she had learned how to reach students through a varied, yet sequentially structured, well-balanced music program in a nurturing way. School reform efforts, however, mandated by the state and focusing on raising standardized test scores to the detriment of the "related arts" (music, art, and drama) had upset her greatly for obvious reasons: They required her, by circumstances not of her own making, to change what had worked for her. She therefore prepared next for a college career to become what she termed "a major decision maker in the field." Aware that research skills were essential in such a career move, she clearly was motivated to take the class.

Muna, seeking an MM degree in performance with music education as a related field, did not have any teaching experience other than her student teaching as an undergraduate. She had disliked that experience and therefore opted to major in voice with music education as her related field of study. She hoped to pursue an opera career but her parents had insisted that she continue her music education studies as well. She definitely preferred practicing over book work.

Is there any person in RC 533 with whom you identify more closely than others in that class? If so, what are the commonalities? Asked differently, what do you bring to the research process in terms of your own biography, professional background, and life experiences that could impact your work as a teacher? Write down your answer(s) and keep what you write; you might need it later.

The Research Process Personalized

Once or twice a month during class time, it was Prof. E.'s practice to meet with his students in a coffee shop on campus. Known as "coffee talk" among the students, its purpose was to allow them to share their plans for the future in a setting less formal than the classroom. Some students might talk about how they hoped to put those plans into reality while others preferred to point out what might stand in their way. At times, the conversations centered on similarities and differences between expectations for a musician, a teacher/educator, and a researcher. Usually, however, the students talked more about parallels between what it meant to make music and to teach than on the place of research in a music educator's life. The subject of "research" only came up when prompted by Prof. E. A patient man, he knew that the students would need time to accept research and scholarship as important complements to becoming well-informed musicians and teachers.

Similar to what it has taken you to become a fine musician and a successful teacher, adding scholarship to your professional skills takes ongoing and engaged practice, much patience, a good dose of self-discipline, imagination and creativity, and a zest for wanting to be the best you can be. Once you couple those characteristics with an inquisitive mind, you have the ingredients that make a musician–teacher–scholar/researcher. An inquisitive mind of that caliber not only asks questions but also tries to answer them. Both the asking of questions and efforts to answer them are learned skills. They consist of reading, documenting your reading, examining evidence in support of specific answers in a variety of ways, and sharing those answers with others.

Throughout the book, the process is visualized as a spiral of ever more focused inquiries and actions. Figure 0.1 shows that spiral in its most basic form, suggesting that research should begin with your own professionally pressing concerns and experiences. They, in turn, undergo a continuing regime of thinking, reading, observing, and sharing with others (ultimately in writing) what it is that you have thought, read, and observed and whether and how it all fits together.

Each of us engages daily in the activities of thinking, reading, observing, and sharing—the latter in conversation or when writing; but we may not always knowingly combine all four actions for the purpose of addressing a specific research problem or question. This is because as teachers we are held to respond through immediate actions to

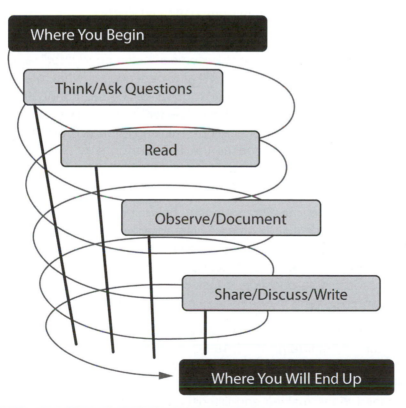

FIGURE 0.1   The Spiral of Inquiry in Its Most Basic Form

what we see, hear, or otherwise experience around us. We generally do not have the time to reflect on the experiences themselves as springboards for examining ourselves, how and why things are done the way they are, or questioning what lies behind those experiences. Research, however, allows us to do just that.

Actively engaging in the scholarly process undoubtedly takes you out of the relative comfort zone of the practice room, the studio, or the rehearsal hall into the perhaps less familiar environments of the university library (be it in person or via Internet), the computer lab, or a bona fide research lab (if your school or department has such a space). You may also spend more time than usual with your peers discussing and examining accepted traditions of teaching, and you may begin to test old assumptions or new ideas about how you think learning might take place. Furthermore, extra time may be dedicated to documenting your own thinking on particular topics and, eventually, to planning out a research study of your own. In addition to time, however, you also need perspective about yourself as a musician–teacher as well as musician–performer, how you see the field of music education, and what has traditionally been done in the name of research and scholarship. Finally, as in studio class, be ready to accept criticism from others for the purpose of improving your own work.

Developing a Scholarly Mind

What follows are three student examples from RC 533 about the connection between disciplined inquiry and thinking, reading, observing, and sharing.

Juan's expressed interest in wanting to become a "better conductor" required a definition of what he meant by "better." What experiences or what role models did he have in mind that suggested what a "good" or "better" conductor–band director was? How well did his definition of "better" fit with other definitions in the world of music and/or music education? Thinking through those questions, it became inevitable for him to consult the literature on how the term "good conducting" was used, if not defined. The combination of thinking, talking to experts, and reading launched Juan's work for the semester.

Christy—no stranger to the library—spent hours browsing through string method books to document and compare different approaches with each other. She did this to get a sense of how her own teaching differed from or was similar to methods "out there." She hoped that such documentation would help her in identifying a researchable question, a task she hesitated to execute because she did not want to commit to one finite question too soon.

Marguerite's interest in outside-of-school learning processes had led her to the work of Christopher Small (e.g., 1977, 1998a, 1998b) prior to any assigned class readings. She had taken a particular liking to his term "musicking" (with a "k" purposefully inserted by Small) because the invented gerund suggested being actively engaged in the making and listening of music rather than in learning

---

about music as a seeming bystander or non-participant. She took to using the term loosely until some of her friends challenged her to articulate why it was a necessary addition to her own vocabulary and that of the profession. When she began pondering that challenge, she thought about studying situations in which students controlled their own musical learning. Perhaps she would observe students in action—she wondered how to go about gaining permission to do so. She also located and examined publications that described in some detail so-called community music processes and what has become known in music education as informal learning among teenagers and young adults. She began wondering about the term informal learning itself and began to realize how many questions could be articulated from just one area of concern.

Driven by personal inquisitiveness at first, each of the three students directed their thinking and reading activities on different issues and zoomed in on them in ways unique to their own perspective of what was important to them individually. However, each of them also connected their personal perspective to the thinking and work by others in music education and related fields.

Because you are now asked to embark on a similar journey as the students in RC 533, be reminded that a researcher and scholar not only thinks about professional interests and concerns but also addresses them in the larger context of the field of music education itself. Taking that step requires discipline and resolve. Just as making music without practicing takes you nowhere fast, simply being inquisitive without having the research discipline to examine what you are inquisitive about can easily become stale rhetoric.

Thinking About Areas of Professional Concern

Undoubtedly, there have been moments in your professional life when you wondered in exasperation why your students reacted in seemingly unpredictable ways and "just did not get it." Indeed, "When will they ever learn?" or "Isn't there anything that interests them?" has been voiced aloud in many faculty lounges. You may also have said to yourself at times: "If I only had more time, I would like to learn . . ." or "I would love to know why my colleagues/my boss/my students/my students' parents react that way."

The scholarly process described in this textbook offers you a chance to respond to any of those questions in a productive and proactive way. You turn general expressions of exasperation or curiosity into articulated *areas of concern* by:

- Recalling situations in which you sighed in frustration or got excited about good things happening;
- Describing the situations with many active verbs;
- Turning your descriptions into actual questions.

Recalling and Describing Teaching and Learning Situations or Moments

The more vividly you can recall critical teaching situations in your recent past and describe them, the more specific any follow-up work can become. If you have not had any professional teaching experience, think of moments where you (as a student) said to yourself, "If I were the teacher, I would do it differently." What is the "it" in this statement and what did the teacher do that prompted you to wanting change?

When you describe those moments, use truly *descriptive* rather than *judgmental* terms. For instance, saying that Teacher X is an *efficient* or even *great* teacher delivers a judgment rather than a description of that teacher's actions. What does Teacher X say, do, or stand for that warrants the interpretation of efficient or great teaching? Does Teacher X always engage everyone during rehearsal? Are her lectures full of real-life examples? Does she know all students by name? Allow for unsolicited questions? Have a recognizable instructional plan—visible for all to see? Summarize the content of the lesson at the end together with instructions for what she expects of the students for the next lesson? Grade fairly? With all of these attributes present, the conclusion might be that "great" is an apt summary of Teacher X's instructional style. However, missing in this assessment would still be how the students themselves assess her teaching: Do all of them feel equally spoken to? Do they understand the points Teacher X wanted to make and were the students able to recall them as a result of the lesson? Clearly, much descriptive evidence is needed before a statement about "great teaching" is more than an assertion. This means that questions, too, should be descriptive rather than judgmental.

Turning Recalled Situations Into Actual Questions

Greg brought up a question many teachers ask: "Why are some of my students not motivated?" Further examination, however, revealed his question to be a lament: "Some of my students are not motivated!" Prof. E. asked Greg to re-word his lament into a question that could be answered by focusing on what the students exhibited that suggested a lack of motivation. Aided by others in class, Greg came up with this list:

- Did all students labeled as "not motivated" exhibit like behaviors and actions?
- Did the absence of such behaviors and actions in other students suggest that they were, indeed, motivated?
- When did students act in the way that Greg attributed to a lack of motivation?
- What do other teachers and writers mean by motivation and are they in agreement with each other?
- How—in various teachers' minds—do motivated students behave?

Greg now had posed "real" (i.e., non-rhetorical) questions that asked for "real" (i.e., information-providing) responses.

Chi-Hui chose to focus on the differences between her experiences in Taiwan and the United States because they impacted on her the most in a personal way as a performer and musician. She therefore came up first with "Why are things so different in the U.S. from how they are in Taiwan?" but soon turned that question into "How does the music teacher training in Taiwan differ from that in the United States?" and "Who determines teacher training curricula in both countries?"

Muna and *Christy* found it difficult to turn real-life experiences into truly descriptive rather than judgmental questions because both had a strong sense of right and wrong. Muna had only taught a little bit during her pre-service experiences and had disliked the experience. Christy, on the other hand, was a long-time studio teacher who had highly developed instructional routines that she did not feel needed questioning. Although coming from very different vantage points, both students needed some extra time for thinking and browsing in the library before they managed to turn their somewhat emotional sentiments into specific questions. Prompted by Prof. E., Muna came up with these questions: "Were all moments of my experience equally negative?" "Which ones caused me the greatest anxiety and why?" "Were there any moments I enjoyed?" "If so, what were they? Did they happen only once or twice or regularly enough that I had something to look forward to?"

Christy began to ask herself: "What were my routines? Did they work equally well for all of my students?" "To what extent does my own teaching approach resemble that of my teacher?" "Were there routines imposed on me by my teacher? If I disliked them then, have I changed them in my own studio routines?" "How do I know that they work(ed)?"

Whether you think of yourself more as a student or more as a teacher, your own questions, too, should articulate moments that bothered or pleased you. When you write them down, describe those moments in active verbs without using judgmental words. For instance, instead of saying that something or someone was really good, happy, or successful, describe actions you saw that were "good," "happy," or "successful." Once you have done that, turn those descriptions into "why–what–how–when" questions and share them with your classmates. Then you are on your way to becoming a researcher.

But actions are not the only source of "why–what–how–when" questions; words are, too. If, for instance, you find that thoughts you read contradict each other or that two historical accounts of the same event describe different occurrences, you have reason to examine why differences exist, what caused two authors to focus on different events, and how or whether the differences have a bearing on current practices in thought and/or action.

Outlook for What Is to Come

This chapter has introduced you to two premises that permeate the research process in general: (1) The way you look at objects, actions, experiences, and ideas tend to influence what you focus on and ask questions about; and (2) the experiences that made you into the professional who you are or want to become, also contribute to defining your researcher-self. Both themes reappear throughout the book because they have an effect on everything else that follows.

Like the two themes, two metaphors will resurface as well: The metaphor of the spiral of inquiry visualized above, and the image of research as a journey with markers that guide the way. The markers are the steps you take from the initial literature search to the writing of a proposal (and possibly an entire study). The steps are reflected by the book chapters, divided into two parts.

Part I (Chapters 1–4) takes you from identifying several areas of concern to exploring a number of research ideas from which a research topic gets selected for detailed study. You learn to turn the topic into a purpose statement and are guided in how to reason out why—in the light of extant literature—your research purpose is important for you to examine and for the profession to know about.

The second part of the book (Chapters 5–12) is organized according to what is referred to as modes of inquiry: The philosophical mode (Chapter 5), defined as the study of *ideas, past and present*; the historical mode (Chapter 6) as the study of *past events, documented actions, behaviors, and experiences*; and the empirical mode (Chapters 7 through 12) as the study of *present events, actions, behaviors, and experiences*. How those events, actions, behaviors, and experiences are expressed, documented, and analyzed as *data* determine whether a study might be called qualitative (Chapters 7 and 8) or quantitative (Chapters 9–12). *Mixed approaches* would combine aspects of all modes with each other. This is why Chapter 13 offers guidelines for constructing *data gathering tools* that may prove useful across all modes of inquiry.

Chapter 14 addresses what often is called "the so what" factor of research: What do your findings have to do with the questions you asked in the first place and with the body of knowledge of music education in general? The chapter directs you in interpreting and writing up research findings for the summary chapter of theses and dissertations and explains how to use that information to prepare poster and paper presentations, articles suitable for peer-reviewed journals, or grant proposals. A Recapitulation reiterates what we consider the most important and recurring themes throughout the entire book and concludes with what we hope marks an exciting beginning in your own career as musician–educator–researcher/scholar.

At the time Rainbow and Froehlich published their 1987 edition, the World Wide Web did not exist. The primary computerized research tools for most investigators were dissertation and journal catalogues on compact disc. Additionally, some libraries offered catalogue access via direct dial-in for users who owned the requisite technology. Since the advent of the Web, the amount of searchable information has increased profoundly.

Researchers now access online journals, self-published works, massive databases of full articles and a host of tools for investigation and statistical analysis.

This book attends to these advances and helps with explanations but where there is plenty, there is also much waste. The Internet is no exception—as valuable it can be with its many search engines. Inaccurate information, questionable sources, and plagiarism require you to be a skeptic first and trusting reader second. This book therefore seeks to offer guidance for responsible travel not only on the information highway but in the entirety of the research process.

Chapter Summary

1. Key elements in good scholarship are tangible and concrete. They range from inquisitiveness and intellectual curiosity to such specific skills as thinking, reading, observing, and publicly sharing the results of such activities. Basic curiosity turns into detailed questions that are addressed by appropriate methods communicated in ways that other researchers accept as good scholarship.
2. Metaphors of the webcam and markers on a lifelong journey can be useful in describing fundamental aspects of research in a field that is diverse and broad-based.
3. Who a researcher is or wishes to become enters prominently into the scholarly process itself. The approaches vary due to the professional allegiances a researcher wishes to hone. This means that decisions vary from person to person as to when and how to (a) zoom in on certain aspects concerning the learning and teaching of music, and (b) omit others.
4. Personal and professional aspirations go hand in hand. Both dimensions therefore need to be considered when developing research skills as an added dimension to the professional person one aspires to be.

Topics for Further Exploration

1. Reflecting back on your Times Square observations and those of your classmates:

   a. How similar were the times and dates that each of you observed?
   b. How closely did you agree with each other on what you saw? Did observations done at the same time show greater agreement?
   c. What could be seen with the lens zoomed in that you could not detect with the lens zoomed out? Is the opposite also the case; that is, are there details you can pick up with the lens zoomed in that you missed when it was zoomed out?
   d. How alike were your observations to those of your classmates? Would you say that you agreed 100%, 75%, 50%, or less? Where were the greatest differences or similarities? What reasons might you suggest as causing either?

e. What is your impression of Times Square based on your observations and those of your peers? How accurate or representative of Times Square as you know it are your collected observations? In other words, can you trust your findings? If so, why? If not, why not?

   i. How might the observations be different if you did them at 9:00 am? 2:00 pm? On December 31?

   ii. If you were to select a few of the observed pedestrians for a casual interview, what kind of questions could or would you ask them about their sense of commercialism in Times Square?

2. Consider the following situation and discuss with each other:

> For a reading assignment in RC 533, *Prof. E.* had planned to lead the students in a discussion of what they had learned from reading a particular study on the effectiveness of two methods of teaching sight singing skills to 8th graders. The first response came from *Greg* who, seemingly angry and somewhat aggressive, stated: "I don't buy that!" Prof. E., believing in the importance of letting students speak their minds, responded with "What do you mean, you don't buy that? I mean, somebody did this study, and they found this. How can you . . . I mean, you can . . ." Greg replied by reiterating what he had said before: "I don't believe in those methods. I use a different approach and know that it works. This study was a waste of time."

Taking Prof. E.'s role, how would you continue the conversation with Greg and the rest of the students? What is your personal position on the subject of the value of research vs. personal teaching experience in music education?

3. Two Games—Choose one!

a. *An Association Game.* In class, or perhaps afterward, ask a few musician–educator colleagues for five words that describe an inquisitive mind and five words that describe a research mind. Collect the responses and write them down in two columns. Analyze your findings and consider the meaning of your collective responses concerning both terms.

b. *Bombardment, or "Throw-the-Question-and-See-if-it-Sticks."* As a group decide on a particular concern and bombard it with questions. Take, for instance, sight reading: Divide the entire group into two teams and see who can come up with the most questions in a specified and agree-upon time frame. We give you a few as start-up:

   ■ What *is* sight reading? What is its purpose?
   ■ Who benefits from it the most?

- Why is it important?
- Who has written about it? Researched it?

Note: Questions asked by both groups do not count in the final tally.

4. Sharpening Your Questioning Skills

Select a few questions from those you have identified as "real" ones and contrast them to pseudo-questions that:

- expect no answer;
- cannot be answered;
- have an answer already known to the questioner.

part one
Entering the World of Questioning

The first four chapters of this textbook are directed at the reader who is about to become a researcher. The chapters describe the search on which "re"-search depends—the "looking again" that is so essential to the spiral of inquiry mentioned in the Introduction. Chapter 1 asks you to apply "who, what, where, when, why, or how" questions to issues that concern you as a music teacher, a student, or both. Chapter 2 describes early steps in finding, analyzing, and selecting pertinent scholarly literature relevant to such concerns. Chapter 3 places those readings into the larger picture of music education as a broad field of many occupations and professional practices. It is the context needed for Chapter 4, in which you get more deeply involved in the process of critical reading and learn to formulate research questions that are succinct enough to guide all subsequent research decisions.

one

The Spiral and Modes of Inquiry

Options, Choices, and Initial Decisions

This chapter describes how your research journey might begin:

- Thinking about professional concerns in the larger context of music teaching and learning;
- Filtering one concern out of several by cursory and reflective reading.

The chapter puts into scholarly perspective what likely originated in personal experience and casual observation. Employing both cursory and reflective reading skills, you learn to look for specific characteristics in a variety of publications.

Introduction

The research journey begins with accepting that "who, what, where, when, why, and how" questions relative to areas of concern are not always easily answered by simply looking them up on the Internet or by asking experts in the field. Second, hardly any answer remains the same once and for all. This is why the "think–read–observe–share" cycle is ongoing: Thinking leads to observing or reading, which may lead to the possible modification of once accepted answers; or reading leads to observations that may make you question previous assumptions or thoughts. Finally, sharing your insights with peers, colleagues and—possibly—the public at large may trigger responses that cause yet more thinking, reading, and observing on your part.

The quest is characterized by exploring and articulating ("framing") researchable questions from which you select any one for further examination. The activities become the filters by which you work toward the goal of selecting a purpose upon which a complete study can be built. You may visualize it as shown in Figure 1.1.

Notice that the illustration actually contains two cone images—one inverted, the other upright—that relate to each other. Its purpose is to point out that when you engage in thinking, reading, observing, and sharing with increasing specificity, your knowledge base about the field broadens; one cannot happen without the other. Early in the filtering process, you may be inclined to spend much time on thinking/reading, less on observing/sharing (preferably in writing) your thoughts and findings with your peers. Ideally,

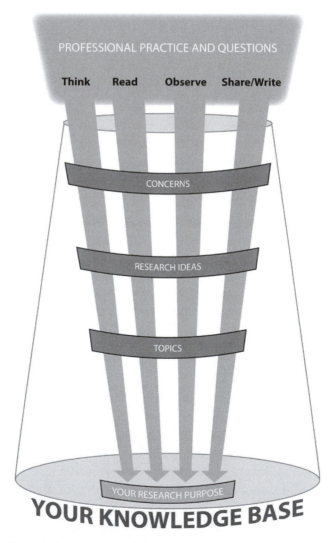

FIGURE 1.1   The Search Process Visualized

however, you should move back and forth between all four activities long before you have fully finalized your plans for executing an actual research project.

Do not be surprised if the spiraling process does not unfold as neatly as visualized in our "textbook description." In fact, at times, you may feel as if the reading and thinking goes in circles, that is, nowhere. This is the proverbial brick wall all scholars run into occasionally, an experience you also know from practicing your instrument. Be assured that moments like that actually may be signs of progress. In the process of exploring, framing, and selecting ideas and topics, uncertainties are inevitable because you do not always feel comfortable in letting one topic go in favor of pursuing another one.

Thinking, reading, observing, and sharing/writing may overlap or take place side by side, albeit at different levels of specificity and clarity. Therefore, share your concerns, ideas, and topics with friends and colleagues so that you learn to frame your thoughts in a terminology familiar to your peers. At the same time, find published evidence in support of your concerns.

Many terms could be used to label the levels of specificity that guide the filtering process. Our labels, chosen deliberately without being necessarily binding, are research *concerns*, *ideas*, *topics*, and *purpose*. Other choices might be equally suitable as long as it is understood that the research process evolves through stages of increasing specificity by which a purpose for your project becomes clear to you.

To describe the aim of a research project, some replace "research purpose" with "research question"; still others refer to it as the "research problem." Consider using the term "research problem" cautiously because it tends to imply that a resolution is expected as the outcome of all studies. In fact, some research, especially in the philosophical realm, may generate more questions rather than solve any one problem in particular. In that case, you might prefer to call the focus of your study the "critical issue" or the "problematic."

Framing Concerns About Music Teaching and Learning

When one defines music education as the study of the learning and teaching of music, the components that foremost frame research in music education tend to be the learner (L), the subject matter of music (M), and the teacher (T), either by themselves or in interaction with each other. To capture this interconnectedness between the component parts, Figure 1.2 shows them as "cogs" (similar to bicycle gears) that cause each other to move, thus resulting in particular processes of learning and teaching.

In the instructional formality of school music in which the teacher guides nearly all musical interactions, the three components shape the interplay of actions in the classroom or rehearsal. Referring to such learning situations as schooling, formal, or instructor-guided learning suggests that they take place wherever teachers, assigned mentors, or otherwise appointed or declared superiors oversee the instructional process. Outside of school—away from teachers, mentors, or mediating guides—the learner interacts directly with the music, which changes the ongoing dynamic between learner and subject matter. Calling such situations informal learning does not imply a learning situation

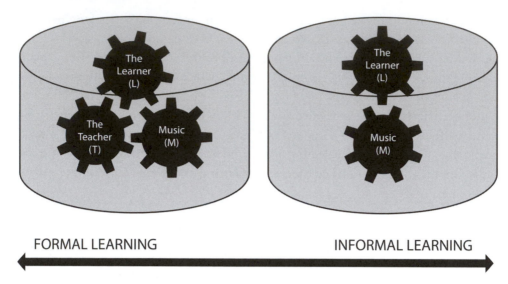

FORMAL LEARNING   INFORMAL LEARNING

FIGURE 1.2   The Interconnectedness Between Formal and Informal Music Learning Situations

that is less important or effective than what goes on in the formality of institutional settings. The opposite may be the case. Presently, both terms—formal and informal learning—are stipulated definitions, still awaiting systematic examination and verification by further evidence. Their presence in this chapter simply acknowledges that the way in which music learning takes place impacts its results.

Some Thoughts by the Students in RC 533

Most of the students in RC 533 were initially more interested in issues related to formal music instructional processes than in informal ones. They thought of themselves as teachers who, with varying degrees of experience, had practical "who, what, where, when, why and how" questions about their own involvement in everyday instructional practices. To illustrate:

Carlos asked about technology as an aid for teaching general musicianship skills, such as composing and music analysis/theory. He also wondered how he could best measure the benefits of technology as a tool for teaching musicianship skills. By looking at the teacher–learner–music model, he realized that focusing on the learners—his students—would prompt him to ask about the technology expertise his students brought to the instructional process. Coming from the vantage point of the music itself, Carlos wondered what type of music would best connect his students' interests to the musical choices mandated by the curriculum. These questions evolved into thinking about the purpose of music appreciation class, at first perhaps a less tangible concern for him, but one that grew in importance the longer he thought and read up about the teaching of music to students of varying ages and diverse musical backgrounds, and interests.

Christy's efforts to articulate several areas of concern stemmed from her question about being an effective studio teacher. "How do I teach differently from what others say or do?" she asked. "What and how do others teach?" "How (and why) do I know that I am effective?" When focusing on music (the music cog in Figure 1.2), Christy—like Carlos—thought about other pedagogues before her. As a result, she moved away from exclusively focusing on herself. Instead, historical questions began to come to the forefront: Who has become known as a string pedagogue? What have they become known for and what approaches did they use? What repertoire choices did they make and how has their legacy influenced today's pedagogies?

Both Christy and Carlos had begun to broaden their interests. Christy's example in particular illustrates how an original concern (her own effectiveness as a studio teacher) can develop into a question (previous pedagogy models) of historical significance (what can knowledge about the past teach us about the present?). Clearly, considering whether your own areas of concern deal with ideas about teaching or specific actions by your pupils, with events of the past or the present adds a new dimension to your inquiries. But Christy could also have broadened her initial concern by probing relationships between herself and her students, possibly even adding issues of repertoire choice, teaching strategies, or her students' home backgrounds to the list of ideas she began to gather.

Exploration: Pause for a Moment and Think

Consider what has come to your mind thus far: Are your interests situated in institutional learning and teaching or in how learning might take place outside of school? Are you looking into the past like Christy had begun to do, or are you more intrigued by what happens in the present? Are you primarily interested in your or other teachers' behaviors and resultant actions or does the world of ideas about music pique your curiosity? If the latter, how does the world of ideas in music relate to thoughts about education and formal instruction? What questions fascinate you and how could you best articulate them?

Answers to any of the questions posed in the above assignment refer to what we call modes of inquiry. Understanding what they are and knowing differences among them may benefit how you might best articulate specific concerns about various learning and teaching settings. The better and more succinctly you frame such concerns, the stronger all subsequent steps in your research are likely to be.

Modes of Inquiry

All research begins with asking questions about that which is to be examined. Now that you have begun that process yourself, scrutinize the nature of those questions. What specifically are you asking about? Are you interested in the past or in the present; in actions, behaviors, and experiences; or in the study of ideas?

A concern about past events, behaviors, and/or documented experiences would likely lead to a historical study; examining past and present ideas would fall under philosophical inquiries; and examining present events, behaviors, actions, and/or experiences would be empirical in nature—regardless of which methods were used. Interestingly, the etymological origin of all three terms goes back to "learnedness, wisdom, and experience."

"Empirical" derives from the Latin empiricus (or from the Greek empeirikos, empeira, and/or empeiros), making reference to experiences that come from "living in the world" as opposed to knowledge that results from studying written documents. A characteristic derived from "learnedness through experience" brings us to the "learned" or "wisdom loving" person. In Greek, philosophos means the same: The person who loves wisdom. The Latin histor means "learned man," suggesting a close connection between "lover of wisdom" and "learned man." A histor, philosophor, and empiricus therefore pursue the answer to a question for the same reason: A need to know. They adhere to principles of both reason and intuition, rely on evidence obtained through the senses as well as through introspection, and engage in the ongoing examination of such principles. In today's understanding of the three modalities, their differences lie mainly in what a question is about: (1) ideas or actions/behaviors/experiences, and (2) those of the past or the present.

Today, each mode has specific conventions and expectations about the nature of the questions asked and the way they are addressed. However, modes of inquiry should never be viewed as being mutually exclusive; one can inform the other. There is no reason, for example, why philosophical inquiry could not draw upon empirical resources or engage quantitatively as well as qualitatively in the examination of unresolved issues concerning beliefs and actions. Any of the choices depend on the perspective you bring to what constitutes a "researchable" question.

If you ask "Why or how did someone do or say something in the past?" you can reconstruct that past either by talking to individuals who witnessed the event or by studying documents that described those events. The same is true if you want to know what took place at a particular moment in time and why. A philosophical examination might ask why a given statement/idea/belief is important in itself or for practices in music education: How does a particular belief or theory compare to other ideas or beliefs prevalent in our field? How consistently have they been expressed over time and actually guided decision-making processes by educators and musicians alike? Do such choices warrant continuous examination today and, if so, why? Are there seemingly irresolvable differences among current ideas that govern our field today?

Finally, if a question addresses current events, ongoing actions as well as experiences, the investigation would most likely fall into the empirical realm of inquiry. It means that the question addresses phenomena that can be described through sense perceptions of seeing, touching, sensing, hearing, smelling—in short, that which one perceives to exist.

Many of the "who, what, where, when, why, and how" questions raised earlier apply here when worded like: Who are the students I am teaching? What is their background? How do they relate to each other and to me? What is their musical taste? How do they spend their spare time? How do any of these questions impact or at least relate to each other and possibly also help me teach better? And, finally, how can I observe "good" teaching? What is it? How do others define it? How was the term used in the past?

To repeat: The lines between research modes are and should be anything but hard and fast. Arriving at good definitions and clear meanings of historical facts and quantifiable behaviors and actions, analyzing different points of view, engages you in more than one mode at various points in your research. This is why an understanding of basic methods, techniques and requirements in all three modes should be considered an important attribute of any good scholar in music education. Making choices requires being informed; honing in on any one mode of inquiry without thinking of all available options limits your scholarship in the same way as does performing only in one style of music or teaching the same lesson for 20 or more years.

Some researchers hold the view that only scientifically (quantitatively) ascertained knowledge should be considered factual. "If you can't see it, label, and measure it," they might say, "how can it be irrefutable evidence on which to base future actions?" Other researchers counter that because there are so many perspectives by which to look at any given question, there also are many approaches to answering it; no one mode is to be valued over another. Still others suggest that as long as the research is beneficial to society and follows scholarly conventions, any mode and, with it, any procedure is appropriate as long as it meets the methodological demands implied by the question itself.

Applying Research Modes to the Learner–Teacher–Music Model

To frame areas of concern so that you can speak about them in terms of modes, ask yourself these questions: Are they about the present or the past? Do they pertain to ideas or actions (behaviors/experiences)? Are the queries about the teacher or the learner? Then consider whether your concerns are driven primarily by the music itself or by matters of teaching and learning that are specific to music, or perhaps also applicable to any other subject matter. Do you have philosophical concerns about purposes of education and schooling in general or do you worry most about gaining better insights about what goes on in rehearsals as music-specific instructional strategies? Do those worries originate from how you think of yourself either as a musician–teacher or musician–performer? Both equally? Finally, what might any one of those perspectives mean for the way you articulate your concerns as having relevance for past or current music education practices?

Figure 1.3 organizes "who, what, where, when, why, or how" questions according to their main focus as suggested by the above questions. The figure is intended to help you ask questions from many different perspectives and angles. These include the three modes of inquiry as well as the learner–teacher–music interactive model portrayed in Figure 1.2.

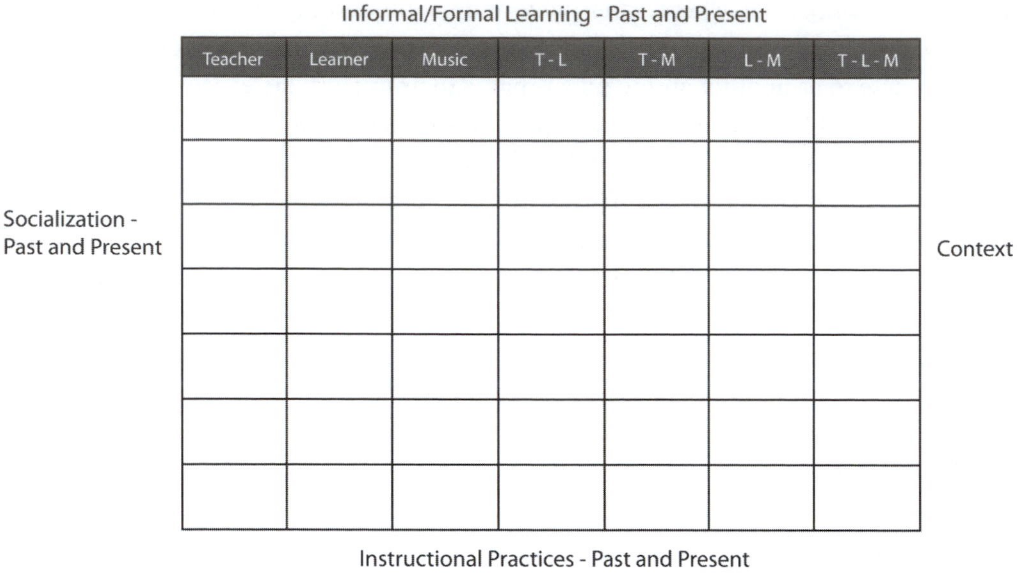

Informal/Formal Learning - Past and Present

	Teacher	Learner	Music	T - L	T - M	L - M	T - L - M

Socialization - Past and Present   Context

Instructional Practices - Past and Present

FIGURE 1.3   The Learner–Teacher–Music Grid for Framing Areas of Concern

Applying Figure 1.3 to their own thoughts, the students in RC 533 worked on an assignment in which they derived questions that looked at the concerns from more than one angle. For each question, they placed a check mark in the appropriate cell. For a complete list of questions, see Appendix A.

Carlos, for instance, had initially worded his concern as "*How* can technology help me to teach general musicianship skills, such as composing and music analysis/theory?" That question, along with another ("*How* can I measure the benefits of technology in the learning of musicianship skills?") were clearly focused on him as the teacher. He therefore checked the teacher/teacher cell twice. To ask the question from a student-focused angle, he came up with "*What* technological knowledge do students bring to the classroom?" A question that combined teacher and learner interests was "*What* can students teach me about technology that might prove useful in class?" For a music-related angle, he asked "*What* type of music is best suited to demonstrate technological advances as compositional tools?" The same question geared toward the learner yielded "*What* kinds of music will motivate my students to want to use technology for performing or composing?" Finally, Carlos came up with a question that combined all three components: "*How* can I use technology to generate a learning environment that is self-guided and provides new approaches that help students master required musicianship skills?" He soon realized that many more questions could be distributed on the grid and encouraged his classmates to take up the challenge.

Carlos was not certain at this point, of course, which of his questions would be his springboard for thinking about such things as modes of inquiry, learning contexts, student backgrounds, or comparing his own situation to those encountered by other teachers. He had simply opened a flood gate of questions, all of which interested him in some way.

When you similarly articulate your own concerns according to their focus on the teacher, the learner(s), and the music that is being taught and/or learned either formally or informally, notice how the wording changes the focus of your concern(s). Because different wordings have consequences for how you might go about answering a question, be sure to write down the questions and your thoughts about them. Your notes become important building blocks for working toward a research question as you move on in the spiral of inquiry that you now have begun.

A Moment for Reflection and Discussion

Should or can all professional concerns be reduced to "who, what, where, when, why, or how" questions that can be answered with certainty? "Not exactly" would be the reply by many experienced scholars inside and outside of music education (e.g., Barrett & Stauffer, 2009; Bowman, 1998, 2002; Deemter, 2010; Elliott, 2002; Keefe, 2000; Sorensen, 2001) who philosophically would favor grey shades over black and white; ambiguity over certainty. Nonetheless, at this point in the process, you should err in favor of exercising precision. Later in the process the rules might relax, akin perhaps to how many music students learn to do counterpoint: First, follow the rules faithfully; once you have something to say musically, step outside certain rules for the desired compositional effect.

When the students in RC 533 looked at their categorized questions together as a class (see Appendix A), some informal conversations arose about career goals and how performing, teaching, and research might contribute to those goals. Certain wordings evoked responses by someone in class who had read materials that seemed applicable to the question at hand or that spearheaded new inquiries outside of the classroom.

Juan asked his conducting instructor what she considered to be signs of "good conducting." She not only talked at length about score study and people skills but also referred him to other conducting teachers. She suggested further that he look at various music trade magazines that regularly publish interviews with successful conductors and instrumentalists about their work. Juan planned not only to look up such articles but also to subscribe to *The Instrumentalist*.

Having already done a master's thesis, *Dale*'s questions were specific enough that he decided to talk informally to some of the colleagues in his own school district about how they felt about their work conditions. His question *"Why do I want to know this?"* prompted him to formulate reasons why knowing about the work conditions of music teachers might be important. As he thought about those reasons, he realized that they triggered further questions and he became excited about what lay ahead.

Not everyone in RC 533 was as excited about what lay ahead as Dale. *Christy*, *Liam*, *Muna* (students who took the course as part of degree requirements outside their major), and Juan wondered why they should get involved in doing research when they sought a career in music performance and/or teaching. How could they possibly benefit from spending precious time on more academic courses when they barely found enough room in their schedule for practicing or working on assignments in music history, literature, and conducting?

Muna in particular felt those pressures more pointedly than some of the other students and did not hesitate to let *Prof. E.* know her feelings. To her, questioning accepted ways of doing things or searching for new approaches seemed to impede on "getting things done." Would it not be sufficient, she asked, to be taught by master teachers who themselves learned through successful coaching and personal experience what to pass on to the next generation of musician–teachers? Had it not already been shown by example that such a master–apprentice model worked especially well in the arts?

Exploration: Consider the Conversation in RC 533

Being open about your own feelings about the issues raised by the students in RC 533, share with each other the past learning experiences, both formal and informal, whose outcomes have most impacted where you are now: Positive, Negative, Undecided.

1. Discuss with each other the benefits and drawbacks of how your lives are impacted daily by the results of scientific research.
2. Talk about the relative benefits of the master–apprentice approach in music as compared to how that approach seems to work (or not work) in other fields.
3. Address the place of scientific thought and research in the arts in general and music in particular. Consider whether spoken language can get at the essence of the artistic process. If so, what—in your opinion—does it try to accomplish? If not, why—in your opinion—do music education scholars continue to insist that you learn skills of scholarly discourse?
4. Finally, find examples for the assertion that research and scholarship have a place in the fields of music, education, and music education and look for commonalities between the process of performing and doing research.

Filtering a Concern/Idea/Topic by Way of Reflective Reading

Reading is most pleasurable when it is "just for fun." It might resemble doodling on an instrument—it feels successful and you already know how to do it. But if doodling was the extent of your musical aspirations, you would never master your instrument. When reading scholarly literature, you should make a similar distinction between "just for fun" and "digging deep." Both are likely to be the case when you embark on reading for the purpose of finding a topic suitable for scholarly research. You may find that research in this context is quite different from the "library research" you did as an undergraduate student when you wrote a report that summarized information about a topic, possibly even in your own words. The purpose of reading and writing in the context of doing scholarly research is not only to summarize but also to scrutinize and analyze how various scholars have addressed particular issues, comparing their thoughts to each other's as well as to your own. Such detailed work is preceded by a phase of browsing and skimming an assortment of literature for the purpose of selecting those sources that meet the criteria required for scholarly work.

If you keep a healthy balance between browsing, skimming, and detailed reading, the result will be a comprehensive view of the body of knowledge related to your professional concern. As a scholar, the library—whether virtual or physical—is your practice room and, like practicing your instrument, you can make the process an enjoyable and even exciting journey of discovery! In the following section, we describe both an exploratory and a detailed approach to reading, likening the latter to having an in-depth conversation with the authors whose works you read.

Exploring Published Sources

One of the first steps in getting an overview of extant sources is browsing; that is, looking over the literature to see what is available. Similar to what many call "surfing the Internet," browsing is a surface-level exploration of sources for the purpose of getting an overview of "what is out there." The result is usually a large list of sources, which is then winnowed by skim-reading, looking through them to determine which ones are truly relevant to your area of concern ("does it speak to what concerns me?"). Prior to actually doing the browsing and skimming (explored further in Chapter 2), consider also the nature of publications that make up the overall body of music education literature (see also Chapter 3). When dealing with information gleaned from books, journals, periodicals, general interest, and scholarly sources, be mindful that any such publications are targeted to reach different audiences and fulfill distinctive functions. The same is true for research, a thought you should keep in mind at this early stage of getting acquainted with the literature.

The Nature of Publications

Books differ according to whether they were written by one author or multiple (contributing) authors, the latter typically compiled and organized by an editor, with chapters that may or may not relate to each other. Edited books also differ as to whether they are collections of papers written by researchers for a conference or whether they contain invited articles in which authors' personal viewpoints are emphasized. Book chapters and articles can be speculative or report original research; they can be aimed at a general audience or a specialized one; and they can express personal opinions or summarize research results. These distinctions hold for online and hard-copy publications. Many journals and trade magazines publish general interest essays rather than technical research reports because the former are easier to read, therefore reaching a larger audience than research articles. Similarly, a good number of popular trade journals and professional magazines prohibit footnotes because the latter take space away from possible advertisements or other, more pressing printed matter. Such restrictions limit the author in specificity of writing and presentation of content. Therefore, as informative as general interest articles may be, they tend not to be as useful for building a body of scholarly literature that is based on tested and documented knowledge.

Because the outer appearance of a published source provides information about its intended audience, also pay attention to a source's layout. Some pieces of writing use words only while others include both words and pictures. Words may be complex or simple, speak to a broad audience or an insider group, or utilize reasoning that is direct or circuitous. Graphics may be simple and easy to follow, or may involve mathematical tabulation and complex figures. Observations regarding the learning and teaching of music may either be somewhat casually stated or may be based on highly specified data collecting methods. References may be many or few, and may be cited as footnotes or at the end of a source. Each of these descriptors provides clues as to an author's intentions.

General interest essays inform you about concerns within the profession and allow you to ascertain where you stand on a particular issue. You find those articles most likely in trade journals and professional magazines that reach a readership with either very specific interests (e.g., *Flute*, the quarterly journal of the British Flute Society) or a comparatively broad readership (e.g., *The Instrumentalist*). Specific to music education, similar differentiations could be made, for example, between *UPDATE* and the *Music Educators Journal*, both published by NAfME (National Association for Music Education, formerly MENC). Both journals contain articles of interest and are purposefully kept non-technical, but one is intended for a broader readership than the other. Technical information, however, helps the reader to determine the validity of a thought process or the wisdom of particular recommendations for action. It is provided in scholarly journals specifically for the purpose of critical reading, allowing readers to follow and critique an author's line of reasoning and investigative choices. We describe in Chapter 14 how your own research might become the basis for you, too, to publish in those and other journals.

Distinctive Functions of Research

The more you peruse different professional journals and books, the more you will appreciate the enormous volume of research relevant to music education. You are likely to find that some publications seem more "esoteric" than others—lacking application to classroom or performance—while other studies speak to those activities directly. That observation will make it easy to understand that research can serve many different functions.

The primary function of all research should be to continue to ask questions about that which is uncertain or unknown and to assure that no one source of evidence dominates over any other without justification. In addition to these fundamental functions, researchers in many disciplines distinguish between basic and applied functions of research. Basic (sometimes also called "pure") research discovers, describes, and/or develops theories for the sake of advancing basic explanations or confirmations of how things work. Research designed to solve a practical problem tends to be called applied (Turabian, Booth, Colomb & Williams, 2008, p. 59). Both kinds of research—basic and applied—are needed for a field of inquiry to move forward.

Disciplines in which research and development are fully integrated components tend to recognize three categories of applied research (Gates, 1999, p. 10). Following Gates, we suggest the following designations for applied research in music education: (1) pedagogical "engineering," (2) field studies, and (3) context studies.

Pedagogical "engineering" would include such areas as testing the advantages of one teaching approach over another, and investigating the usability and appropriateness of tests and other measurement tools. Field studies would comprise observations in natural settings, curriculum development, action research, and the advancement of instructional technologies. Context studies would be those that include surveys of specific practices or opinions on practices, policy studies, and the articulation of rationales for music education, as well as biographies and historical accounts of important events. The four-level research structure (basic, pedagogical-engineering, field, and context studies) might explain why one study investigation speaks to you immediately while another seems further removed from your interests. However, as in other disciplines, each function is needed and contributes to the field as long as the research is well done and its findings correctly interpreted.

In music education, studies geared toward advancing our knowledge about music and learning as theoretical constructs function as basic research. Many such investigations exist on the nature of specific responses to a variety of musical stimuli, often describing, comparing, and experimenting with them. Basic research also examines the validity of psychological, physiological, and sociological constructs on music teaching and learning, and questions traditions and practices in light of philosophical worldviews. The primary purpose of such investigations is not so much to solve the practical problems each of us encounters in daily teaching as to direct our attention to principles of thought that might help us understand why we encounter the realities we do. Through such deeper understanding, then, even basic research has the potential of impacting practical matters in the classroom.

While basic research may sometimes be applied to practice, it may also happen that the desire for easy applications to everyday life problems results in the misinterpretation and misuse of basic research findings. As an example, we offer the story of the popular response to the "Mozart Effect" studies.

In the early 1990s, three neuroscientists—Frances Rauscher, Gordon Shaw, and Katherine Ky—designed an experiment to test a possible connection between music cognition and mathematical reasoning. They subjected 36 college students to three listening conditions (Mozart's Sonata for Two Pianos in D Major, K. 448, a relaxation tape, or silence), and immediately followed each listening experience with a published test of spatial reasoning. The researchers found that the students' performance on the test improved more after listening to the Mozart sonata than after the other conditions (Rauscher, Shaw & Ky, 1993). Published in the journal *Nature*, the results were embraced by music educators and the music industry as evidence for the practical importance of music education. Subsequent attempts to replicate the research, however, were not successful. Dr. Rauscher later indicated that this was because the results of the original study had been misinterpreted. The evidence from the original study supported only the three spatial-temporal tasks that had been reported in the original report, as measured by a specific test, and were not intended to represent an improvement in general IQ or other aspects of intelligence. In other words, practical applications of this research misinterpreted both its purpose and its results (Steele et al., 1999).

Reading as Conversation

Whatever you read, whether a journal or magazine article, book, pamphlet, or website, always guard against initial reactions such as "I like this, therefore it is good" or "I do not agree with the author and therefore find this information useless." Instead of relying on such a gut feeling, take the next step and become an active partner in conversation with the author.

As you react to what you read, examine your reasoning: Are you responding to a poor quality of writing and research or because your ideas are being challenged by evidence that does not match your experience or your beliefs? Do the author's ideas express personal opinions entirely or are they backed up with reliable and valid evidence? Does the author acknowledge contradictory evidence and how is such evidence presented?

When you ask these questions and look for answers to them in the text you are reading, you begin the process that scholars call critical reading. Do not confuse the word critical with negative. It is understandable if at first you feel uncomfortable with actually questioning the work of published authors. After all, you have possibly learned to consider printed word as coming from experts who presumably know more than you do. While that may be true, it should not stop you from analytically examining what you read.

Just as critical listeners pay attention to how particular structural elements in a musical performance give it cohesiveness and musical sense, critical readers look for the building blocks that hold a publication together. Learning to think and read critically requires from scholars "seeing both sides of an issue, being open to new evidence that disconfirms your ideas, reasoning dispassionately, demanding that claims be backed by evidence, [and] deducing and inferring conclusions from available facts" (Willingham, 2007, p. 8).

Critical reading, then, is the trademark of a good scholar, regardless of the mode of inquiry one is engaged in. We suggest you begin with the tangible step of determining the frame of a published piece: What is it about? What is its purpose? How does it contribute to your own thinking about the concern(s) you have formulated? In subsequent chapters, we recommend more specific questions but at this point we ask you to consider: (1) the function of a particular publication in the larger context of music education research; (2) how the authors made use of referenced evidence by which they articulated their own questions; (3) whether and why those sources and their content can be trusted; and (4) how the authors themselves adhered to accepted principles of scholarly inquiry. Later chapters detail those considerations; this chapter outlines the first of several steps in that process: Identifying trustworthy sources of evidence.

Identifying Trustworthy Sources of Evidence

"Consider the source!" means having background information about the source itself. When a trusted friend tells you a first-hand experience, you are likely to accept that information as true. If, however, you believe your friend's perception to be biased, you will seek proof from another person that the friend's description of the experience was trustworthy. Of course, it is possible that the second person's testimony stems only from hearsay; it may not be a good source of information at all. Similar situations can be present in published sources.

Good scholars also give credit where credit is due. In the context of writing, this means that all thoughts not the author's own should be acknowledged by reference citations—either parenthetical (cited in parentheses within the narrative), footnotes or endnotes, or in a reference list at the end of the publication. There should be consistency between page numbers at both places; sloppy work at this level suggests poor quality work. This is one of the first things you should check as you decide whether the sources you examine meet the criteria for scholarship.

Next, follow a select number of references to their originals. If the information in both places coincides in all cases, trustworthiness in the author's work is at a higher level than if you find several mistakes. Carelessness may not weaken an author's overall message but, as in a musical performance, technical mistakes tend to lessen the overall appeal and—possibly—its trustworthiness. Because the quality of a publication depends on whether it is published in a peer-reviewed source—that is, it was judged by a committee of scholarly peers prior to publication—some of those cross-checks should have been done by the reviewers and thereby give you greater confidence in the work you are reading.

Another indicator of good scholarship is the use of sources that are as close to the original as possible. Generally, the further removed a piece of writing is from the original source, the less one should trust it as reliable. You know this principle of research from being a performing musician: When you want to understand a composer's rather than an editor's intent, you try to find an edition that is as close as possible to the manuscript itself (also called the *urtext*, the first published source of a composition).

The principle of "considering the source" is as important in research as it is in daily communication or in your work as a performer. A key question should be: Is the information in the source original and consistent with other accounts of same events? An affirmative answer means that the information obtained can be trusted and should be considered useful for further research steps.

Common sense suggests that the original, first source, called in research terms a primary source, is the most trustworthy. A source that uses information from the primary source as a reference in its own context is known as a secondary source. Tertiary sources, accordingly, are references that utilize secondary information about a primary source. Research ethics as well as good scholarly sense suggest that an author utilize primary rather than secondary or tertiary sources as much as possible.

Secondary or tertiary sources can be very helpful in finding primary source material. However, if a publication is full of secondary and tertiary source citations at the expense of primary ones, confidence in a writer's scholarship level might decrease. One of your first investigative tasks, therefore, should be sorting out primary from secondary and tertiary sources. It is a skill at the center of historical research in which primary documents are such data sources as birth and death certificates, marriage licenses, bills, notebooks and diaries, letters, newspaper clippings, and other mementos of the topic under investigation (for more, see Chapter 6). For right now simply keep in mind that a primary source is always the one closest to an actual event or observation. That knowledge can serve as a good gauge by which to judge the nature of referenced information in any mode of inquiry.

Exploration: Consider the Source

To practice what is usually called source verification, locate, read, and compare Vaughn and Winner (2000), Deasy (2002), and Ruppert (2006). All of them speak to the issue of arts advocacy but the last two publications rely on the first as one of their sources. Below you see a summary of Vaughn and Winner's article.

One of many music educators' ongoing concerns is to establish evidence that academic achievement in school is positively tied to participation in the arts, including music. Vaughn and Winner's study involved multiple statistical analyses of 10 years of data gathered by the United States College Board from students taking the nationally standardized *Scholastic Aptitude Test* (SAT). Results indicated that students who were involved in arts courses had higher test scores than students who were not involved in arts courses, and that students with more high school arts experiences (according to the number of years they had taken arts courses) tended to score higher than lower scoring students. Because these results were derived from survey data, however, the authors suggested merely a correlation, not a causal relationship. In addition, the authors suggested that their study results should be viewed with caution because "an even stronger link exists between SAT scores and study of academic subjects" (2000, p. 87).

In light of Vaughn and Winner's caution, ascertain how Deasy (2002) and Ruppert (2006) presented the findings of the original study in their respective works.

Chapter Summary

1. Personal questions about the learning and teaching of music become professional questions when they are examined in the context of what already has been researched by others—be it in the field of music education or in other disciplines.

2. Placing your own concerns into an interactive framework of learner–teacher–music allows you to see the connection of your work in the larger context of the learning and teaching of music.

3. The cyclical nature of research as "think–read–observe–share" demands that no one action stand on its own. One calibrates the other, thereby moving the process forward.

4. Many different kinds of books, articles, and trade magazines make up the body of literature music educators have at their disposal. To sort through them and organize them for use in your own professional quests is an important step in becoming a music education scholar.

5. Critical reading does not mean to find fault; instead, it means seeking the building blocks that make a publication fit the bill of scholarly work. When reading, therefore, one determines how accurate, complete, and dependable (trustworthy) newly found information is.

6. Filtering your own concern, idea or topic by way of critical reading requires both cursory and detailed reading. Focusing on the purpose of a publication and verifying the accuracy of referenced sources should be the first two of several steps that are to follow.

7. Many commonalities between the processes of teaching, performing, and doing research exist. They should be stressed over seeming differences because one set of skills informs the other and can provide guidance in how to become the best music educator possible.

Topics for Further Exploration

1. Characteristics of critical reading.
2. Similarities and differences in the contents in the *Music Educators Journal, The Instrumentalist,* the *Journal of Research in Music Education,* and the *Bulletin of the Council for Research in Music Education,* or a similar combination of scholarly and professional periodicals.
3. *Library of Congress* classifications and other possible classification schemes using a minimum of six to eight of the books in a particular Library of Congress number (i.e., MT1). Categorize according to purpose and targeted readership(s).

Suggested Assignments

1. Create your own music education questions grid and develop a plan of action as described in Figure 1.3.
2. Reflect on how your musician, teacher, and researcher selves worked with each other as you developed your areas of concern and began to take them through the filter of thinking–reading–observing–sharing.
3. As you begin to look through printed source material, keep your eyes open for primary, secondary, and tertiary materials about same information. Keep track of those sources for later reference.
4. Find an example of basic research in a music education research journal. Summarize it and report to your colleagues.
5. Find an example of each type of applied research in a music education research journal. Summarize them and report to your colleagues.
6. Select and locate three of the sources listed in the References and find the authors' purpose statement(s). Skim each selected text and determine the steps the author(s) took to fulfill the purpose(s) as stated by them. Share with your colleagues what you find.

two

Finding and Mapping Sources of Information

This chapter guides you through steps that make as efficient as possible the reading tasks involved in conducting research. The steps include:

- Exploring further one area of concern;
- Framing a research idea;
- Collecting scholarly evidence related to your research idea;
- Constructing a literature map.

Placing the search for scholarly literature in both the "bricks and mortar" and "virtual" library, this chapter portrays this phase of the process as identifying, describing, and evaluating relevant literature. You progress from having voiced a concern to specifying a narrowed research idea situated in an organized body of literature.

Introduction

The professional expertise of most musicians and teachers is acquired by a combination of formal and informal knowledge, obtained from former teachers, reviewed in previous studies, and solidified with personal experience. Professional expertise may be distinguished from any formal knowledge that is collectively shared by the profession as a whole because such knowledge is expected to be based on fact and tested evidence. What constitutes fact and what qualifies to be called evidence continues to be under debate by many scholars. There seems to be considerable agreement, however, as to what constitutes scholarly communication; that is, scholarly writing. This chapter is about recognizing those characteristics in what is known as the body of literature relevant to a given field.

Obtaining some understanding of that body in reference to your chosen area of concern is a necessary first step in any scholarly endeavor. Subsequent to that step, the process of finding and using literature for a research project generally occurs in three phases as illustrated in Figure 2.1: You (1) explore preliminary sources; (2) use the vocabulary from those sources to frame a research idea; and (3) find and collect literature relevant to that idea. Later, you will assess each source you have collected, describing its contents and evaluating how well it adheres to scholarly conventions and addresses your research idea. Most often this results in a review of the literature—an analysis, evaluation, and synthesis of how other scholars have studied your research interest. Such a review can stand on its own as a term paper or article, or provide background for the topic and purpose of a thesis, dissertation, or grant proposal.

Exploring Your Area of Concern

If you are like most new researchers, you will begin the information search at the level we call *area of concern*. As already suggested in Chapter 1, such concerns are often derived from "burning questions" about your work as a music educator. At this level, most new researchers are able to name their research concerns in general terms—"music

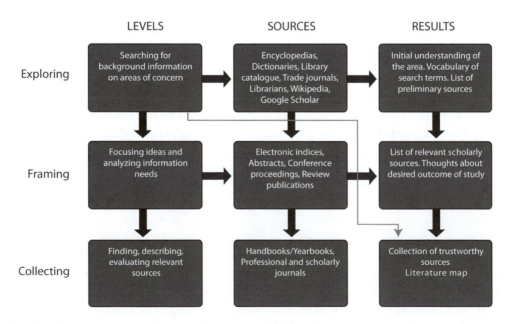

FIGURE 2.1   Steps in Exploratory Reading

technology in the high school music program," "the history of scat singing," or "string pedagogy"—but may not know the terms used by scholars to discuss that area, or the best sources for information. The exploration stage of the literature search therefore involves preliminary searching: locating sources, browsing to see what is available, taking note of specific vocabulary and terminology, deciding on a record-keeping strategy that works for you, and skimming the literature to see what is relevant.

Locating Sources in an Academic Library

Most literature searches begin in a university's "bricks and mortar" library or its electronic equivalent. Whether you visit a library building or a virtual library, you can search for information about any subject you wish, including music and education. The efficient use of a professional library requires learning the location of the libraries you will need, the organization of the holdings in each building, the types of holdings that will best serve your needs, and the procedures for finding materials. Using a virtual library requires similar skills: navigating your university's online library, learning which search indices are available, distinguishing reliable from unreliable websites. Either way, you must develop an efficient way to keep track of your findings at each stage of your search. This skill will serve you for a lifetime.

Getting Around in the Library—Virtual and Physical

When you consult library holdings via the Internet, the electronic catalog traditionally refers to hard-copy holdings, such as books and periodicals housed in the library building, as print holdings. Electronic holdings refer both to computerized databases and to subscriptions to online journals. (These are further described later in this chapter and referenced in Appendices B and C.) Library buildings have specific areas for such resources as reference materials, books (fiction and non-fiction), periodicals, media, electronic sources, special collections, archives, and often rooms for reading or working on computers. Common items as, for example, standard dictionaries, encyclopedias, professional yearbooks, and conference proceedings are generally located in the reference section, which may be found in a central place in the library. Books are housed in "the stacks," classified either according to the Library of Congress system (academic libraries in the U.S.) or the Dewey Decimal System (school and public libraries). You may find it helpful to become familiar with the music classifications in one of these systems. Periodicals, typically including scholarly research publications, trade journals, magazines, and newspapers, are often found in a special reading room, although they are increasingly published and accessed electronically. In addition to the physical organization of the library, make sure to learn about the procedures for viewing microfilm and microfiche. Many libraries also provide an interlibrary loan service by which books, articles, and other media can be obtained from other institutions.

Some college or university libraries have separate facilities for undergraduate and graduate students; others decentralize library buildings according to disciplines. The education library, for instance, may not be in proximity of the music library; and music scores, sheet music, music books, and anthologies may be at a different place from professional journals in music education or books on music teaching. Many large university libraries also house special collections and archives that are useful for historical research (Chapter 6). Be prepared, therefore, to spend time in more than one locale.

Libraries employ trained personnel who are very good at helping researchers make sense of the available search options for print and electronic sources—make sure to seek their help. Although many libraries also offer online help through email and instant messaging (so that patrons do not always have to actually visit the library), it is best to make personal contacts with library personnel early on.

Finding What You Are Looking For

At the exploration stage, your purpose is to learn to find the literature that will support and guide your project. Scholarly sources should therefore be your primary focus. These include research handbooks, research periodicals, conference proceedings, and occasionally anthologies that are peer-reviewed (meaning a manuscript was reviewed and accepted for publication by a committee of professionally established experts in the field). Peer-reviewed sources are expected to contain a clear and well-defined line of reasoning, utilize appropriate methods for data gathering and analysis, and have findings and conclusions that speak to their stated purpose.

Although you should focus mostly on peer-reviewed sources, do not ignore other professional publications—peer-reviewed or not. Trade journals or magazines, whether intended primarily for performers (i.e., *Horn Call, Flute, Percussive Notes*, etc.) or music educators (i.e., *Music Educators Journal, Teaching Music, Music Teacher, Instrumentalist*, etc.) can give you insights that might contribute to further inquiries or help to clarify your thoughts on a subject. Do not let them form the bulk of your sources. Even belletristic books and public-interest newspaper articles can serve the purpose of clarifying your concern and ideas. Likewise, lexica (encyclopedias and dictionaries—subject-specific as well as general) should never be far from your fingertips or desktop.

Exploration: A Library "Scavenger Hunt"

- Use a campus map

  - Find all the libraries on your campus. How many are there?
  - Visit the music library or the library that holds music education materials. Find a librarian, introduce yourself, describe your research interests, and find out about his or her area of expertise.
  - Locate the following and give an example of each:

    - Music holdings (call numbers starting with M, ML, MT);
    - Education holdings (call numbers starting with L);

- Periodicals (both professional or trade journals and scholarly journals);
- Reference section;
- Reserve section;
- Information about electronic holdings;
- Information about Interlibrary Loan (ILL);
- Enter the library URL_____;
- Do an electronic search of the library holdings related to your area of concern;
- Do an electronic search of at least one electronic database related to your area of concern.

- Go to your local public library and find out about their services.

Exploratory Searching

In the process of looking for sources that will guide you to appropriate materials, you must discover and take written notes about which terms and key phrases are most fruitful. At this stage, therefore, review a wide variety of general sources seeking to find out what exists in your area of concern. Skim (look through) those materials that look interesting to you and let them give you an idea of how others in the profession have studied and/or explained the nature of your area of concern.

Begin the search by entering your area of concern into a familiar source such as Google or Wikipedia. Note, however, that these sources are acceptable only for preliminary searching. Subject-specific indices, described briefly below and in more detail in Appendices B and C, are more trustworthy for finding reputable sources (and, when accessed through your library, provide sources free of charge). Because it is not peer-reviewed, Wikipedia is not a dependable source for scholarly research, and should not be used beyond this preliminary stage.

As you explore these and other online sources, approach them thinking as a researcher, reasoner and skeptic rather than a receptive acceptor. Start keeping track of questions raised by what you read and pursue answers to those questions through continued search. These links represent starting points to help you to begin to question.

Discovering Search Vocabulary

Discovering the appropriate search vocabulary is an important aspect of finding relevant literature. Whether you are using an electronic database such as Google, a library catalog, or a subject-specific index, the correct vocabulary can make or break your search. If you type in your research concern in your own words, your search may not necessarily result in any "hits," or useful sources. Dividing your initially worded concern into its component parts, that is, nouns and/or verbs, is the first step in finding the most useful search terms.

Jeannette was interested in learning more about whether students' perspective of choir varied according to their ethnic background, so she Googled "minority students in choirs." Immediately, at the very top of the computer screen, appeared three links to scholarly articles that dealt either with ethnically diverse students in general or specific to music.

Juan's search was not quite as fruitful—at least not at first. Googling "improve conducting skills," the entries were of little interest to him because they were too basic to be of much use. However, when he broke his initial concern into "research, conducting, music, improvement," he received, as Jeannette had, links to scholarly journal articles, one by Yarbrough (1985) in the *Journal of Research in Music Education* and the other by Johnston (1993) in the *British Journal of Music Education*. Of course, Juan would not know until after reading the articles themselves whether they were going in the direction that he had in mind. But their references, along with additional sources listed by Google Scholar would clearly get Juan further into the spiral of inquiry.

Dale, a more experienced critical reader already, developed terms that would help him find literature related to work conditions in general. Thus, he broke his initial interests into the following search terms:

- Band Director: instrumental music teacher, conductor, music director, bandmaster;
- Work Conditions: occupational/job satisfaction, fulfillment, labor relations.

By coming up with synonyms, related terms, and broader alternatives, the combined terms of "occupation/job satisfaction music" and "labor relations, music, teacher" yielded enough "hits" that Dale felt he could move forward in his search of relevant literature.

Using Publication Indices

Sources known as publication indices are intended to provide trustworthy information about scholarly sources in particular fields of study. Following your initial search, you should seek out one or more of them. Libraries subscribe to such indices, enabling patrons to use them for free—usually online as well as in the library building.

Publication indices vary greatly by purpose and content. You might use WorldCat ("the world's largest network of library content and services" www.worldcat.org) to find books and other library materials in your area of interest and learn where they are housed. Academic Search Complete indexes and abstracts over 8,000 journals in the social sciences and education. The RILM Abstracts (short for the French term Répertoire International de Littérature Musicale) is a music bibliography search engine, holding records for a variety of musical sub-disciplines. These and other indices are listed for your information in Appendix B.

Using electronic indices effectively often requires learning additional "subject term" vocabulary. For instance, Academic Search Complete uses the phrase "music—instruction and study" to designate "music education." In most cases the website that hosts such an index will have a web-based "button" or other symbol where you can search for the terms used by that source. Figure 2.2 displays the interface for that index. You may also want to look ahead to Figure 3.1 (Chapter 3), which lists many such key terms, fields of study, and subject headings.

As can be seen in Appendix B, web-based indices may be organized by content area (such as arts and education) or according to whether they are free or require a subscription. If you have university access, for instance, the RILM Abstracts of Music Literature (for music) or Academic Search Complete (for education) are efficient preliminary

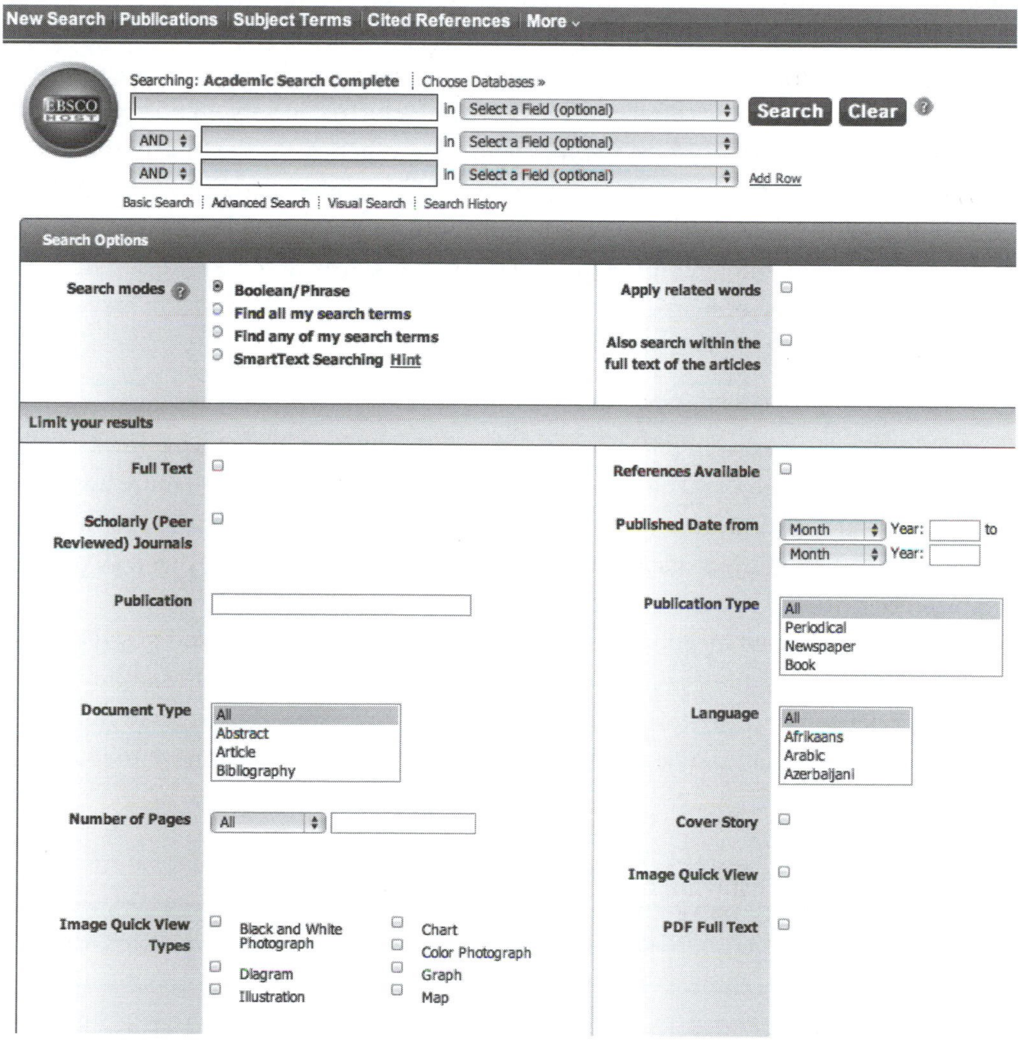

FIGURE 2.2 Sample Search Page from Academic Search Complete

Note: This illustration is used by permission of EBSCO Publishing.

sources. If you lack such access, you may wish to try the Music Education Search System (MESS) or the Education Resources Information Center (ERIC). Google Scholar tends to straddle this distinction; you may use it for free to find citations, but accessing those sources usually requires a fee. In such a case, check with a university or public library about interlibrary loan (ILL) services.

A well-planned search of publication indices should yield a long list of publications of potential interest to you. Keeping track of the indices you search and the terms you use will make your search more efficient in the long run. A form similar to that in Figure 2.3 may be useful for keeping track of which terms are most useful for each index.

While some indices offer access to articles, this is not their purpose. They are designed to help you locate sources related to your topic and tell you where to find them, not simply to provide access to articles. Some records give minimal information: an article title, author and source, leaving you to find the journal through another search. Many records link to an abstract (synopsis) of the article, helping you know rather quickly if the source will be worth locating for your investigation. A few records will link to the full text of an article, either an electronic (html) publication or an electronic version of a print article that is stored online for access, sometimes with a fee attached. At the time of this book's publication, many but not all print publications offer online access to recent and past articles. It is neither acceptable nor wise to limit your search to articles that can be found in full text online. As noted on the University of North Texas Wired Music Education Page, "If you want the best articles, not the ones that are easiest to get, you may have to go to a library to look at print journals" (Justice, 2008).

Keeping Records of Your Search

Even this early in the search process it is necessary to devise a way to keep track of what you have found and how you have found it. Note-taking becomes much more important at the next stage of project development, but at this point we recommend a two-part record-keeping strategy: a database of search records and a project diary. A possible template for setting up such a record is shown in Figure 2.3.

Enter time, date, and location of each search as well as the name (and possibly URL) of any search engines, the search terms used with each search engine, the author(s) and, if you can determine it by browsing, the quality of each source. Also take note of all bibliographic information related to each source so that you do not have to look it up

Topic/Research Interest:			
Date	Source	Terms	Results

FIGURE 2.3   Keeping Records of Your Search(es)

again later. This includes: (1) the full name of all authors or editors, in the order they are written in the source; (2) the full title of the source and, if applicable, the work in which the source appears (such as a chapter in an edited book or the volume, issue and year of an article in a periodical); (3) the publisher and place of publication; (4) the genre of the source (book, periodical, doctoral dissertation, website, etc.); and (5) the page numbers you are interested in (or paragraph numbers for html sources).

You will typically be required by your university to use one of several specific formats for what you are writing, usually based either on the style requirements of the American Psychological Association (APA) (2009), the Chicago Manual of Style (2010), or the Modern Language Association (MLA) (2009). Speaking from experience, we suggest that you learn these rules early and make even preliminary bibliographic notes in the appropriate format. Each organization publishes a style manual, and you should add the one required by your university to your personal collection. In addition, several online sources provide free access to style guidelines; Purdue University's user-friendly Online Writing Lab is used by many graduate students for that purpose (http://owl.english.purdue.edu/).

You may wish to collect other kinds of information at this preliminary stage. Some full-text databases allow users to save the entire contents of an article for their personal files. You may also be able to find the table of contents for a source on the Internet. If neither of these is possible, consider copying or scanning the table of contents and the conclusion of key works. You may also wish to copy or scan important pages or lengthy paragraphs that are particularly interesting. Note that page numbers should accompany any direct quotations, no matter how small. There is nothing worse than having to return to a source at the end of a project to find the page number for a key quotation, or even having to delete that source from your reference list for lack of an appropriate citation. Taking brief but careful notes at this level sets the stage for a successful search. As you gain expertise in locating and reading sources, your skills of analysis and critical discernment become greater.

Many scholars also keep a project diary to track their progress. Such a diary may be kept in a word-processing file or a notebook. Entries generally include the date, time, location, goals for that work session, and notes about the process. Such record-keeping may help you stay on track and provide a gauge for how the project has developed over time.

Skimming Preliminary Sources

The most important publications at this early stage of the search are likely to be "overview" sources, usually from within the scholarly music education literature. These can often be recognized by the word "review" in the title of the article or chapter. Overview sources can be found in handbooks and scholarly journals that specialize in reviews; in fact, many of the examples in Chapter 1 came from overview sources. NAfME (formerly MENC) has published a number of music education research handbooks since 1992, as has the American Educational Research Association. These and other text-based review sources can be found in your university's library. Appendix C lists a number of additional sources that you should become familiar with during this stage of exploration, including journals that specifically publish literature review articles as well as major lexica (encyclopedias and dictionaries) in music and education. In Appendix D, you see a list of scholarly research periodicals you may want to consider later in your search.

Jeannette's experience with review sources was fairly typical. At the request of *Prof. E.*, she sought information from Colwell and Webster's (2011) *MENC Handbook of Research on Music Learning*. Specifically, she found a chapter by Phillips and Doneski entitled "Research on Elementary and Secondary School Singing." Clearly written and well organized, it offered a great deal of information about the musical voice, even including a section that discussed cultural impacts on singing. After reflecting on her reading, Jeannette realized that even though she did not find many leads to help with her own interests as a choral conductor, she had learned a lot about the terminology used by scholars and researchers to discuss choral and vocal issues. In fact, Jeannette observed that she had been using the word choral (implying a group experience) when what she wanted to know had to do with individual vocal production. This insight helped her specify her research interests more clearly.

Like Jeannette, you may find that overview sources help you place your research interests into a larger and/or better defined context within the field of music education.

Once you have located a good number of preliminary sources related to your concerns (between 10 and 20), you should skim-read them to determine whether they are relevant. If you are new to scholarly reading, this can appear to be a daunting task: "I have to read 20 sources in a week?!" You can manage such a number if your focus stays on the question whether a publication is relevant to your area of concern. You do this by reading selectively.

Beginning with the initial paragraphs that may be labeled "introduction," look at the first sentence or two in each paragraph. Go through the entire paragraph only if something interesting is stated in the opening sentence. Finally, read the last paragraphs, which are often but not always labeled "conclusion." If your reading of the conclusion indicates that you missed something, go back and find it. Otherwise, make note in your database of what you found—broad ideas, terms, and subject areas—and move on to another source. Later in the process you will read in a much more detailed and, thus, critical way, but at this stage, skim-reading is both necessary and efficient.

Both browsing and skimming the literature can help you develop a good overview of what is accepted knowledge in a field and what questions still await answers. Sometimes, however, an area of concern changes as a result of this reading—the topic may become substantially broader than the initial question, or branch off in another area entirely. This is appropriate at this stage but be careful that you do not lose sight of your area of concern. If that happens, you may literally wander around in the library or surf the Internet with no end in sight. For this reason, it is important to keep track of the steps you followed, because you may need come back later to the very first sources you found.

Also be reminded to cast your net of key terms wider than you first believe necessary. For instance, a search for "sight reading in the middle school choral rehearsal" may produce fewer results than "research, sight reading, choir." The opposite can occur as well: Your initial search terms yield "thousands" of seeming hits but none of them prove to have any relation to your actual interest. In such a case, you need to devise more limits and narrow your search by adding more keywords.

It may occur that sources seem scarce because you have come up with a relatively new territory of exploration. In such a case, you may have to look for literature beyond music education sources. If that search also yields only a few results, document that lack of evidence and work with your course instructor or project advisor to develop a plan of action. It may be that your literature search will set the stage for a new area of music education research.

Framing a Research Idea

After you have found and consulted a variety of overview sources, get ready to move to the next level in the spiral of inquiry. This means bombarding your original concern with real questions (see Introduction Chapter, this volume) in light of: (1) what you have found in your exploratory literature search; and (2) what you find in further, more detailed reading. Similar to the first level, this involves examining, re-wording, thinking ahead, and specifying further the nature of your research interest. Because scholarly reading is less about trusting in any one answer to a problem or question than examining suggested answers for their validity, trustworthiness, or usefulness, asking the right questions is more important at this stage than finding the "one right answer." At this stage, your questions should be about specifics ("where, why, when, how, what") and also include practical, mediating factors that may impact your project and the breadth (parameters) of your search.

Examining Your Original Concern in Light of the Exploratory Search

In your initial browsing and skimming of the literature, you most likely encountered differences in the ways authors addressed your concern. You may even have found discrepancies between their concerns and your own. At this point of the search, your purpose is not so much to resolve those differences or to mediate between them as to analyze them and determine whether they are worthy of further study and which ones might be most suitable for further investigation.

Michelle had begun her literature search with the hope of being able to come up with a proactive proposal for how fine arts teachers could work together to influence school board members in her school district. She discovered very quickly, however, that she could not address her frustrations about school practices without learning how policy makers operate and how decisions about arts education policies are made. As a result of that insight, she decided to learn more about music education and educational policy in general before trying to mobilize others to join her cause.

Considering Multiple Perspectives

Most initial research questions are broad and touch on many areas within the field of music education. To find answers to those questions, you must break them into more specific sub-questions. The sub-questions are more likely to correspond to a body of literature, and a critical assessment of that literature will help you to define and narrow your questions still further. This process continues until your question has become so focused that its potential answer may be considered a contribution to knowledge in music education.

Mode of Inquiry

One way of focusing your area of concern for further study is to imagine how it might change if it were asked from each mode of inquiry.

> Despite her ongoing interest in relating race and ethnicity to the vocal production of adolescent choral singers, *Jeannette* also contemplated writing a history of the National Association for the Study and Preservation of African-American Music (NASPAAM) and debated this option with her peers. She clearly felt pulled to address what might be called culturally appropriate, culturally responsive, and/or culturally equitable music education for students from different kinds of communities. She also considered whether she could use a qualitative or quantitative approach to examine music education in different communities. In fact, she contemplated replicating a qualitative study such as Ladson-Billings' *The Dreamkeepers* (2009) with a focus on music instruction. Eventually, influenced by Chinn's 1997 study, she returned to the question of vocal production, wondering whether it would be possible to observe, or even measure the relationship between ethnic identity and vocal skills for high school or collegiate non-music-major singers.

Thinking Ahead

At this point of sorting through the literature, it might be useful to ask yourself some pertinent questions about the search process itself: What do you hope to get out of this project? What are realistic limitations of your time, financial resources, expertise, and professional aspirations? Are you working toward a doctorate or are you about to finish your master's degree?

> *Michelle*'s decision to examine policy sources proved more costly and time consuming than she had thought, but she still felt that a detailed reading of extant studies concerning arts policies and education would be useful. She also realized how broad her area actually was; her search needed to be focused substantially if she wanted eventually to conduct a study herself. Because Michelle

found that she enjoyed the reading process, she got permission from *Prof. E.* to continue reading and produce as her semester project a comprehensive literature review, always remaining open for eventually focusing on a more limited research topic.

Greg did not feel nearly as good about this stage of his literature search as Michelle. Still uncertain about pursuing the degree, he found it difficult to commit to the research process in full. Somewhat aimlessly, therefore, he amassed information on publications concerning string education in public schools. He collected the titles and call numbers of method books and articles in professional journals and magazines and even took notes on many of them. But he still was not sure of the purpose of that activity because he found it difficult to ask further questions about what seemed to him to be obvious and known information.

Dale, quite clear about his career path, had the following practical and personal concerns:

- My desired outcome is to be a music education professor. Focusing on popular music or jazz as a way to diversify the band curriculum might mean I am labeled as a "popular music" scholar. Is that what I want?
- I want to finish the doctorate as quickly as possible.
- I want to make use of expertise I gained while working on my master's thesis.
- I have young children at home. It is important to me to choose a topic that does not take me far from home for long periods of time. What kind of study would allow me to work mostly from home?

Quite set on continuing with his interest in the use of technology for teaching compositional and music analytical skills, *Carlos* was not sure why he needed to ask further questions. How much more specific could he get? Getting a bit frustrated with the slow process of finding good sources and more "doable" questions to ask, he turned to Dale for additional advice. Going beyond Dale's questionnaire, he began to read the entire thesis. Doing so made him gain confidence that he could move forward because he saw possibilities that made sense to him.

Because *Chi-Hui* was to return to home after completing her master's degree, she made the practical decision, together with Prof. E., to focus on literature in the field of Comparative (or International) Music Education. Not only did that decision shorten the initial broad-scaled search process, but it also provided Chi-Hui with a subject—music education in the United States—that she could report to her colleagues in her home country.

Whether you are doing a literature review that is limited to a few weeks, expands over several weeks or a semester, or—as in a doctoral dissertation—might take a year or so, avoid rushing this phase of your project. The more and better informed you are about the literature, the easier you may find it to articulate what interests you professionally. And, as it is with the musician in you, the more passionately you care about something, the better you are as a professional. Try to frame an idea that truly interests you, contributes to your professional growth, and has broad applicability to future work.

At the master's level, make sure that the research idea you choose has sources that are relatively easy to find and do not involve trips to academic libraries far from home. Consider also whether and how your topic is related to your present job and whether it may be applicable to future jobs. At the doctoral level, take into account that you are at the beginning of a research agenda which might prove useful in your future career as a college professor. If that is your plan, practical concerns may be less important than topics that address larger issues.

Specifying the Parameters of Your Search

Based on the considerations above, decide on the parameters—the boundaries—of your literature search. What approaches seem to hold promise for explaining your articulated concern? What aspects addressed by others are of less interest to you personally? If the purpose of your literature review is to lead you toward proposing and conducting your own study, what methods and procedures seem manageable to you and which ones require a commitment of time or money beyond what you are able to do?

Dale decided on the following parameters:

- He was interested in knowing about band directors' work conditions.
- The general education literature connected job satisfaction in education with issues of faculty retention.
- The literature on job satisfaction interested him more than the literature on faculty retention.
- Several research studies purported to measure job satisfaction in different professions. He wanted to obtain those studies and see what type of approaches the researchers had taken to examine job satisfaction.

Michelle began to build a bibliography of research studies on arts policy and education by paying attention to the chapters in three music education research handbooks (Colwell, 1992; Colwell & Richardson, 2002; Colwell & Webster, 2011). She planned to examine all of the studies mentioned in the various chapters on arts policy and music education and, in the process, also skimmed many of the other chapters. She also discovered a periodical, *Arts Education Policy Review*, which had many articles of interest to her. Michelle was amazed at the amount of information collected in those sources and at the differences they revealed between the perspectives of so-called music education advocates and scholars. As a result, she began to pay attention to similar handbooks in education and psychology.

Collecting Evidence from the Research Literature

By now you have learned to distinguish various source types and genres from each other. You know how to separate overview articles from indices and hard copies from electronic research sources. You also have begun to pay attention to layout and format differences between textbooks, professional literature, and scholarly publications.

The phase that follows involves what was referred to in Chapter 1 as critical or reflective reading. Having drawn some boundaries around a research idea and decided on a first set of project parameters, it now is time to describe and then evaluate the content of what you read. Both steps require detailed note-taking.

Describing Source Content

Notes at this stage of the literature search are more comprehensive than the basic information you began collecting earlier. Now you must keep track of the bibliographic information that identifies the source (explained earlier in this chapter) and also write an annotation or abstract that describes the source. For note-taking, use any format and medium that is convenient for you—most important is that your record-keeping is systematic and detailed. Commonly used are computer data files, pages in a spiral binder, or even 5x7 inch note cards. Many universities subscribe to *RefWorks* (www.refworks.com), an online service where notes and information can be stored; *EndNote*, a computer software product, and *Evernote*, an Internet-based note-taking service, are also used by many writers.

When describing a source, use the author's own words or a close paraphrase with page citations to address its structure. To do this, you need to:

- Locate basic question(s) the source purports to examine. Sometimes this is an explicit "purpose statement"; other times you must deduce it from the author's words or the title of a publication.
- Establish the mode of inquiry addressed by the source; that is, whether the source deals with ideas or describes present or past actions, events, and experiences. If you cannot clearly identify the primary mode in which a study is conducted, identify it as such.
- Find a logical explanation about the importance of the author's purpose in the context of related literature.
- Trace the author's use of referenced sources and determine their trustworthiness.
- Identify the author's description of the approach used to answer their research question.
- Take note of the reported reliability and validity (or absence thereof) of any data-gathering tools (i.e., tests, observational systems, attitudinal and rating scales, questionnaires, formal or informal interviews).
- Paraphrase or quote the study's results. Assess the extent to which the study's results address its stated purpose.

Ideally, it is advisable to describe the content of a source in enough detail to keep from having to return to the original source later for more information. Realistically, however, since your reading purpose changes over time and according to the project you are working on, you should leave enough space in your notes to add further details as the need arises.

Evaluating Source Content

If you find that the author uses trustworthy evidence and logical arguments, you may conclude that the source is suitable for use in your own quest—either to support your research, or as the basis for a new way of thinking about an issue. If you find a source lacking in the qualities just described, you may also be able to use that "verdict" for arguing why more research on the same subject might be needed. In both cases, you now have reason to use the publication in your own work. Depending on the purpose for which you are reading, of course, your evaluation of the content of a publication may differ in depth and focus. Your "verdict" should be based on the presence or absence of clear principles of scholarship as established by the research community in music education (see Chapters 5–12).

Once you have found a number of studies that clearly connect to your research idea, analyze each source in light of that idea. This turns a collection of individual sources into a related body of knowledge. When you establish categories and sub-categories within that body, you are on your way to finding possible researchable topics within the idea. Jeannette's experience may serve as an example. It led her to the creation of a so-called literature map (see Hart, 2007; Creswell, 2009), a graphic representation of the categories and relevant publications in a literature collection.

> *Jeannette* initially cast a wide net to find scholarly sources, which resulted in a large collection. Jeannette found that the sources fell into five basic groups: choral music, vocal production, minority adolescents, cultural relevance, and measures of student perceptions of ethnic identity or musical preference. Would literature from any of these categories help her to address her initial research interests? The most appealing idea was bringing together vocal production and ethnic identity, similar to Chinn's (1997) study. Analyzing the literature to see how her sources addressed related ideas was her next task. *Prof. E.* suggested that a literature map might help clarify further directions of her work.

Constructing a Literature Map

A literature map can: (1) show you visually which studies are most pertinent to your evolving research topic; (2) help you to recognize important sub-topics within your literature collection; and (3) bring to light some possible connections between sources that may not be obvious when you consider them individually.

Jeannette built her map by first labeling it with a tentative title ("Relationships between Racial/Ethnic Identity and Vocal Production for Adolescent HS Students") and then naming the two main categories within her literature collection: "racial and ethnic identity" and "vocal production for high school adolescents." She then examined the sources in each category more closely, which helped her to define sub-categories for each of the main categories.

Within the category of vocal production, Jeannette found that the sources in her collection tended to address either the developing voice or the impact of vocal models on vocal production. Within the category of racial/ethnic identity, studies either discussed theories of racial/ethnic identity or they evaluated or reported on measures of racial or ethnic identity. A third sub-category explored relationships between racial or ethnic identity and musicianship or organizational involvement, both of which she equated to the choral experience. The map helped her see that additional evidence was needed for the construct of ethnic identity. Consulting the *Encyclopedia of Multicultural Psychology* (Jackson, 2006), therefore, she located references to several related sources, which she then added to her map.

Jeannette's complete literature map can be seen in Figure 2.4.

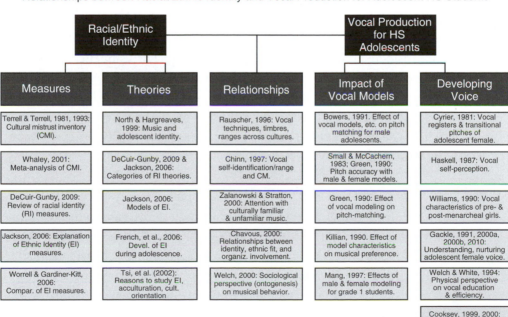

Relationships between Racial/Ethnic Identity and Vocal Production for Adolescent HS Students

FIGURE 2.4   Jeannette's Literature Map

Organizing the body of knowledge relevant to your research concern into a literature map can help you clarify the researchable topics within your concern. It may also point out strengths and weaknesses in your literature collection:

- Which studies are most pertinent to your evolving topic;
- What sub-topics are dealt with by particular researchers;
- Whether there are any "holes" in the literature that still need answers;
- How other researchers designed studies for topics similar to yours.

Such clarification requires, however, that only well-conducted studies be included in the map. These are studies for which you know the exact purpose statement, pertinent terms and their definitions, mode of inquiry, research methods, data gathering and analysis tools, and results and conclusions as stated by the author. It should be clear that the results of each study address the author's stated purpose; the conclusions are truly based on the results; and any limitations in design are properly acknowledged. If all of those characteristics are not included in a research report, you may suggest that more work should be done. Recognizing gaps or contradictions in the existing evidence is the start of identifying possible topics for research.

A literature map can also help you to tie together or synthesize the findings from your literature search. Chi-Hui, for instance, might have used the literature map to reorganize her literature collection by categories. Jeannette's approach, however, was more innovative. By integrating cultural identity and vocal production to answer questions about the singers in her high school choir, she brought previously disparate ideas together (Strike & Posner, 1983, p. 346).

If you construct a literature map, use only those sources that most closely relate to your evolving topic. This means re-assessing the value of each publication as it pertains specifically to what you have chosen to pursue further. You may find that some information you once considered relevant are no longer applicable. For Jeannette, for example, this meant discarding references related to choral music and cultural relevance—ideas that had been important in the earlier phases of her search, but were no longer needed. If your literature map does not end up looking as neat as Jeannette's, keep in mind that its purpose is to help you think about: (1) what you are looking for; and (2) what you expect to do with the information once you found it.

Taking the Next Step in Your Research Journey

The form in which the findings from your literature analysis are communicated differs according to why the review was undertaken in the first place. If your purpose is simply to gather and organize extant research related to a topic of interest for an introductory research course, you may write a scholarly literature review paper as a class project. If you are designing a research study, your analysis of the literature will become the basis for your research purpose and rationale (discussed in Chapter 4) and suggested research design (elaborated in Chapters 5–12). For publication, scholarly articles frequently combine the discussion of related literature with the rationale, while master's theses and doctoral dissertations typically have an entire chapter, frequently titled "related literature," where the writer establishes his or her place in the topic under consideration.

If your purpose is simply to gather and organize the literature about a topic of interest, it may be acceptable to create an annotated bibliography. You do this by collecting the notes about your sources, following the guidelines for annotation suggested in this chapter, and organizing them in a way that is useful to you: alphabetically, historically, or by sub-topic, for instance. For most scholars an annotated bibliography is the starting point of a literature review, however, rather than the end product.

Do not be intimidated by what may seem an overwhelming task. Remember that it took years to become an accomplished musician, but you began the process of learning and never looked back. We think the same will happen now that you have begun the journey into doing research. After having evaluated and abstracted a number of publications, we are confident that you will begin to develop a sense for what separates strong and trustworthy publications from weak and less convincing ones. Developing such a discerning ability is one of the most crucial skills in your preparation as a competent researcher. It requires expertise that grows over time.

Chapter Summary

1. Exploring an area of concern involves: (a) getting to know the library—bricks and mortar and/or virtual; (b) preliminary searching to discover search vocabulary and preliminary sources; and (c) keeping track of search terms and results.
2. Framing your research idea prior to your formal search makes for a more efficient search. You do this by considering the results of your preliminary search, imagining multiple perspectives from which your idea might be examined, thinking ahead to the outcomes of the project, and specifying the parameters of your search.
3. Collecting literature-based evidence involves both describing and evaluating the literature you collect.
4. Constructing a literature map can help you identify: (a) studies that are pertinent to your research ideas; (b) sub-topics within your literature collection; and (c) connections between sources that might not otherwise be obvious.

Topics for Further Exploration

1. Preliminary sources versus research sources.
2. The formatting requirements of your institution or publisher.
3. Differences between taking notes and critically evaluating articles.

Suggested Assignments

1. Team up with a colleague and label yourself as A or B. Interview your partner about his or her experiences in exploring the literature. Be as specific in your interview as possible, covering as much of the process as possible. After about

20 minutes or so rotate to another colleague and be interviewed about the same subject. Each class member should have been interviewer and interviewee at least once. Compare the answers and experiences and identity commonalities and differences among all answers. Assess how the questions were asked and which questions yielded the most detailed responses.

2. Locate in the library the major indices relevant to research in music education.
3. Locate the various Handbook(s) for Research in Music Education (i.e., Colwell, 1992; Colwell & Richardson, 2002; Colwell, 2006; and Colwell & Webster, 2011). Briefly describe their similarities and differences. Compare them to at least one similar handbook in education or the social sciences.
4. Initiate a computer search for references.
5. Read three articles from research journals and evaluate them according to the criteria described in this chapter.
6. Construct a literature map for your literature collection. Explain it to your colleagues.

Recommended Reading

On literature mapping:
Creswell, J.W. (2009). *Research design: Qualitative, quantitative, and mixed methods approaches* (3rd ed.). Los Angeles: Sage.
Hart, C. (2007). *Doing a literature review: Releasing the social science imagination.* London, England: Sage. (Reprint of 1998 edition.)

On literature reviews:
Cooper, H.M. (1985). *A taxonomy of literature reviews.* Paper presented at the annual meeting of the American Educational Research Association, Chicago. ERIC Document Reproduction Services No. ED254541. Retrieved September 19, 2008 from http://www.eric.ed.gov/

On print and electronic music sources:
Gottlieb, J. (2009). *Music library and research skills.* Upper Saddle River, NJ: Pearson/Prentice Hall.

three

Reading and Thinking in Conceptual Frames

This chapter asks you to place your research ideas into the contexts of:

- Historical and conceptual developments in research on music learning and teaching;
- Established scholarly ways of thinking;
- Identifiable laws, theories, paradigms, or belief systems.

The perspectives and concepts described in this chapter introduce you to thinking as a research activity. Such intense form of reflection includes what we refer to as "writing to learn."

Introduction

Thinking as a research activity cannot be done in a vacuum. Rather, making critical judgments about extant studies in music education, an umbrella term for broad areas of diverse practices and study, requires context knowledge. When, where, and why a study was conducted provides you with historical and conceptual information about research perspectives, purposes, and methods that have shaped a field.

The history of music education scholarship, while relatively young, adds a particular dynamic to what researchers have accepted as more and less important constructs about the learning and teaching of music. You can think about those constructs as they developed over time or you can compare their likenesses and differences across time, thereby sorting them conceptually. In either case, you can get a sense of where a study fits in the body of knowledge established by the research community in music education.

The chronology may help you see how ideas have changed or stayed the same over time. Conceptually, that knowledge determines whether what the profession "knows" requires ongoing validation in the light of new insights and findings. You may even discover that there really are no "old" ideas and/or questions; only old answers. New contexts may require new studies.

Because of the distinct research traditions and scholarly predilections that describe music education as a field of study, how a study contributes to the building of knowledge or to the strengthening of beliefs in our field represents the current body of research. When examining it, you will soon discover that historical and conceptual precedents shape your own way of thinking. Therefore, as you read this chapter and think about its content, place your own articulated and mapped research interests (see Chapter 2) into the larger frame of where the field is historically and conceptually. Visualize where you belong in the broad field that makes up music education practices.

A Brief Chronological and Conceptual Overview of Music Education Scholarship in the United States

Both chronological and conceptual contexts have shaped our professional field and literature. As brief and possibly oversimplified as this overview may be, it is intended to illustrate that what has transpired over time impacts the how, why, and what of today's research.

The Chronological Context

The first peer-reviewed research publication in the field of music education appeared in the United States in spring 1953 with the *Journal of Research in Music Education*. In 1963, the *Bulletin of the Council for Research in Music Education* made its debut under the supervision of the College of Education and School of Music of the University of Illinois and the Office of the Superintendent of Public Instruction, Urbana, Illinois. Both journals provided music educators with a research forum of their own and an avenue for disseminating information pertinent to the research community. Prior to the establishment of those two publications, observations about musical actions and ideas, present and past, were gathered by researchers of many different disciplines and published in journals specific to education, psychology, musicology, and music theory.

A third publication representing music educators' early efforts to establish their own field of study was *Basic Concepts in Music Education* (Henry, 1958). This book contains a selection of articles that describe the scope of concerns paramount to and typical of music education as a field of study in the middle of the 20th century. Specifically, the book acknowledged the multidisciplinary characteristic of the field, stressing the relationship of music education to such disciplines as philosophy, psychology, and sociology. A second edition of the book was edited by Richard Colwell in 1991.

Comparing both editions to each other, Colwell (1991) asserted that the basic concepts prevalent in the field of music education remained the same between 1958 and 1991 (p. x). In the 1991 edition, Colwell also observed the rapid growth of the field, an observation that can be substantiated by the following advances:

- The number of journals publishing research-based articles (either online or in hard copy) has steadily increased (see list in Appendix D). This may be due in part to efforts by music education researchers and the cooperation of MENC in the late 1970s and early 1980s to constitute so-called Special Research Interest Groups (SRIGs) whose members either meet or communicate with each other on a regular basis.
- The Internet and World Wide Web enable music educators to share publications from around the world, resulting in a larger international involvement of readers and authors than was the case even 50 years ago.

Between 1953 and the 1990s, research on the pedagogy of jazz, singing, and various instrumental specializations increased as well. This can be documented by the emergence of peer-reviewed journals in which performance specialists examine pedagogical techniques and repertoire according to scholarly principles (e.g., *Journal of Band Research*, *Journal of Research in Singing*, and many others).

Two comprehensive research handbooks on the learning and teaching of music (Colwell, 1992; Colwell & Richardson, 2002) and a two-volume handbook, called the *MENC Handbook of Research on Music Learning* (Colwell & Webster, 2011) have further changed the landscape of published music education research in English-speaking countries. Referencing a much larger number of peer-reviewed research studies than were available in the mid-20th century, the topics range from research methodology to the status of knowledge in particular subject areas. The entirety of studies collected in the handbooks conveys the kinds of questions music education researchers have addressed since the publication of the first *Basic Concepts* in 1958.

The topic areas deal with (to name a few): cognition and perception, both from a socio-psychological and biological/environmental perspective; teaching and learning strategies, singling out skills in listening, singing, and music reading; musical development and learning for able-bodied and challenged autistic learners; music teacher education as well as neuro-scientific approaches toward the study of processing musical sound; and the relationship of social contexts to curricular decision making about the learning and teaching of music.

What began as a small field with a single journal has continued to expand in form and function as additional journals (both in electronic and in hard-copy format) have become available. Professional symposia and conferences have also multiplied beyond those that were common in earlier years, adding a far greater number of professional papers and documents (again, both in e-format and as hard copies) to the published body of knowledge currently accessible to music scholars and practitioners alike. The ease of communication via the Internet and international air travel has made this expansion virtually exponential, as music educators frequently communicate with peers from around the world.

The plethora of information available brings forth another question: How does a researcher prevent information overload, keeping track of the many ideas in the field, and placing them in categories that make sense? Over time, scholars have developed conceptualizations for obtaining a "bird's eye view" (a macro view) of what otherwise might appear to be an enormous and unwieldy amount of isolated information held in studies that bear little relationship to each other.

One methodological approach to handling the growth of published information in our field is that of conducting so-called *meta-analyses*. They are statistically driven examinations of large pools of data derived from discrete studies. A meta-analysis requires, however, not only a careful examination of each study included in a pool but also a solid grasp of statistics so as to avoid the old adage among statisticians of "garbage in, garbage out." Once you have established that a pool of "good" data exists, various software programs are available for their analysis (for further information and reference see, for instance, Borenstein, 2009; Cooper, Hedges, & Valentine, 2009).

A Conceptual Perspective

Central to our definition of music education research as the study of the learning and teaching of music are the terms *learning*, *teaching*, and *music*. This is why in Chapter 1 we provided a visual model in which we called the learner, the teacher, and the subject matter music "interacting agents." Figure 3.1 is a macro perspective of the same three "cogwheels," now surrounded by the fields and areas of study that, over the years, have become the body of professional literature informing us about the learning and teaching of music in its many different settings. In the case of school music, all three cogs may be visualized in constant motion. In situations where the learner interacts with the music without an intervening expert (called here the teacher), interesting questions arise as to whether the learner perceives a need for the third (missing) cog.

Figure 3.1 lists numerous themes and subject areas in which questions about the teaching–learning processes have been examined. In the figure, the themes and subject areas are named as key terms, fields of study, and subject headings under which specific investigations may fall. The terms may aid you in searching for relevant literature but may also guide you in placing each study you read into the mosaic of extant research.

The mosaic that represents research in music education ranges from issues specific to the learner, the music, and the individual teacher to queries that focus on the dyadic or triadic relationship between these three interacting agents. Whichever aspect you investigate, the results have consequences for the entire body of knowledge.

All communication occurs in specific contexts that are created by circumstances not under the control of any of the three "agents." Researchers therefore consider contextual factors as interacting with what goes on in teaching–learning processes. In the model depicted in Figure 3.1, context provides the background for what is to be studied. You

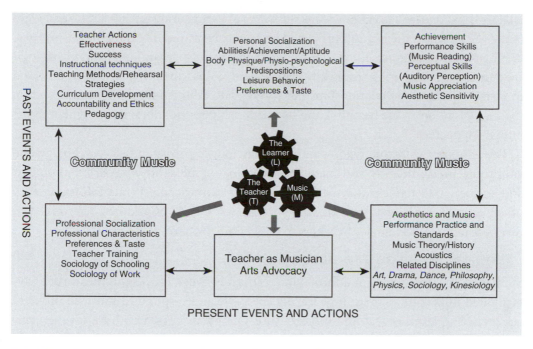

FIGURE 3.1 Suggested Fields, Areas of Study, and Selected Key Terms Relevant to the Study of the Learning and Teaching of Music

might, however, elect to focus on those "contextual" factors as your main concern. The options are indeed limitless when you consider the amount of research that has already been conducted on each of the component parts in the interactive web (and how much still needs to be done).

Music as an Interactive Agent

Research in and about music is often seen as the purview of musicologists, theorists, and ethno-musicologists, and scholars in cultural studies as well as anthropology. Music educators rely on such work because what we know musically is a considerable part of the core of our profession. The musical knowledge and skills we have shape our instructional choices and thereby influence our students' musical knowledge and skills.

The origins of music have been discussed and speculated on by many scholars and in many cultures for thousands of years. A most interesting research account of music in pre-historic times may be Steven Mithen's (2006) evolutionary hypothesis about a "music-like communication system" among the Neanderthals "that was more complex and more sophisticated than that found in any of the previous species of Homo" (p. 234). For later times, Cho (1975, 2003) refers to early writings on the music of China dating back to about 122 B.C.E., in which the pentatonic pattern and the 12 semitones within the octave are described. Today, thanks to the work of many musicologists, ethno-musicologists and anthropologists, we have knowledge of musical traditions as they have shaped diverse cultures in Africa, Asia, India, the Mediterranean, and Middle Eastern countries.

Hardly anyone fails to acknowledge the works of Pythagoras (ca. 500 B.C.E.) and Plato (427–347 B.C.E.) as the beginning of modern concepts of studying the physical and aesthetic properties of music in relationship to their cognitive, emotional, and physiological dimensions. Both Pythagoras and Plato sought to describe physical aspects of sound in terms of arithmetic relationships but it was Plato who, additionally, speculated on the manifestation of the beautiful and its relationship to the moral development of the human character.

Today, many academic fields—anthropology, music theory, music psychology and education, music therapy and medicine, neurology, philosophy, physics, physiology, and sociology, to name a few—shape our musical knowledge. While informing each other, each discipline has its own scope of research questions and has determined its own research methodologies by which to answer the former.

The Learner as an Interactive Agent

Studies on the immediacy of informal interactions between music and the learner have facilitated information about how learners perceive and respond to music at different age levels and levels of training and exposure. Out of such research have sprung questions as to whether different kinds of music might cause different kinds of responses among listeners of all ages, gender orientations, and music backgrounds. Matters of technology in the classroom, both virtual and real, and in application to music are more important than ever.

A major difference between instructor-guided and self-monitored learning may lie in the impact that educational institutions have on the articulation of teaching rationales, curriculum theory, and political practices. Issues of power and control among groups of unequal standing deserve attention as much as a learner's socio-economic conditions, socialization, and enculturation. In light of those issues, informal learning gains have been contrasted to formal gains and self-guided learning strategies to teacher-designed instructional strategies. Philosophically, questions prevail about what it means to "educate musically" (Bowman, 2002) both inside and outside of school and about the multi-faceted nature of curriculum that guides formal instruction.

Studies exist on the appropriate sequence of learning tasks for children of different age groups as well as on the measurement of musical ability and achievement. Scholars in various disciplines have addressed issues specific to aesthetics and aesthetic education as they become evident in matters of musical identities, preferences and taste in and out of school settings have been investigated by music psychologists, educators, sociologists, and philosophers alike. Theories have been developed to explain how the brain functions and how it may process musical stimuli. The theories come from studies directly related to music as well as from work in child and adult psychology, education, medicine, and neurology.

Methods of measuring performance output through quantifiable tests have been studied separate from and together with qualitative methods that use personal, verbal-comparative judgments in assessing achievement and aptitude. Reaching consistency in both measurements and judgments has been central to relating performance outputs of learners and teachers to each other. In the name of arts advocacy, researchers have collected data with the purpose of documenting the benefits of music instruction on general learning skills, notably literacy and mathematical comprehension. Such investigations have often led to public debates about the purpose of the arts and music in the curriculum as well as in society.

The Teacher as an Interactive Agent

In efforts to increase instructional effectiveness, researchers have measured the time teachers typically devote to activities that routinely shape a lesson or rehearsal. Such an approach can determine, for instance, how much time a teacher spends on warm-ups, on reviewing old and introducing new materials, on speaking versus making music, and on summarizing the lesson objective(s) for the day. Proportions of time spent on specific lesson components are related to the use of verbal and non-verbal instruction in a lesson and on the relationship between forms of instruction and classroom management. Research conducted by school music supervisors has compared teachers to each other or has related their teaching skills to student performance.

As representatives of the two worlds of music and education, teachers are often considered the best advocates for music and the arts in the curriculum, yet most music educators find themselves challenged to articulate publicly why music plays an important part in a learner's formal education. To make that case skillfully and convincingly, data are needed in support of that claim. Presenting such proofs, however, can be a challenge that requires careful thought, because what may be in the best interest of a student educationally may not be of the best interest musically. Resultant conflicts have only begun to be debated in the music educational research literature and among cultural theorists.

An area of more recent interest among researchers has been the study of how music teachers become who they are. Using terms such as *music teacher identity construction*, *social psychology*, and *sociological studies*, you might find investigations about connections between identity construction, instructional values, and the actions that shape what goes on in classrooms and rehearsal halls across the country. Such knowledge is considered relevant for decisions about needed curricular reforms in music teacher training programs.

Contextual Factors as Interacting Agents

Spearheaded by researchers interested in the application of social-psychological and sociological theory to music education, instructional contexts of varying kinds have become major investigative topics. These are broad and, at times, unwieldy; requiring interdisciplinary approaches that span from music to political science, psychology to sociology, and physiology to ethics. The questions they have raised and examined ask how educational goals and purposes are set and processed within different institutional and political settings; how musical values are socially acquired; and how upbringing, social status, and cultural/artistic opportunities impact learning styles, patterns, and motivations. Any decisions about educational goals are as dependent on those forces as they are about decisions about music repertoire selections, disciplinary measures in the classroom, and what constitutes appropriate instructional sequences at various levels of schooling.

As in the case of research on other "agents" listed in Figure 3.1, considering the music education research literature over several decades makes you aware that certain questions come up repeatedly but are viewed differently by researchers from different generations and philosophical perspectives. You may also notice that certain facts in the field have changed whereas others have remained constant. To conclude, no single answer is ever satisfactory for very long because perspectives change. To respond to such changes and remain useful, research must be ongoing. However, do not reject a study because it is old; similarly, do not put trust into findings just because they are recent.

Ways of Thinking: Perspectives and Their Consequences

In the Introduction to this textbook, you conducted observations by zooming in or out of Times Square via webcam images. Dependent on the position of the lens, you either obtained a "bird's eye view" of the entire scene or were able to pay attention to minute details about a few people in the picture. Looking at the large picture is sometimes called a macro view; correspondingly, zeroing in on details becomes a micro view. The choice in between—the mesa view—articulates how the minute details fit into the larger picture.

Describing views "from a higher plane" (Popper, 1945, p. 3) can be as necessary and beneficial as detailing one part of the larger picture from the ground up. Each approach is important because one is needed to inform the other. But each view also has drawbacks because in either case important information can become lost. After all, you might fail to see the proverbial "trees in the forest."

Figure 3.2 pictures two observational positions similar to those just described. However, rather than dealing with micro and macro perspectives, the images speak to the role the observer takes in different research settings. Image A portrays a curious, but personally uninvolved bystander—a *non-participant* observer—in a research setting. By viewing the setting from the outside, the researcher is expected to remain personally detached from that which is being observed. In Image B, the researcher is accepted as integral to that which is being examined; she becomes part of the setting. Presumably "objective" observations change into personal accounts of self-knowledge, the probing of feelings and sensations, and interpretations of "lived" experiences.

Image A stands for the classic scientific model of research which, in most instances, guides the quantitative approach to inquiry. It is representative of what philosophers call a modernist point of view, a firm belief in the power of "objectively" reasoned and observed evidence (the data) in support of what is factual and therefore true. If the observed evidence is measurable (i.e., quantifiable) in the form of *variables* and can be replicated, a belief becomes factual. Philosophically known as "empirical" or "logical positivism," this trust in tested evidence as truth favors physical observations and mathematical logic over intuitive insights or spiritual and otherwise intangible beliefs.

Image B stands for those theoretical perspectives that favor qualitative approaches to data gathering and analyses. Believing objectivity to be impossible, researchers recognize and acknowledge the contextuality of what they themselves experience as they seek to

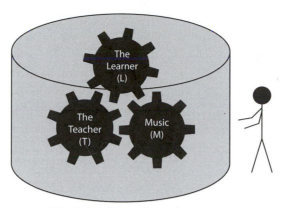

The Researcher as Bystander:
Non-Participant Observer, Involuntary
Contributor to All Observed Interactions

IMAGE A

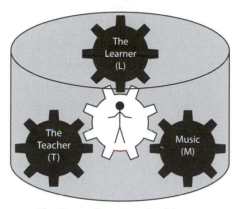

The Researcher as Involved Agent:
Conscious Contributor to All Recorded Interactions

IMAGE B

FIGURE 3.2 The Researcher's Role as Participant and Non-Participant

observe what goes on around them. Philosophically, Image B illustrates what are known as postmodernist beliefs. More recently, new labels for such viewpoints have sprung up in response or reaction to the variety of different philosophical positions about what constitutes research, knowledge, fact, and truth (for more, see Chapters 5 and 7).

The research modes as defined (see Chapter 1) emphasize that empirical approaches may be quantitative or qualitative in nature so long as they look at present-day events, actions, and experiences. This means that, just as in the case of macro or micro views, neither the quantitative nor the qualitative way of thinking is "right" or "wrong"; instead, each has consequences for how research findings become part of what we know as the body of knowledge of music education. Researchers are expected, however, to share with their readers how their ways of thinking has resulted in their respective methodological choices.

Empiricists might at times decide to combine quantitative and qualitative approaches. For example, an investigator who identifies herself as a non-participant observer might nevertheless use intuitive language to explain the meaning of her data. Or, a quantitatively orientated empiricist may conduct informal conversations with a few likely research participants prior to developing a large-scale measurement tool, such as a multiple-choice test or a questionnaire (for qualitative approaches, see Chapters 7 and 8; for quantitative, Chapters 9 to 12).

Historians, viewing music teaching and learning through the lens of the past, are expected to maintain detachment and avoid bias on the one hand and to show intuition and empathy for the social and political circumstances of the time frame under investigation on the other. When interpreting people's words and actions on the basis of printed and pictorial evidence, for example, such intuitive knowledge would stem from being well grounded in knowledge about how people lived and thought during the time period in question (see Chapter 6).

Philosophers, too, understand that both quantitative and qualitative research approaches are necessary to explore the world of ideas fully—be they of the past or in the present. Philosophically, in fact, their connection is crucial to appreciating the relationship between the angles chosen to pose a question, the methods used to address it, and how the findings are interpreted. Both the lens and the role a researcher chooses for a specific project have therefore become important philosophical topics of debate in and of themselves (see Chapter 5). When you read critically, you should be familiar with those debates at least to some extent.

For instance, always think about the angle from which an author has approached a study and ask yourself these questions:

- What are the acknowledged roles and lenses you recognize in a piece of writing?
- How have they contributed to the question(s) asked and answered in each reported investigation?
- How do you yourself think about a particular idea?

Any serious efforts to address such questions turn your reading into thinking as a research activity.

Thinking as a Research Activity

As a discipline, the art and science of thinking has been subject to systematic study in many countries, by many individuals of different scholarly disciplines, and for many centuries. You might say the body of scholarly knowledge—across disciplines, around the world, and over time—is the depository of those efforts. You join in on the scholarly conversation by learning to discern how researchers:

- Draw valid inferences from observations, statements, or sources;
- Think about things in a deliberate way;
- Know whether or when they present "certain" knowledge as compared to belief or perceived reality;

- Reflect their own worldviews in comparison to those held by others;
- Approach and describe ethical decisions in the course of their reported work.

Philosophically, the bulleted points have much to do with the way researchers see and describe the world. Quantitative empiricists and scientifically trained philosophers, for example, may look for indisputable and replicable facts as their data whereas many qualitative empiricists and postmodern philosophers may accept that shared knowledge and beliefs represent certain truths only for the time being, if at all. Each study you read reflects any such perspective even if it is not always spelled out clearly. But you will be able to tell whether or not: (1) a report is clearly written and logically convincing; (2) methodological decisions seem to be ethical; and (3) beliefs about teaching and learning are theoretically grounded as well as evidence-driven.

A major tool in obtaining answers to these questions lies in your knowledge and use of logic, an important domain (or branch) of the field of philosophy. Logic is also an indispensable tool in many other aspects of doing research and should therefore be seen as the foundation of all scholarship—whether in the so-called hard or soft sciences, music education included.

Logic as a Major Research Tool

As "the study of the principles of reasoning" (*American Heritage Dictionary of the English Language,* 2011, p. 1031), the application of rules of logic to your own and other people's thinking and writing is key not only to good scholarship but also to everyday living (e.g., Allen, 2004; Cannavo, 1998; Hult, 1996). However, as Leonard (1957), Tragesser (1977), and a number of other logicians have pointed out, there is not only one logic but, instead, several. Foremost among them are formal/informal, propositional/inferential, dialectic, phenomenological/interpretive, and combinations of each of these (see Chapter 5). One such combination is informal–propositional logic, also referred to as Aristotelian logic, and perhaps implied most often when people refer to "logic" as "clear thinking." However, not all scholarly writings follow that approach. We therefore contrast it below to additional forms of scholarly reasoning; namely, *dialectic* and *phenomenological* thinking as well as *interpretivism.* Your increasingly critical eye will likely discern these and similar forms of reasoning in current music education literature. Take note of how each speaks to you.

Aristotelian Logic

Very common to Western thinking, Aristotelian logic underlies how most students are taught to think and write. In the English language, for example, sentences that contain "because," "since," or "although" suggest linear inferences from one point to another. "Because it rained last night, therefore the street is wet" is an argument that contains evidence and a conclusion. Grammatically, inferences make use of adverbs such as "therefore," "hence," or "consequently" to assert a claim.

A claim, to be convincing, should be followed or preceded by a reason that contains sufficient evidence to qualify as such. If the evidence is weak, the reason is weak as well, which then questions the veracity of the claim and, therefore, the argument. Hart (2007) defines a claim as "an arguable statement" and evidence as "data used to support the claim" (p. 88). This definition allows the building blocks in the argument to go in any order as long as all of them are present. To build a valid line of argumentation, then, weave several arguments together in such a way that the final conclusion seems inevitable. It makes the argumentation linear because only that evidence is being used that contributes to the conclusion.

As an example, think of what lawyers do in their roles as prosecutor and defense attorney, respectively: Each start from the same Point A, the defendant being accused of being guilty. Then both lawyers argue in a straight line toward two very different end points in their respective argumentations: The prosecutor ends with "therefore, the defendant is guilty" and the defense attorney with "therefore, the defendant is not guilty." Both lawyers build their reasoning on different evidence (in both cases presumably air-tight) spiced with emotional rhetoric (often quite graphic), by which to make the jurors believe that each Point B is inevitable (and, thus, a "logical") conclusion.

Dialectic Logic (Dialectics)

Dialectic reasoning moves from a claim (the *thesis*) to a counterclaim (the *antithesis*) to a synthesized claim (the *synthesis*). Still inferential, the reasoning takes argument and counterargument into consideration when making a case. The *American Heritage Dictionary of the English Language* (2011) defines dialectics as: "The contradiction between two conflicting forces viewed as the determining factor in their continuing interaction."

"Being—not-being—becoming" is such a dialectic (Mautner, 2005, p. 159), but the synthesis ("becoming") is not so much a conclusion as it is the new thesis which immediately creates its own opposition, "not-becoming." Again, in the tension between becoming and not becoming lies the next synthesis.

Some writers in music education describe as dialectic the tensions that lie in such binaries as product–process, informal–formal learning, or teacher-guided and student-initiated learning. While possibly very descriptive, such polarities do not in themselves represent dialectic reasoning as long as the assumption prevails that tensions created by the polarities can be resolved.

Rather, dialectic reasoning tends to question the possibility of any permanent resolution of such forces. Think, for example, of music not only as an aesthetic but also a social object; as an artistic product as well as a subjective, entertaining "doing"; a social–political, yet highly personal, emotional force; a self-serving but also an educational instrument. Critical theorists in music education would place such polarities into further structural contradictions and perpetual conflicts that can be found in institutional learning: the call of social justice in unequal class structures; knowledge as selected by and for specific social groups in society; and unequal economic and socio-cultural conditions within a country and across the globe that impact on personal choices and freedoms. Any solutions to such detected incongruities can hardly ever be more than temporal which, however, should not render them any less important in a critical reader's eyes.

Figure 3.3 portrays both propositional and dialectic logic as described above. As straightforward as the images appear here, their equivalents in scholarly literature are not always easily identified. Rhetoric and stylistic "fillers," while at times important writing tools, can also cloud the clarity of reasoning intended by the writer. But, if at all possible and where applicable, identify claims, reasons, and data as well as original claims, counterclaims, and synthesized claims.

Phenomenological Logic

As a second alternative to informal–propositional logic, phenomenological reasoning (or phenomenology) has been "practiced in various guises for centuries" (Smith, 2011, para. 2). It is an intentional "first-person view" (Smith, 2011, para. 1) by which the quality of an experience is described. Such description allows for speculation, emotion, and reason to be used as equally important means to convey meaning. Such "free form" investigation combines observation with personal insights to fully understand the phenomenon as it presents itself to the researcher.

The term "understand" in this context has a special connotation and is therefore often referred to by phenomenologists as *verstehen* (fer-shtee-hen), the German word for understanding. Although not much different in its meaning from the English term, the German word as used by German philosopher Martin Heidegger implies that you bring to life the relationship between what you observe and your role in it. Such descriptions of "lived experiences" become both claim and evidence (data) because what a writer claims to be true should be accepted as long as the descriptions are honestly delivered (phenomenology is covered in more detail in Chapters 7 and 8).

Interpretivism

Similar to phenomenology but not necessarily written in a first-person view, interpretivism is at the heart of many qualitative studies in which the researcher does not separate

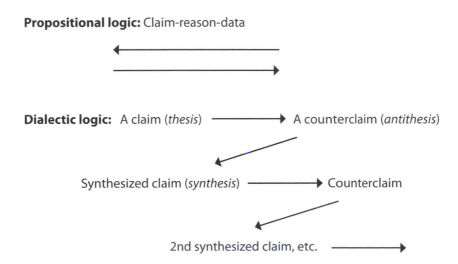

Propositional logic: Claim-reason-data

Dialectic logic: A claim (*thesis*) ⟶ A counterclaim (*antithesis*)

Synthesized claim (*synthesis*) ⟶ Counterclaim

2nd synthesized claim, etc. ⟶

FIGURE 3.3 Diagrams of Propositional and Dialectic Argumentation

herself from that which she studies (Image B in Figure 3.2). In its strictest sense, the technique derives from *hermeneutics*, a term that means text analysis or interpretation. Originally coming from the field of theology, hermeneutics keeps close to the text which means that it only seeks to explain what is there rather than question or speculate beyond it.

Interpretivism is applied to qualitative data in music education that require honest and reflective interpretation (Elliott, 2002) in response to the research questions posed. Unlike in phenomenology, broader speculations, while perhaps feasible and interesting, should be avoided. However, some qualitative researchers who base their work on the tenets of interpretivism insist that no method of reasoning should ever override the need to deal with a particular phenomenon in its own way and language (for more information, see Chapters 7 and 8).

Consequences for Scholarship in Music Education

Because not all "logics" (Leonard, 1957) are the same, it becomes necessary to look at extant studies in terms of not only what they are about but also how their respective authors structured the written word. Once you have ascertained the answer to those two questions, follow up with: What perspective or perspectives seem to be most suitable for particular questions and their examination? Do certain topics lend themselves to particular paths of reasoning? And, does the primary data gatherer take the role of participant or non-participant observer?

If you read studies in which the focus is on music as a non-verbal means of communication, how did specific researchers address sound images by means of the written language? Did they capture important nuances of meaning that could not have been described verbally? If you detected any distortions that resulted from the process of transposing the meaning of one set of symbols to another set, what means and avenues would have been open to the researcher to minimize such distortions?

Many such questions should guide your reading before you settle on your own research purpose. We urge you to couple much of what you reflect about with writing down your ideas as a way to clarify your thoughts. We call that process "writing to learn." Returning to the think–read–observe–share spiral, putting your thoughts down on paper—that is, sharing them with yourself—might be one of the best ways to learn how and what you think.

To guide you in the task of writing to learn, always reflect on your own position in the field of music education. Place what you examine into historical as well as conceptual contexts and articulate how your own interests resemble or are different from other researchers' perspectives, roles, and angles. Accept that your own beliefs about the learning and teaching of music may be challenged as you examine other writers' beliefs.

Fact and Belief in the Study of Music Learning and Teaching

Scientists couch facts that have remained constant over time in phrases known as "laws." Many such laws exist and have been with us over time as, for instance, the law of gravity or Newton's law of motion (in short: to any action there is an equal reaction). A musical law might state that sounds are physical waveforms traveling by air. The law might further assert that sound waves are perceived differently by young and old adults due to age-related, physical changes in the ears. Either of the two musical laws can be confirmed repeatedly by means of observations of many kinds. However, laws can be disproven if new evidence makes such a move inevitable.

Laws that have changed over time may be called *paradigms* (Kuhn, 1970). A field is paradigmatic when it accepts and acts upon extant laws uniformly and consistently. Because disciplines in the humanities allow many viewpoints to live side by side, Kuhn called research in the humanities *non-paradigmatic*. Whether or not that assessment is entirely true anymore may be subject to debate among scholars. But it certainly seems to be true that music education scholarship is characterized by the co-existence of theories, models, and beliefs about the learning and teaching of music. As a reader of research you should know how a particular work contributes to what the profession declares to be its accepted body of knowledge. As a researcher, you should be clear in your own mind whether a question contributes to affirming a law or expressing a belief. In addition, you should have an informed opinion on how evidence functions in either case.

About Scientific Laws, Paradigms, Theories, Models, and Beliefs

Physical laws are paradigms—accepted principles of operation; so are many agreed-upon principles in the medical field. For example, the medical community holds to a common paradigm about the distinction between a cold and the flu. One should not be treated like the other. But it can also happen that certain scientific paradigms change over time. Bloodletting by way of leeches, once a medicinal paradigm, has long been abandoned for newer treatment conventions.

Following Kuhn, we define a paradigm as a theory with tested laws that are widely believed to override others in a scientific field or discipline. As such, a paradigm should be time-proven. However, you probably know by now that what is or is not factual is considered subject to debate among philosophers and physical scientists alike. Beliefs and the principles guiding them, then, play an important role even in scientific research.

Like paradigms, principles emerge once similar findings for like questions get confirmed over time and give you reason to trust a researched explanation as long as no contradictory evidence emerges. Beliefs require the largest amount of trust in what is merely at the earliest stage of testing or still is untested personal experience, common-sense knowledge, or casual observation.

A paradigm (or principle) of importance to music education researchers might be that humans process sounds cognitively and emotionally in different ways regardless of any physical hearing acuity. What triggers different levels of processing in the listener or performer then becomes the subject of further research, possibly leading to new theories and/or new questions. The angles that inform how we ask new questions are the theories.

Educational psychologist Guy Lefrançois (2000) describes a theory as:

> a statement, or more often, a collection of related statements whose main function is to summarize, simplify, organize, and explain observations and to permit prediction about events relating to this set of observations. Some of those statements may be described as laws, others as principles, and many as beliefs. (pp. 10–11)

Lefrançois' definition separates laws from principles and beliefs. Again, how much each of them contributes to the building of a theory depends on the strength of the evidence behind them. Just as accepted facts get either confirmed or refuted because of newly gathered evidence, so do theories because new insights can either question or reaffirm old explanations. Explanations should simplify rather than complicate the observations (or known facts). Therefore, a theory should always be "practical," that is, provide insights you did not have before. If a theory is less clear than its underlying observations, you may have reason to question its need.

You can find different, at times even conflicting, theories in the music education literature about levels of processing music. The theories come from various disciplines, often even proposing interdisciplinary ways by which to explain how humans respond to music. You have, for instance, theories of perception, musical taste, and aesthetics. Some of them originated in psychology, sociology, and philosophy; others are from musicology, ethnomusicology, anthropology, and culture studies.

The image of the interacting cogwheels used in Chapters 1 and 3 illustrates our understanding of a theoretical framework known as *social interactionism*, a belief system derived from *pragmatism* as an interdisciplinary way of looking at how individuals and groups of individuals interact with each other in particular contexts. It certainly is not the only or perhaps not even the best theory, but it can be useful for grasping the breadth and diversity of our field. It groups its many parts according to a perspective derived from a social-psychological theory (for more about interactionism and other philosophical perspectives, see Chapter 5).

Lesser-known theoretical frameworks generally require more detailed documentation than do familiar or commonly known theories. For instance, the theory of behaviorism, widely applied to research in music education over many years, may require less explanation than its underlying framework of *Cartesianism*, a thought process going back to philosopher René Descartes and instrumental for understanding behaviorism.

To word your own thoughts and questions according to the language common to a particular theory, familiarize yourself with the field(s) integral to it. Subsequently, think about how you might describe your own thoughts either verbally, visually, or even artistically.

Considering the Interdisciplinary Nature of the Field

As a composite of at least two disciplines (music and education), questions about the learning and teaching of music tend to be situated between the research traditions and concerns of several fields of study. For a long time, such fields have not only included psychology but, ever since the middle of the 20th century, also neuroscience, medicine, and sociology. Most likely, therefore, many of the studies you read have an interdisciplinary twist.

For example, an investigation of the effect of hearing loss on performance acuity may deal with musical, neurological, and physical constructs of sound perception and its measurement. Research on motivation probably includes relevant sources in psychology, education, sociology, and social-psychology. Researchers interested in past events and actions may draw from the political history of a particular time frame to distill questions that deal with relationships between population statistics and major cultural movements that may have influenced music instruction in the schools. Other researchers may originate relevant questions by examining thoughts in sports psychology, marketing, and other fields that address various forms of skill training, communication, and motivation.

When researchers draw from one discipline to investigate questions in another, you should expect that they show familiarity—at least rudimentary—with the technical know-how of the secondary field. Of course, having your expectations fulfilled requires, similarly, your own familiarity with the terminology and ways of doing things in other fields. Staying abreast of the broad array of research traditions that connect to the study of the learning and teaching of music is not only necessary but also exciting; consider it an added bonus of becoming a music education scholar.

Articulating Your Choice of Model

You can model your thoughts in a variety of ways. You may describe them verbally and take the reader through a carefully crafted process of defining constructs and terms important to an investigation. You can also present it in the form of a graphic or otherwise artistic rendition that reflects your viewpoint of how observations or ideas are connected to each other.

One model was visualized earllier as interacting cogs. Whether or not you find the image useful depends on how you think about the field known as music education. Do you see music as the non-changing subject matter in the middle of the instructional process or do you consider repertoire an interactive force that determines the nature of all communications between learner and teacher? Do you place the learner or the teacher in the center? Are there other forces you consider more important than those accounted for in the interacting cogwheel image?

A different model was briefly introduced in Chapter 1 as distinguishing between various functions of research. Similar to how scientists draw such distinctions, Gates' (1999) labels of basic research as engineering, field, and context studies categorize investigative findings according to their usefulness in advancing specific kinds of knowledge—the why, what, how, and when of researched facts. As you read the literature to sharpen your own ideas and take them to the next level of specificity, you may look for how other researchers' studies function within the suggested model as basic, engineering, field, or context studies.

A third approach toward organizing extant studies in music education research might be the kinds of observations that provide the data in a particular investigation. Called the *descriptive–relational–causal loop*, it is a three-level, sequential model in which the observations (the data) have distinctly different purposes. Introduced to researchers in education in the 1970s (e.g., Gage, 1963; Rosenshine & Furst, 1973) as a quantitative model alone, it may be useful also in sorting and categorizing other kinds of research.

The first level comprises those studies whose purpose is the careful description of behaviors and actions either verbally (qualitative) or numerically (quantitative). Level 2 subsumes investigations whose purpose is the determination of (a) relationships among observed behaviors and actions, and/or (b) the association of observed behaviors/actions to external events. Both purposes fall under the label of *relational research,* a term applicable to certain quantitative (Chapters 9–12) and many qualitative studies (see Chapters 7 and 8). Level 3 represents those inquiries which estimate or test the causal effect of one set of observations on another set. Causality between events, actions, and behaviors of the past is the purview of historical research (see Chapter 6); experimental studies (see Chapter 12) are about measured causality between current events, actions, and behaviors.

The model emphasizes that the three levels should inform each other so that one level becomes the prerequisite to the next. Qualitative studies might be best suited for identifying and describing important actions and behaviors in their actual contexts, keeping them connected to what goes on in specific situations without disturbing the integrity of the interactions studied. Quantitative studies become important once valid descriptors of learning and teaching behavior have been identified as quantifiable variables and can therefore be hypothesized as being either relationally or—eventually—causally connected to clearly defined outcome variables. When you accept this way of thinking, the descriptive–relational–causal loop can become useful for theory building because the evidence has the potential of getting stronger with each level.

Certain music educator–artists who define their work as rooted in the artistic field of music hold that valid research in the arts should be exclusively situated in the artistic product itself. Composing, then, is "doing research"; understanding a musical work by performing it means to grasp its underlying theory. This belief (and theoretical position) recently has gained momentum among scholars and should be acknowledged. Often referred to as "arts-based living inquiry" or "arts-based educational research" (e.g., Jevic & Springgay, 2008; Springgay, Irwin, Leggo, & Gouzouasis, 2007; Barone & Eisner, 2006), theory formation lies in the doing of music, in the doing of art. When it expresses what it is supposed to express, theory and evidence become one.

The Function of Evidence in the Research Process

Some scholars hold that the more observations a researcher has in her data pool, the better the findings corroborate extant theories and beliefs. An opposing viewpoint is that certainty of belief is in itself impossible because uncertainty is a basic principle of human existence. In between those two viewpoints (for which there are many philosophical labels, see Chapter 5) are a considerable number of others which speak about the place of science, knowledge, the arts, and teaching in relationship to each other.

A recurring theme among scholars in many disciplines is the question of how evidence functions as contributor to theory. Asked more directly: What comes first? A basic "hunch" (or assumption) of what causes certain behaviors and actions to occur, or many observations that lead to conclusions as to why the observed behaviors or actions might have occurred in the first place? Does evidence contribute to knowledge *inductively* or *deductively*? Does the theory drive the observations (deduction) or do the observations drive the development of a theory (induction)?

To illustrate that question, Figure 3.4 (inspired by and indebted to Pidwirny and Jones, 2010) shows how the elements of observed reality might lead to an understanding of that reality. Like Figure 3.3, it illustrates the relationship between data and claim in lines of reasoning.

Inductive and Deductive Reasoning

Deduction seeks to confirm theory by collecting evidence after the fact (the theory occurs *a priori*); induction formulates a theory in advance (*a posteriori*). Although you may recognize in this description elements of the proverbial "chicken and egg" question, you may also realize the implications of such a distinction: When you begin with a theory

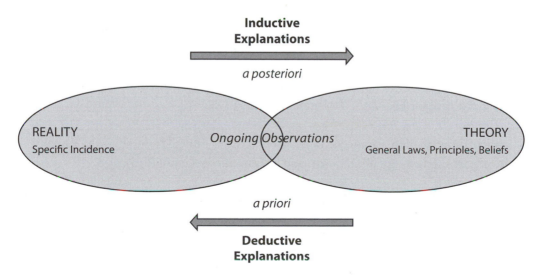

FIGURE 3.4   Scientific Understanding: Inductive and Deductive Reasoning

and collect data to test it, you run the risk of only looking for those data that support the theory from the onset. When you collect data to eventually formulate a theory, you never can be certain that another set of data will not falsify the theory.

The following story, as told by the late Irving Rothchild (2006), professor emeritus of reproductive biology at Case Western University, is a reflection on an essay by Vicky Hearne (1995) that contrasted the behavior of highly trained primates. Rothchild's story concludes with questions we want to ask you as well:

> A chimpanzee and an orangutan, housed separately, were each given a small hexagonal block of wood and an assortment of differently shaped openings into only one of which the block would fit. They knew they would be rewarded for making the right choice. The chimp examined every detail of the floor, walls, and ceiling; the openings and every side of the hexagonal block; smelled it, tasted it, and, after trying one opening after another, found [an opening] the block would fall into. The orangutan scratched his back with the block, and then sat with a far-away look in his eyes for what seemed to the human observer like forever. He then put the block directly into the hexagonal opening. Was the chimp an inductivist? Did the orangutan consider the problem, form a hypothesis, then test it? Which one was the scientist? (Rothchild, 2006, p. 2)

At the center of the process in both cases are ongoing observations. To return to the chimp, the orangutan, and Rothchild's questions: "Were both scientists? Yes. Was the orangutan more so than the chimp? No. He was only different" (p. 4).

Popper (1968) argued that no observation can ever be made without a pre-conceived perspective (theory), thereby rendering the distinction between inductive and deductive research a moot point. Rothchild (2006) objected to that point of view and used Hearne's story to argue, instead, that:

> Induction and deduction are two, usually different but never contradictory, approaches to problem solving. The problem must be solved by testing the validity of the conclusion or inference, etc. reached from either direction. Induction and deduction are thus valuable, often complementary, tools that facilitate problem solving. (Rothchild, 2006, p. 3)

Scientific inquiry, then, can occur in a variety of ways, but all holding to the same principle of learning through observation and examination. Again, Rothchild:

> The only true scientific method is to use whatever tools we can to make observations, ask and answer questions, solve problems, test a theory, etc., and it doesn't matter whether we use induction, deduction, or any other kind of reasoning to do so; it would be a heresy to deny the validity of *any* method that helps us learn to know. (Rothchild, 2006, p. 4; emphasis in original)

Exploration: Articulating Your Thoughts

State in writing what you believe as a teacher, a student, and a researcher about the relationship of knowledge to fact, beliefs to truth, and "subjectively" perceived to "objectively" measured experiences. Connect your thoughts to readings from your research class and elsewhere. Give your essay a title that reflects its content.

Chapter Summary

1. Much interesting and exciting material has been accumulated over the hundred-year-plus history of music education as a field of study.
2. At every stage in the spiral of inquiry, consider the benefits and drawbacks of your perspective. Apply this understanding when you read studies of many kinds and in a variety of disciplines.
3. How we come to perceive the world, know the world, and judge and justify our own actions and those around us as good and desirable should become the starting point for any question we consider important enough to ask. Discern the answers to such questions from the writings you examine.
4. Researchers disagree with each other about the veracity of worldviews and beliefs; about what is factual and what is not. Nonetheless, they respect scholarly argumentation when it is forthright and clear.
5. Different forms of logic guide the way in which authors articulate their beliefs. Examine those forms and apply them to the way you yourself think.
6. Stating your own thoughts clearly requires "writing to learn" when using philosophy as a tool for thinking. Increased writing skills have the potential of making you a more discerning reader than thinking alone would do.
7. To organize the material you read, you might want to keep in mind the model of learner, teacher, and music and how the three relate as interactive agents to each other.
8. Other models and organizing principles than the model the authors suggested exist. Inform yourself about them as you advance your reading and comprehension skills pertaining to research.
9. Distinguishing between theories, paradigms, laws, principles, and beliefs in music education research might allow you to determine the respective strength and weaknesses of many studies you read.
10. As a critical reader and novice scholar, you should strive to locate evidence that:

   ■ connects to and supports extant research;
   ■ provides further explanations for or provides confirmations of evidence that strengthens specific theories and their explanatory power.

Topics for Further Exploration

1. Obtain copies of: Colwell's (1992) *Handbook of Research on the Teaching and Learning of Music*, Colwell and Richardson's (2002) *The New Handbook of Research on Music Teaching and Learning*, and Colwell and Webster's *MENC Handbook of Research on Music Learning* (2011).

   a. Examine the Tables of Contents for recurring themes that could be placed into the schematic of Figure 3.1.
   b. Read comparable chapters from two or more of the textbooks and trace advances in research between 1992 and 2011 as portrayed by the chapter selections. (For example: Compare Swanwick's chapter "Musical development: Revisiting a generic theory" with Runfola and Swanwick's 2002 chapter "Developmental characteristics of music learners.")

Suggested Assignments

1. Take a recent written assignment from a recent class and show it to trusted colleagues. Ask them to honestly critique the logic and argumentation you used in the paper, looking at the relationship between claim and evidence. Even if you received a good mark for the assignment and are proud of the document, invite questions that may clarify what you said and ask for suggestions to improve your work.
2. Find sources comparable to the music education *Handbooks* in education and psychology and look for: (a) similarities and differences in these sources as compared to those mentioned above, and (b) themes and topics not addressed in the music education handbooks.
3. Examine the Tables of Contents of a random selection of the *Journal of Research in Music Education* (JRME) since 2002 and place each title into the schematic of Figure 3.1.

Recommended Reading

Fieser, J., & Dowden, B. (Eds.). (2003). Deductive and inductive arguments. *The Internet encyclopedia of philosophy*. Retrieved January 12, 2012 from http://www.iep.utm.edu/ded-ind/

Forster, M. (1998). Guide to Thomas Kuhn's *The Structure of Scientific Revolutions*. Retrieved on January 6, 2012 from http://philosophy.wisc.edu/forster/220/kuhn.htm

Mackenzie, N., & Knipe, S. (2006). Research dilemmas: Paradigms, methods and methodology. *Issues in Educational Research, 16*. Retrieved January 6, 2012 from http://www.iier.org.au/iier16/mackenzie.html

Pine, R. (2011). *Essential logic: Basic reasoning skills for the twenty-first century (online ed.)*. Retrieved January 6, 2012 from http://home.honolulu.hawaii.edu/~pine/EL/Essential-Logic.html

Trochim, W. M. (2006). *The research methods knowledge base* (2nd ed.). Retrieved February 4, 2012 from http://www.socialresearchmethods.net/

four

Toward a Rationale and Research Plan

Writing a Contract With Yourself

This chapter suggests developing a research plan according to the following steps:

- Name a research topic;
- Craft a purpose statement;
- Construct a rationale.

Having collected literature related to a topic and examined the place of your topic and literature map in the broader scope of music education knowledge, you now develop a rationale and plan that points the way to your research proposal and study.

Introduction

In the fourth week of RC 533, *Carlos* announced to *Prof. E.* that he had made arrangements with teachers in his home school district to distribute a question-naire. He had therefore drafted one (similar to what he had seen in Dale's thesis) about issues concerning technology in the music classroom. Proudly showing Prof. E. a draft created with SurveyMonkey.com, Carlos was surprised (and somewhat frustrated) when Prof. E. did not even look at the questionnaire items but simply asked for clarification about his research topic and purpose, expressing concern that his plan seemed vague and also had not been "approved" by certain committees. As he tried to answer Prof. E.'s questions about topic and purpose, Carlos realized that he was not able to articulate either of them clearly. Reluctantly, he had to admit that he had "put the cart before the horse" by trying to start gathering data before his research plan—purpose, rationale, and methods for data collection and analysis—was fully complete.

A research plan divides a project into specific tasks that, once carried out, assure that you have done what was necessary to complete it. Such a plan directs future action and serves to remind yourself and others what needs to be accomplished. In Appendix E we provide guidelines for completing such a plan, separated respectively for a research course project and final graduate degree requirements such as a thesis or dissertation. Once formalized in writing and accepted as a research proposal by your department or institution, it is a *bona fide* contractual agreement: You have indicated what you will do to meet the institution's research requirements and the institution has approved your proposed actions. The reason for this requirement is the following: Anyone conducting research in the United States that includes interaction with other people (called "human subjects" in research terms) is obliged to seek the approval of the Institutional Review Board (IRB). As an appointed committee within each public institution, the IRB is tasked with assuring that all institutional research complies with the requirements for ethical conduct as outlined by the Federal government. Further information is included later in this chapter.

Your Preliminary Plan

Do not rush into submitting an official proposal or seeking IRB approval without having laid out a "plan in progress" first. Continually tighten and revise your plan as you learn more and more about methods and designs common to each respective research mode (see Chapters 5–12) and about different proposal formats (see Chapter 14). Dealing with each aspect of the plan systematically will move you forward in the spiral of inquiry. This is so even if, at times, the demands of critical reading, working on class assignments, and continuing life outside of class may look insurmountable, particularly in the context of a one-semester course. Remember that you became an accomplished musician step by step; the same is true for becoming a researcher. Learning to do research is a process—one that requires, like musical performance, continuous refining.

A good first step is to begin to formulate in writing:

■ A clearly articulated research topic;
■ Rationale (and literature review);
■ Purpose statement.

Then think about:

- A possible research design, including:
  - any purpose specifications (i.e., research questions, sub-purposes, hypotheses);
  - proposed methods for study and analysis;
  - expected findings or answers.

   As you develop your research plan, whether for an introductory research course or for the completion of an original research project, keep in mind the experiences of the students in RC 533. Like them, some of you will focus more on the "search" aspect of thinking and reading, with a *review of the literature* as your desired outcome. That may be the extent of your work for the time being, while others will turn from reading to doing original research, with the literature collection laying the foundation for their research plan. If you are a master's or doctoral student, this plan may become the basis for the formal research proposal that will guide you through your thesis or dissertation.

   In a single semester, you may expect to get a good start on your literature collection, purpose, and rationale. If planning to do original research for a thesis or dissertation, you will learn the basics of the research methods with which you will plan the design of your research. No student in RC 533 completed an entire research study in a single term, and the same is likely true for you.

Articulating Your Research Topic

Liam came to class one evening rather upset. His mapping of the research related to the scat singing techniques of Louis Armstrong had led him to question the basic premise he voiced at the beginning of the semester: Rather than viewing the music of Louis Armstrong as a technical singing accomplishment, his non-musical sources (i.e., historical, social science) suggested that the practice of scat singing was the result of a long line of African-American musical and social factors. The sources seemed to suggest that Louis Armstrong used scat singing to build up his own stage persona, but that he did not originate the practice. After sharing this new perspective with his colleagues in RC 533, Liam realized that bringing together these seemingly disparate ideas would make his research stronger. "So now, what I want to know is: What are the differences between the reality of the origins of scat singing and the myths surrounding it?"

Contradictions like the one Liam encountered between assertions in the research literature or among experts in various fields can be the basis of well-defined research topics as well as purposes. A similar contradiction was the basis of a research question pursued by Montemayor and Moss (2009). Several professional sources (among them, Battisti &

Garofalo, 1990; Lisk, 1991) suggest that musical score study without a recorded model is preferable to study with a recording. Montemayor and Moss (2009), however, found an inconsistency between that belief and the research literature, with some studies suggesting pitch and rhythm error detection by student conductors to be superior when recordings were used, whereas other studies did not report such findings. Their topic thus became error detection skills with and without the use of recordings. Already quite well defined, articulating the actual purpose statement would be a matter of clarifying the context of the research, its specific questions, design, and methods. It eventually reads, to investigate "effects of aural-supported rehearsal preparation on selected behavioral and evaluative elements of novice teachers' rehearsals" (p. 236).

Crafting a well-defined purpose will ultimately help you create a title that clearly communicates your intent. The published title of the study above, for example, reads "Effects of recorded models on novice teachers' rehearsal verbalizations, evaluations, and conducting" (p. 236). You may think that deciding on a title may seem a "final" activity, but we suggest even at this preliminary stage of the process to come up with a "working title" that you will sharpen as your project takes shape.

Not all projects move quite as smoothly from topic to purpose to title. However, the more clearly you pinpoint your research topic, the more likely it is that a well-articulated purpose and rationale follow. Narrowing your research ideas to a single topic, therefore, means becoming ever more exact about what and how you wish to observe, describe, or examine. You may also consider several options before committing to a single topic. Carlos's earlier struggles illustrate this process: Did he wish to know what teachers did with technology—how they organized their curricula or their classroom activities? Or, was he more interested in understanding how students used technology at home, so that he could better gear his curricula to meet their needs? Was he interested in documenting changes in musical achievement with and without technology in the music classroom? Or did he just want to describe what he observed? From what perspective would he consider this issue?

Because the research journey differs from person to person, there is no single way to narrow your thoughts from general to specific. We therefore return to three of the RC 533 students to illustrate what it means to commit to a research topic. As you will see, this was easier for some students than for others:

> *Chi-Hui* hoped to limit her search to studies in International (also called Comparative) Music Education. From cursory reading on that subject, she learned that investigating similarities and differences in the development of formal music education in different countries was a legitimate research project.
>
> *Christy* had begun the semester wanting to study string pedagogy. Interested in the history of that area, she had narrowed her research idea to a study of how evolving thoughts about educational pedagogy had influenced string pedagogues from 1800 to 1900. But there was little explicit mention of pedagogical

thinking in the literature she found. Should she expand her search in some way, or narrow it to focus more on individual pedagogues? Her interest was piqued and she began to look more carefully at the pedagogues that had originated the methods. As she did so, she took note more about the historical context of those methods than about their contents and pedagogical strategies.

Thinking and reading about connections between the component parts of her topic led *Michelle* to visualize music education policy as a game. She came to view it as a "seesaw" (if not "tug-of-war") between arts education advocacy organizations, the concerns of special interest groups (such as the music industry), state and national politicians, and the policy makers in her state. The teachers and students seemed to be left on the sidelines. This image gave her the idea to look for similarities and differences in decision making and actions between the groups involved at both ends of the spectrum: The policy makers and the policy implementers.

Imagination caused the three students to think broadly, yet in ever more specific terms. Your own imagination, too, should allow you to envision your project as a concrete "thing" rather than a nebulous whim. Becker (1997) calls that process "visualizing" your research, imagining what a study might literally look like when the topic is worded this or that way. Think creatively about new ways of seeing what seemed fully examined before. Make concrete connections between what you read and think about as well as what you begin to observe, describe, and examine. Live with the ideas for a while so that they take on a life of their own.

Initial interests in practical matters such as musical actions in the classroom can be addressed philosophically when you turn them into quests about ideas and constructs of thought. Marguerite might transform her excitement about Christopher Small's ideas into a research study by exploring how relationships are affirmed and celebrated "every time we take part in a musical performance" (Small, 1997, p. 4). She especially liked the question: "What does it mean when this performance takes place at this time, in this place, with these participants?" (p. 3). Her research idea became concrete enough to imagine a context where it could be explored. Although to an uninvolved bystander the idea might still sound abstract, for Marguerite it would likely be a natural and practical outcome of her earlier voiced concerns.

Crafting the Research Purpose

The purpose statement communicates the intent of a particular study. As such, its wording should be succinct and unambiguous. It should clearly state the functional scope and boundaries of your research project—nothing more and nothing less. Returning to the functions of research, described in Chapter 1: Are you more interested in examining theories and principles applicable to music learning and teaching in general or do you favor inventing technological and other learning tools? Is your perspective that of an "engineer-type" educator or a philosopher–educator? Do you want practical answers to "how to" questions or are you primarily interested in generating more questions?

How you respond to any of these queries guides the wording of your purpose statement. If you are not sure about your stand on those questions, consider replicating an existing study or taking up a question posed by well-established researchers in the conclusion of one of the pivotal studies in your literature collection that led you to your topic to begin with.

Initially, you may begin simply: "The purpose of this study is to investigate/examine/ explore . . ." Fill in the component parts of your topic as outlined in the literature map and as they speak to your expectations of what the study should accomplish. Provide a sense of: (1) the mode of inquiry (i.e., historical, empirical, or philosophical) employed in the study; and (2) whether the study is based on descriptive (qualitative or quantitative), relational, experimental or mixed approaches, but avoid specific reference to any particular data-gathering device unless the purpose is the development of a tool. As your purpose takes shape, make sure to share it with colleagues in and out of class, as their perspective will help you to make sure your purpose is as clear as possible.

Below are first attempts by many of the students in RC 533 to formulate purpose statements. What feedback would you give them?

Carlos—to examine the effects of music technology on high school music classes.

Chi-Hui—to explore research related to the formal teaching of Western art music in Taiwan and North America.

Christy—to investigate the historical contexts of influential string methods between 1800 and 1900.

Dale—to investigate how band directors in his home state perceive and describe their work conditions.

Jeannette—to relate vocal style and singing range to a measure of ethnic identity in adolescent females.

Keisha—to study the effects of speech-based rhythm patterns on the rhythmic achievement of young children.

Liam—to explore stories about the cultural and musical origins of the practice of jazz scat singing.

Michelle—to compare music educational policy publications from the business, policy, and public education communities.

Note how a purpose statement triggers expectations about what a proposed study might look like. Make suggestions for clarifying and sharpening the focus where necessary and ask about the implications of the words each student used. Consider your own developing purpose statement in light of the advice you give to the students in RC 533.

Purpose Specifications

It is common for researchers in all modes of inquiry to specify the parts of their purpose with research questions, sub-purposes, or hypotheses. Many students who are preparing a research plan for the first time find this activity helpful for delineating the scope of their research project. Writing down your purpose specifications can clarify whether you have: (a) addressed all necessary variables or questions; (b) chosen the appropriate mode of inquiry and research methods for collecting and analyzing data; and (c) learned the requisite skills or techniques for completing the research successfully.

What you choose to call your research specifications is a matter of personal choice, and depends somewhat on the mode of inquiry and methods with which you work. "Research questions" are typically used by philosophical, historical, and qualitative researchers; quantitative researchers may also use that term or may call the delineations of their purpose "sub-purposes" or "hypotheses." The latter term—hypotheses—has a specific mathematical connotation and is used most frequently in ex post facto and experimental research (see Chapter 9). Once your purpose statement and any specifications have been clearly written, you use the evidence from your literature review to make a case for your research plan.

All aspects referred to in the purpose must be investigated if the topic is to be handled adequately. Consider, for example, the purpose statement suggested by Jeannette earlier in this chapter "to relate vocal style and singing range to a measure of ethnic identity in adolescent females." At least four aspects inherent in that purpose should be identified by appropriate research questions after all terms have been defined: vocal style, adolescent female singing range, ethnic identity and specific measures of that construct, as well as any relationships between these.

If this kind of specification is not clearly stated, you risk wandering into territories not pertinent to the purpose of the study. That danger is particularly strong in studies where purpose statements are rather general in nature. When researching the essence of ideas and philosophical concepts, the purpose specifications provide the parameters that determine, beyond the purpose statement, the major line of argumentation. A preconceived line of argumentation is essential if you wish to avoid a thinking-while-you-work approach. A word of caution is also in order for the word "effect." It suggests causality between what is being observed and leads to particular considerations about research method and design—whether quantitatively or qualitatively, historically or philosophically.

Regardless of the form in which purpose specifications are presented, they should express what aspects of the topic the investigator intends to study. They should not reflect, however, how these aspects are to be investigated. Issues such as the development of a measurement tool, test, questionnaire, or observational system belong to the method section of an investigation because they refer to the procedures by which a purpose or quest is addressed. You may face difficulties in developing a measurement tool or test, but facing those difficulties is generally not the purpose of your study. Of course, there are exceptions to nearly all rules. For instance, you might think of yourself as an engineer who tries to work out technological difficulties in some music hardware or software. As a result, you eventually might find new ways of doing things, truly a sign of leadership in music education scholarship.

Constructing a Rationale for Your Research Purpose

A rationale is a logical explanation of the fundamental reasons why something exists. In research, it is usually an argumentation constructed to underscore the importance of the research purpose in light of the literature. The rationale has a dual function: (a) for you as researcher it represents the logical framework for the stated purpose of the investigation; and (b) for your readers it serves to explain the purpose of the study, and establish the theoretical framework by which its results can be interpreted.

A good way to learn how to construct a rationale is to analyze rationales written by other researchers. As noted in Chapter 3, research argumentations (or rationales) tend to be constructed using claim–reason–evidence/data in any order. In the Recommended Reading at the end of this chapter are references for research articles that vary according to philosophical, historical, and empirical modes of inquiry, and represent qualitative, relational, and experimental methods. Despite their seemingly different formats, each contains the elements of rationale and purpose in some explicit form. For the sake of brevity, each of these is from a published research article.

Begin by skimming multiple dissertations and research articles related to your research purpose so you can see: (1) how authors often present the same information (rationale, purpose) in unlike ways; and (2) the difference between the breadth, depth, and length of a thesis or dissertation rationale as opposed to those printed in published studies. Once you have examined several rationales written by other researchers, it is time to begin to construct your own. As you get involved in crafting your argumentation, you will come to understand more clearly how your research should be designed. What follows are two examples—one by Moga, Burger, Hetland, and Winner (2000) and the other by Miksza (2006).

After citing two political figures in support of the arts in general, Moga et al. (2000) began their article as follows:

> The view that studying the arts makes people more creative and imaginative is part of our folklore. Arts education at its best includes open-ended inquiry, creative problem finding, and creative solving. It is reasonable to wonder, therefore, whether studying the arts helps develop creative thinking skills that can be developed in other areas besides the arts. (p. 91)

Circular as it may be, the rationale opens the path to the authors' inquiry. It is a writing tool to set the tone for what is to come.

After a thorough summary of reviewed literature, Miksza (2006) ended the review as follows:

> Conclusions regarding which specific behaviors predict improvement in performance achievement cannot be made on the basis of the existing research. Additional studies with carefully controlled conditions (e.g., length of time, musical material) are necessary if valid generalizations are to be made. The current study [therefore] was an investigation of practice effectiveness as one component in a broader psychosocial model of music learning. (para. 6 and 7)

Mikza's rationale suggests his study to be based on the need to obtain further evidence in support of a particular psychological theory.

Other rationales may be derived from such reasoned needs as:

1. The exploration of seeming contradictions in empirical, philosophical, or historical studies.
2. The synthesis of ideas from disparate sources, resulting in a new way of thinking about a familiar issue.
3. The creation of a narrative about a particular aspect of music teaching and learning in the past.
4. The systematic exploration of constructs of thought related to the learning and teaching of music.

Differences in the written forms of a rationale depend on the kind of document you are working on, but the basic structure and purpose of the rationale should remain the same.

To summarize: Consider whether your research is guided by one of the reasons listed above. Ask your peers to review the plan and check your reasoning. Sharing your research purpose and rationale with your colleagues can assure that your thoughts are logical and you are not missing any factors of importance. But discussing your plans with others may also help you in considering practical matters, such as:

- What group(s) of people do you have access to? How will you gain access?
- How much time do you have to complete the study? Is there a best or worse time of year for you? For your participants?
- Will your topic involve travel or other expenses? How will you pay for these?

You are likely to answer these questions in a variety of ways. Some may want to wait until later to make such decisions; others will find that answering this kind of question overrides theoretical concerns. Because it is always advisable to consider practical issues from the beginning, such considerations as the number of individuals in your study, the perspective from which you observe, the type of data you collect, and the time frame within which to observe, measure, or otherwise collect and analyze data are important.

Formalizing the Contract

As was true with Carlos at the beginning of this chapter, it is premature to suggest a design for collecting and analyzing data until you have fully developed your research plan and presented it in writing. That plan is called the research proposal, an official document that requires approval from various university committees as well as from the aforementioned Institutional Review Board (IRB).

The specifics of the proposal depend upon policies of the institution under which you conduct your research as well as on your objectives as a researcher. If, possibly for a thesis topic or paper in lieu of thesis, you are completing a literature review alone, such a contract is probably not needed. More formal proposals, however, require at least an outline of your topics and subtopics and an explanation of your plan for collecting, analyzing, and evaluating data. Additional information about preparing and submitting a formal research proposal is included in Chapter 14 and Appendix E.

The "Institutional Review Board" (IRB)

If you plan to conduct research on "human subjects," you will be required by your institution to submit the details of your plan to an Institutional Review Board (or IRB). All research that is done under the auspices of an institution that receives funding from the United States government is subject to the Code of Federal Regulations for the Protection of Human Subjects (Department of Health and Human Services, 2009). It is administered by the Office for Human Research Protections (OHRP). Because of the law, most if not all educational institutions have policies for compliance with the code. Whether you are a professor at a research university, an itinerant music teacher working in a school, or someone working with a community arts organization that receives government funds, research that involves interaction with people other than yourself is subject to these rules (as is research done by your students, if you teach research in some capacity). Other federal governments around the world have similar laws; if your research is being done outside the United States, you should become familiar with the laws of the country in which you are working (and that which is funding your research, if different).

This board reviews proposed research to make sure the research plan adheres to the government's requirements for ethical research: respect for persons, beneficence, and justice. One key element of these requirements is the idea of informed consent; that is, that research participants have been informed of the procedures and risks involved in a given study and have consented to participating. Research done in a school district is typically subject to approval by the board of education. Smaller community arts organizations may not have research policies, but this does not release researchers from the obligation to make sure their research is safe and ethical. Fortunately, many of the contexts music educators typically study are exempt from a full IRB review. Note, however, that it is your institution's IRB that makes the determination of exemption, usually through an expedited review process. Note also that as of November 2011 these regulations are under review and may change; however, as a researcher it is your responsibility to know the law and abide by it. More information can be found in the sources under "Recommended Readings" at the end of this chapter.

Chapter Summary

1. Deciding how you will do your research—that is, the method by which you want to carry out the study—is premature until you have completed the other parts of your research plan. This will enable you to communicate with other researchers, as well as with a departmental committee, Institutional Review Board, or other policy bodies.

2. Clearly articulating your research topic means being ever more exact about what and how you wish to observe, describe, and/or examine. This takes imagination, thinking broadly yet in ever more specific terms.

3. Paying attention to the wording of the purpose statement is essential for communicating the intent of your study in an exacting and clear way.

4. A research rationale serves two purposes: Representing the logical framework for the stated purpose of the investigation, and explaining the purpose of the study and the theoretical framework by which its results can be interpreted.

5. The design of your research should not be determined until the other aspects of your study are in place. It is useful, however, to consider practical and theoretical elements of the design prior to making final decisions. If you plan on working with human subjects, your research must be reviewed by your institution's Institutional Review Board.

Topics for Further Exploration

1. The characteristics of a clear purpose statement.
2. The relationship between research purpose, rationale, and methods.
3. The varying ways scholars construct rationales.

Suggested Assignments

1. Apply steps similar to those followed by Carlos and other students to narrow your research topic as much as possible.

2. Articulate in writing at least three possible *research purposes* that originated in your chosen *research topic*.

3. Write a preliminary purpose statement for your research project. Explain your choice of wording to your colleagues.

4. Construct a rationale for your research project.

5. From a source in your literature collection, trace an author's stated purpose through their rationale, research design, results, and conclusions.

6. Use your imagination to suggest one or more possible designs for achieving your research purpose.

Recommended Reading

About Research Proposals:

Kilbourn, B. (2006). The qualitative doctoral dissertation proposal. *Teachers College Record, 108*(4), 529–576. Retrieved June 13, 2008 from http://www.tcrecord.org/Home.asp

Locke, L. F., Spirduso, W. W., & Silverman, S. J. (2007). *Proposals that work: A guide for planning dissertation and grant proposals* (5th ed.). Thousand Oaks, CA: Sage.

On U.S. Government Research Regulations:

National Commission for the Protection of Human Subjects of Biomedical and Behavioral Research. (1979). *The Belmont report: Ethical principles and guidelines for the protection of human subjects of research.* Washington, DC: Author. Retrieved October 7, 2011 from http://www.hhs.gov/ohrp/humansubjects/guidance/belmont.html

National Science Foundation. (2008). *Frequently asked questions and vignettes: Interpreting the common rule for the protection of human subjects for behavioral and social science research.* Washington, DC: Author. Retrieved October 7, 2011 from http://www.nsf.gov/bfa/dias/policy/hsfaqs.jsp#exempt

Sample Research Rationales:

Allsup, R. E. (2003). Mutual learning and democratic action in instrumental music education. *Journal of Research in Music Education, 51*(1), 24–37.

Fitzpatrick K. R. (2006). The effect of instrumental music participation and socioeconomic status on Ohio fourth-, sixth-, and ninth-grade proficiency test performance. *Journal of Research in Music Education, 54*(1), 73–84.

Froehlich, H. C., and Cattley, G. (1993). Language, metaphor, and analogy in the music education research process. In E.R. Jorgensen (Ed.), *Philosopher, teacher, musician: Perspectives on music education,* pp. 243–258. Urbana and Chicago: University of Illinois Press.

Hewitt, M. P. (2001). The effects of modeling, self-evaluation, and self-listening on junior high instrumentalists' music performance and practice attitude. *Journal of Research in Music Education, 49*(4), 307–322. Retrieved September 29, 2011 from Sage Journals Online.

Miksza, P. (2006). Relationships among impulsiveness, locus of control, sex, and music practice. *Journal of Research in Music Education, 54*(4), 308–323. Retrieved March 22, 2008 from the Academic Search Premier database.

Moga, E., Burger, K., Hetland, L., & Winner, E. (2000). Does studying the arts engender creative thinking? Evidence for near but not far transfer. *The Journal of Aesthetic Education, 34*(3–4), 91–104.

Montemayor, M., & Moss, E. A. (2009). Effects of recorded models on novice teachers' rehearsal verbalizations, evaluations, and conducting. *Journal of Research in Music Education, 57*(3), 236–251.

Reichling, M. J. (1990). Images of imagination. *Journal of Research in Music Education, 38*(4), 282–293.

Volk, T. M. (2007). "Charts and other paraphernalia": Charles H. Congdon (1856–1928) and his music teaching materials. *Journal of Research in Music Education, 55*(4), 302–312.

part two
Methods in Modes of Inquiry

Part II is about specific methodological considerations imbedded in different modes of inquiry. The distinction between traditions within those modes and their respective methodological requirements is detailed in Chapters 5 through 13, following those suggested by Gall, Gall, and Borg (2007) and Creswell (2003). Whether your questions are about the past or the present, events, actions, behaviors, experiences, or ideas, you now learn about methods by which to address them in the most appropriate way. Your task lies in finding the best possible approach among several options by which to collect and examine the evidence you need to fulfill your stated study purpose. Such decision requires careful thought and analysis.

The chapters that follow begin with philosophy because choices about research paradigms, theories, and beliefs are the purview of philosophical reasoning and impact all modes of inquiry. You best understand the relationship between modes and their respective methods once you grasp philosophical differences about what constitutes knowledge and evidence in any form of research. Furthermore, all modes of inquiry demand the ability to convey your thoughts convincingly and in a well-reasoned manner. As already suggested in Chapter 3, logic becomes an essential research tool in whatever you choose to investigate.

Following the philosophical mode of inquiry is the chapter about historical research in music education (Chapter 6). This chapter provides a glimpse into the rich world of examining past events, actions, behaviors, and documented experiences in music and music education. The chapter also sets the tone for the broad scope of qualitative research methods as described in Chapters 7 and 8.

Conceptually, research purposes that suggest the use of qualitative research methods require knowledge of specific traditions and philosophical underpinnings that have guided and continue to guide the researchers of today. The methods continue to evolve as new thought processes bring about new questions and ideas for study. Chapter 8, although about specific procedures common to particular traditions, must be understood as a snapshot of currently favored qualitative research designs.

Chapters 9–12 introduce you to basic research designs common in many quantitative–empirical investigations. Purposefully brief, Chapter 9 addresses measurement theory as it might aid you in understanding the meaning of numbers in statistical analyses. More advanced philosophical and mathematical theory are kept to a minimum. Chapters 10–12, too, are limited to basic information about descriptive statistics, simple correlations, ex post facto, and quasi-experimental designs. Advanced knowledge about more sophisticated options and measurement procedures should be gained from sources outside the purview of the type of class for which this book was written.

Chapter 13 describes "basics of content and construction" of commonly used data gathering tools across the research approaches described in the previous seven chapters. This is done to emphasize that all modes of inquiry can benefit from carefully developed observation forms, interview schedules, tests, and/or tools for content analysis. Furthermore, mixed methods, already used successfully by a number of music education, seem to lend themselves well to the many questions typically found in the wide span of issues concerning the learning and teaching of music.

Chapter 14 addresses the "so what?" factor of a completed study. It is the question most everyone asks after the data are gathered and analyzed. The chapter, however, is not only about interpreting your findings but also about making your original research accessible to different audiences. Such sharing can be in the form of specialized research or general interest articles, scholarly papers or workshops, grant applications or designing new or ongoing research. The book ends with a "Recapitulation"—a review of those components in scholarship that should be considered essential in all modes of inquiry.

five

Approaches in the Philosophical Mode of Inquiry

This chapter focuses on philosophy as a tool for research in music education:

- Understanding and using skills of reasoning;
- Examining key ideas from the past and present;
- Articulating your own beliefs in light of new or established belief systems.

The "doing" of philosophy is covertly or overtly imbedded in all scholarship. But as a mode of inquiry in music education, its main function lies in the analysis of theories and their underlying constructs of thought as well as practice. Common to the many possible approaches should be the presence of traceable lines of argumentation with well-defined and consistently used key terms.

Introduction

We may note one peculiar feature of philosophy. If someone asks the question what is mathematics, we can give him a dictionary definition, let us say the science of number, for the sake of argument. As far as it goes this is an uncontroversial statement . . . Definitions may be given in this way of any field where a body of definite knowledge exists. But philosophy cannot be so defined. Any definition is controversial and already embodies a philosophic attitude. The only way to find out what philosophy is, is to do philosophy. (Bertrand Russell, 1959, p. 7)

You likely believed that you were engaged in "doing philosophy" when you applied for a teaching job and the principal or other designated school official asked about "your philosophy of music teaching/education." You may also have been asked the same question in several of the classes you are taking in preparation of becoming a music educator. In either case, your answers are expected to be in support of music in the curriculum.

During one of the coffee talks the students enjoyed so much, *Liam* spoke up about what he hoped to accomplish as a jazz musician. *Christy* then asked him how those plans fit into his "philosophy of music education." Usually quiet during those conversations, *Prof. E.* interjected, "Christy, what exactly do you mean by that term?" Not only Christy looked at him incredulously: Surely he knew what a philosophy of music education was! After all, there is hardly any music teacher who is not required sooner or later in his or her career to articulate "a philosophy," that is, to give a personal statement on the importance of music in the curriculum. And, was it not Prof. E. who repeatedly had stated how important philosophy was for research? Why, then, his question?

Prof. E.'s question had been asked with the intent to bring up a difficult topic—the distinctions between simply stating an opinion, engaging in philosophical discourse, and conducting research in the philosophical mode of inquiry. Stating an opinion is usually the result of having thought about things in the past or developing a thought at the spur of the moment. Both can contribute to philosophical discourse in its best sense, especially when others around you enjoy serious conversations about topics that are of equal importance to you and them.

Focused on young children's ability to accurately perform pitch and rhythm patterns, *Keisha* had narrowed her interests to looking at speech patterns as a tool for learning; patterns commonly found in words and musical phrases by which melodic patterns could be reproduced and internalized. Having discovered Gordon's Music Learning Theory in the process, she now thought about using those rhythm and pitch patterns in her planned research. But she also realized that holding to those patterns might mean ignoring practices linked to other theories. She decided to slow down on formulating a research purpose and, instead, opted for exploring other learning theories that might prove useful for her interests.

In its most popular usage, *philosophy* means "love of wisdom" (philo: "loving," sophia: "knowledge, wisdom"). In popular usage, it is demonstrated by any train of thought articulated as a deliberate point of view, sometimes shared with others for the purpose of debate, and at other times carefully articulated as a personal statement about what is important to you in the way you see the world.

What sets any such "trains of thought" apart from doing philosophy as a mode of inquiry in the context of research? How is sharing your ideas with friends or writing out your own belief system different from choosing philosophy as a tool to publicly address a pressing professional concern? When would such thinking qualify to be called research?

Imagine an informal gathering of like-minded friends who make music together. Intuition and the immediacy of personal judgments of "what sounds right" define the moment of performing. Even an occasional mistake or unwanted chord progression does not diminish your satisfaction with the experience. You and your fellow musicians set the parameters, unencumbered by scrutiny from a body of professional critics.

Impromptu performances like the one described have shaped the creative life of most every music lover, but loving music does not necessarily equate with being a professional musician. That happens once your performance withstands expert scrutiny and you meet external musical and technical standards set by outside experts and audiences. Similarly, expounding a train of thought at the spur of the moment generally "does not a philosopher make." Philosophy must reach beyond an "arbitrarily held opinion" or "personal views rooted in nothing more substantial than sentiment" (Bowman, 1998, p. 5). Rather, you "perform" philosophically by employing skills of reasoning that have been established by the collective of the profession. Such skills include versatility in dealing with the details by which ideas are systematically probed in light of empirical and historical evidence. Many such details exist and have been developed over centuries of scholarship all over the world. Knowing and understanding them is but one of the many requisites for good philosophical scholarship.

Why and When to Engage in Philosophical Inquiry

Several reasons may prompt you to consider philosophical study. They may include the discovery of discrepancies between others' ideas and your own, contradictions in accepted practices and beliefs you wish to examine or even resolve, or concepts that impact specific practices but are in need of further clarification. You might also want to illuminate or strengthen extant musical and educational theories, constructs, and paradigms. Any of these or other reasons can be turned into a particular research purpose, question, or (as some philosophers might call them) a problematic. Even examining the place of rational thought in the arts continues to be the subject of examination and scholarship.

As is the case with other modes of inquiry, systematically conducted philosophical research—despite or across differences in approach—is intended to convince. Readers should be able to confirm that: (1) stated questions are true rather than rhetorical; (2) they are addressed exhaustively and in good faith; and (3) the conclusions drawn from presented evidence either answer the questions or lead to new ones. You, the researcher, therefore should:

- Be consistent in wording the purpose, questions, or named quest throughout a study;
- Conceptually frame the questions and place them into the larger body of extant professional literature;
- Use a recognizable form of argumentation that is explicitly laid out so that the reader can easily follow it (see also Chapter 3);
- Share with the reader how key terms were defined throughout the entire research process;
- Use those definitions consistently from beginning to end of the written document.

Most of the spelled out expectations for philosophical inquiry fall under the broader term of logical reasoning, the activity that most directly defines various forms of "philosophizing." Your reasoning should correspond to your worldview, the way you see knowledge, truth, and fact to interact with each other.

The remainder of this chapter describes working with different forms of logic, defining terms, and articulating the worldview that likely prompted your chosen form of logic. Contrasting your own beliefs to other systems of reasoning relevant to music, education, and music education concludes the chapter. It emphasizes that philosophizing as a research activity and philosophy as a discipline come together because, historically as well as conceptually, both inform each other.

Skills of Reasoning as Research Tool

At the end of Chapter 3, you were asked to trace lines of argumentations by various authors. You also analyzed definitions for clarity and consistency. Both—traceable lines of argumentation and consistently defined terms—should be present in all systematically conducted research. They are, however, the backbone of philosophical reasoning as a research method for examining past and present ideas and thoughts.

To describe both skill sets beyond what you read about in Chapter 3, this chapter relies in large part on Copi, Cohen, and McMahon (2011); Hart (1998, 2001); van den Brink-Budgen (2010); Weston (2009); and Wheelwright (1962). Details about how to construct lines of argumentation are provided about informal–propositional (called, in short, informal) and dialectic logic. Other forms of reasoning are addressed in Chapters 7 and 8.

Using Informal Logic

You likely have used components of informal logic in composing term papers and other written assignments for various classes. You made claims (philosophers call them premises or propositions) that you strung together to make your final point. Each sentence you wrote was supposed to have been derived from the previous one, thus leading to what you concluded to be true.

Philosophers call any writing that contains at least one premise and a conclusion a *syllogism* (e.g., "if p, then q"). It is the building block for entire lines of propositional argumentation in which q (as conclusion) becomes the proposition (p) in the next argument. There are many concrete guidelines about the "do's and don'ts" of informal–propositional logic because centuries of scholarship have helped systematize this form of reasoning. Figure 5.1, adapted from Weston (2009, pp. 1–57) provides a summarized guide to developing valid lines of argumentation in informal logic. Any entries that have an asterisk before or directly behind them are additions by the authors.

All cells in the figure advise you how to think and subsequently write: Start with reliable premises, outline your line of argumentation as well as possible, use representative examples, be cautious about claims of fact, remember the relational–correlational–causal loop, consider objections and alternatives, and be mindful of the fact that definitions do not substitute for arguments. When you extend an argument by exploring a sideline issue, make sure you inform the reader of such a "side trip." Finally, be clear in your own mind whether you reason from specific cases to general conclusions (inductive reasoning) or whether you take a broader—theoretical—perspective and wish to provide specific evidence for its veracity (deductive reasoning). If you find that initial efforts at this sort of writing sound a bit stifled or stiff, be reminded, once again, that writing is like performing: You are likely to get better as you practice. To examine

	RULE 1	RULE 2	RULE 3	RULE 4	RULE 5
Short Arguments	Identify premises and conclusions	Develop your ideas in a natural order	Start from reliable premises	Be concrete, concise, and consistent	Avoid rhetoric when it gets in the way of an argument*
Generalizations	Use more than one example UNLESS: ⬇	Use representative examples	Be cautious about claims of fact (including numbers and statistics)*	Think of ratio between examples that fit **and** those that don't fit your point	
Arguments by Analogy	One example suffices if it is used as an analogy	Make sure the analogy holds	Use analogies sparingly*		
Arguments About Causes	Causal arguments start with correlations	Correlations may have alternative explanations	Work toward the most likely explanation	Expect complexity	
Deductive/ *Inductive Arguments	Syllogisms [If p, then q] or: p. Therefore, q.	[If p, then q] Not-q. Therefore, not-p.	Hypothetical syllogism: If p then q. If q then r. Therefore, if p then r.	Dilemma: p or q. If p then r. If q then s. Therefore, r or s.	Reduction to absurdity ("Reductio ad absurdum") To prove: p; Assume the opposite: not-p. Argue q as the conclusion. Show that q is false (not true). Conclude p as being true.
Extended Arguments	Explore the issue	Spell out basic ideas as arguments	Defend basic premises with arguments of their own	Consider objections & alternatives	Definitions don't replace arguments

FIGURE 5.1 Basic Rules of Propositional Argumentation (adapted from Weston, 2009, pp. 1–57)

your own skills in propositional writing, we suggest you determine the extent to which you followed the rules of informal–propositional logic faithfully and completely in your own written work. In previous assignments (Chapter 3), you were asked to examine some past essayistic papers you had written for logical strength. You now may revisit that assignment, this time paying attention to what philosophers call *fallacious argumentations.* Once you recognize fallacious arguments, you will learn to appreciate valid ones.

Fallacies of Argumentation

Fallacies tend to be caused by logical and structural weaknesses in arguments in which you can detect: (1) missing, incomplete, inadequate, irrelevant, ambiguous, or even inaccurate evidence; and/or (2) deficient, weak, or inconsistently used definitions of key terms. Generally unintentional, omissions or deficiencies happen because a writer takes short cuts in trying to make persuasive arguments. For example, one author may refer to "big names" or known experts in support of a given statement, suggesting that because so-and-so said so, it therefore must be true. Such appeal to force or authority renders an argument invalid and is not permissible as evidence in any scholarship, regardless of mode. When a writer claims that "research has found" but only gives one study as reference, clearly, he or she has not provided a convincing amount of data upon which to build a premise. Your task as a philosopher, then, might be to pinpoint such fallacies and show how they impact the writer's conclusion(s).

Of the named fallacies listed in many available textbooks on logic, the most commonly mentioned seem to be:

1. An *ad hominem* argument, also called a *straw man* fallacy: An idea is attacked more on the grounds of what person holds the idea rather than on the specifics of the idea itself. This can take two forms: An idea is assumed wrong simply because it came from a person *non-grata* (undesirable, un-liked, considered inept); or, an idea is believed to be good because it is expressed by a person everyone holds in high esteem. Neither option is sufficient a reason for accepting or rejecting the stated premise.
2. An *ambiguous* argument: The meaning of a word or phrase in one premise is inconsistent with that in another premise in the argument. This can happen quite easily when definitions are complex and/or are assumed to be understood by the profession. There are many such terms in all fields, and music education is no exception (for more information, see section "Approaches to Defining Terms" in this chapter).
3. A *circular* argument (see also "*begging the question*"): Something is declared good or bad because the writer says so. This happens quite frequently in the above mentioned, opinion-rich "philosophies" (justifications) many of us have been asked to articulate in various situations. Because we want to believe that something is true, we declare it to be so—often passionately and with personal conviction. It is what some call wishful thinking.

4. A *slippery slope* argument: Causal relationships are drawn where there are none. "A boy who blows his horn does not blow a safe" is an old saying that refers to the assumed causality between musical training and morally upright behavior. Very little evidence, if any, exists to confirm that causality but statements of similar meaning can often be found in arts advocacy documents (see the Mozart effect studies referred to in Chapter 1).

5. *Begging the question*: The strength of a belief becomes the evidence in support of that belief (see also circular argument and ad hominem). Enthusiasm and strength of conviction, both needed in the work music educators do, should not be assumed to replace factual evidence derived from well-conducted investigations of various kinds.

Exploration: Knowing a Fallacy When You See It

1. If you were to simply take the authors' word for the list of fallacies compiled from a variety of sources (see *Recommended Reading* and *References*), which fallacy (or fallacies) would you commit?
2. Comparing the above fallacies to the entirety of those listed in the referenced sources, why do you believe the authors made those choices?
3. What other steps could you take to strengthen your own knowledge about fallacies of argumentation in music education research?

Dialectics

Already briefly explained in Chapter 3, dialectics use opposites, conflicts, or contradictions that are stated as thesis and antithesis and serve as evidence in a temporary resolution called synthesis. A simple example might be the thesis that "music can do no harm." Contrast that statement with "music can be harmful to the ears." Both statements together form the basis for which the synthesis might be that "music can have differential effects on the listener's or performer's ears." However, do not conclude your analysis here because the synthesis, as the next thesis, calls for a further antithesis, again qualifying the synthesis. You might do that by saying that below a certain decibel level, the differential effects are negligible. And so you continue the process by inductively examining the complexities of music performance as an art, craft, practice, medicinal issue, and business.

The example may seem simple, but the technique is not. It goes back to a lineage of dialectic philosophers of the late 19th and 20th century, notably G. W. F. Hegel, K. Marx, F. Engels and, later, critical theorists, such as J. Habermas, P. Bourdieu, P. Freire, I. Illich, and others. Dialectic reasoning is a method well suited to taking a macro view (see Chapter 3) of the many antithetical forces in society that seem to stand in the way of providing equal access to all resources a society has available. Critical theorists examine such given polarities in their meaning for taking action: Calling for social justice in unequal societal class structures; pointing to how knowledge as social capital is selected by and for the economically ruling class(es); and attributing unequal economic and socio-cultural conditions within a country and across the globe to unequal access to knowledge as social capital. Critical pedagogues carry this analysis into calls for transformation of formal education in society rather than mere revision or reform.

Because of the inferential nature inherent in dialectic reasoning, proponents of the method—particularly those following in Hegel's (1929) footsteps—view it as the most stringent scientific form of philosophical inquiry. No other approach, they argue, is as inductive in nature as dialectic reasoning. Needless to say, there are philosophers who dispute that claim.

In summary, along with thinking and writing and working with words, dialectic reasoning demands:

- Detailed knowledge of the literature in support of and contradiction to particular theories, practices, thoughts, and beliefs;
- Understanding critical theory as a philosophical position and worldview;
- Remaining open to the irresolvable tension between wanting to draw finite conclusions even if the inquiry promises to be ongoing.

Approaches to Defining Terms

Regardless of the form of argumentation you choose, a second component of good scholarship in any mode is the presence of explicitly defined terms and their consistent use throughout a piece of writing. Ambiguous or poorly worded definitions weaken any argumentation although even the best definition does not replace an argument.

Figure 5.2 shows several approaches to defining terms, labeled *synonymous-stipulated*, *synonymous-lexical*, and *operational* definitions as well as those by *genus and difference*. Each kind carries with it a certain level of convincing power, suggesting that not all definitions should be equally trusted, or are equally strong.

Types of Definitions

	Synonymous	*Operational*	*by Genus and Difference*
Stipulated	Author-generated	Author-tested over time	Definition follows scientific format/ structure of class and sub-class
Lexical	Published and literal translation of foreign and/or unusual terms	Professionally agreed-upon definitions	Definition follows scientific format/ structure of class and sub-class

FIGURE 5.2 Types of Definitions

Stipulated and/or Operational Definitions

When you find it necessary to attach a meaning to an uncommon or unfamiliar term, you either stipulate or operationalize it. A stipulated definition simply replaces one term with another. Such may be the case when you define "good music" as that which you like. Perhaps not very strong and possibly quite different from what music theorists or philosophers would support or stipulate, the definition may serve its purpose for what you speak or write about.

An operational definition requires more than a simple word or phrase replacement. For example, Gordon (1980) coined the term "audiation"; Small (1995/1997, 1998) the gerund "musicking" (with a "k"); and Elliott (1995) "musicing" (without a "k"). Each of these authors took measures to explain their choices in detail, thus defining the terms operationally. As the profession at large gradually began to include the terms in its vocabulary, the definitions found entry into other authors' writings and, later, into dictionaries as well as peer-reviewed, published glossaries. The operational terms became lexical. An important task of good scholarship is to verify that the lexical use is in keeping with how an author first stipulated either a new term altogether (as in the case of audiation and musicking) or a new meaning for an already known term.

Operational definitions often describe how a term may be used in a particular context. Such is the case, for example, when "music achievement" is defined by the tasks included in a particular music performance or theory test. A collection of tangible behaviors, observable and themselves defined, provide the meaning of the word to be defined. Such a practice, not uncommon in quantitative studies, can run the risk of making a definition circular.

Because of the context-dependency of operational definitions, it is conceivable that different authors provide dissimilar definitions for the same term. In that case, you might choose to examine such differences systematically and make suggestions for further clarifications. Such differences and contradictions can become the raw material (the raw data) for much needed philosophical studies in our field.

Avoid stipulating circular definitions, meaning that you define a word with itself: For instance, stipulating "aesthetics as the study of appreciating an aesthetic object" makes the definition circular, thus useless. Surprisingly, you find many such examples in lexica, dictionaries, and encyclopedias. Look out for them; it's easy to fall into that logical trap.

Definitions by "Genus and Difference"

Definitions by "genus and difference" include operationally defined terms when the latter speak to: (1) the class or family to which a term belongs (the *genus*); and (2) the specific attribute(s) that separate(s) the term from the class or family (the *difference*). A somewhat simple example might be to define a violin as an instrument in the string family with four unfretted strings, tuned from highest to lowest as e, a, d, and g. You first state the larger category (string family with four unfretted strings), followed by what sets the violin apart from the viola, the cello, and the double bass (the tuning of the strings).

Constructing the actual definition works best if you first list everything that falls under a term (the denotations), and then find the characteristics that are common to all denotations. Those commonalities (the connotations) become the building block for the definition itself. Order the connotations from broadest to most specific so that all qualities are accounted for. Then you craft one or several sentences in which the connotations describe the term. Your task is to assure that the term itself is not broader than the definition or that the definition is not broader than the term itself.

How different researchers have stipulated or operationalized terms in their respective works can result in fruitful philosophical investigations. You might, for instance, address how specific terms have been adopted, adjusted, or changed in various scholarly documents; findings that could serve as a springboard for new queries.

In their reading, *Juan*, *Keisha*, and *Marguerite* found many terms and phrases requiring more clarity than was often provided by an author. Specifically, they identified: aesthetic education; creativity and imagination in the learning and teaching of music; social justice, power, and behavior modification in the class- room; student empowerment and teacher control. The three students also won- dered which of these terms actually belonged to or were derived from specific theoretical frameworks. Did the studies they read provide enough evidence for claims made by an author?

Looking for Strength of Evidence Behind a Claim

How you reference any evidence in your arguments is important. So is the question of whether the content in a source actually speaks to the claim made. Differentially worded referencing may have consequences for the validity of a claim.

It is easy to verify the truth of the following statement:

In 1987, Rainbow and Froehlich published a research book.

The evidence is available in some libraries and book stores. Similarly, you can validate the statement:

Rainbow and Froehlich (1987) listed five sources of truth.

The statement is true because you can document the page numbers for that list; namely, pages 7–8. Whether you agree that there are five rather than six or ten sources of truth would be another matter and required sources in support of your own position.

Next consider:

There are five sources of truth (Rainbow & Froehlich, 1987, pp. 7–8).

You now stipulate a truth that—to be convincing—calls for far more evidence than pro- vided by one reference. Its content rather than the source becomes the issue.

In looking through research relating children's multi-sensory responses to learning rhythmic and pitch patterns, *Keisha* realized that there were many different theoretical frameworks underlying the studies she read. Some articles were cited in support of perception and cognition theories, others within theories for learning and teaching. Although a connection between the theories was likely and reasonable, the tested tasks did not always seem comparable. She therefore began to wonder how permissible it was to group many studies as evidence for one claim when, actually, the tasks in the studies might not be comparable. Only a study-by-study analysis of the tasks seemed to be able to answer that question.

It might be tempting to rely simply on the title, type, or abstract of a publication to determine its strength of evidence. However, only the data themselves, not their summary, can assure that content rather than format or guesswork become the evidence by which to make a valid claim. Therefore, be careful about lumping the results of one study together with those reported in other investigations.

Examining Key Ideas

Philosophy is no mere marshaling of views, no mere purveyor of irrefutable, absolute truths. It is, rather, a messy and disquieting process in which cherished beliefs and comfortable assumptions are subjected to critical scrutiny. (Bowman, 1998, p. 6)

You might think of philosophers in music education as "watch dogs" because one of their tasks lies in questioning taken-for-granted theories, concepts, and terms that are widely but, at times, somewhat indiscriminately used in music education. Isolating, examining, and systematically comparing ideas in all modes of inquiry can bring out similarities and differences in meanings and findings across studies, and point out weaknesses and strengths in applying certain concepts to practice. Such inquiries can:

raise issues; question assumptions; open new vistas on what error, or truth, or belief consist of; reassess our realities within newly conceived frameworks; or any of the other ways to stimulate reconstructions of our theories and practices that rigorous examination might reveal as being unproductive or dehumanizing. (Reimer, 2008, p. 195)

However, philosophy as "a systematic, *reflective* discipline" (Bowman, 1992, p. 3; emphasis in original) can and should not be prescriptive, not so much a guide for action as an examination of "the *grounds* for belief and action" (Bowman, 1992, p. 3; emphasis added. See also Bowman, 1998, p. 5). Such grounds are nearly limitless whereas their consequences, the actions themselves, might not be.

Beginning with questions about the nature of music, society, education, music education, and principles of learning and teaching, your options of what to examine philosophically are practically endless. They also far exceed issues of arts advocacy or the articulation of personal statements in defense of music in the school curriculum. While a worthy pursuit, such statements should likely be superseded by queries about the nature of school knowledge in general and what sets such knowledge apart from what is learned outside of school. You can examine the grounds for what is or is not considered important social and musical capital (what may constitute valuable musical knowledge and skills) and what various thinkers may mean by schooling and education as societal mandates.

Questions About the Nature of Music and Education

Many music educators believe that "philosophy of music" means thinking about aesthetics. This is a misconception because, as important as it may be, aesthetics is merely a sub-branch of philosophy, either categorized by itself or belonging to axiology as the study of values (see Chapter 3). Although possibly one of the most examined constructs of thought in music and music education in the United States since the early 1970s, other issues of concern have been integral to philosophical inquiry as well.

Critical theorists and constructivists in particular reject the notion of reasoning about and examining music educational practices from an aesthetic angle alone. Instead, they address the relationship between music educational goals and purposes within the axiological context of ethics and politics. Because musical values are socially acquired, they reflect upbringing, social status, and cultural/artistic opportunities. Any decisions about educational goals are as dependent on those forces as they are about decisions about what "good music" might be or what a "well-rounded musical education" might mean.

While grounded in music making, any musical practice should be more "than an understanding of pieces or works of music." Instead, it should be guided by "actions[s] that [are] embedded in and responsive to a specific context of effort." Such music practice is termed *praxis*, signifying that "'music' pivots on particular kinds of human doing-and-making that are purposeful, contextual and socially-embedded" (Elliott, http://www.davidelliottmusic.com/music-matters/what-does-praxial-mean/).

Both philosophers and empiricists have examined such issues as: (1) a teacher's role as indoctrinator or facilitator of learning; (2) gender inequalities as manifested in instrument and repertoire choice; (3) social justice toward marginalized students who do not "fit" neatly into the reality of public schooling; (4) race and gender discrimination in curriculum construction and teaching practices; and (5) differences in urban versus rural versus suburban instructional settings. A few examples are those by Arnold (2004), Bleiker (2009), Bradley (2007), Corey (2006), Duvenage (2003), Gould (2007), Lamb, Dollof, and Howe (2002), Macarthur (2002), Redfield (2003), vanWelden (2004), and Williams and Shannon (2004). Use these or similar examples to sharpen your questions on comparable topics; link them to educational contexts with which you are familiar or which you care about.

If you are interested in the study of aesthetics, be aware of ethics and socio-political contexts as potentially important contributors to how individuals and social or cultural groups interact with each other in society. Consider the consequences of such social–cultural facts on any recommendations you make for action. Indeed, whatever problematic you choose to investigate, you are well advised to always consider opposing data sets and viewpoints before drawing any conclusions that result in guides for action.

Exploration: An Invitation to Think About Music and Education

Review and compare thoughts by Dickie (1997), Scruton (1997), and the contributing authors in Regelski and Gates (2009). Focus on whether and how constructs of musicianship should or should not be connected to socio-cultural and educational traditions of schooling in general and institutions of learning in particular. Reflect on the influence, positive and negative, of hierarchies of power on your own learning. Determine how interdisciplinary ways of thinking may conflict with what subject-specific curricula focus on.

Clarifying Constructs and Theories

The clarification of constructs and theories in our field is a much needed dimension of philosophical scholarship as it could contribute greatly to setting a somewhat paradigmatically orientated research agenda for the profession. Efforts to that effect have been spearheaded by many music educators of different philosophical persuasions and research preferences. A few of those names are listed in the Recommended Reading at the end of this chapter. Their contributions may give you a sense of how systematic reasoning has and can impact action in the classroom or how it furthers empirical and historical research.

Another example of such systematic reasoning may be seen in *The Oxford Handbook of Philosophy in Music Education* (2012). Edited by Bowman and Frega, the collection of essays displays a wide spectrum of issues concerning the aims and purposes of philosophical inquiry as applied to the value of, respectively, music and education, music education instruction, curriculum development, and instructional practices. The ideas expressed by 27 experienced scholars from ten different countries reflect a great diversity of opinion as well as style of reasoning, but always invite you to re-consider your own viewpoint on any given topic.

To get started in asking your own questions that clarify philosophically extant constructs and theories about music education, take a look at how past novice scholars have proceeded. Begin by looking at dissertations in which biographical and historical information about the lives and contributions of particular philosophers, musicians, and music educators were connected to their respective beliefs about music, education, culture, and society (e.g., Bowman, 1980; Chandler, 2004; Helfer, 2003; Lee, 1982; Mortyakowa, 2011; Orrel, 1995; Revkin, 1984; and Whalen, 2008). You might examine studies in which specific instructional actions were described and analyzed from a variety of theoretical angles (e.g., Bassett, 2010; Benton, 2002; Garberich, 2008; Kedem, 2008; Kuehmann, 1987; Louth, 2008). The descriptors came from such areas as cognition and perception; creativity and inspiration; power and ideology in music instructional settings; metaphor and imagery in music; multiculturalism, globalization, and musicianship; age-specific processes of learning; and curriculum theory.

A third group of studies is characterized by the researchers having combined empirical and philosophical methods to examine particular instructional settings. Often, terms used to describe what was going on in private studios or music classrooms from kindergarten through college were derived from the investigator's own philosophical worldview or that of known philosophers inside or outside the field of music education. Examples are investigations by Cho (2010), Dees (2005), Eshelman (1995), Field (1997), Jensen-Hole (2005), and Williams (2010). In some instances, the focus was less on philosophical methods than on empirical ones, thereby concentrating a study more on pedagogical actions than on clarifying underlying theoretical constructs.

Only recently (and much encouraged by critical theorists in music education) have young researchers begun to address any apparent dissonances, tensions, or incongruities between specific thought processes and key terms in extant theories of instruction and music pedagogy. Such efforts require your willingness to step outside the relative comfort zone of accepted ways of instructional practices. Your scholarship skills, too, need to be strong because questioning extant practices is more difficult than building on them.

Finally and concurring with Vogt (2003), "it should not be beyond the scope of [philosophical inquiry in music education] to investigate . . . topics like 'child development' or 'learning'" even if some music educators might place such topics under the research umbrella of psychology and/or sociology of education (p. 15). If you followed Vogt's advice and chose to examine psychological and sociological constructs that shape music educational practices, apply what you would do in any other mode of inquiry:

- Articulate your research question(s) and chosen line of reasoning clearly.
- Define key terms and place them into your question(s) and argumentation without replacing either.
- Use those definitions consistently throughout your work. If your study is actually about defining a term, say so as part of your research rationale.
- Document strength of evidence in specific arguments; point to divergent, contradictory, or even unclear philosophical positions that emanate from different forms of reasoning.

When examining controversies or challenging problematics that result from different meanings attached to constructs by the same name, you face additional challenges: Determine whether the evidence (the data) used to address the controversy consists of ideas and thoughts publicly expressed by others or whether they are primarily your own thoughts. If the former is the case, ask yourself the following questions:

- Do you have access to the primary documents in which those thoughts are/were first expressed or spoken to?
- Have those original thoughts changed over time and can you document that change?

When relying primarily on your own thoughts in voicing a question or problematic:

- Determine how sure are you that others have not published comparable ideas that deserve acknowledgment;
- Back up the validity of your thoughts by evidence from historical and empirical (both qualitative and quantitative) research;
- Be cautious about generalizing beyond the evidence you have;
- Place your own beliefs within extant worldviews

Articulating Your Own Beliefs Within Extant Worldviews

Juan, after examining the references in Yarbrough's (1985) study on basic conducting skills, "discovered" behaviorism, a worldview generally associated with a positivistic (modernist) perspective. A practically minded performer, he found the theory to match his own inclinations and convictions better than what he heard many of his classmates discuss. He decided to look up references to various psychological theories that derived from B. F. Skinner's stimulus-response theory imbedded in behavior modification. Any of these theories seemed to set clear boundaries about what was and was not possible to do in research and scholarship. Juan found out about researchers who focus their observations on overt behaviors rather than deriving them from inferred or interpreted meanings. Because he felt such research approaches matched his own thinking, he wondered whether behaviorism might be an avenue by which to learn more about skilled conducting.

Over centuries, articulated beliefs by individuals and groups of individuals have shaped what today is the discipline of philosophy. It informs how each of us thinks. This means that how you think and what has been thought about over centuries is connected. Juan discovered that fact when he recognized the connection between personal actions, predilections, and beliefs (also called worldviews).

Like the term "behaviorism," worldviews have labels that describe their key tenet. For instance, *absolutism* professes to an unconditional belief in true, right, and desirable standards of actions and behaviors over false and undesirable judgments and values. *Relativism*, on the other hand, acknowledges that differences in context should allow for differences in judgments about right and wrong, good and bad, or appropriate and inappropriate. *Behaviorism* is a short term for a complex belief system in the power of observable actions ("behaviors") as the basis for what may be considered scientific data.

Just as centuries of making and composing music have resulted in a defined body of musical works, describable in styles, genres, and ways of thinking (the discipline of music), so have centuries of thought and argumentation about beliefs contributed to the discipline of philosophy. Systematized as philosophical branches (or domains), the discipline reflects what philosophers have done and continue to do: Examine the relationship between reality, perception of reality, knowledge, fact, and truth from many angles and perspectives. By which perspective you address a particular topic constitutes your worldview or belief system. Both the philosophical branch within which you place your work and the worldview that guides your thinking signal to the reader the contextual boundaries that define the scope of your argumentation. Be sure you state both succinctly.

Philosophical Branches

You already know about the branch of logic as the study of reasoning and you also know that the branch (or domain) of axiology comprises ethics, aesthetics, and politics. Just as these domains inform all research in music education, so do the remaining branches of:

- Epistemology as the study of knowledge;
- Metaphysics as the study of the nature of reality;
- Phenomenology as the study of experience.

Each of them contributes to the questions you ask and the methods you use to answer them or generate new queries. Sometimes difficult to separate one from the other, one branch informs the other. Grasping the terminology of each makes you a stronger philosopher and researcher in general. That is only true, however, if you have a clear understanding of the meaning behind what a particular branch stands for. Thus a word of caution: Only use terms with which you are familiar. Scholarly sounding multisyllabic words do not make you a better philosopher. Clarity of thought does.

Epistemology and Music Education

As the branch of philosophy that reasons about the nature and origin of knowledge, epistemology is central to investigations of what constitutes knowledge in the music classroom and in music teacher training. Different answers about what might be considered accepted canons of musical choices on the one hand and learner preferences on the other shape that discourse in music education.

Recent writings in what has become known as social epistemology focus on "the social dimensions of knowledge or information," in which the "central role of society in the knowledge-forming process" (Goldman, 2006, para. 1) is emphasized. Philosophy, sociology, and education intertwine in this discourse, challenging music educators to connect what pupils learn musically outside of school, what they might bring to such learning processes from home, and what school music instruction has to offer them. Thus, social epistemology applied to music learning takes you directly into the middle of what many music educators have talked about and researched for many years: The why, what, and how of developing music curricula and community programs that are both transmitting knowledge and transforming minds for the betterment of society. These, however, are practical questions that also connect to axiological questions of aesthetics, ethics, and political power structures in society.

Metaphysics and Music Education

The branch of *metaphysics* investigates the nature of ultimate reality and is generally divided into *ontology* (the study of being) and *cosmology* (the study of the structure of the universe). Finding a clear-cut definition for the term itself is not easy because, like aesthetics, it has undergone major changes of meaning since Aristotle first used it as a label for the treatise that followed *Physics*, a collection of eight philosophical lectures (books) on nature itself; that is, about "space, time, causality, and so on" (Pigliucci, 2009, para. 2).

In more recent times and in everyday language, the term is used most often to refer not to the physical world but to what may lie beyond it. In that sense, metaphysical questions have theological or teleological bents which cannot be explained by scientific means alone. Tangible connections between metaphysics (as it is understood today) and ontology become clear when you think systematically about music and the arts as aesthetic phenomena whose explanation may extend beyond intellectual understanding alone. Emotions, feelings, values, and how these come about take you back to axiology. Ethics and politics enter into educational and artistic decision making.

Metaphysical examinations of what constitutes aesthetic responses to music often take you to the self and its place either in the realm of social realities or connected to spiritual experiences. When connected to social realities within the nature and purpose of music schooling, it becomes essential to ask not only what makes a composition great rather than merely good, but also to inquire about whether, when, and where such judgments are "teachable."

Phenomenology and Music Education

Chapter 3 described phenomenological writing as a method of reasoning. This explanation is expanded in Chapters 7 and 8. Philosophically, it is the branch that studies self and "consciousness" (Smith, 2011). The term itself, however, has undergone changes in meaning across different disciplines and times and therefore requires ongoing clarification. Music education researchers tend to refer to it mainly in the context of qualitative research in which data gathering and interpretation are both equally situated in the consciousness of the observer and the observed, "not of anything independent of human consciousness" (*American Heritage Dictionary of the English Language*, 2011, p. 1031). Philosophers who subscribe to this approach place themselves into that which they examine.

Phenomenologists accept given perceptions as factual so long as their descriptions are trustworthy. Thus, personal experiences and viewpoints are as valid in phenomenological reasoning as are recallable facts and agreed-upon measurements in quantitative research. Phenomenological scholarship realizes perhaps more clearly than any other philosophical branch that your worldview determines the investigative steps by which to address the questions you may have. Knowledge originates in the viewer, rather than the viewed. Such an approach invites the "I" form of writing, a style not always condoned by scholars who favor a formalist, functionalist, or modernist view of the world.

Extant Worldviews or Belief Systems

Your belief system (or worldview) reflects who you believe you are and why you think the way you do. Many such belief systems exist and range from relatively well-defined religious or theological beliefs to casually formulated secular ideologies. Either form describes what you consider important in life—both personal and professional. Figure 5.3 lists a select few of the many "-isms" you can find in the literature. Those listed, sometimes by themselves and also in combination with each other, seem to have shaped music education discourse in the United States over the past 50 years.

Terms like "absolutism," "formalism," "functionalism," and "relativism" may seem more familiar than others because they readily say what they represent. Others are not as easily defined because they seem to have distinct every day and philosophical meanings. An example is *idealism*, often used in everyday language to mean beliefs only a dreamer or unrealistic person might hold. Philosophically, however, the meaning is more complex.

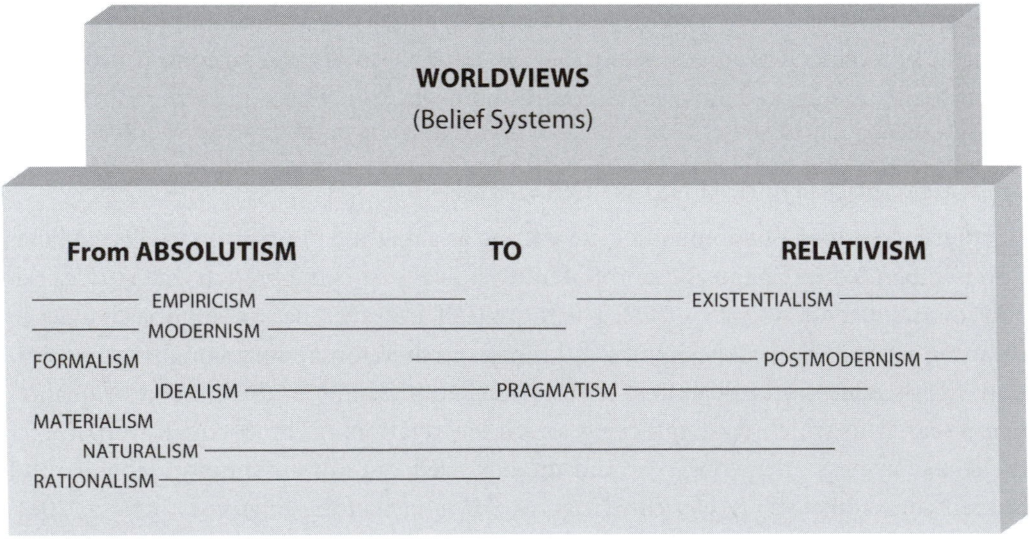

FIGURE 5.3   Selected Worldviews

Going as far back as Plato's theory of idea, "idea-ism" suggests that the idea of a thing is more real than the thing itself. Thinking "tree" gives you a clearer concept of what a tree is than any one tree you see in the forest or in the parking lot. The concept—the idea—is more concrete in its comprehensiveness than any physical object that represents it. It is this "idealism" as a philosophical construct that can be found in metaphysics, epistemology, and their respective sub-domains. German philosophers of the late 18th and early 19th century further added to the meaning of the construct, thereby creating even more definitions (and, possibly, more confusion).

On one hand, you have the belief that the "idea" of any material thing is more "real" than the observed object itself. On the other hand, idealism may also mean that concepts ("ideal values") rather than physical realities should serve as guides for your thoughts and actions. Acknowledging that there will always be a schism between the experienced and the ideal world, an idealist in either sense is not a dreamer but a thinker with a particular worldview about reality as the tension between that which is conceptualized and that which is physically "out there."

You may encounter a similar discrepancy between the philosophical and everyday usage of the term "pragmatism." If you examine the term's definitions in Appendix G you may notice that "practical" and "pragmatic" appear to be used interchangeably. Exploring pragmatism in greater depth, however, you find the term's philosophical meaning to be more complex than what some of those definitions suggest.

Only theories that account for the ongoing and undeniable interaction between organism and environment, between context and action, are believed to truly explain human behavior in all its forms. Such thinking is inter- and multi-disciplinary, reaching across artificially set boundaries of subject matter and knowledge.

One of the best-known pragmatists in education was John Dewey who always thought in interdisciplinary terms. Connecting education with the arts, politics, psychology and social-psychology, he—along with other pragmatists in various fields—set the course that later led to the theory of *social interactionism*, the theoretical position that formalizes the "web" of interactions between individuals, social groups, their actions, and specific contexts. It is also the basis for the theoretical model of music education throughout this book.

A more recent term not in Figure 5.3 but considered an important socio-philosophical addition to previously known worldviews is "feminism," defined by the authors in *The Stanford Encyclopedia of Philosophy* as:

> [B]oth an intellectual commitment and a political movement that seeks justice for women and the end of sexism in all forms. However, there are many different kinds of feminism. Feminists disagree about what sexism consists in, and what exactly ought to be done about it; they disagree about what it means to be a woman or a man and what social and political implications gender has or should have. Nonetheless, motivated by the quest for social justice, feminist inquiry provides a wide range of perspectives on social, cultural, economic, and political phenomena. Important topics for feminist theory and politics include: the body, class and work, disability, the family, globalization, human rights,

popular culture, race and racism, reproduction, science, the self, sex work, human trafficking, and sexuality. (Haslanger, Tuana, & O'Connor, 2011, para.1)

Note that feminism has had a role in questioning traditional "-isms," which historically were created predominantly by European male scholars and therefore represented particular socio-political and cultural perspectives. It is quite conceivable that new perspectives, new "-isms," emerge as the globalization and democratization of education systems and cultures continues.

Your Place in the "-isms"

It is time now for you to articulate your own beliefs about what constitutes truth, knowledge, and fact in your own life and work. Begin by talking about those beliefs with friends and peers; then put them in writing, support them with evidence you can trust, and connect them to your research concerns that you have articulated thus far. To find appropriate terms that describe how you think about things, begin with the continuum of worldviews presented in Figure 5.3. Look up their respective definitions as provided in Appendices F and G.

Appendix F shows the definitions as Rainbow and Froehlich presented them in 1987 and had selected them from three reputable, refereed, professional dictionaries. The sources listed in Appendix G are *The Internet Encyclopedia of Philosophy* (Fieser & Dowden, 1995), the *Wikipedia Free Dictionary/Glossary of Philosophical Isms* (n.d.), Chrisomalis' (2007) online compilation of 234 *philosophical "-isms,"* and the online *The Ism Book* (Saint-Andre, 1996). The first of the four dictionaries is peer-reviewed; the other three are not but invite contributions to the respective websites. Some definitions in all four sources are well crafted and compare favorably with entries in *The Stanford Encyclopedia of Philosophy* or similar refereed, professional dictionaries in various disciplines. Other definitions are circular and clearly require further work.

Exploration: Working with "-isms"

Compare all definitions in Appendices F and G to each other and note similarities and differences among them. In instances where you recognize same, but unreferenced definitions in two or more sources, mark them as examples of possibly questionable scholarship.

Examine all definitions carefully and, where applicable, make suggestions for their improvement. Most importantly, however, discuss: (1) where each of you stand on the issues alluded to by the "-isms" listed; and (2) how the issues may be of relevance to your work as a musician, teacher, and researcher. For example, where would you place yourself on a continuum between absolutist and relativist? Idealist and empiricist? Pragmatist and formalist?

In the course of the suggested exploration, you may find it best to speak about your beliefs when you compare one position with another. Begin by pairing them as shown in Figure 5.4.

Be mindful that some pairs of terms may represent opposite worldviews; others complement each other. If you find any one "-ism" alone to be insufficient to describe your worldview, which combination would you favor? Could you combine some "-isms" in a way that they form more differentiated viewpoints? Many philosophers have done so and you can read about them in the literature. But always remember that the level of detail with which you describe your beliefs should be considered more important than the label you give them.

Finally: Earlier we defined absolutism as the unconditional belief in the existence of true, right, and desirable standards of actions and behaviors over false and undesirable judgments and values. Relativists would question that certainty of truth by pointing to context as an important dimension of determining what is right, desirable, or perceived as truth. When you apply this seeming duality to matters of music education, how would you respond to the following questions?

- In your view, does everyone have an inalienable right to be taught about the music of their choice?
- Should it be a music teacher's role to guide students in the acquisition of musical taste? Is such guidance even possible? If so, in whose view? If not, who would say so?
- What should be the purpose of music in a public school curriculum?
- Should there be a national music curriculum?
- Is there a right way to teach music?

Thinking about these questions in what Elliott (2002) calls a "sustained, systematic, and critical" way (p. 85), examine your answers carefully. The term "sustained" implies that your reasoning can be followed even if one did not share your belief. "Systematic" means that your efforts are methodical and follow a plan. "Critical" suggests that you maintain a questioning and analytic attitude toward examining what has contributed to your thoughts and to those by other thinkers whose works you cite.

Absolutism	··········	Relativism
Rationalism	··········	Existentialism
Empiricism	··········	Idealism
Modernism	··········	Postmodernism
Materialism	··········	Naturalism
Formalism	··········	Pragmatism

FIGURE 5.4 Selected Paired Worldviews in Comparison to Each Other

Your individual and collective responses may go beyond one paired continuum alone. You may find also that it is not always easy or even possible to be fully true to a once articulated philosophical viewpoint. After all, as work circumstances and contexts change, so may your beliefs (this statement, of course, signals that at least one of the book authors is a relativist at heart). When you spend time with the "-isms" and consider how you think, the result may well be a stronger perspective about yourself. A strong perspective, however, is likely to influence the way you ask questions and pursue their answers.

Being and Becoming a Philosopher

Working in philosophy as a research mode means spending time on thinking through many of the tasks outlined in this chapter. Perhaps these tasks alone have convinced you that doing philosophical research is not for the "faint-hearted." But then, neither is music performance! As a philosopher, your research field is the library—both digital and real—and the workspace where your computer is located. In most cases you do not need to attend to such demands as finding subjects for your study and/or having to depend on your/their schedules and availabilities. Quite free, therefore, from external restraints and obligations toward others, the relative isolation in which you work may pose its own challenges.

Internal restraints can be caused by thinking about things in the quiet of your study rather than talking to others. Feeling the responsibility to articulate your thoughts exactly as you mean to say them, you can never be fully certain that you are successful until you submit your writing to peer review. In that process, you are likely to discover that trying to describe the writings of others as they were intended to be understood takes time and repeated re-drafting. That can lead to occasional writer burn-out, insecurities, and "brick walls." Therefore, allow yourself ample time for re-writes, self-selected peer reviews, and the continuous re-vamping of drafts. Think of yourself as a sculptor chiseling away at the marble within which lies the form that you want to bring out.

If you enjoy reading and writing in scholarly ways and cherish asking questions in and about the world of ideas as they pertain to your field of expertise, you can and will succeed. Do not be discouraged when answers remain inconclusive, trigger more questions, or set your world apart from the world of others. Engaging in philosophical inquiry is a form of literary creativity, full of discoveries and opportunities but also relentless in making you more and more aware of the many thoughts that await articulation. In fact, philosophy may choose you instead of you philosophy. And, even when you end up conducting research in other modes of inquiry, once a philosopher, always a philosopher!

Chapter Summary

1. Philosophy as a research mode should be distinguished from stated opinions whose claims may be unwarranted or expressed as "wishful thinking."
2. Examining publications (both in music education and in other disciplines) for unwarranted and warranted claims as well as probing contradictions in extant answers are important tasks of a philosopher–scholar.

3. Identifying both fallacious and strong argumentations in published works can lead to new questions and "problematics." Attention should be paid to the relative strengths of definitions of terms in each argument.

4. Defining terms should be part of any form of reasoning as definitions reflect varying degrees of information.

5. A purposefully chosen form of argumentation and explicitly defined terms should also be central to your own scholarship. Depending on the choices you make as a researcher, the reader might expect documentation of how the definition came about.

6. Different worldviews impact forms of argumentation. As a multidimensional tool in all of research, familiarity with various forms of logic is essential for matching your worldview with the most appropriate form of reasoning.

Topics for Further Exploration

1. The role of the philosopher in music education.

2. A comparison of the various schools of thought described in Figure 5.3 and their application to education, music, and music education.

3. Arguments for and against Bertrand Russell's assertion that value and dogma should not be the subject of philosophical inquiry because their truth cannot be probed by methods of logical argumentation.

4. A brief review of the main differences in propositional and dialectic argumentation, highlighting their respective strengths in music education scholarship.

Suggested Assignments

1. Of the titles given below (for full citations, see References), select two that pique your interest. Imagine/envision: (a) what each of them might be about; (b) how you would do the study in your own mind; and—after skimming the sources—(c) how close your own vision came to the actual work:

   ■ Bowman, W. D. (1980). *Tacit knowing, musical experience, and music instruction: The significance of Michael Polanyi's thought for music education.*
   ■ Froehlich, H., & Cattley, G. (1993). *Language, metaphor, and analogy in the music education research process.*
   ■ Glover, A. (2002). *The unreasonable logic of Western epistemologies: Rhetoric, writing and the affective domain.*
   ■ Gould, E. (2005). *Nomadic turns: Epistemology, experience, and women university band directors.*
   ■ Helfer, J. A. (2003*). Susanne K. Langer's epistemology of mind as an interpretive resource for music education.*
   ■ Lamkin, J. R., II (2003). *Beyond the podium: A phenomenological investigation of the lifeworlds of experienced high school band directors.*

■ *Music as Epistemology: From a letter to a Finnish theoretician.* (n.d.).

■ Rao, D. (1988). *Craft, singing craft and musical experience: A philosophical study with implications for vocal music education as aesthetic education.*

■ Savage, J. (2010). *A phenomenology of contemporary flute improvisation: Contextual explications of techniques, aesthetics, and performance practices.*

■ Whale, M. (2009). *Music as the between: The idea of meeting in existence, music and education.*

2. Randomly select a chapter in any of the three referenced *Handbooks* by Colwell (1992), Colwell and Richardson (2002), and Colwell and Webster (2011). Then select a paragraph in which an author cites at least three different studies in support of one claim. Determine whether terms in those studies are used interchangeably despite theoretical/epistemological differences.

3. In a small group, find a seemingly simple object (e.g., a table, chair, or musical instrument) and work out a definition by genus and difference that seems satisfactory to each person in the group. Note issues that seem hard to resolve.

4. Outline major points that describe your own belief system about what should constitute "quality music" in the curriculum. Take a key term from one of those collected points and define it lexically, operationally, and by genus and difference. Write about any changes in thought in your own mind as you incorporate each of those respective definitions in your described belief system.

5. Select three published articles in the realm of philosophical inquiry and determine:

   a. Purpose(s) and/or questions;
   b. Line(s) of argumentation;
   c. Definitions of terms;
   d. References to pertinent literature divided into primary and secondary sources;
   e. Conclusions drawn.

   Evaluate the studies according to the criteria described in this chapter.

6. Find or develop examples that fit the fallacies of argumentation provided in this chapter.

7. Examine and try to label the variety of definitions you find in a selected number of published research studies, particular theses and dissertations.

Recommended Reading

On Philosophy in General:

Abel, R. (1976). *Man is the measure: A cordial invitation to the central problems of philosophy.* New York: Free Press; London: Collier Macmillan.

Durant, W. (1961). *The story of philosophy: The lives and opinions of the world's greatest philosophers.* New York: The Pocket Library.

Harris, E. E. (2000). *Apocalypse and paradigm: Science and everyday thinking.* Westport, CT: Praeger.

Hoffman, L. (2008). Premodernism, Modernism, & Postmodernism: An Overview. In *Postmodernism and psychology* [website]. Retrieved January 6, 2012 from http://www.postmodernpsychology.com/Philosophical_Systems/Overview.htm

Longino, H. E. (1990). *Science as social knowledge: Values and objectivity in scientific inquiry.* Princeton, NJ: Princeton University Press.

Russell, B. (1945). *A history of Western philosophy* (14th ed.). New York: Simon and Schuster.

Ryder, M. (n.d.) *Contemporary philosophy, critical theory and postmodern thought.* Retrieved January 6, 2012 from http://carbon.ucdenver.edu/~mryder/itc/postmodern.html

Whitehead, A. N. (1929). *The aims of education and other essays.* New York: Macmillan.

On Logic:

Allen, M. (2004). *Smart thinking: Skills for critical understanding and writing* (2nd ed.). New York: Oxford University Press.

Crosswhite, J. (1996). *The rhetoric of reason: Writing and the attractions of argument.* Madison: The University of Wisconsin Press.

Perelman, C. (Ed.). (1975). *Dialectics.* (International Institute of Philosophy, Entretiens in Varna, 15–22 September, 1973). The Hague: Martinus Nijhoff.

Popper, K. R. (1959). *The logic of scientific discovery.* New York: Basic Books.

Popper, K. R. (1968). *Conjectures and refutations: The growth of scientific knowledge.* New York: Harper and Row.

Salmon, W. C., & McLaughlin, R. (1982). *What? Where? When? Why? Essays on induction, space and time, explanation: Inspired by the work of Wesley C. Salmon and celebrating his first visit to Australia, September–December 1978.* Dordrecht, NL: D. Reidel Publishing.

On Aesthetics (and Music Education):

Macarthur, S. (2002). *Feminist aesthetics in music.* Westport, CT; London: Greenwood Press.

Meyer, L. B. (1956). *Emotion and meaning in music.* Chicago: Chicago University Press.

Meyer, L. B. (1994). *Music, the arts, and ideas: Patterns and predictions in twentieth-century culture.* Chicago: Chicago University Press.

Pike, A. (1967). The phenomenological analysis and description of musical experience. *Journal of Research in Music Education, 15*(4), 316–319.

Pike, A. (1972). A phenomenological analysis of emotional experience in music. *Journal of Research in Music Education, 20*(2), 262–267.

Prince, W. (1972). A paradigm for research in music listening. *Journal of Research in Music Education, 20*(4), 445–455.

Reimer, B. (1962). Leonard Meyer's theory of value and greatness in music. *Journal of Research in Music Education, 10*(2), 87–99.

Reimer, B. (2002). *A philosophy of music education: Advancing the vision.* Upper Saddle River, NJ: Prentice Hall.

Reimer, B. (2009). *Seeking the significance of music education: Essays and reflections.* Lanham, MD: Rowman & Littlefield.

Schwadron, A. A. (1970). Philosophy in music education: Pure or applied? *Bulletin of the Council for Research in Music Education, 19,* 22–29.

Schwadron, A. A. (1975). Research directions in comparative music aesthetics and music education. *Journal of Aesthetics, 9*(1), 99–109.

Soellner, G. E. (1971). Formalism as an aesthetic theory for music education (Doctoral dissertation). *Dissertation Abstracts International, 32*(4), 2123–2124A.

Other Recommended Sources:

Amedco, G. (2008). Difficulties encountered in the application of the phenomenological method in the social sciences. *Indo-Pacific Journal of Phenomenology, 8.* Retrieved on January 6, 2012 from http://www.ajol.info/index.php/ipjp/article/viewFile/65428/53118

Barrett, J. R. (Ed.). (2009). *Music education at a crossroads: Realizing the goal of music for all.* Lanham, MD: R&L Education.

Jorgensen, E. R. (2008). *The art of teaching music.* Bloomington: Indiana University Press.

McCall, C. C. (2009). *Transforming thinking: Philosophical inquiry in the primary and secondary classroom.* London & New York: Routledge.

Pirsig, R. M. (1974/1999/2005). *Zen and the art of motorcycle maintenance: An inquiry into values.* New York: HarperCollins Publishers.

six

Historical Inquiry

Getting Inside the Process

Marie McCarthy

This chapter describes

- Historical research as a mode of inquiry;
- Contemporary trends and developments;
- Steps for conducting a study:
  - exploring topics of interest and framing research questions;
  - locating, selecting and verifying sources;
  - organizing, critiquing and interpreting sources;
  - making inferences and drawing conclusions.

Numerous studies as well as the cases presented in this book illustrate the variety of approaches common in the historical mode.

Introduction

Doing historical research in music education takes you on a journey into the past for the purpose of collecting evidence and creating a historical narrative. The evidence comes in many forms, from documents to photographs, recordings to artifacts. Using such primary sources, the researcher creates a critical account of the past by analyzing and interpreting the evidence in the larger milieu in which actions and events occurred and developed.

Aware of the importance of bringing historical research to life in the classroom, *Prof. E.* frequently had students examine and evaluate primary source materials. To illustrate the value and power of visual media in historical research, he brought to class two books that contain photographs and images of music education in past eras: *The Music Educators Journal*'s "Special Issue: The Sesquicentennial" (MENC, 1988) that marked the sesquicentennial of the introduction of music into the public schools in the United States (1838–1988), and *MENC: A Century of Service to Music Education 1907–2007*, a book that marked the centenary of the founding of the Music Supervisors National Conference, forerunner to what today is known as NAfME: The National Association for Music Education.

Prof. E. presented a selection of photographs from the books and asked the members of the class to share questions that arose from examining them. Organizing the class in groups, he then asked each group to choose a particular photograph. Reminding the class that "who, what, where, when, why, and how" questions had guided discussion in other sessions, he presented these questions:

- Who is in the photo? Where was the photo taken, and by whom?
- When was it taken? What was the occasion and context?
- How does the content reveal the culture and values of the time period?
- What questions does the photo elicit?
- What can I learn from this photograph?
- How might the source be useful for research purposes?

The discussion of the photographs spoke to the power of visual media to stir the imagination, to provide a window into the past, to stimulate questions, and to cause self-reflection about one's assumptions and biases.

Exploration: Thinking About History in Your Professional Life

Before proceeding to choose a topic to research, think about what "history" means to you and what you believe about its function and value in the lives of music educators, individually and collectively.

Historical Research as a Mode of Inquiry

To possess a historical sense does not mean simply to possess information about the past. It means to have a different consciousness, a historical consciousness, to have incorporated into our minds a mode of understanding that profoundly influences the way we look at the world. History adds another dimension to our view of the world and enriches our experience. (Wood, 2008, p. 11)

The word "history" has etymological roots in the ancient Greek word *historia*, translated as "inquiry" or "knowledge acquired through investigation" ("History," 2011). This meaning is resonant of the Latin *histor* – learned person. Both terms refer to someone who is intellectually curious and seeks wisdom through inquiry. The historical researcher creates a narrative by chronicling past actions and events, finding relationships and patterns among pieces of evidence, and inferring meaning from them.

Historian Lawrence Stone defined narrative as "the organization of material in a chronologically sequenced order and the focusing of the content on a single coherent story, albeit with sub-plots" (1979, p. 3). Narrative is descriptive in form and provides an account of how a complex event unfolded in time. Through narrative, the researcher connects, interprets, and creates a sequence of events across time, and provides a causal explanation of the outcomes of actions and events. Several challenges and tensions can arise in presenting history in and through narrative. Among others, the researcher might make connections that are not true to what actually occurred, or tell the story as he thinks it should have happened, or gather some evidence and neglect to find or include evidence that presents an alternative viewpoint or line of reasoning. As you can see, there is considerable responsibility associated with historical research and writing, a point that will be explored later in the chapter.

What kinds of narratives emerge from historical study in music education? We learn about the lives of persons who contributed in important ways to music education; the development of curriculum, pedagogy, and programs at local, regional, and international levels; and, the evolution of institutions and organizations. Researchers also investigate the emergence and demise of trends and practices; the participation of particular groups and sub-cultures in formal and informal music education; and, the transmission of music in various contexts as it relates to political, social, and cultural history.

Overview of the Historical Research Process

Research based on historical inquiry is similar to that of other modes in some ways. All research involves systematic documentation of evidence, methodological rigor, scholarly standards of citation and sourcing, interpretation of evidence, and contextualization and evaluation of findings. Historical research also has unique processes and challenges. With the exception of oral history, the historian uses data sources from bygone times, and thus relies heavily on imaginative and intuitive strategies to make connections between pieces of evidence. The historical researcher may use multiple fields of literature in the arts, humanities, and social sciences to support interpretation of evidence—for example, education, musicology, history, psychology, sociology, and cultural studies. The focus is on crafting a narrative to convey a chronological sequence of events and actions and infer meanings from multiple layers of evidence gathered from primary sources. Collingwood (1946/1994) captured the essence of doing history when he wrote that history is a science of a special kind, whose business is:

to study events not accessible to our observation, and to study these events inferentially, arguing to them from something else which is accessible to our observation, and which the historian calls "evidence" for the events in which he is interested. (pp. 251–252)

As a historian, you study the actions and events of human beings through examination of evidence, navigating between investigative work on the one hand and humanistic interpretation on the other. You are guided in this process by critical thinking skills which are key in moving the historical account from a mere chronicling of past actions and events to uncovering the thoughts and motivations of those whose stories are being narrated. Throughout, you recognize your own biases and assumptions, evaluate related research studies, and identify a topic that leads to a research purpose. You question the veracity of sources, examine evidence for motivation, error and bias, corroborate pieces of evidence, and make inferences.

All of these moments of critical thought contribute to a historical narrative that is communicated to the reader in a voice that is, on the one hand, detached in the presentation of chronological facts and sequences and, on the other hand, personally engaged in description and interpretation. The manner in which you achieve this balance varies. Traditional approaches to history tend toward dispassionate reporting, whereas contemporary approaches are more oriented toward the inclusion of the author's voice and worldview. The change resulted in part from a movement away from the idea of history as a singular set of facts and truths to a view of history as a set of perspectives that can be re-examined and revised.

Visualizing the process can help you to develop a historical consciousness and a sense of the uniqueness of historical inquiry. Which of these metaphors would you likely draw upon when engaging in historical inquiry: History as a window or lens into the past; a map or a canvas on which a story is framed; a jigsaw puzzle to be solved; a sculpture not yet realized, waiting for a sculptor to chip away extraneous material and bring it to life? As you proceed with your topic, visualize the past and create your own image or metaphor for the process of doing historical research.

Why Engage in Historical Research?

The creation and dissemination of knowledge about music teaching and learning in the past, in all its forms and contexts, is an important task of the music education profession. Historical knowledge can deepen understanding of the past, develop self-knowledge in the individual music educator and in the profession, and serve to inform present problems with the wisdom gained from past experience. It can foster community, identity, and continuity.

As we come to know the past, we develop a sense of how music education today came to be—for example, why music was valued in education and society, how instructional practices evolved, what stimulated change in curriculum, and how music in schools interacted with musical cultures outside of school. This kind of professional knowledge can influence the perspectives of individual music teachers and the professional body at large. Historical knowledge can serve as a source of inspiration and an advocacy tool. Learning about the conditions under which teachers taught in bygone times can generate a sense of admiration for their accomplishments and gratitude for the resources available today. It can highlight how you are part of a lineage of professionals working in the name of music education. Historical knowledge can also provide a foundation for understanding trends in music education and for evaluating new curriculum materials. Historical insights allow us as music educators to see who we are, where we came from, and to what we belong (Wood, 2008, p. 8), thus lending a sense of continuity and depth to our work. For these reasons, it is a professional responsibility for each generation to augment the body of literature on the history of music education.

Doing History in Contemporary Times: Trends and Developments

> The music educator must operate with a proper realization of his present and past place in society not only for the sense of pride that such realization brings with it but also for the fund of wisdom thus made available with which to deal with contemporary problems. (Britton, 1969, pp. 109–110)

The nature of historical inquiry has changed in recent decades, resulting in part from developments in philosophy of history, expansion of intellectual paradigms, and advancements in technology and media. Philosophy of history is part of the larger area of historiography, the study of history—its past achievements, approaches, methods, and effects. The functions and uses of history came under scrutiny when scholars in a number of disciplines began to evaluate its political effects. Questions arose such as: Whose stories have been told? Whose voices have been heard and whose voices remain silent?

The idea that there is one universal or master narrative of the past, one story that produces *the* historical truth for all time, was challenged in the latter half of the 20th century. Influenced by postmodern thinking, critical theory, and other intellectual paradigms, historians began to acknowledge the importance of documenting multiple historical narratives, using different vantage points as starting places and different lenses to examine and analyze what remains of the past. This approach is referred to as *revisionist history*.

Revisionist Views of the Past

Revisionist approaches to history focus on bringing values and ideologies of the present to bear on investigations and interpretations of the past. Recognizing the limitations of depending on one grand narrative, revisionist historians are therefore critical of earlier interpretations of the past, particularly those written from the perspective of dominant political groups that view the past through a narrow window. Revisionists remind us that historical study is dynamic and always evolving. As values change, new perspectives call us to look again into the past for new stories and new ways of re-framing and re-telling old stories. Thus, revisionist historians have expanded the paradigms used for interpretation, brought forth alternative and marginalized viewpoints, and created new narratives out of evidence that was previously kept silent due to neglect, or worse, oppression.

For an excellent discussion of revisionist history, read Carol Pemberton's (1987) article on the topic, in which she uses the life of Lowell Mason to illustrate how perceptions of his contributions during his lifetime contrast with those of the late 20th century. She concludes that when we recognize influences on historical writing, our own and others, "we become more perceptive readers and more insightful writers" (p. 213).

Expanding the Scope of Historical Research

Parallel to the introduction of revisionist approaches, historians have expanded the paradigms and disciplinary bases they draw on to include sociological, feminist, cultural, and post-colonial perspectives (see Cox, 2002, pp. 695–706). These trends and developments have influenced historical study in music education (McCarthy, 1999, 2011). They also have contributed to fundamental changes related to where we look for topics, what we look for, how we look, and why we are motivated to study certain topics. Thus, the scope of historical research is expanding. An increasing number of studies account for political, cultural, economic, and social influences on music education (e.g., Goble, 2009; Volk, 2007; Warnock, 2009). Insights from such studies enlighten our understanding of the relationships between music, society, and education.

Furthermore, studies about the history of music education in settings outside the public school serve to establish a more complete picture of music learning and teaching. And, the lives of all music educators are under consideration, not just those who taught in public schools or held leadership positions, although such work remains important. Similarly, the stories of all social groups and classes, ethnicities, and marginalized groups are beginning to receive the attention they deserve. Their stories are being told, some for the first time (e.g., Handel & Humphreys, 2005; Howe, 2009; Lee, 1997; May, 2005). Increasingly, historical researchers contextualize their studies within the social norms and cultural values of the time period under study.

Contemporary Approaches and Methodologies

The expansion of research approaches and methodologies in the late 20th century influenced historical research. When Rainbow and Froehlich (1987) were writing about historical research in the mid-1980s, they referred to a broadening of approaches coming from the social sciences and the natural sciences—comparative historical research, oral history, psychohistory, and quantitative (social-scientific) history. With the exception of psychohistory, these approaches are increasingly present in historical studies in music education.

Comparative Historical Research

The topic of comparative and cross-cultural research has entered the mainstream of music education in the past two decades (Kemp & Lepherd, 1992; Cox, 2002; McCarthy, 2011). In addressing "historically grounded comparative work," Cox (2002) argued for its value when he concluded that, "music educators in a variety of countries and cultures can be encouraged to question what they take for granted in their practice" (p. 703). After carrying out a cross-cultural historical study, Gruhn (2001) recommended further studies that engage in cross-cultural analysis, arguing that such studies "could result in better understandings of the roots of ideas and practices that are or have been implemented in another cultural context" (p. 18). Cox and Stevens (2010) adopted a cross-cultural approach in their edited volume, *The Origins and Foundations of Music Education: Cross-Cultural Historical Studies of Music in Compulsory Schooling*. This collection of national case studies can stimulate thinking about other topics to study cross-culturally. As comparative and cross-cultural historical research develops, it reveals the predominant factors that impacted music education practices internationally, in particular the spread of European music and music pedagogy across the world during various colonial periods.

Oral History

The Oral History Association (2012) defines oral history as "a field of study and a method of gathering, preserving and interpreting the voices and memories of people, communities, and participants in past events" (www.oralhistory.org). Those voices and memories are collected in oral form through in-depth interviews and recorded in audio or video format (Ritchie, 2003). An interview becomes an oral history "when it has been recorded, processed in some way, made available in an archive, library, or other repository, or reproduced in relatively verbatim form for publication" (Ritchie, 2003, p. 24). Oral history, then, can be understood as both process (the act of interviewing) and product (the record that results from the interview) (Shopes, 2011). The purpose of an interview could be either to document a person's account of his or her life or to examine a particular time frame or series of events from the perspective of those who lived through them.

The interviewee is referred to as the narrator or the informant. Topics may address what it was like to live or work with an influential figure, or may focus on the interviewees' own reflections about specific recollections of experiences or events. The focus of such research may be on famous musicians or music teachers, or music education leaders, but oral histories of the "common person" are also revealing, providing a sense of how ordinary people experienced life or a particular moment in the past (Bogdan & Biklen, 2003, pp. 56–57). Oral history can also document the experiences of groups, institutions, and communities. Such oral histories can serve, for example, to document traditions and cultures that are disappearing, to tell the stories of groups that have been neglected in mainstream history, or to chronicle a community's response to a major event.

Techniques for conducting interviews in oral history follow those advocated in qualitative as well as quantitative research methods (see Chapters 8 and 13 for further information). Key to good interviewing is careful preparation. Know as much as possible about the interviewee so that your questions are to the point and invite responses that open the dialogue for rich exchange. Remember that interviewees are often recalling events that took place many years ago and their memories may not be clear and accurate. The oral historian brings that awareness to the timing, planning, and analysis of the interviews. In sum, oral history is "both the oldest type of historical inquiry, predating the written word, and one of the most modern, initiated with tape recorders in the 1940s and now using 21st-century digital technologies" (www.oral history.org). The possibilities for using oral history research in music education are many and varied. Consider how such an approach might be valuable in relation to your research topic.

Psychohistory

The study of historical subjects engages the researcher in understanding people and their actions and behaviors. It is not surprising, then, to learn that historians find resonance in disciplinary concepts from psychology. Psychohistory is a relatively new approach in historical research, with roots in the work of psychologists Sigmund Freud, Eric Fromm, Carl Jung, and Erik Erikson. While clinical psychologists research the history of their subjects to gain insight into development over time, historians have drawn on developmental psychological theories, among others, to explain the emotional origins of human motivations and actions, individually and collectively, across time.

Psychohistorical approaches assume that by applying insights from human psychology, one can better explain why certain events or changes occurred. The psychological make-up of an individual is studied in great detail and an in-depth psychological profile is developed using the most up-to-date theories and clinical practices to understand the past. This bio–socio–psychological approach to history has not been formally employed in music education research, but it may prove useful when historians research or re-visit the lives and contributions of individuals and groups whose influence effected the development of the field.

This approach to the past also locates human actions and behaviors in the context of social and cultural contexts of the time, examining interactions between an individual's or group's psychological make-up and the worldviews and values within which those beliefs were constructed. One can imagine using such an approach when studying pedagogical lineages in music where continuity and change can be traced from one generation of performer–teacher to the next. Similarly, in a group setting, the approach might be useful in developing insights into the psychological make-up of school board members of past generations who supported or opposed music instruction in the schools.

Some historical studies focus on topics that seem well suited to psychohistorical analysis, for example, Warnock's (2009) study of the anti-Semitic origins of Henry Ford's arts education patronage, or Nagao's (2000) synchronous approach to the lives and contributions of Peter Dykema and Koji Nagai, leaders in music education in the United States and Japan, respectively, who lived at the same time. As a psychohistorical study, one could attempt to access the relationship between the individual and his cultural environment in each of the two cultural settings, and then compare the relationships across cultures. Similar to other research methodologies, psychohistory is a specialized domain with specific techniques and it demands extensive study and careful implementation (Loewenberg, 1983/1985/1996).

Quantitative History

Records based on quantitative data (typically used to illustrate the occurrence or frequency of events, trends, etc.) have been used more frequently in recent years as a form of historical evidence. For example, Wasiak (2000) included statistical data from department of education records in his study of school bands in Saskatchewan. In her study of the inclusion of women composers in college music history textbooks, Baker (2003) presented her data in tables to show frequencies of representation. Handel and Humphreys (2005) used population statistics in their study of the Phoenix Indian School Band, while Preston and Humphreys (2007) conducted a quantitative analysis of dissertations in music education and music therapy completed in the 20th century. Quantitative data can serve in a number of different ways in historical studies, among them: to create an initial picture of the size and magnitude of a trend or development, to ground or refute other kinds of evidence, to provide precise data to complement other primary sources, to compare statistical data from one place or region with others, or to back up claims leading to conclusions.

Developments in Technology and Media

Technological advances greatly enhance possibilities for creating and "re-presenting" the past. For example, digital video recording of oral history interviews is a superior source for biographical study and an effective way of preserving recent history for future researchers. Digitized recordings of archival media present a clear record of the past that allows you to move closer to the historical event or action. The availability of online archival materials and serials, among other resources, provides easy access to sources. When working with archival material, the researcher can use a digital camera to capture images and later include them in a study. Such developments have changed the face of historical narrative.

Visual images in historical studies are coming into their own, in part because advancements in technology have facilitated their inclusion in publications. The power of visual images to bring the researcher to the heart of a historical moment, to stimulate questions and wonderings, and to reveal the values and priorities of a group and its surrounding culture cannot be underestimated. Overall, the inclusion of audiovisual media in historical narrative can contribute to deepening the reader's encounter with the past. A brief list of Internet sources for historical research is included at the end of this chapter.

When one considers the expanding scope of historical research topics, the new approaches and techniques that support historical inquiry, and changing views of the purpose of history, it is clear that the nature of historical research in music education is poised for change. At no other time in our professional history has there been a more dynamic and comprehensive array of topical and methodological resources available for the historian. The field of historical research in music education is vast, the task is noble, and the outcome can be fulfilling and valuable.

Initial Steps for Conducting a Study

It is important to point out that the "steps" described here do not necessarily imply that one happens after the other in the research process itself. Some steps obviously occur before others—an initial review of the literature before the formation of a research purpose, or the reading of sources before writing the narrative. However, the process is equally cyclic, similar to "think, read, observe, share" as described in Chapter 1. As you read sources, you make connections with other sources; as you critique evidence, you make initial interpretations; or, as you interpret, a logical organizational structure for the narrative is created.

Topic, Purpose, and Research Questions

Historical researchers differentiate between choosing a topic, writing a purpose statement, and creating specific research questions. All three aspects are of equal importance and require your careful attention.

Choosing a Topic

Sources that inspire historical questions are many and varied: teaching experience, historical papers or artifacts that are close at hand, your cultural background, a source that you stumble upon and that piques curiosity, or a sense of professional responsibility to document a particular topic. For example, Christy's research interest originated in her extensive string teaching: She was curious about the works of string pedagogues since 1800 for continuity with teaching strings today.

With similar origins in practice, Isbell (2006) found his inspiration for a research study while he was teaching at Steamboat Springs High School in Colorado. He became curious about the history of the unique high school Ski Band (a band providing entertainment for skiing festivals in Steamboat Springs) that he conducted. Subsequently, he documented its history and addressed these questions: "What factors contributed to the Steamboat Springs high school ski band's creation in 1935? What changes have occurred in performance practice since its creation? What is the relationship between the ensemble and the local community?" (p. 25).

Inspiration for a study often originates in our own backyard, in historical documents or artifacts that are close at hand. Ward-Steinman (2003) drew on a treasure trove of historical data that she found in family archives. Her father and grandfather managed Madura's Danceland in the greater Chicago area, and she had access to their papers and used them "to gain unique insights into big band musicians' compensation during the Big Band Era" (p. 167). Cultural background, too, can be a motivating factor in choosing a topic. Chi-Hui's research interests originated in her first point of reference for music education, her home country of Taiwan, as she compared her experience there with music education in her adopted country, the United States. She anticipated that such a study might give her insights into prevailing practices in her own country and possibly strengthen her professional philosophy and pedagogy.

Scholars also stumble upon topics that pique their curiosity and inspire them to pursue a study. For example, when McCarthy was reading Birge's *History of Public School Music in the United States* (1928/1966), she noticed a reference to an "international gathering" of music educators in London in 1928 and a forthcoming meeting in Switzerland in 1929 (p. 270). She was surprised to read this reference because prior knowledge had caused her to believe that organized international activity began with the founding of the International Society for Music Education (ISME) in 1953. Curious, she decided to solve what puzzled her. Thus, she searched for published studies describing these earlier events and determined that they had not been documented, at least not in English-language sources. She established the need to trace the roots of international activity in music education and that led to two studies, which documented the history of international music education prior to the founding of ISME (McCarthy, 1993, 1995).

Inspiration can also arise out of a sense of professional responsibility for documenting the story of music education in a community, state, or region. A striking example is the compilation of essays on music and music education in the state of Rhode Island that started out as a project in a graduate class and developed into an edited book. *Rhode Island's Musical Heritage: An Exploration* (Livingston & Smith, 2008) provides testimony to the musical and cultural diversity that comprises the state's musical heritage and confirms the value and importance of doing local history. When you choose your topic, pay similar attention to the origin of your curiosity. Such knowledge will sustain your interest and motivation to complete the study.

While searching the literature, you come to appreciate the breadth and variety of research topics in published studies of music education history. Until the late 20th century, historical researchers documented primarily the chronology of events, the development of music programs in public education, and the contributions of leaders in music education. Studies included questions such as: What was the rationale for introducing music into the public schools in 1838? When was the first professional organization of music educators founded and how did it develop from a small group to a national body of music educators? Why did music appreciation enter the music curriculum in the early 20th century and how did Frances Elliot Clark, leader in the development of music appreciation curriculum and media, contribute to the movement? Although questions of *who, what, when, where, how,* and *why* remain relevant, contemporary researchers are beginning to question patterns of thought, motivations for actions, and causes for change with greater intention and focus.

New research techniques evolve all the time, which also allows us to ask new questions. A content analysis of articles in the first 20 volumes of *The Bulletin of Historical Research in Music Education*, 1980–1999 (McCarthy, 1999) yielded the following categories of topics: development of music education programs (local, national, international), biography, curriculum methods and materials, and historiography. A similar study of more recent volumes (21–30) in the newly titled *Journal of Historical Research in Music Education* resulted in the addition of two new topic categories—cross-cultural studies that focus on a topic in more than one national setting, and studies whose primary focus is the political and/or cultural context in which music and music education developed (McCarthy, 2011).

Finding a Purpose

When you have found a topic that has inherent value and is likely to hold your interest over time, you are ready to carry out some preliminary research to assess its feasibility.

Begin reading sources that others have written about the topic, thereby expanding your knowledge of the research base. Confirm the existence of a substantial number of relevant primary sources, and identify specific "holes of knowledge" about the topic under study. Examining a selection of primary research sources will provide the foundation for assessing the feasibility of a study.

Becoming familiar with the time period and the people and events involved will build confidence and develop a sense of ownership of the topic. Questions will arise as you engage with sources. Write them down and begin to shape a purpose statement based on them. Initial wonderings and hunches give way to a more focused topic of inquiry. All of this vital work leads to a purpose statement that provides a frame for a historical question you intend to resolve in the study.

As *Chi-Hui* explored her topic of comparative music education in the context of Taiwan and the United States, *Prof. E.* suggested that she examine several books containing investigations on music education in different countries or discuss music education internationally (Cox & Stevens, 2010; Hargreaves & North, 2001; Kertz-Welzel, 2008; Lepherd, 1995; McCarthy, 2004). He advised Chi-Hui to focus on countries close to her homeland in East Asia (Ho, 2000; Kou, 2001; Lee, W.R., 2002). During her review of these and related sources, Chi-Hui realized that although she was educated in the Taiwanese school system, she knew little about how the system worked. She became fascinated with accounts of the educational system in Taiwan and felt she should have a formal knowledge of that system before comparing it to those of other nations. The topic of her study thus evolved: Western influences in primary and secondary music education in Taiwan since music became a compulsory subject in the curriculum. She was close to having a purpose identified.

Christy, after an initial phase of searching in secondary sources, found that the chronological scope of the topic she started out with—string pedagogues since 1800—was too broad, given time constraints and available resources. She was not finding literature from the 1800s, other than biographical sketches of string performers. Based on her initial search, she decided to focus on pedagogues of the 20th century whose works were more readily available to her. The next task was to choose which pedagogue(s) to study and to identify which aspects of their contributions she wanted to investigate.

Exploration: From Purpose Statement to Research Questions

Choose either Chi-Hui's or Christy's purpose statement (see Chapter 4) and compose two to three research specifications (sub-problems/questions) that would fulfill the study's intent. Compare your suggestions with those of your classmates.

Finding Sources and Verifying Evidence

There are two principal categories of sources from which historical evidence is gathered: primary sources and secondary sources (see Chapter 2). Although the categories are presented as discrete, there can be overlap between them depending on the context of the study. For example, a dissertation can serve as a primary source when its author is the topic of a study or as a secondary source if a researcher uses its findings for a related study. A researcher typically encounters secondary sources first—dictionaries, annotated bibliographies, and foundational texts in music education that provide useful bibliographic information, and books and articles directly related to the topic. Such sources serve an important role in establishing the need for and value of a proposed study. They also serve to build a case for the feasibility of the study, to refine the research purpose and question, and, most importantly, to guide the researcher to relevant primary sources.

Primary Sources

Primary sources are "the gold standard of historical research" (Danto, 2008, p. 62). Generated by someone who witnessed or participated in the historical event under study, they provide firsthand evidence to the researcher. Criteria used to determine the value of a primary source include originality, veracity, relevance, and evidentiary value.

- Originality: How close was the witness to the subject of the study when an event was documented? As a historical researcher, you work with sources that are as close as possible in time and space to the "origin," that which is being studied—the person, institution, organization, curriculum, program, or cultural group.
- Veracity: What is the relationship between the person providing the evidence and the subject under study? This question helps you judge a primary source in terms of its "competence," that is, if the witness is capable of understanding and describing the situation, shows impartiality, or has something to gain from distortion of the record (Felt, 1976/1981, pp. 7–8).
- Relevance: How is the content of the source related to the research questions? In historical research, it is possible for a researcher to become fascinated with interesting sources that are at best tangentially related to the purpose of the study. To determine data relevance, therefore, you should ensure that each source can be placed in some meaningful way onto the collage of sources that is being assembled and that contribute to the story you are about to tell.
- Evidentiary value: How does the piece of evidence contribute to the overall collection of data? Does it contribute to increasing the variety of evidence, the multiplicity of voices, or elaborating on different dimensions of the topic under study? Evaluate the overall corpus of primary sources used to ensure that they represent different perspectives on the topic achieved from different vantage points. In studying the life of one person, multiple voices may be found, for example, in various roles that the individual played in her profession over her life time.

The Infinite Variety of Primary Sources

Historical study engages you in examining different kinds of evidence. Barzun and Graff (2004) categorize evidence into "the Verbal and the Mute," the verbal referring to the majority of sources which contain words and the mute consisting of "any physical object bearing no words" (p. 117). Some sources fall between or outside these broad categories. Visual media reside primarily in "the Mute" but can have elements of "the Verbal"—for example, a photograph with a caption and/or description of its contents or a plaque with an inscription. Quantitative data have numeric attributes but could be accompanied by verbal description. Perhaps a more inclusive approach to source categorization is as follows:

- *Written documents* (e.g., autobiographies, diaries, letters, scrapbooks, memoirs, magazines, newspapers, government documents, institutional records, quantitative records such as school music enrollment numbers, demographics, test scores, music festival ratings).
- *Oral records* (e.g., interviews, audio and visual recordings of school concerts or festivals, recordings of student compositions).
- *Artifacts* (e.g., photographs, textbooks, instructional media, musical instruments, trophies, music scores, costumes and uniforms, concert props).

Locating Primary Sources

As already stated, the scope of research topics in music education history is expansive. Thus, the primary sources related to such varied topics are deposited across several kinds of libraries and special collections, public and private. A review of articles in Volumes 21–30 (2000–2009) of the *Journal of Historical Research in Music Education* indicated that researchers draw on primary sources from a range of public records and documents, private collections and personal papers, oral history interviews, journals, proceedings and yearbooks, concert programs, textbooks, songbooks, tune books and tutors, and autobiographies (McCarthy, 2011). Materials were accessed in a number of different public libraries and archives; for example, the Library of Congress, Special Collections in Performing Arts—University of Maryland, U.S. Government Archives, and the Naval Historical Center. While it is true to say that more and more documents and serials are available online, the majority of topics will require the historical researcher to visit archival collections.

Using Archival Material

The use of archival material (a collection of historical records) is unique to historical research and deserves special attention since it involves policies and procedures that you will typically not encounter when gathering data for other kinds of research studies. Due to the care required for accessing and handling archival materials, each institution that houses archives will have its own policies for making materials available to patrons.

The Special Collections in Performing Arts at the University of Maryland is the largest and perhaps most comprehensive repository of music education archives in the United States (for access to website, see http://www.lib.umd.edu/PAL/SCPA). The collections are divided into the following categories: band, media, music education, professional organizations, performer and scholar, and score collections. Music education researchers use sources primarily from the Music Education Collections and Professional Organization Archives, but they may also find sources in other categories (e.g., the Alice Parker Papers and the Charles Fowler Papers are located in the Performer & Scholar Collections). The Special Collections website provides clear guidelines on how to get in touch with the curator and gain access to the materials.

In writing a history of the first 50 years of ISME (McCarthy, 2004), the author examined sources in the ISME Archives that are part of the Special Collections. The content of the ISME Archives is listed in a *finding aid* (a document describing in detail the content and context of a specific collection within an archive), which was useful in gaining an overview of the collection and identifying which records to read. The records of some individuals who held office in the society were located elsewhere in the Special Collections (e.g., Marguerite V. Hood who was active in ISME and also president of MENC, and Vanett Lawler, a key figure in the founding and early development of ISME and also executive secretary of MENC).

Historical research can involve travel in order to access primary sources in archival collections. Reconstructing the history of ISME required correspondence with individuals internationally, and a trip to Perth, Australia to read the papers of Sir Frank Callaway that are housed in The Callaway Centre at the University of Western Australia. Callaway played a significant role in the development of ISME during its first 50 years, and papers related to his work in the society are held with his other papers at The Callaway Centre. Additionally, the author corresponded with or interviewed several past ISME officers through letter, email, telephone, or in personal interviews held during biennial conferences between 1996 and 2002.

It may take some readjustment to be at home with archival research. It is frequently less convenient to access historical sources than it is to conduct research online, and this reality may challenge your patience and lead to frustration. Focus on the positive aspects: the sensory information that is afforded by handling an original piece of historical evidence; the closeness you feel to the subject of your study when you have that tactile experience with sources; or, the excitement that is found when you turn a page to find a photograph that captures an essential aspect of your investigation. Furthermore, there is the satisfaction gained when you begin to grasp the spirit of a time and place through reading newspapers and locally produced print media; the immediacy of listening to a recording and hearing the performances of those whose musical accomplishments you seek to document; and finally, the overall sense that you are touching the humanity of a bygone age by studying these historical sources.

Engaging With Primary Sources

It is vitally important that you experience historical sources firsthand. This can be achieved in a number of ways—visiting a library that has an archival collection and looking at some primary sources, finding a historical artifact in your family records, visiting a historic building, or reading an old music textbook that is in your school library.

Exploration: Bringing a Primary Source to Life

Appendix I contains a reprint of John Curwen's account of observations of Sarah Glover's classroom in Norwich, England. John Curwen (1816–1880) is commonly known as the creator of the Curwen hand signs, a sol-fa system of hand signals to represent pitch. He based the system on a method known as Norwich Sol-fa, developed by Sarah Glover (1785–1867). Read Curwen's account and reflect in writing on the following questions: What images form in your mind as you read the document? What sounds do you hear? What emotions do you feel? What do you imagine was the intention of the writer who created the document? Do you detect any biases on the writer's part? If so, what does that tell you? Finally, what makes this source a primary source?

Reading and Recording

The next step in the research process is to select and read sources, and record the evidence. Choose some method of recording the data—note-taking, photocopying, scanning or whatever technology seems appropriate and useful for the material at hand. It takes considerable time to immerse yourself in a particular place and era in order to grasp the *Zeitgeist* ("the spirit of the times"). Thus, it is necessary to examine carefully the evidence—let each piece speak to you. Contemplate the words and the use of language, the modes of communication, the visual images where they apply, and the underlying assumptions. As you read, be prepared for the unexpected, and keep a watchful eye for inconsistencies between data sources and ambiguities that may arise. In addition to reading the sources directly related to your topic, read "around" the topic, and when possible watch movies about the era or talk to people who lived at the time. Become an insider to the time and place you are studying just as you would when conducting other forms of qualitative research. At all times, use a journal for recording questions that arise when you read or listen to sources and for writing responses.

Verifying the Evidence

Verification of primary source material is essential to all historical investigations. Each source undergoes what historians call external and internal criticism. Both serve the purpose of establishing that evidence should be considered trustworthy.

External Criticism

The term refers to the authenticity and reliability of a source. Both qualities are ascertained by questions such as:

- When was the source produced?
- Where was it produced?
- Who produced it?
- Is it in its original form? If not, where is the original?

- Is there any reason to suspect that this source may not be genuine?
- Could it have been written by someone else?

External criticism may not be as great a challenge for documents of the 19th and 20th centuries as it is for documents of earlier time periods. There may be instances, however, when essential information is lacking because a date of origin cannot be found, information is inconsistent with other sources, or handwriting is not legible.

W. R. Lee (2002) used external criticism as one aspect of examining an essay by Charles Farnsworth (1859–1947), a pioneer in American music teacher education in the late 19th and early 20th centuries (p. 39). When scrutinizing Farnsworth's papers at the Thetford Library and Archive in Thetford, Vermont, Lee found an unpublished paper with a questionable date of origin. The Thetford document was labeled as a speech titled "Music in the Secondary School," given on September 21, 1898. Lee was aware that the archive at the University of Colorado mentioned a speech of the same title, given at a meeting of Colorado teachers a year earlier, in 1897. The Thetford manuscript contained typewritten revisions pasted over the handwritten speech, and was signed and dated by Farnsworth. An expert on Farnsworth's life, creative output, and scholarly work habits, Lee made the following claims about the manuscript: Since Farnsworth rarely made substantive changes in revisions of his work, the 1897 version would likely have differed little in content from the later version. Further, Lee suggested that typewritten revisions must have been added after 1899, since Farnsworth's essays and speeches were not typewritten until after his move to New York City in 1900. Since Lee based his article on this one essay and he found evidence of two speeches of the same title, it was necessary for him to provide a detailed account of its provenance.

Internal Criticism

Establishing accuracy and credibility of information contained in a source requires such questions as:

- What motivated the author of the information to produce this statement/image/object?
- What is the author's role in relation to the information provided?
- Are facts included in the piece consistent with other writings of the time period?
- Does the author show bias in the way thoughts and ideas are expressed?
- Are the stated thoughts and ideas consistent with other writings by the same author?
- What is the evidentiary value of the content? Can this evidence be corroborated with evidence from other sources?

Ethics and Historical Research

In other research modes that involve human subjects, ethical standards are established and reported. Similar standards are applied when doing oral historical research (see

Chapter 3 and 4 for discussion of ethical issues and Chapter 7 for a discussion of human subjects in qualitative research). You request the written consent of persons being interviewed and have the study approved by the Institutional Review Board at your college or university. Transcripts of interviews are shared and the interviewee has the opportunity to make changes. In oral history, typically, the interviewees will be older and have much life experience. Their ability to recall accurately will vary, and you will sometimes need to corroborate evidence received in this way with that of other sources. Consider how the interviewee is positioned in relation to the topic and how recollections may be biased, inaccurate, or emotionally charged. Furthermore, when researching the lives of individuals or groups, some negative information or attitudes may come to your attention. When that occurs, you need to be particularly sensitive, and diplomatic. Listen closely to the dynamics of human relationships as presented in the sources. Corroborate the evidence with other sources and evaluate its place in your study.

There are additional ethical guidelines that apply to the conduct of historical research beyond interviewing oral history participants:

- Exercise care in interpreting sources. The persons and groups under study are no longer present to respond to how their words or actions are interpreted. Thus, care must be taken to examine the evidence with sensitivity, to corroborate evidence with that of other sources, and to remember that you have obligations to the individuals or groups you study.
- Acknowledge the values of the time period and evaluate evidence accordingly. This principle is related to the idea discussed earlier that it takes considerable time to become an insider to the time period, to get to know all the contextual factors that influenced the mentality and shaped the values of the people who lived at the time.
- Honor the historical record without distorting it—for example, filling in holes in the records without adequate evidence or not disclosing records.
- Read widely about the history of marginalized groups you are studying, gain perspectives from insiders when possible, and bring the stories of such groups into mainstream history in a balanced and sensitive way that does not patronize them.
- Present a holistic interpretation of the past that includes both glorious achievements and painful or contentious actions. Remember that individuals and groups have memories that, for example, may contain pain and animosity caused by political suppression. As African-American novelist and political activist James A. Baldwin (1955) put it, "People are trapped in history and history is trapped in them" (p. 163). The cause of pain may no longer exist but memory carries its traces into the present where it may surface in the process of recalling the past.

Interpreting the Evidence, Organizing and Writing the Narrative

No piece of evidence can be used in the state in which it is found. [Emphasis original.] It must undergo scrutiny of the researcher's mind according to the rules of the critical method. (Barzun & Graff, 2004, pp. 119–120)

Interpreting and writing go hand in hand as historical evidence is collected, analyzed, and incorporated into the unfolding narrative. In a sense, you begin to interpret when you write your first observations about a primary source. Such observations are useful later when it comes to connecting various pieces of evidence, inferring meaning from them, and placing them in chronological order as well as thematic sequence.

Interpreting the Evidence

There is no history without interpretation. The mere reporting of facts in chronological order or the categorization of evidence into themes is not sufficient in itself in order to complete a historical study. Primary sources are not authorities but only sources, as Collingwood points out, and "the historian's attitude towards them must consist neither in acceptance nor in rejection, but in interpretation" (1946/1994, p. 377). Criticism is integral to all interactions with historical data. Recall the discussion of internal and external criticism when verifying sources. It is particularly vital in the interpretive phase of doing history as the researcher creates a narrative of the past from the evidence examined in the sources.

Senses and Sensibilities at Work

Although the researcher is working with materials that were produced in the past, doing history can be a concrete and tangible encounter when sources are approached interactively. Listen for the intention of the writer, look for connections with other pieces of evidence, imagine why the writer or speaker thinks and feels as she does, and identify places where the source is silent about something and speculate why, given the content and context of the evidence. Ask numerous questions of each source and pursue answers elsewhere if necessary. Assume that human motivation is complex and that the words or visuals before you reveal only part of the story. Pemberton (1999) alludes to that complexity when she writes: "As historians, we have to look around corners, expecting circular and zigzag progressions. After all, history is the record of human endeavors, and those endeavors don't run in straight lines" (pp. 117–118). Therefore, it is necessary to read multiple sources of data, to juxtapose their insinuations and implications, and to place their meanings in the larger social and cultural context in which they occurred.

Acknowledging and Minimizing Bias

It is important to keep in mind that when you interpret historical evidence, you are influenced by your own background. Clarify your relationship to the topic you are studying, and the values and beliefs that underlie your reading and interpretation of the sources.

In doing so, you may bring to the surface some biases inherent in the way you listen, look and evaluate what you see and read.

When *Christy* discussed her reading of sources with *Prof. E.*, she tended to be overly critical of string teaching in the past. Prof. E. asked her several questions about what she thought it was like to be a string teacher in the early 20th century: How were teachers educated? What was known about child development? What curriculum materials were available? What was the quality of instrument available to students? What was known about group process string teaching? Responding to these questions, among others, helped Christy to build awareness of the realities of string teaching in the past. It also helped her to critique it with a more informed and compassionate perspective.

Similar to Christy's initial response to historical string method books, consider the lens that you bring to investigating your topic. In what ways are you using values, beliefs, and experiences to critique past events? Do present-day ideas and perspectives dominate your interpretation of the past? It would be impossible to remove such bias totally, but it is important to acknowledge it. Collingwood (1946/1994) suggests that the historian re-enacts past thought (p. 215) as she processes it. Situate yourself in the past by asking questions such as: What was it like to be a music teacher at the time of the study? Who valued the teacher's work? What was considered to be a successful music program? What kinds of music were valued at home, in the community, in the culture at large?

Making Inferences and Drawing Conclusions

According to some historians, the study of history is a study of causes, and Pemberton (1992) sees it as "a tangle of causes and effects diffused over time and space" (p. 96). How does one make sense out of this "tangle of causes and effects" in the process of making inferences and drawing conclusions? This is a challenging task that demands rigor, reason, and critical thinking. Ensure that the evidence is pointing strongly in the direction of the inference and argue for its credibility in the larger context of the time period. Is the inference based on evidence from multiple sources? Do those sources represent different dimensions and perspectives? Is the cause–effect relationship insinuated in sources of evidence, and if so, by whom and how frequently? Are there alternative explanations?

Similar to other forms of research, historical inquiry can lead to the emergence of new questions about the persons, events, or developments that were studied. It can bring to the surface contradictions or ambiguities that were not evident to the researcher at the beginning of the study. Certain pieces of evidence can be identified as central to the development of further study.

The trend to use findings from the past to inform problems and issues in the present day is noteworthy (Cox, 2002). This approach brings the past into the present and makes vital connections between past, present, and future (McCarthy, 2002). For example, both Kennedy (2000) and Nelson (2004) examined the history of creativity in U.S. music education and used historical perspectives gained from their studies to comment on the present status of creative music making in the schools and to make a prognosis for the future. Hash's (2008) recommendation to conduct further studies into "school band contests in individual states and other parts of the world" (p. 20), if implemented, may contribute valuable insights into the ongoing discussion about their value and role in music education.

Organizing and Writing the Narrative

A good narrative engages the reader intellectually and emotionally with the topic, reflecting the combined scientific and humanistic dimensions of historical inquiry. While the presentation of a historical article or dissertation may differ in form from that of a quantitative study, the essential features—rationale, purpose, research questions, literature review, and description of methodology—must be included. A literature review will typically contain contextual information about the topic, findings of prior studies, and an overview of relevant primary and secondary sources.

Following are some guidelines for writing historical studies:

- Use an organizational structure that is true to the purpose of the study and the research questions.
- Engage the reader in the details of the story by including quotations from primary sources.
- Honor the chronology underlying the topic by including dates and historical facts and presenting events in chronological order.
- Elaborate on and interpret ideas that emerge from the evidence.
- Make connections between pieces of evidence and locate them in related contexts.
- Above all, in your role of storyteller animate the persons, places and events being described using active verbs, descriptive adjectives, dramatic language, and poetic imagery to sustain the tension of the narrative throughout.

There are several ways to organize the narrative, among them chronological order, topical or thematic order, or a combination of both. The degree to which these approaches are employed depends on the topic under study. In a biographical study, the researcher might organize the individual's life around periods that represent distinct phases of that life. In a study that has a narrow chronological time line, the emphasis may be on interrelated events and actions that developed simultaneously. A combination of chronological and thematic approaches is recommended in most cases; combining them effectively presents one of the challenges of writing history, moving the chronology forward while addressing the topic in an exhaustive and complete manner.

The following three examples show a diverse range of possibilities for organizing historical narrative. Karpf (2002) reported on William Bradbury's observations of European music educators, 1847–1849, using Bradbury's letters from Europe as published in the *New York Evangelist* as her primary sources. She organized the narrative around Bradbury's descriptions of teachers and schools and presented them in the order in which he wrote about them—from London, Leipzig, and Switzerland.

May (2005) studied the early musical development of African-American jazz musicians in Indianapolis in the 1930s and 1940s. She presented her findings using three overarching themes: formal music education, informal music education, and the contributing political, social, and cultural influences. Her organization around themes was effective in achieving the goals of her oral history study.

W. R. Lee's (2002) study of Charles H. Farnsworth's unpublished essay mentioned earlier further illustrates the diversity of ways historical evidence can be presented. After an in-depth description of the essay's context, both internal and external, Lee presented an edited and annotated version of Farnsworth's speech. He added side notes and footnotes to provide commentary on the manuscript and suggested possible sources of influence.

In conclusion, historical writing must present a compelling story and convince the reader that evidence was collected according to the highest standards of historical scholarship. The author must present conclusions as an outcome of precise and painstaking documentation, empathetic and critical reading of evidence, and careful interpretation that is supported by multiple sources and argued by reason. Historical research demands both the rigor of the scientific method and the humanistic qualities needed to interpret the significance of events and actions of persons and groups in the context of time, place, and culture.

Chapter Summary

1. Writing history is an interdisciplinary activity, drawing on the sciences and the humanities.
2. The historical process involves reconstructing the past in narrative form.
3. The values of historical research are diverse and findings can be made relevant to contemporary music education.
4. Contemporary trends and developments in history are rooted in philosophy of history, expansion of intellectual paradigms, and advancements in technology and media.
5. Primary sources represent the data of historical research. They are varied in form: written documents, oral records, and artifacts.
6. Criticism is key to historical research, especially in the examination of primary sources: external criticism to test the authenticity and reliability and internal criticism to test accuracy and credibility.
7. Interpretation of sources stands at the core of the historical process.

Topics for Further Exploration

1. Compare and contrast the role and use of various kinds of primary sources (written, oral, artifacts).
2. Discuss the nature of ethics in historical research as compared to other modes of inquiry.

Suggested Assignments

1. Consider the following purpose statements chosen from historical studies and identify a number of research questions that would need to be asked to fulfill each respective purpose.

   a. *Title:* Political Influences on Curriculum Content and Musical Meaning: Hong Kong Secondary Music Education, 1949–1997
   Purpose: The purpose of this article is to examine the history of secondary school music education in Hong Kong, with emphasis on a period of major socio-political change: from 1949 to the transfer of Hong Kong's political sovereignty from the United Kingdom to the People's Republic of China in 1997. (Ho, 2000, p. 5)

   b. *Title:* The Use of Creativity in Music Textbook Series, 1900–1950
   Purpose: The purpose of this paper is to investigate the type of creativity included in U.S. music textbooks during the first half of the 20th century. Did students have access to music creativity in music textbooks of the first half of the 20th century, and if so, what was the nature and scope of the creative experiences presented in the textbooks? (Nelson, 2004, p. 129)

   c. *Title:* History of Illinois School Band Association: 1924–1941
   Purpose: The purpose of this study is to document the history of the Illinois School Band Association (ISBA) and the contests this organization sponsored between 1924 and 1941. It examines questions about the origin, leadership, rules and procedures, impact, growth, and decline of the organization. It also discusses how these findings can be used in modern practice. (Hash, 2008, p. 4)

2. Review a historical study of your choice. Identify the rationale, purpose, and research questions, and critically analyze them.

3. In small groups, select two source readings from Michael L. Mark's book, *Music Education: Source Readings from Ancient Greece to Today* (2008). Choose one from Part 1 (Greece and Rome, The Middle Ages, Later European Views) and the other from a later period in Part II or III. Compare sources in relation to authorship, time period, context of production, language and tone, and content.

4. Go to the Performing Arts Encyclopedia at the Library of Congress website (http://www.loc.gov/performingarts) and browse by subject (e.g., folk music, conductors). Search for a photograph or image that is of interest to you. Use Prof. E.'s questions from page 121 as prompts for examining it. Share your findings in class.

5. Find an artifact or oral record that may be used to begin a conversation about the history of music education (e.g., musical instrument, textbook, photograph, certificate, recording). Spend time with the artifact, looking or listening with intent, interrogating the evidence and forming questions around it. Bring to class and share the findings.

6. Visit a place or building that has some historical connotations or connections (e.g., an elementary school you attended, a library with archival material, a historical building, a graveyard where you can read the headstones and imagine the lives of the deceased). Write a reflection on the experience.

7. Visit an archive on or near your campus. As a class, select a historical figure for study based on materials found in the archive. Work together to compose a historical vignette (see above) that helps the reader to engage with the topic. Consider how you could include visual and/or audio media.

8. Compare two articles written about the same historical topic. (See example below.) Use these guiding questions: What is the purpose of each study? What primary sources are used? What is unique about each author's treatment of the topic? How are conclusions drawn? What did you learn about interpretation by doing this exercise?

   a. The Music Educators National Conference and World War II Home Front Programs (Mark, 1980)

   b. American Music Education 1941–1946: Meeting Needs and Making Adjustments During World War II (Beegle, 2004)

Recommended Websites

History of Education Society, UK: http://www.historyofeducation.org.uk/
History of Education Society, US: http://www.historyofeducation.org/
Organization of Educational Historians: http://www.edhistorians.org/
Special Collections in Performing Arts, University of Maryland: http://www.lib.umd.edu/PAL/SCPA
United States Library of Congress, Music Division Finding Aids Online: http://www.loc.gov/rr/perform/special/gd-index.html
United States National Archives and Records Administration: http://www.archives.gov

Recommended Reading

Barzun, J., & Graff, H. F. (2004). *The modern researcher* (6th ed.). Belmont, CA: Wadsworth/Thomson Learning.
Cox, G. (2002). Transforming research in music education history. In R. Colwell & C. Richardson (Eds.), *The new handbook of research on music teaching and learning* (pp. 695–706). New York: Oxford University and MENC.
Heller, G. N., & Wilson, B. D. (1992). Historical research. In R. Colwell (Ed.), *Handbook of research on music teaching and learning* (pp. 102–114). New York: Schirmer.
Janesick, V. J. (2010). *Oral history for the qualitative researcher: Choreographing the story*. New York and London: The Guilford Press.
Marius, R., & Page, M. E. (2010). *A short guide to writing about history* (7th ed.). New York: Longman.
Pemberton, C. A. (1987, Winter). Revisionist historians: Writers reflected in their writings. *Journal of Research in Music Education, 35*(4), 213–220.

seven

Purposes and Questions in Qualitative Research

This chapter:

- Describes how research purposes and questions emerge from an interpretive perspective;
- Summarizes distinct characteristics of various qualitative research traditions typically used in music education research; such as ethnography, phenomenology, case study, grounded theory, narrative research, and arts-based research.

Questions situated in qualitative research contexts come from different traditions and worldviews. Their diversity leaves open the possibility that other and new qualitative research practices already exist, are thinkable, or may be on the horizon.

Introduction

Qualitative research is a situated activity that locates the observer in the world. It consists of a set of interpretive, material practices that make the world visible. These practices transform the world. They turn the world into a series of representations, including field notes, interviews, conversations, photographs, recordings, and memos to the self. At this level, qualitative research involves an interpretive, naturalistic approach to the world. This means that qualitative researchers study things in their natural settings, attempt to make sense of, or to interpret, phenomena in forms of the meanings people bring to them. (Denzin & Lincoln, 2005, p. 3)

Researchers who use qualitative research methods do so based on a belief that reality is socially constructed, complex, diverse, and not reducible to mutually exclusive, "objective" observations. Any documented observation is also an interpretation, which cannot and should not be separated from the researcher's way of knowing the world. Such epistemological underpinning makes necessary awareness and acknowledgment of the researcher's own perceived realities.

Because qualitative research is contextual, many researchers prefer to guide their work with questions instead of or in addition to statements of purpose. The questions and themes, typically based on such tasks as describing, analyzing, and theorizing about human action and interactions, are derived from "phenomena in forms of the meanings people bring to them" (Denzin and Lincoln, 2005, p. 3). Descriptive questions posit: "What is happening here?" Analytic queries ask "What does this mean?" Theoretical analyses propose new holistic ways in which observations and descriptions might be interpreted and understood within the entirety of their respective contexts (Roulston, 2006, p. 156). All three analytic processes may be involved from the onset of the study. To do the data full justice, researchers visit and revisit them repeatedly throughout a project.

When you think of music education in its broadest sense as the learning and teaching of music, countless questions lend themselves to consideration and study, especially when applied to qualitative empiricism. Here, all aspects of observing music learning and instructional processes may be embedded in systematic reflection about and interpretation of the research process itself. Participation means involvement; research questions therefore mirror that involvement.

Take, for instance, the following selection of research purposes and questions. Each of the approaches reflects to varying degrees the connection between rationale, purpose, and the researcher's role in the investigative process:

Mutual Learning and Democratic Action in Instrumental Music Education
Dissatisfaction with the "false dichotomy" caused by "the disconnection between the music studied at school and the hidden or private musical world of our students" (para. 4) inspired Allsup (2003) to create and study *mutual learning communities*, defined as "workable space[s] where students and educators [come] together to share and create music" (para. 4). Allsup's research questions

> were both philosophical and pedagogical: How would the participating groups evolve and define themselves through the practice of composing and analyzing music? What would our choices reflect or signify? How might this experience affect individual growth as well as community-making? And finally, how is such a project congruent with philosophies of democratic education (Dewey, 1916; Freire, 1970, 2000; Greene, 1988, 1995, 2000; hooks, 1994). (para. 5)

Music Education in Home Schooling: A Preliminary Inquiry

In order to "delve deeper" into reasons for and practices of music education among homeschooling families, Nichols (2005) "examined the music education curricular choices of parents who homeschool children . . . ."

The following research questions guided the study:

1. How do parents' philosophical positions on education influence their reasons for including music in their homeschool?
2. When parents make a specific effort to include music as a part of their homeschool curriculum, why do they choose to do so?
3. How do these parents conduct music education at home as a part of the homeschool curriculum? (pp. 29–30)

Custom and Cherishing: The Arts in Elementary Schools

Wishing "to establish what is happening, both within arts courses and activities but also in the many contexts: curricular, administrative, fiscal, political, historical and social" (p. 3) Stake, Bresler and Mabry (1991) studied eight "ordinary" (p. 3) schools from across the United States. The sample was intended to represent a cross-section of the United States rather than to highlight outstanding arts programs (p. 3). The intentions that guided their study "were not so much 'What are the children learning?' but 'What are the schools providing as opportunities for learning?'" (p. 4)

You Can't Be in My Choir if You Can't Stand Up: One Journey Toward Inclusion

Wondering about the perspective of special needs students involved in school music led Haywood (2006) to focus research on "Deborah," a physically challenged student participating in the high school choir. Her primary research question was: "How does the process of including an individual with special needs in choir create change in that individual?" (p. 407). Her stated research purpose was, therefore, "to gain a greater understanding of the possibilities and potential benefits of including individuals with special needs in choirs" (p. 409).

Stories from the Front

A year of teaching music in a civilian elementary school that serviced a U.S. military base during a time of war inspired Walker (2009) to collect and tell her own story and imagine the stories of the students with whom she worked. The following questions guided her inquiry:

> What is the relationship between the musical worlds we attempt to create in our classrooms and those the children experience? Over time, how closely do the shadows cast in memory by those experiences characteri[z]e the experiences themselves? Can teachers know which will loom large and which will fade quietly from memory? Then there is the grand question for teachers: Is there any way to know, while experiences are still malleable, how to fine tune them so they provide the maximum possible lifetime output of warmth and enlightenment? (pp. 179–180)

Second Chair: An Ethnodrama

To explore and express "the underlying symbolic and metaphoric significance of first and second chair's status" (p. 188), Saldaña (2008) wrote and performed "Second chair: An autoethnodrama." His rationale, stated in commentary after the script: If musicians can understand the feelings accorded to someone of "second chair" status, they can hopefully understand the feelings of the marginalized individual in a competitive mainstream society: "it's always feeling and sometimes being treated as lesser than, second best, like playing a cheap-ass plastic Bundy when you'd rather be playing an ebony wood Selmer with a glass mouthpiece" (p. 188).

When you consider the topics and approaches featured in the above questions, you may notice that each of the examples reflect what philosophers would call an interpretive worldview. The following section of this chapter further discusses the meaning of this worldview in the context of qualitative research. The final section of the chapter summarizes the characteristics of the qualitative research traditions that are most frequently used to investigate topics germane to music education in its many forms (i.e., ethnography, phenomenology, case study designs, grounded theory, narrative research, and arts-based research). Chapter 8 then outlines major procedural considerations for qualitative research in music education. The information provided in both qualitative chapters rely on such sources as Barrett and Stauffer (2009), Charmaz (2006, 2008a, 2008b), Denzin and Lincoln (2005), Glaser and Strauss (1967), and Strauss and Corbin (1990, 1998). Other sources are acknowledged where quotations are directly attributable to them.

Research With an Interpretive Perspective

Since the qualitative researcher shapes what is documented from a personal point of view, research questions take as a given that all research reflects a particular worldview in a specific setting. Each research participant (including the researcher) is assumed to construct a unique reality. Thus, individual understandings of experiences and knowledge can only be shared with the researcher present, or "embodied" in the space in which a conversation or observation takes place. Many researchers who share in such a worldview reject the notion of universals of truth. Rather, they believe in the "here-and-now" of knowledge, temporary from moment to moment. This viewpoint distinguishes it from quantitative and even from historical inquiry.

However, belief in the temporary nature of knowledge and perceived reality does not prevent the researcher from gaining insight into that which is being investigated. As the construction of knowledge involves continual unfolding and decision makings, change may therefore be considered as a constant in the work of a qualitative researcher who should acknowledge, if not welcome, it. Signifiers of the ongoing construction of knowledge, changes of mind and unanticipated actions often turn into the source of unanticipated insights. Thus, for many scholars, guiding research purposes and questions are temporary at best. But they are necessary nonetheless, to provide direction and a basis for documenting and examining changes in knowledge.

In addition to purposes and/or questions, all qualitative investigations must be framed theoretically. Such a framework argues the purpose for the investigation, articulates the researcher's reasons for design choices (see Chapter 4), and presents the literature-based and/or philosophical perspectives that guide the study (see Chapter 5). Even an inductive approach requires such a frame, if only a declared intent to remain open to what transpires in a particular situation.

The partnership that arises when researchers ask questions as both data gatherer and participant requires attentiveness to both roles. This partnership can occur on a continuum from fully involved participant to (mostly) detached observer (see Figure 3.2). Becoming aware of one's place on that continuum is part and parcel of the qualitative research process and requires articulation.

Campbell (2003) describes the phenomenon, referring to the Greek terms *emic* and *etic* as capturing the ongoing tension between what we know as insiders to a situation (*emic*) and what we can know as outsiders (*etic*). Derived from the Greek word "phon*emic*," the insider is "akin to the perspective of one born and raised within a culture." "Phon*etic*" reflects "the perspective of someone born outside the culture of study" (p. 23). "Emic" and "etic" always work in tandem; at times in conflict, at times living smoothly side by side. Exploring the duality of insider–outsider can be a particular strength of qualitative research. In certain contexts, the duality can even lead to *dialectic* prose and argumentation (see Chapters 3 and 5), based on a belief that no matter how hard any of us try to understand the people we study, the best we can do is to acknowledge that reality resides somewhere between our outsider view and that of the insiders we study.

The principle that emphasizes contextual knowledge as essential for understanding human action suggests that one can only know that with which one is fully involved. This means that research should be done in places where the actions and interactions suggested by the research purpose occur naturally. The "place" of a researcher in such a setting varies, depending on his or her purpose for being there. Some researchers strive to minimize any interventions that their presence might cause, whereas others make no such effort, but acknowledge in their field notes any interruptions or changes that may have occurred in the setting as a result of their presence. A third group may purposefully become integral to what is being observed and therefore let the research questions themselves account for the investigator's presence. Being thusly "situated" in the research means acknowledging one's role as an interpreter rather than reporter of the investigative context. This premise is assumed to strengthen rather than weaken the veracity of qualitative observations.

Qualitative writing requires imagined dialogue with readers, expanding the connection between researcher and participants by anticipating how readers might respond to and engage with the writing both thoughtfully and emotionally. Thus, the charge of the researcher–writer is to develop skills not only of observation, but also of clear and evocative writing, weaving data, analysis, and interpretation together. That subject is described, along with other more technical considerations, in Chapter 8.

The characteristics described above are markers of excellence in qualitative research (Tracy, 2010; Malterud, 2001; Elliott, Fischer, & Rennie, 1999): A *coherent* study stitches all components into an interconnected and engaging whole whose parts (research questions, appropriate methods, related literature, theoretical perspectives, and interpretations) are clear yet connected. *Credibility* is demonstrated by the use of multiple data sources (called *triangulation*, which hints at a specific number and shape, or *crystallization*, suggested by Richardson and St. Pierre in 2005 to signify multiplicity without constraints in shape or number). A detailed "thick" representation of observed actions, events, and related reflections also brings credibility to a research account. *Reflexivity* is demonstrated when an author acknowledges and reflects upon personal biases and preconceptions, and *rigor* is present when data are sufficiently plentiful, rich, and varied. *Resonance* can address the extent to which a writer's work evokes a response from readers; and for some studies, the degree to which findings suggest a theoretical model. Finally, *trustworthiness* speaks to the relevance and timeliness of the research. Researchers reach that goal by being honest with themselves and their readers, and ethical toward others—both participants and peers.

Evolution of Interpretive Research

This *interpretive* perspective arose from philosophical disagreements in the late 19th and early 20th century about the validity and applicability of specific scientific paradigms to examining questions in the human sciences. In contrast to the view of positivists, interpretivists suggested that understanding human actions is best approached by observing and/or experiencing such action in the settings where they occur (rather than manipulating behavior in lab settings), and at the same time trying to "grasp the meanings that constitute that action" (Schwandt, 2003, p. 296).

Primarily inductive in nature, methods developed to systematize observations and reflections are derived from and situated more in the study of text interpretation (*hermeneutics*, see Chapter 3) than in forms of experimental empiricism common to behavioristic research models. The often-used term "thick description," brought to anthropology by Geertz (1973) exemplifies the difference between the two worldviews: Explaining a physical act such as winking merely as behavior (i.e., contracting the eyelids) ignores its meaning. To get at intention, a researcher's interpretation of human action must include the perspective of the actor(s); in this case, the winker.

The belief systems that undergird interpretive research questions have evolved from post-positivist roots to the vibrant and multi-faceted interpretive community of the present. As outlined by Denzin and Lincoln (2005, p. 3, 14–20), eight "moments" mark those philosophical changes:

- Traditional, 1900–1950: The time of "classical ethnography," usually involving white researchers studying non-white "others" as objects "to be archived" (p. 15). The "Chicago school" of sociology emerged toward the end of this "moment."

- Modernist or golden age, 1950–1970: As new interpretive theories (ethno-methodology, phenomenology, critical theory, and feminism) became popular, researchers "were drawn to qualitative research practices that would let them give a voice to society's underclass" (p. 16). Glaser and Strauss's (1967) *The Discovery of Grounded Theory* provides a model for systematic analysis of qualitative data.

- Blurred genres, 1970–1986: Spurred initially by Geertz' *The Interpretation of Culture* (1973), the distinction between fiction and fact, art and science, was blurred by the realization among theorists that all research is interpretive.

- Crisis of representation, 1986–1990: "A profound rupture" (p. 18) in previous beliefs, this three-way crisis involved "representation, legitimation, and praxis" (p. 19): Is it really possible to represent the lived experience of another? If not, how does one defend the legitimacy of research as practiced?

- Postmodern, 1990–1995: To make sense of the crisis, writers experimented with techniques like auto-ethnography, stories, and in general "more action, participatory, and activist-oriented research." Instead of "grand narratives," researchers sought "local, small-scale theories fitted to specific problems and particular situations" (p. 20).

- Post experimental inquiry (1995–2000), methodologically contested present (2000–2004), and the fractured future (2005–): Journals and publishing houses emerged to bring new authors into the interpretive community. Shortly thereafter, the *No Child Left Behind* education laws challenged the legitimacy of qualitative research for education, making the present time a period of conflict and tension in the research community. (For further discussion of these conflicts, see Lather, 2006 and St. Pierre & Roulston, 2006.)

Topic Areas and Selected Questions

As you think about topics and their underlying questions, pay attention to the close relationship between both. Also consider the following: (1) How could you research similar topics in your own environment? (2) What would it take for you to be truly open to the perspectives of others? (3) What might your own place in the research site be, and how would you account for it in your design decisions? and, (4) Why would you choose that specific location as opposed to others?

About Places, Perspectives, Participants, and Practices

Nearly everything opens up as a research field when you consider qualitative research approaches: locations such as playgrounds (e.g., Harwood, 1993; Marsh, 2008; Campbell, 1998), phenomena like non-traditional schooling (e.g., Bose, 2008; Nichols, 2005; Seddon & Biasutti, 2010), experiences of individual novice teachers (e.g., Schmidt & Knowles, 1995) or multiple teachers in specific settings (e.g., Frierson-Campbell, 2003). Even school reform as a result of policies, a topic of interest to Michelle, has found its way into qualitative research (e.g., Craig, 2003; Kos, 2007).

The researcher's perspective, in the form of a theoretical framework, may use new or existing philosophical ideas as a lens for interpretation. Feminist theory, examined from the broad philosophical perspectives of postmodernism, may be applied to questions of activism toward transformation rather than mere reformation of *praxial* curricula and politically controlled school knowledge (Lather, 1991). (The term "praxial" means theoretically informed practice, a phrase important to constructivists and pragmatists alike; see also Chapter 5.) Other critical and postmodern philosophies that might frame research range from constructivism to critical race theory to queer theory and even "post everything" (Lather, 2006, p. 37). Qualitative researchers believe such "epistemological diversity" helps to guard against methodological fundamentalism (p. 35).

In terms of perspectives, you might ask questions about the music classroom as seen from the participants' points of view (e.g., Beegle, 2010; Gouzouasis, Henrey, & Belliveau, 2008; Reese, 2006; Silvey, 2005), or that of the teacher (e.g., Reese, 2006). You might examine research questions through a construct such as gender (Abramo, 2011; Hoffman, 2008; Legg, 2010; Roulston & Misawa, 2011), a pedagogical practice like assessment (e.g., Latukefu, 2010; Niebur, 1997), or a cultural issue, such as war (e.g., Walker, 2009). Most important is crafting a framework that allows you to be clear about your own biases and subjectivities while taking great care not to force them on participants.

Qualitative Research Traditions

Qualitative research traditions have evolved from many disciplines: the humanities as well as the social sciences, evaluation research, and even literary and linguistic theory. The traditions used most often for qualitative research in music education focus on methodology (i.e., ethnography), philosophy (i.e., phenomenology), research design (i.e., case study), analysis (i.e., grounded theory), and even the medium in which the researcher works (i.e., narrative and arts-based research). These distinctions reflect the decisions researchers make about their work.

While it is useful to understand the various research labels, avoid seeing the "traditions" as fixed. Like the boundaries on a map, they are more obvious in theory than on the ground. There are many examples of "border crossings": ethnographers who write from a phenomenological perspective, case studies that use grounded theory for analysis, and so forth. Why, then, do the distinctions matter? Because the various qualitative traditions evolved from different disciplines. Within each sub-discipline are conventions for representing knowledge, making and backing up assertions, and communicating with the community of scholars (Shulman, 1999). In Schoenfeld's words,

> The application of any research method is only as good as the match between the assumptions underlying the method and the set of circumstances being explored. And if there is a mismatch, the findings may well be either meaningless or wrong. (1999, p. 180)

Ethnographic Research

Ethnographic procedures were first developed by Western anthropologists to study the culture of "other" people as described earlier in the chapter. This perspective tended to privilege the Western view as uniquely authoritative (Clifford, 1983, p. 118). Prodded by the interpretive turn along with the dissolution of colonialism and subsequent human rights and ethnic power movements that occurred in the early and mid-20th century, ethnography evolved into a more "generalized" tradition that acknowledges difference as a human invention (p. 119).

Ethnographers learn about and describe observed actions and interactions between individuals in an in-depth manner known as *immersion*. They spend extended time, often a year or more, observing and interviewing participants in natural settings. Data are collected by way of observation, interview, document analysis, and personal reflection. Ethnographies may be written from the researcher's point of view or that of the participant(s), who are often called *informants* in this research tradition. While ethnography is primarily a qualitative tradition, some ethnographers also use quantitative methods, such as tests or other measures, to gather evidence (Creswell, 2007, p. 72).

Doing ethnography requires identifying and approaching one or more groups who represent the researcher's purpose. Guided first by the rules of research ethics (described in Chapter 8 as well as in Chapter 4), access is often gained by contacting a member of the group who mediates between the researcher and the group members—ethnographers call this person the *gatekeeper*. Living in the research environment (known as *the field*), it is sometimes difficult for the researcher to navigate a balance between the shared roles of researcher and participant. This challenge can compromise a study if the researcher is unaware or unreflective of its impact on their work.

Ethnographic questions in music education might ask: "What is the nature of musical culture among . . .?" Or "What cultures and sub-cultures emerge in a typical (or elite or underserved) middle school choral (or band or other musical) setting?" Allsup's (2003) study, featured above, added what he called an "experimental" component because he created the small democratic musical ensembles whose evolving cultures he studied.

Influenced by philosophy, sociology, and anthropology, *ethnomusicology* is a discipline whose data comprise music performed and/or notated along with the researcher's experience of becoming part of a musical culture. The researcher is therefore as much a "participant performer" as a participant observer (Campbell, 2003, p. 23). In addition to the traditional qualitative procedures of observation, interview, and document/artifact analysis (see Chapter 8), ethnomusicological research involves transcribing musical activities with the goal of describing the transmission of musical traditions. Contemporary researchers use modern tools such as hand-held digital recording devices, but the earliest ethnomusicologists carried such things as Edison wax cylinders and heavy battery-operated recorders (p. 23). Watch, for instance, the film *The Songcatcher* (2000) and notice what happened as the researcher immersed herself in the Appalachian sub-culture.

Like ethnographers, ethnomusicologists typically spend at least a year immersed in a musical culture, more if the study involves short visits rather than a long residency. The distinction for music educators is whether exploring the musical aspects of a given situation will provide new information about music teaching and learning.

Often music educator/ethnomusicologists begin by studying with a master teacher, using this experience to get to know a musical culture. This might mean recording and analyzing the music of a culture from an exotic and distant location, but it could just as easily be closer to home (p. 13). For example, a pioneering ethnomusicological study of a kindergarten designed for musical creativity was undertaken by the Pillsbury Foundation in the 1940s. Researchers Moorhead and Pond (1978/1941, 1942, 1944, 1951) investigated how children developed as musicians through musical play by observing young children in that setting. A more recent example, published as *Songs in their Heads*, is Campbell's 2010 study of the meaning young children have for the music in their lives, as demonstrated by musical play at school and at home.

Phenomenological Research

As a philosophical worldview, phenomenology dates back many centuries (see Chapters 3 and 5). The German philosopher Husserl is credited with spurring the philosophical movement in 1913, with the publication of his book entitled *Ideas* (see Gearing, 2004, p. 1430). In the United States, such scholars as van Manen (1990) and Moustakas (1994) first applied phenomenological research traditions to investigating mental and physical health issues, studies that also impacted research in education.

Moustakas (1994) describes the approach as "a process of internal search through which one discovers the nature and meaning of experience." This quest places the "self of the researcher" into the process of inquiry, thereby increasing the depth of understanding a phenomenon. The positioning in the process also leads to a researcher's "growing self-awareness and self-knowledge" (p. 17).

The questions guiding phenomenologists' work vary. Van Manen (1990) suggests the following in application to the study of learning:

> What is the nature or essence of the experience of learning (so that I can now better understand what this particular learning experience is like for these children)? The essence or nature of an experience has been adequately described in language if the description reawakens or shows us the lived quality and significance of the experience in a fuller or deeper manner. (p. 10)

A phenomenological researcher, therefore, seeks to get at the core of what makes a lived experience what it is (p. 10).

Because phenomenology is really a philosophical approach by which to reflect upon human experience in the empirical world (Jorgensen, 1995, p. 1), systematic reflection rather than a search for explicit themes may be the result. Closely connected to dialectics, interpretivism and hermeneutics, phenomenological research allows for an open-ended research process. Its degree of scholarship rests in the rigor of carefully probing and analyzing diverse viewpoints and examining different "understandings" of the "life world." Sorting through such understandings becomes the body of knowledge from which new questions emerge. The phenomenological perspective was the guiding tradition for Nichols (2005, see above).

Case Study

Case studies are conducted in many disciplines, reflecting the traditions of the fields in which they are used: business, law, medicine, political science, psychology, and sociology, to name a few. They differ in definition, structure, and purpose but have in common the selection of one or more cases for study that represent a researcher's purpose.

A "bounded" case is specific; it may be an individual, a group of individuals, or one particular setting during a prescribed period of time. It may not, however, be a process such as a relationship, a method, or a belief system—these may emerge as factors within case studies but do not themselves constitute a case. More design than method, qualitative case studies can involve ethnographic or phenomenological procedures. Dependent upon their focus, they may be referred to as collective, intrinsic, instrumental, and comparative (Stake, 1995).

Unique cases tend to be *intrinsic* or *instrumental* (Stake, 1995). An intrinsic case might be chosen because of its uniqueness (p. 3); for instance, a teacher whose background or current position is compelling and distinctive, a group of amateur or professional musicians who have found an unusual performance niche, or other one-of-a-kind examples of music teaching and learning. An instrumental case illustrates a common situation that may have transferable value beyond the case itself; it serves to make a point beyond the situation examined. Such might be the case when a researcher chooses an individual music teacher or a single music program as a "case" that exemplifies a common issue such as school reform or assessment.

Studies that involve multiple cases may be *collective* or *comparative* (Stake, 1995, p. 3–4). In a collective case study, each case is examined descriptively without comparison to the other cases. The result is a comprehensive picture of multiple cases as they relate to the research purpose. In contrast, a comparative case study utilizes multiple cases for the purpose of looking at similarities and differences among them. Such projects can be cross-cultural and even international, although some researchers might question the wisdom behind such broad-scaled comparisons. Kos' (2007) study of two Wisconsin schools "with different characteristics and different policy contexts" (p. 2) was a comparative case study. For quantitatively schooled researchers, serious validity issues would arise from the use of a small sample; for qualitative researchers, however, the question would be completeness of data and, thus, trustworthiness of findings.

Grounded Theory

Grounded theory is unique among qualitative traditions because it suggests specific guidelines for gathering and analyzing data in the form of "interrogating" them (see Chapter 3). The procedures enable the researcher to theorize about relational questions.

Research questions might ask about relationships between human actions: How do teachers respond to school reform? What relationships exist between musical education and musicians' eventual non-musical career choices? How do music teachers navigate between shared identities such as musician and teacher?

The grounded theory process was initially developed by two sociologists, Barney Glaser and Anselm Strauss (1967) to provide a transparent method for inductive theorizing from qualitative data. Expanded and further codified by Strauss and Corbin (1990, 1998), Charmaz (2006), Corbin and Strauss (2008), and others, these procedures enable qualitative researchers to stake a scientific claim for their work, supported by the long-held belief that inductive and deductive reasoning are equally valid for scientific discovery (Rothchild, 2006). Note, however, that while qualitative researchers develop themes inductively, many (if not most) make no claim of scientific veracity.

Despite or perhaps because of its "modernist" beginnings, grounded theory is used by researchers with a wide variety of worldviews, the result of which has been of consequence for other qualitative traditions as well. Concurrent data collection and analysis, now a common qualitative procedure, was an innovation when Glaser and Strauss suggested it in 1967 (Charmaz, 2008b, p. 162). It systematizes the qualitative research process, thereby providing concrete guidelines for the novice researcher (see Chapter 8).

Haywood's (2006) questions, included in the examples above, represent a hybrid of several research traditions. She applied grounded theory to analyze and interpret the data because "grounded theory is used to explain phenomena in light of a theoretical framework that evolves during the research itself, as opposed to a previously developed theory that may or may not apply (Strauss & Corbin, 1990)" (p. 412). The study was designed as an *instrumental* case study: she chose an individual in the high school choral setting to represent the topic of special needs students in school ensembles. Her stated philosophical perspective was phenomenological, intended "to elicit the phenomenon of the individual's experience" (p. 411). Eventually (separate from the study described here) she analyzed correlations and connections between this case study and two others: "an ethnographic case study of an entire choir of individuals with typical needs as well as individuals with multiple and varied special needs" (p. 412) and "an historic case study of . . . a choral conductor who had been including individuals with special needs in her choirs in the U.S. since the beginning of her teaching career in 1962" (p. 412).

Narrative Research

Throughout history, people have used stories (or narratives) to construct their understandings of the world (Barrett and Stauffer, 2009, p. 7), explaining not only the facts, but also what those facts mean to them (Bowman, 2006, p. 8). The human tendency toward narrative is so strong that psychologist Jerome Bruner (1986) has called it a "way of knowing" (in contrast to "logico-scientific" or "paradigmatic" knowing, which seeks universal truths). Thus, the term "narrative research" (sometimes also called narrative *inquiry*) specifically denotes "the study of experience as story" (Clandinin, 2006):

Story, in the current idiom, is a portal through which a person enters the world and by which their experience of the world is interpreted and made personally meaningful. Narrative inquiry, the study of experience as story, then, is first and foremost a way of thinking about experience. Narrative inquiry as a methodology entails a view of the phenomenon. To use narrative inquiry methodology is to adopt a particular view of experience as phenomenon under study. (Connelly & Clandinin, 2006, p. 479)

Rooted in the philosophies of John Dewey, there are three "commonplaces" of narrative inquiry: interaction, continuity, and situation. Narrative researchers must simultaneously explore all three:

- Interaction, describing the personal and social elements of the situation;
- Continuity, recognizing past, present, and future implications;
- Situation, or place, depicting the physical details of the place where the research takes place, and acknowledging its impact on the stories and their interpretation. (Clandinin, 2006, p. 47)

This three-dimensional "metaphoric narrative inquiry space" (p. 47) distinguishes narrative research from other qualitative traditions.

Narrative researchers focus on a combination of *telling* stories and *living* them (Connelly & Clandinin, 2006, p. 478). A researcher focused on telling, concentrates on stories conveyed by participant(s), or on their own interpretation (or re-telling) of those stories. The emphasis may be on the story or on its meaning. Research from the perspective of "living" includes an ethnographic dimension, the researcher's recounting of being involved in the life or lives of the other participants. As McCarthy (2007) notes, exploring how music learners and teachers tell their stories and live their lives can reveal "threads of continuity and discontinuity," between the professional and the personal lives of participants (p. 7). Walker (2009), whose questions are included in the examples above, both told and lived her own story, documenting the details with field notes, lesson plans, performance records, seating charts, and "other typical classroom artifacts" (p. 193).

The line between doing qualitative research for an aesthetic purpose and using aesthetic tools for qualitative research is, like other boundaries, open to interpretation. In particular, two sub-genres that straddle that boundary are worthy of mention. *Autoethnography* is a research method that focuses deliberately on the researcher's point of view. An "autobiographical genre of writing and research that displays multiple layers of consciousness, connecting the personal to the cultural" (Ellis & Bochner, 2000, p. 739), autoethnography focuses on the "self" within specific cultural contexts. Ellis and Bochner suggest that autoethnography is particularly pertinent when "the success of your work depends on developing some degree of intercultural understanding" (p. 760). Frierson-Campbell and Newman (2008), for instance, used autoethnography to explore how their individual beliefs about research and scholarship impacted their collective approach to teaching master's level jazz performance majors to do research. Ultimately, they came to realize that differences in their "'hyphenated identities' (Tim as performer-scholar and Carol as musician-educator-scholar)" (p. 100) led them to dissimilar perspectives about uses of research-based knowledge for performing musicians.

The sub-genre known as *literary non-fiction* or *critical storytelling* (Barone, 1992) has much in common with investigative journalism (p. 145). Written from the perspective of critical theory, "the responsible story . . . adopts an openly political stance" (p. 143). A well-known example is Barone's (1989) "Ways of Being at Risk: The Case of Billy Charles Barnett." Following Sartre's claim that it is the writer's responsibility to "speak for those who cannot speak for themselves," Barone explored the many iterations of "riskiness" that threatened the future of an adolescent boy who was failing in a rural southern school. Telling the Billy Charles story led Barone "to rethink my tired notions about such fundamentals as, oh, the meaning of life, the purposes of schooling, and the various ways in which an adolescent can be at risk of not being educated" (p. 147). By turning a qualitative case study into a story with a beginning, middle, and end, Barone reached an audience that might not otherwise have been aware "of the locations of [the] characters' thoughts, beliefs, desires, and habits, in the webs of contingencies that constitute their life-worlds" (p. 142).

Arts-Based Research

The word *research* typically brings to mind the hard-core sciences, library or Internet search work, or both. But why should those sources be the sole purveyor of knowledge? Are the arts not equally as valid as the sciences for making statements about what is true or necessary to know? In response to these questions, educationist–scholar Elliot Eisner articulated a theory of *arts-based educational research* (ABER) that draws on artistic as well as scholarly practices. Arts-based research does not oppose the underlying assumptions of scientific research, but instead acknowledges the continuum of scholarly and artistic knowing on one end and knowledge that is purely scientific on the other (Barone & Eisner, 1997, p. 73).

Arts-based research is typically undertaken by scholars who use an artistic medium to express their work. Working to obfuscate traditional boundaries between scholarship and artistry, such "scholARTists" (Cahnmann-Taylor & Siegesmund, 2008, p. 6) believe the arts "stretch a researcher's capacities for creativity and knowing, creating a healthy synthesis of approaches to collect, analyze, and represent data in ways that paint a full picture of a heterogeneous movement to improve education" (p. 4). In other words,

> the contribution of arts based research is not that it leads to claims in propositional form about states of affairs but that it addresses complex and subtle interactions and that it provides an image of those interactions in ways that make them noticeable. (Barone & Eisner, 2012, p. 96)

In concept, arts-based research could result in musical composition or production. In practice, perhaps because most music educators are trained as performers or conductors rather than composers or arrangers, arts-based music education research tends to have more of a literary than compositional basis in terms of the arts discipline that is used. For example, Johnny Saldaña's 2008 autoethnodrama is "an autobiographical cultural story in play script format intended for performance" (p. 177). In it, Saldaña, now a successful professor and playwright, explores the many meanings he had ascribed to being "second chair" in his high school band.

Arts-based research may stand alone as art, or its artistic nature may be sandwiched between sections of social science prose. Even when ABER appears in the guise of formal social science research, however, its evocative nature draws the reader into an experience much as a story or poem or play would do. For some researchers the artistic element is part of the data collection and analysis, such as turning narrative data into poetry. Others share their findings in an interactive or artistic way, such as through ethno-drama or even painting. Writing about the tensions inherent in the arts-based approach, Eisner (2008) cautions researchers to make sure that arts-based research is not just about doing something different:

> Arts-based research needs to pursue novelty without sacrificing utility. It needs to be more than a projective test. And this creates a tension between achieving the shock of the new and, at the same time, genuinely communicating. (p. 24)

There is no specific process for designing or producing arts-based research; it is a matter of considering one's own artistic skills and goals in light of what one wants to say. Arts-based research is judged by how well it "broaden[s] and deepen[s] ongoing conversations about educational policy and practice" (Barone & Eisner, 2006, p. 102). This includes: (1) illuminating the situation it explores; (2) generating new "puzzlements"; (3) focusing on important issues that are relevant to phenomena beyond itself (p. 102); and (4) remaining open to the possibility that new questions and methodological challenges require methods of examination not even yet discovered.

In sum, curiosity and inventiveness, coupled with stamina and persuasiveness, are the factors that ultimately propel qualitatively acquired knowledge forward. But what may or may not be considered factual, what qualifies as evidence, and what deserves to be called truth are ongoing questions that have not only been debated for centuries but have also triggered an ever increasing pool of methods at the profession's disposal. Because the conversation is ongoing, it also stands to reason that new developments in theory and methodology will occur in response.

Chapter Summary

1. Qualitative research methods tend to be used by researchers with an interpretive worldview. This includes the belief that reality is socially constructed, complex, diverse, and not reducible to mutually exclusive observations.
2. Because qualitative research is contextual, many researchers prefer to guide their work with questions instead of or in addition to statements of purpose.

3. The merit of qualitative research studies depends on coherence, credibility, reflexivity, rigor, resonance, and worthiness.
4. Interpretive research is done in a naturalistic setting and involves a situated research perspective.
5. The philosophical underpinnings of interpretive research have evolved from post-positivism to a multiplicity of postmodern perspectives.
6. The labels used most often by music educators for specific qualitative traditions focus on methodology (i.e., ethnography), philosophy (i.e., phenomenology), research design (i.e., case study), analysis (i.e., grounded theory), or even the medium in which the researcher works (i.e., narrative and arts-based research).

Topics for Discussion

1. Compare several published research studies that use one or more of the traditions described in this chapter.

    a. Discuss the extent to which each source exemplifies the shared characteristics described at the beginning of this chapter.
    b. Make note of how the authors adhere to the traditions they claim to use. Discuss the pros and cons of keeping the traditions separate and of combining them.

2. What would you be looking for in a study to ascertain excellence based on characteristics of coherence, credibility, reflexivity, rigor, resonance, and worthiness? Discuss a study you are reading in light of these terms.

Suggested Assignments

1. In light of what you have already done to articulate your research topic, consider how you might address your own interests using one or more of the research traditions described in this chapter.
2. Peruse research articles related to studies that used the qualitative traditions described above. Try to find sources that address similar topics with different traditions. Write a response to each of the studies: What are the similarities and differences? The strengths and weaknesses?

Recommended Reading

Arts-based Research:
Barone, T., & Eisner, E. (2012). *Arts-based research*. Los Angeles: Sage Publications.
Cahnmann-Taylor, M., & Siegesmund, R. (2008). *Arts-based research in education: Foundations for practice*. New York: Routledge.

Case Studies:
Stake, R. (1995). *The art of case study research*. Thousand Oaks, CA: Sage.

Yin, R. K. (2003). *Case study research: Design and methods* (3rd ed.). Thousand Oaks, CA: Sage.

Ethnography/Ethnomusicology:
Bresler, L. (2010). Ethnography, phenomenology and action research in music education. *Visions of Research in Music Education, 16*(4). Retrieved June 20, 2011 from http://www-usr.rider.edu/~vrme/ (Reprinted from *The Quarterly Journal of Music Teaching and Learning, 6*(3), 4–16.)
Campbell, P. S. (2003). Ethnomusicology and music education: Crossroads for knowing music, education, and culture. *Research Studies in Music Education, 21*(16), 16–30.
Wolcott, H. F. (2008). *Ethnography: A way of seeing* (2nd ed.). Lanham, MD: AltaMira Press.

Grounded Theory:
Charmaz, K. (2006). *Constructing grounded theory: A practical guide through qualitative analysis.* London and Thousand Oaks, CA: Sage Publications.
Corbin, J., & Strauss, A. (2008). *Basics of qualitative research* (3rd ed.). Los Angeles, CA: Sage.

Narrative Research:
Barrett, M. S., & Stauffer, S. L. (2009). *Narrative inquiry in music education: Troubling certainty.* Dordrecht, NL: Springer Science + Business Media.
Connelly, F. M., & Clandinin, D. J. (2006). Narrative inquiry. In J. L. Green, G. Camilli & P. Elmore (Eds.), *Handbook of complementary methods in education research* (3rd ed., pp. 477–487). Mahwah, NJ: Lawrence Erlbaum.

Phenomenology:
Gearing, R. E. (2004). Bracketing in research: A typology. *Qualitative Health Research, 14*(10), 1429–1452.
Manen, M. van (1990). *Researching lived experience: Human science for an action sensitive pedagogy.* Ontario, Canada: The Althouse Press.
Moustakas, C. (1994). *Phenomenological research methods.* Thousand Oaks, CA: Sage.

Overview of Qualitative Research:
Bogdan, R. C., & Biklen, S. K. (2003). *Qualitative research for education: An introduction to theory and methods* (4th ed.). Boston: Allyn and Bacon.
Creswell, J. W. (2007). *Qualitative inquiry and research design: Choosing among five approaches.* Thousand Oaks, CA: Sage.

Theoretical Underpinnings of Qualitative Research:
Denzin, N. K., & Lincoln, Y. S. (2005). Introduction: The discipline and practice of qualitative research. In N. K. Denzin & Y. S. Lincoln (Eds.), *The Sage handbook of qualitative research* (pp. 1–32). Thousand Oaks, CA: Sage Publications.
Lather, P. (2006). Paradigm proliferation as a good thing to think with: Teaching research in education as a wild profusion. *International Journal of Qualitative Studies in Education, 19*(1), 35–57. Retrieved January 12, 2012 from http://people.ehe.ohio-state.edu/plather/files/2008/11/qse-06-me.pdf

eight

Selected Procedures for Gathering, Analyzing, and Reflecting on Qualitative Data

This chapter:

- Emphasizes that ethical conduct should guide all research decisions in qualitative research;
- Suggests how to proceed when planning a qualitative study;
- Describes the initial process of gathering data and labeling them;
- Singles out key analytical approaches for reflecting on and reporting research findings.

Respect for those with whom you work as well as trustworthiness and credibility are the main criteria by which all research decisions should be made. They also become the standard upon which procedures of planning, data gathering, analysis, and sharing findings with the field should be based.

Introduction

When you prepare for a musical performance, you are guided by the intent of presenting a cohesive, finely polished product. The selection of the piece itself, together with the resources you have available and the other musicians with whom you work, contribute equally to that goal. Some choices you make are based on your skill level; others are imposed on you by the composer and the needs of other performers. The type of performance venue and what a certain composition means to you are additional elements that determine how you prepare for the final presentation.

While learning the music, the study of specific elements like tone quality, pitch and rhythm, technique, and expression helps you to comprehend and communicate the overall essence of the work. When working with others, your awareness expands to include not only what your partners are playing, but also how and when your parts interact with theirs. In fact, the entire process—including the performance—involves weaving between the whole and the parts, attending to interactions with the music, with other performers, and with the audience (Bresler, 2005).

In qualitative research, all investigative phases are similarly intertwined; interpretation is the thread that binds them together when you, as researcher, become the "research instrument" (Barone & Eisner, 1997; Merriam, 2002; Barrett, 2007). You craft a plan based on your purpose and question; gather and analyze data, always exploring their meaning. As you come to know the people and settings, further interrogations (possibly beyond those planned at first) become part of the fabric. New issues arise as codes and themes that need to be woven into the original visualization. The final account, much like performance, combines these seemingly disparate elements into a comprehensive whole. The outcome is neither fully predictable nor replicable. Even when adhering to the same standards of quality and excellence, no two researchers follow the same process from beginning to end.

Prominent among standards of excellence is a firm commitment to ethical integrity. While applicable to all research situations, the individuality of philosophical and procedural choices within the qualitative research traditions make ethical guidelines for investigative conduct particularly important and relevant. This chapter therefore suggests ethical conduct as a major gauge by which procedural decisions of planning, data gathering, analysis, and presentation of findings are reported and their appropriateness eventually judged. The questions you ask impact on how you observe people and settings, interview participants, or review related materials. The questions also set the tone for how you label and organize data based on your own understanding of the situation under study. That understanding, however, is the result of your own worldview (Chapters 3 and 5), the demands set by particular research traditions (as described in Chapter 7), and how you navigate the continuously interacting roles of participant, observer, interrogator, and reporter.

Always keeping in mind the interplay between paying attention to the whole and the parts of your work as well as your various interpretive roles in it, this chapter speaks to the parts one by one; from ethical conduct to planning the study, gathering and labeling data, then analyzing, reflecting on, and communicating about them. In reality, however, you bring to your findings a vision of the whole. It comes to life aided by your writing skills, storytelling ability, empathetic understanding, creativity, and imagination as you invite readers to engage in that vision together with you.

Ethical Conduct as Gauge in Research Choices

As his class project, *Greg* hoped to investigate college music drop-outs and self-identity. His motivation was to understand why some of his most talented college classmates had left the music program early in their college careers. Greg saw the qualitative approach as a way to "get to the bottom" of this issue. It would be fairly easy to contact his former "buddies" and ask them to take part in his research project. In fact, he was concerned that participants he did not know well might not be willing to talk to him as openly as his friends would.

When he shared his ideas with the class, however, *Prof. E.* cautioned him about ethical concerns: "Remember that you will be asking your friends for personal information with the express purpose of sharing that information with others. Sharing personal information with a researcher can put participants at risk in their jobs, their communities, or their families and deciding how to manage this can be awkward and even painful for everyone involved."

When you think of "risky research," medical and pharmaceutical research may come to mind. But, as Greg learned, gathering qualitative data in music education, too, can reveal vulnerabilities in the people you study—called "dangerous knowledge" by Glesne (2011, p. 42). Formal protection of research participants regarding respect for persons, beneficence, and justice is part of the role of the university's Institutional Review Board, or IRB (see Chapter 4). Such boards require a *research protocol*, a form they usually provide. In it you explain your plans in detail. Your expectations regarding observations and interviews must be described clearly, including procedures for gaining access and securing permission to do the study. All participants must be given an opportunity for "informed consent," meaning that they are informed about the purpose of the research, know about any risks (physical or mental), and consent to being part of the study. If your study involves a vulnerable population, such as underage students, written permission is also required from parents or guardians.

Research ethics demand that you are sensitive to the difference between confidentiality and anonymity. Decisions about confidentiality are typically made based on the likelihood of harm to research participants. A promise of confidentiality is a serious statement and should be treated as such. It means details shared in your research report cannot betray the identity of research participants to the reader. In such a case you may not mention by name the location(s) of your work or any of your participants to anyone other than the IRB and the committee reviewing your proposal.

Video recording and photography for the purpose of research requires written permission from authorities at the site as well as the participants you wish to record. In the request for permission, key questions are usually required including how long and in what format you will store the recorded information. Typically, observational research pertaining to an adult (such as a teacher) in which children may be seen but are not part of the research, does not require parental permission. Such decisions, however, are ultimately made by the institution directing the research and the site in which the research is being conducted. At the risk of being repetitive: Any audio- or video-recording and photography must be cleared first with your own institution (and IRB, if appropriate) and also with the institution where you will be working. These recommendations apply equally to the use of formal video equipment and seemingly informal smart phone videos, snapshots, and voice recordings.

Because complete confidentiality is hard to maintain, a promise of anonymity is more common in qualitative research. This means that individual participants may be known to be part of a given study, but will not be specifically identified by name or other distinguishing characteristics. In either case, your IRB protocol should be clear about the level of anonymity or confidentiality promised.

If during a conversation a participant asks you to turn off the recording device when discussing a sensitive matter, or talks more freely when the device is off, you must clarify what aspects of that "sensitive" discussion is "on the record" or "off the record," and confirm the details of what that means. Most research reports utilize changes in names and contextual details to protect confidentiality; nonetheless, if a participant tells you not to use certain information, you may not use it—either in the research report or on other occasions. Keep those restrictions in mind from the very beginning of articulating any research questions. It is pointless to come up with fabulous ideas that are not based on realistic ways of implementing them.

Increasingly, qualitative researchers undertake "member checks" to present their interpretations to their research participants before presenting any findings to the public. A first step in those "member checks" is to provide the transcript of an interview or observation to the participant(s) described in those transcripts. A follow-up step would be to ask for specific feedback about the transcribed material. Disagreements between participants and researcher(s) must be noted and acknowledged. Such a practice ensures that the participants continue to have a "voice" in the research. It is part of doing *credible* research.

Planning a Study

As described in earlier chapters, it is premature to plan research activities until you have reviewed the body of literature relative to your topic and developed a research purpose or question. In the case of qualitative research, you add to these an interrogation of personal motivations for developing a given project (see Chapter 7). The procedural plan then follows naturally from the parameters suggested in your research question. It involves making decisions about: (1) what people and sites you wish to study; (2) the required period of time; and (3) how best to gain access to them. Considering a pilot study to test your research ideas will improve your data gathering skills and make the project stronger.

The analytical procedures highlighted in this chapter are based on those described by Glaser and Strauss (1967) as part of their *grounded theory* approach (see Chapter 7), and further developed by other scholars in sociology as well as social psychology.

Although grounded theory is viewed by some researchers as connected to a positivist worldview, many of the suggested procedures are followed by qualitative researchers across the positivist–interpretivist spectrum (see Figure 5.3). For this reason, the steps commonly found in grounded theory are a good starting place for anyone new to qualitative research.

Phases of analysis, suggested by Charmaz (2006, 2008a, 2008b), are built on Glaser and Strauss's principle of *constant comparison* between collected data and analytical interpretations from the onset of the first data to the written research product. It is a method also known as the *constant comparative method*. Other methods may use only certain aspects of those described here; but the sequence of events in its entirety gives you a sense of the ongoing aspect inherent in the qualitative research process.

Analytical examples come from a study by Frierson-Campbell (2003) of music teachers whose schools (all in low-income "urban" areas) had been identified as "low performing" by the U.S. law known as *No Child Left Behind* and were part of a university-based school reform effort. The study began as a needs assessment, exploring the role played by music educators in the schools. Data were gathered from interviews and observations. Interviewees included music teachers as well as building administrators and district-level arts administrators. The author used grounded theory to analyze the research; analytic vocabulary has been adapted for the purpose of illustration.

Making Research Decisions

Decisions about research are based on the parameters set by your research question and/or purpose. For instance, Haywood (2006) asked "How does the process of including an individual with special needs in choir create change in that individual?" (p. 407). The parameters suggested by her question include "an individual with special needs," "choir," and "change in that individual." Clear parameters make it easier to decide on the focus of a study (also known as the unit of analysis), and then make detailed plans about participants, locations, and gaining access to either. Using a pilot study to try out your ideas will help assure the success of the formal study.

Unit of Analysis

Refining your research purpose into more specific questions provides clarity about the intended focus of your research: individual teachers, a classroom, an entire school, a school district, or a local community, etc. Each answer would suggest a different *unit of analysis*, the basis for analyzing what you see, hear, or otherwise experience through observation and participation. Be aware, however, that persons, places, and other contexts both inside and beyond the boundaries of that unit provide contextual information for your investigation.

It may be helpful to consider the units of analysis suggested by the research questions and purposes of some of the authors featured in Chapter 7. Regarding groups of student musicians, Allsup (2003) asked: "How would the participating groups evolve and define themselves through the practice of composing and analyzing music? What would our choices reflect or signify? How might this experience affect individual growth as well as community-making?" (para. 5). Allsup's unit of analysis was a group of musicians involved in "the practice of composing and analyzing music." He instigated and then studied two such groups.

Stake, Bresler, and Mabry (1991) asked "What are the schools providing as opportunities for [arts] learning?" (p. 4). Their unit of analysis was individual schools—to be specific, eight elementary schools. Haywood (2006) asked "How does the process of including an individual with special needs in choir create change in that individual?" (p. 407). Her stated research purpose was "to gain a greater understanding of the possibilities and potential benefits of including individuals with special needs in choirs" (p. 409). Her unit of analysis was the individual special needs student, and she studied one such student in a choir setting. Once you are clear about the focus of your research, you may consider how to select and recruit participants.

Participant Selection

Choices about research participants (often called sampling) are guided by your research purpose and question(s). For this reason, sampling choices are traditionally labeled *purposeful*. Most researchers begin by identifying an initial sample that meet the parameters of their purpose, with tentative plans to add participants as additional issues emerge (King & Horrocks, 2010, p. 30). Since potential participants may not all agree to be part of the research, it is necessary to identify more participants than you expect to need, ranking them in some way according to those you will approach first.

Among options for finding participants are *snowball sampling* and *theoretical sampling*. Snowball sampling entails asking participants you have already recruited to help you identify additional volunteers. Theoretical sampling involves making theoretical choices about what participants to include in a study. Either of these techniques may be used to recruit an initial sample or to find additional participants as your research evolves. It is advisable, therefore, to make allowances for recruiting additional persons when submitting a research plan to your IRB and any other gatekeepers. Asking for more time and access than you expected at the beginning of your work is a better strategy than asking for limited access and then having to ask for additional permission later.

You might see the latter as "fishing," or starting a study without knowing the details of its intent. Interpretivist research, however, suggests that the researcher is the tool that makes analytical decisions from the initial research plan, to the organization of the data into appropriate categories or themes, to decisions about when to stop gathering data altogether. Credibility and trustworthiness depend on the researcher's clarity and reflexivity about the process.

Details of Engagement

As you may recall, New York City's Times Square is a different place on December 31 from what it is on most other days. It would therefore be necessary to experience Times Square on many different days, including December 31, to get a "real" sense of what goes on there throughout the year. This example, while extreme, suggests that prolonged engagement and repeated observation are important for the credibility of research. Ideally, the timing of visits will be varied enough to provide a complete sense of the site as it pertains to your research purpose. If visitation times are limited to those that are convenient for your schedule, you may not get an accurate sense of what goes on at the site. Likewise, if you visit only when special events occur, you may get an unrealistic view of the site.

At the planning stage, consider several issues regarding time. How long (weeks, months, years) do you imagine it will take to gather the data you need? (While there is no "hard and fast" rule, it is best to over- rather than under-estimate.) What elements of your own or participants' calendars have to be considered? And, what is the ideal length of time for each visit? Such estimates are part of the stated plan, and participants are likely to want this information as a condition of participating in a study.

Gaining Access

Once the sample and site have been chosen, the time frame estimated, and the proposal approved, the next step is to recruit participants from within the sample. Known as *gaining access*, it may be as simple as speaking to one or more individuals, or it may involve going through a bureaucratic hierarchy that is controlled by "gatekeepers" or even by carefully constructed rules for conducting research. The latter is more common with schools; however, gatekeepers are not always the holders of official titles. Sometimes they are simply the people whose "okay" is needed if you want to reach potential participants in an identified sample.

Many people are suspicious of strangers coming into their daily activities. Glesne (2011, p. 53) suggests that sharing the details of your study in the form of a *lay summary* will help to allay the fears of those you work with. The information you provide should be similar to that provided on your IRB protocol, but stated in the vernacular of your participants. Whatever you do, stress in all cases that your role is not to judge or evaluate, but to understand. Different levels of involvement (or access) allow you to do that. Even if you want to be seen as an "insider" to the situation because you were (or are) a teacher, your participants may not see you that way. To them you may be a more distanced "outsider," essentially a stranger who, by his or her mere presence, changes the "normal" classroom environment.

Doing a Pilot Study

A pilot study is a "pre-study" that allows you to try out the methods and procedures you plan to use. Applicable to nearly all research methods, it follows the basic elements of research design, but has fewer formal requirements. Pilot testing of sampling and data gathering procedures is highly recommended. It allows you to try out your ideas prior to the official start of the project, demonstrating that you have made efforts to cultivate the skills needed for rigorous research.

Is the setting unfamiliar? Are you unaccustomed to qualitative interviewing and observing? Would you like to try out some of your questions, to see how well they work? Do you wonder whether your ideas for the research will work at all? Even if you feel confident about the answers to these and similar questions, plan on conducting at least one pilot study.

Conducting a pilot study is a realistic and attainable goal for a semester research course, enabling you to prepare a well-thought-out proposal for a subsequent semester. If you are a student in such a course or a degree program, however, you should not begin a pilot study without the knowledge of your instructor or project advisor, and without getting the approval of the Institutional Review Board (IRB) at your institution, if required. Check with your instructor or IRB to be sure you follow the proper procedures.

Gathering and Labeling Data

Qualitative data comprise recorded interactions (observations and/or interviews) with human participants or with documents, artifacts, and/or electronic media that represent human action in some way. Data may be recorded electronically or in writing. Non-written recordings are transcribed into text for the purpose of analysis.

Because data collection involves thinking analytically from the outset of a study, pre-liminary labels are attached from the moment you begin gathering data. Memos, written immediately after gathering data, provide a way to reflect on possible meanings of your experiences, examining initial labels, revising some and combining others into focused codes and themes (Charmaz, 2006). This corresponds to rules suggested by Glaser and Strauss (1967) for the reflexive process of *constant comparison*: First, continuously weigh codes used for new data against those used to label previous incidents (p. 106), and second, "*stop coding and record a memo on your ideas*" (p. 107; emphasis in original). These two rules are key elements in grounded theory.

Not all qualitative researchers support the use of coding. Especially postmodernists and post-structuralists see the practice of coding as a carry-over from positivist con-ceptions of knowledge and question its primacy in traditional qualitative research as decontextualizing and fragmenting discourse (St. Pierre & Roulston, 2006; St. Pierre, 2008). There is no question that any naming is a form of coding, albeit less structured and tested than is typical of coding in quantitative research (see Chapter 13).

Obtaining Data by Observation, Interview, and/or Document Review

As mentioned above, the procedures traditionally used for collecting qualitative data have been interview, observation, and document or artifact review. One type of data may inform the others or each may be dealt with as a separate collection tool. To assure the credibility of your research, however, data should be gathered in more than one way, and from multiple sources. The development of digital technologies has made additional media available for study; despite their constant development, however, the basis of col-lecting and using information for research purposes remains similar.

During any given observation, interview, or document review, the researcher records data electronically and/or manually, resulting in what is known as "raw data" (electronic recordings or *field notes*). The episode is not complete until data are transcribed, initial labels are applied, and a memo has been written about the experience. Written memos that document procedural and analytical decisions and reflections on those decisions are part of the research and are included as data. This ongoing interpretive cycle continues throughout the data gathering process. The following section describes this cycle with a discussion of observation, interviewing, document or artifact review, transcribing, naming and labeling, and memo writing.

Observation

When used in this chapter, "observation" refers to deliberately viewing and listening to human action and interaction in the context of a research study. Below we discuss qualitative observation as it typically unfolds, from the first observations in the field to determining and navigating the observer role.

The observation process   Whether as a teacher or student, you have experienced entering a new school. The first few days can be overwhelming, as navigating between unfamiliar spaces and asking directions makes you feel out of place. Remembering the names of colleagues and of students may be similarly challenging. After a few days, however, you learn details that help you proceed through the daily schedule. You may find a schematic design that helps you to understand the layout of the building and the placement of the rooms. You may create a seating chart, or develop other ways of keeping track of names and other details related to your students. What was once a sea of unfamiliar faces in a confusing space becomes a classroom full of students whose names, instruments or voice parts, and personalities are familiar.

Coming to know a research site follows a similar sequence, but instead of (or in addition to) finding your way around a building, you are trying to get to know the people you study as both an outsider and an insider. Who do you need to talk to? Where should you look? What questions should you ask? Tentative patterns begin to emerge when you recognize and begin naming a few threads or themes that bind your observations together.

The observer's role   Qualitative observations exist on a continuum from *direct observation* (see Chapter 12) with little interaction with the site or participants, to *participant observation*. Remember the images shown in Figure 3.2, contrasting the role and view of the non-participant observer with that of the participant observer. In qualitative research, knowing your place on this continuum is part of the research. In classroom research, for instance, you may intend to be an "observer," while the teacher you observe may wish to engage you as a student or assistant in their classroom. Be aware that accepting such an offer could change your role from "visitor" to that of "helper" or even "judge." You will have to decide whether such a role will limit what you learn or help you gain access. Regardless of the role you ultimately choose, children are likely to ask why you are there and expect you, as an adult, to act like a teacher or classroom aid. Be prepared with a simple explanation for them, and make note of your own actions, including the reasons behind them and what you perceive to be their results—all of these are data and should be written into your memos.

Recording observational data   Observational data are usually recorded both with researcher notes and with video recording. Some researchers develop an *observation form* to provide structure for taking field notes. (For more information, see Chapter 13.) Details such as the date, time, and place of the observation, the participants involved, space for a brief schedule of activities observed, and room to jot both notes and diagrams are common in such a form.

If you gather data via video recording, do so in the most natural setting possible. Note that there is no perfect camera position—a better view of the teacher may obscure students, and vice versa—but once the camera is running, "set it and forget it." Remember that the camera cannot capture everything; in fact, its placement suggests what you believe it is important to see, and you should reflect on the reasons for your choices. If possible, while the video camera is recording you should record your own field notes, to provide context and meaning for the details that the camera will provide. Writing while recording can, however, be perceived as more intrusive by research participants, whether they are students or teachers.

Recording equipment varies from traditional film-based video cameras to "smart phones" and other types of electronics. Make sure to choose equipment that will make a clear recording of action as well as sound. Many researchers use an external microphone to assure that sounds are picked up clearly. When choosing equipment, consider how you will store the originals. Large amounts of video data can clog up a computer hard drive very quickly, so you may wish to invest in a secure digital (SD) card or external hard drive.

Taking notes   Note taking involves using all of your senses to grasp as much about a setting as possible. During each visit, keep records of what you hear, feel, and smell (and even taste, if applicable to your research purpose). In addition to verbal notes, you may wish to draw pictures or diagrams or take photos, if possible. Make an effort to view familiar phenomena as an outsider would: How is the room organized? Why is the schedule organized one way as opposed to another? Pay attention to gestures as well as words, to tone of voice as much as what is said, and to who is not there as much as who is.

The worldviews that underlie most qualitative traditions suggest that it is not possible to truly separate your observations from your impressions of them. Thus, notes taken in the field require *narrative accuracy*—recognition that empirical perceptions (what you observe or learn through interview) reflect personal beliefs and preconceived knowledge about the situation under study. Field notes may therefore acknowledge your position in the setting, question how you may have disturbed the usual routine, and examine what personal biases have kept you from seeing some things. Reflective notes made in the field are often designated by "O.C." (observer comment) in the margin or by typing in upper case type or a different font to separate them from notes intended as descriptive.

Interviewing

It is difficult to get through a single day without hearing or reading about media figures being interviewed for their view on politics, entertainment, or sports (King & Horrocks, 2010). But the purpose for most media interviews is to promote entertainment or share opinions. Research interviews have a different purpose: to develop an understanding of an experience from a variety of perspectives. Qualitative interviews still involve one-on-one or small group conversation, but with the purpose of understanding multiple perspectives rather than persuading an audience toward a point of view.

The interview process The most common approaches to interviewing include: (1) informal conversations, typical in participant observation fieldwork; (2) interviews based on a *guide* or *schedule* (see Chapter 12), where you work from a set of possible topics but do not have predetermined questions; and (3) formal interviews in which respondents provide answers to predetermined questions (Patton, 2001). Open questions may enable researchers to uncover perspectives about aspects of music learning and/or teaching that formal questionnaires and structured interviews can miss. Be aware that different disciplinary perspectives and/or theoretical assumptions suggest a variety of interview procedures—for a discussion of these see Brenner (2006).

Initial topics are derived from four main sources: your experiences with and knowledge of the topic; the theoretical framework you develop from the literature or as the study unfolds; questions derived from any preliminary information you gathered in a pilot study (King & Horrocks, 2010, p. 37); and previously held knowledge about participants. While avoiding a linear "ask-this-then-that" process, research interviews typically include the following as part of the conversation: (1) backgrounds of the respondents relative to the topic; (2) details of actions observed by or shared with the interviewer; (3) motivations for those actions; (4) questions about (a) emotional reactions to an experience or action, (b) knowledge held by the participant, and (c) things observed by the participant.

Interviews should be scheduled at a time and in a place that are comfortable both for you and for your participants. If possible, let the interviewee choose the setting. While interviews always involve issues of power, avoid settings that explicitly suggest a power relationship, such as an office where one of you sits behind a desk. Choose a setting that is private and make an effort to minimize any possibility of interruption. When you schedule the interview, allow additional time for introductions and parting words. Caution is in order if you are going to an unfamiliar place: For your own safety, tell someone where you are going and when you will return.

The interviewer's role As interviewer your task is to elicit responses that reflect the participant's perspective. Think of it as an opportunity to learn from participants rather than to tell them what you think. It is important, therefore, to ask questions that "prompt," but that do not assume a particular perspective on the part of the interviewee. For instance: "How did you feel about that?" is a prompt, while "Didn't that make you mad?" is a leading question because it assumes a specific emotion. You may also wish to plan "probes" to seek additional information—possible reasons, for instance, for an action or a response (King & Horrocks, 2010, p. 40). Learning to interview without "leading" takes practice. If you plan to interview, make sure to practice first, both informally (perhaps with colleagues in your research course) and as part of a pilot study.

Empathetic listening is important in qualitative interviewing. Particularly when talking to someone who differs from you—whether by age, race or ethnicity, class, gender, sexuality, or some other way—you should try to become attuned to their style and speed of speaking, and even their breathing rhythm, to put them at ease (Norkunas, 2011, para. 13). To practice this skill, set up planned, separate interviews with selected classmates who you perceive as being different from you in some way. Ask them to tell you about a sad or a joyous story, or about an important milestone in their life. Do not respond with your own story, but instead learn to be comfortable with pauses and silences. Follow this activity by journaling about your experience as a listener, noting your reactions and assessing your skills (para.12).

Recording interview data   Successful interviews require the development of rapport, and that can be difficult to do if you are trying to take notes or type every word of a conversation. For this reason interviews are typically recorded electronically with manual note-taking as a back-up. In a case where the setting is particularly important, you may wish to use a video recorder, but an audio recording is generally sufficient. Use a digital device whenever possible so recorded interviews can be copied to your computer without conversion, allowing you to use transcription software if you wish. Digital audio recorders have become relatively inexpensive, and many smart phones and PDAs come with a recording function. Make sure to try out a recording device before your scheduled interview, and have both a back-up recorder and a notebook and pencil in case of a technical malfunction. When you make the interview appointment, ask permission to use recording equipment, and clarify for your participants how long you will keep the recorded data. Such information is required for an IRB protocol.

Document or Artifact Review

Document review has to do with studying how "things and our knowledge of things are structured and represented through text and talk" (Prior, 2008, p. 114). "Documents" include written materials, published or unpublished, that help to shed light on your research. "Artifacts" comprise non-written documents such as photographs, audio- or video-recordings, or memorabilia that represent your research participants.

Personal documents such as diaries or a collection of letters written by a participant can also reveal unique aspects of their point of view. Such primary source materials are critical for historical research, as they provide an intimate personal view of the past. Photographs and other artifacts can provide a window into present-tense data as well: Viewing a participant's collection of photographs can give you a sense of what they want to remember, or of how they want to be remembered. Research participants may not voluntarily offer them to you, so you may have to ask whether such documents exist and whether you can have access to them.

As Yin (2003) notes, such materials have several benefits for the researcher. They are stable because they are frozen in time. You can view them on your own time. But because documents are often preserved selectively by participants, they may not completely represent the person or situation you are studying (p. 86). For these reasons, documents and artifacts should be viewed in the context of other available data unless the purpose of your study is to study documents alone.

The process for reviewing documents and artifacts for research is similar to that used for observations and interviews. Keeping a written record is required. Include a description of each item and the time and the location where you encountered it. If possible copy, photograph, or scan each item. Take notes about what you see, and reflect upon your impressions as you would with any research experience. These notes become part of your data and are treated in the same way as other field notes.

Electronic or virtual documents   Electronic documents provide a new area of study. Web pages, for instance, can be studied for their content alone: What is their structure? How do they communicate their purpose? Beyond individual web documents, however, are questions about connections that emerge from relationships between websites (via hyperlinks). Researchers may examine associations between interactive materials people view, use, or even order on the Web. Prior (2008) cites a web crawler designed by Richard Rogers to facilitate such a study. (For more information see Prior, 2008, pp. 120–125.)

The relatively recent widespread availability of digital indices and online document repositories has had a major bearing on all qualitative research, not just that involving extant documents. While not yet widely used, new computer-based procedures will make it possible to combine sophisticated computer analysis with the interpretive perspective of qualitative research for the examination of field notes, transcribed data, and memos (Altheide, Coyle, DeVriese, & Schneider, 2008).

Transcribing Raw Data

Turning recorded information (observations as well as interviews) into text is known as *transcribing*. A fairly straightforward process, it involves viewing or listening to each recording and creating a verbal transcript of what was recorded while it is fresh in your mind. Combining the details of the recording with your reflections on what you remember from being in that setting, transforms your raw data into text that is ready for analysis. A labor-intensive process, manually transcribing a single hour of observation typically takes about four hours.

If you are transcribing a great deal of data, consider using a computer assisted transcription program. Two packages are worth mentioning: *Transana*, an open source transcription and analysis software for audio and video data can be downloaded from www.transana.org; *Dragon Naturally Speaking* is a commercial product that can be ordered from online or brick and mortar software dealers.

Requirements for transcription vary: some researchers transcribe only the elements of an observation that are pertinent to their research questions while others transcribe everything that occurred. We recommend that you begin with full transcription in the early stages of your study, gradually moving toward transcribing only what pertains to your research purpose. Make sure to copy original recordings and store them in a safe place so you can return to them as the study evolves. What you define as important can change over the course of the research.

Naming and Initial Labeling

The first or *initial* stage of analysis involves applying names (or labels) quickly, during or immediately after transcribing data from a research experience. From the moment that you begin taking in information your mind begins to conceptualize and label what is going on in order to make sense of it. The qualitative researcher pays attention to those preliminary labels and notes them for later analysis.

Labels are typically devised either on your own (based on ideas that emerge from the data) or borrowed from the words of participants (known as *in vivo*). Sections, sometimes called *units of data*, may be marked word-by-word, line-by-line, paragraph-by-paragraph, or in a scheme devised by you. Choosing a specific unit for labeling may seem arbitrary but can help assure that nothing is missed (Charmaz, 2006). Figure 8.1 displays the initial labels applied sentence-by-sentence to an interview transcript. One of many possible ways to store and code data, this two-column table displays interview data on the left, with each sentence placed in a different row. The column on the right holds the initial labels developed by the researcher.

The example illustrates Charmaz' advice that gerunds suggest action within labels. See, for instance, the labels "*excluding* music," "*trying* to get along with everyone" and others in the field notes shown in Figure 8.1. The latter phrase is also an example of *in vivo* coding, which means using participants' words to capture their interpretations of

Raw Data	Initial Label
1. I often think that sometimes they have grade level meetings … um … I'm not included in them.	Excluding music from grade level meetings
2. And–I get along with everybody around here.	Trying to get along with everybody
3. But–so I don't take it personally.	Not taking things personally
4. It's just that we tend not to be included.	Excluding music
5. And whenever we have been included . . . .see, what they do, in here, is that they put together the music teachers, the art teachers, and the gym teachers, and we all sit together and say "what are we doing here" and we write down some issues that nobody reads.	Isolating special area teachers
6. You know … and that's not right.	Responding to isolation

FIGURE 8.1 Initial Labeling of Interview Notes

an experience. *In vivo* labels are particularly appropriate for initial coding, as they stay close to the data, but it is important to confirm their meaning with participants. For instance, probing further into another teacher's concern about "the right thing to teach" during a later interview enabled Frierson-Campbell (2003) to understand more fully the motivation behind that teacher's approach to the classroom.

Writing Memos

Scheduling specific time for notating your thoughts is a required part of gathering data. Such notes, written after and separate from data collection instances, are known as *memos*. These comprise written reflections on what is heard and seen; questions about the parameters of promising categories and how well they fit the data as well as thoughts about what theories might be emerging as findings. As with other types of data, keep track of the time and place of any writing you do (even if the computer gives you dates as well).

The content and purpose of memos will likely change as a research project evolves. Early memos, like early labels, are exploratory. Later memos examine analytical possibilities. The following memo (condensed for illustration) was written by Frierson-Campbell early in her research. A later example is included in the section on analysis.

> I need to look into research about worker productivity and morale and the like. It seems to me that it's a basic human need to talk about what you do and network with peers. What effect will simply allowing these teachers to do this have on their work? (2.7.2001)

Memos are written quickly, to get thoughts down on paper. Editing for clarity and grammar will happen later if the notes turn out to be important for the research.

In the shared role of researcher and interpreter, one cannot help but bring one's own lived experience into the analysis of what is heard. A researcher following the *phenomenological* tradition uses memos to acknowledge and "bracket" biases and prior knowledge, setting them aside in order to fully experience the perspectives of the research participants. Because *bracketing* means different things to different researchers, part of this process is explaining in detail its meaning and how it was used in the research (Gearing, 2004, p. 1432). This process is not complete until the bracketed data are reintegrated back into the final analysis and interpretation (p. 1433).

Managing Data

Qualitative research produces a great deal of data. Each data-gathering episode requires a transcription, often representing 45 to 60 minutes of talk or more, plus field notes and reflective memos. With that much information to keep track of, most researchers need some kind of organizational strategy. A so-called codebook is a frequently used option.

Keeping a Codebook

The collection of computer files or the notebook in which qualitative data are organized and housed is traditionally called a *codebook*. This term is somewhat confusing, as the term refers more to keeping track of data in its various forms than to anything resembling a book. The format and contents of the codebook differ for each researcher. Assuming the use of a computer, the codebook is likely to include the following:

1. A folder that contains files of raw data in their most original form. (Files containing audio or video recordings should be copied and stored in a second location for safe keeping.)
2. A folder consisting of multiple data files that organize transcribed data by code, category, date, and participant (see Figure 8.1 and Appendix J). You may wish to include a file that lists initial labels and the focused codes and groups with which they are organized.
3. A "memo" folder that holds ideas that occur to you during the research.
4. A folder to store drawings and diagrams that help explain things non-verbally.
5. A file that keeps track of all of the information described above.

The analysis itself may be done by hand or with a computer program. Whether to use specialized or general purpose software or work with word-processed or hard-copy notes is a matter of personal preference; there are benefits and drawbacks to each. With a small project, time may be better spent working manually rather than in learning a complicated software program; however, if you have a lot of data to analyze, the software may make the workload more manageable. See Koenig (2009) for a review of available qualitative data analysis software programs. Researchers who want to explore further use of a spreadsheet program for data storage may wish to see Meyer and Avery (2009).

Analysis, Reflection, and Reporting

As already emphasized at the beginning of this chapter, researchers go back and forth between the interpretive–analytical processes described in this chapter. This is because qualitative analysis is recursive rather than linear. In practical terms, separating this chapter into various consecutive headings and sub-headings (to be read one after the other in a textbook) is not true to the way qualitative research is done. Hyper-text (rather than print) might be a better medium to describe the process, in which you navigate through the interpretive spiral of gathering and analyzing data. As you read, therefore, imagine that you can "click" on each description, learn how and whether it applies to your research or reading, and then click the "back" button to return to the point you started from and choose a new path.

Despite the fact that every researcher defines his or her own personal research path, the process shares certain commonalities. The first of these, gathering and initially labeling data from individual research events (observation, interview, or document/artifact review), was described earlier in the chapter. This section describes more in-depth analytical and reflective processes, such as (1) bringing together the data from several research events, re-visiting and re-coding the labels to focus them, and grouping similar focused codes together, (2) seeking themes that connect codes to the original research questions or theories (inductive or deductive) that offer insight, and (3) writing an account of the process to share findings with the field. Researchers who distrust coding as too restrictive nonetheless seek to connect their data gathering and analysis through inductive and deductive themes. How those themes come about is, again, a matter of naming, labeling, and—ultimately—coding.

Focusing and Grouping Analytic Codes

After several transcripts have been coded and a relatively stable list of labels captures the essence of the data as you understand them, a second phase of analysis begins. Assuming the use of data collected from multiple sources and in different ways, this phase typically has at least two stages: refining initial labels into *focused codes*, and *grouping* like codes together for further analysis. (Note that there is no "right" labeling and coding scheme; your task is to develop a system that works for your research purpose and questions as imbedded in your worldview.) Frierson-Campbell's research (see Figure 8.1) is used here to illustrate the process of focusing codes.

After reflecting on initial labels given to data from several sources, she chose the phrase "professional isolation" as a focused code because it seemed to capture the collective meaning of the various labels attached earlier to the raw data. Returning to the labels with that code in mind, she looked for additional instances of "professional isolation" expressed in the data. At the same time, she reviewed other initial labels to create further focused codes.

Grouping similar codes together helped her to "reduce" the data by allowing patterns to emerge across sources. Grouping is an analytical decision that should be explored in a memo, such as the one found in Frierson-Campbell's notes:

> What other professional expectations do music teachers describe when talking about their work place? What is "professional isolation" a part of? (4.4.2001)

Eventually, she devised the phrase "Professional Music Teacher Expectations" as a name for the grouped data (see Appendix J). The codes that fell into this group included (1) Isolation, (2) Time resource/"Coverage teachers," (3) Discipline, (4) Enjoyment, and (5) "Neat people." (The phrases "coverage teachers" and "neat people" were terms used by administrators to describe the music teachers in the study. They were used by the researcher as *in vivo* codes.)

Labeling, focused coding, and grouping of codes continue together for as long as data are collected. Once data are analyzed, however, they are usually stored in a new file so they can eventually be sorted by code and category. Appendix J displays one possible method for data storage: using a spreadsheet or word-processed table to organize text (in this case, transcribed interviews and field notes) by code and group, as well as by other characteristics. Housing data in such a file enables a researcher to sort data by any column: date, file, line, speaker, role, code, or group.

Thematic Analysis

Inductive analysis builds themes from individual codes and groups of codes that emerge from the whole of the data. The memos by which your thoughts were documented during data collection; that is, your data interrogations provide guidance for thematic analysis. Based on the research tradition that informs your study, codes may be examined inductively or deductively, dialectically or propositionally. Phenomenological interpretation deliberately avoids theorizing, striving instead to present the essence of the experience as communicated by the research participants themselves. Grounded theory, on the other hand, would endorse attempts to induce a new theoretical framework out of the codes emerging from the data.

To approach thematic analyses, ask yourself the following questions: When I look at the entire body of data, what relationships might exist between insights noted in my memos and the codes that have emerged most frequently from my data? Do stages uncovered in my research suggest a chronological description? Is there a particular story or incident that illuminates my findings in a particular way? Are concepts and constructs from an underlying discipline (i.e., anthropology, history, psychology, sociology) useful for explaining such illuminations? Answers to any of these questions may form the basis for your written interpretation.

Writers use a number of strategies for thematic analysis. Many write analytic memos to explore how their findings illuminate the questions that guided the research or expand upon findings from other studies. Some researchers use tools such as chart paper to list, organize, and re-organize themes. "Mapping," a process that is somewhat similar to literature mapping as explained in Chapter 2, is a non-linear approach that allows you to consider various organizational schemes. (For an example of mind-mapping, see Bachwani-Paritosh, 2007.)

The following analytic memo explores thematic connections between Frierson-Campbell's data and sociological constructs from the literature:

> If music teacher identity is realized/actualized/recognized at the intersection of musicianship and teachership, what can we learn from the first group about identity and/or need? Very little about musicianship—almost no mention of it. And very little about teachership or musicianship in relation to student learning. I learned more about music teachers interacting very little with their schools, but instead acting as isolated adults in a professional world that they perceive as hostile to them. Based on the first year's interviews, it does not seem to be clear to anyone what the music teacher's roles are or what their needs are. (5.3.2001)

The terms "role" and "professional identity" are sociological constructs; this memo therefore suggested tying her thinking to sociological writers in and out of music education (i.e., Becker, 1973; Bouij, 1998).

True "grounded theorists" add an additional step to the process of analysis. *Theoretical* coding involves conceptualizing and even hypothesizing possible relationships between codes and/or themes. This involves re-visiting codes and groups of codes in search of those that "carry the weight of the analysis" (Charmaz, 2008b, p. 164). While initial labels may reflect action, and additional analysis may group common actions together, theoretical codes seek to make sense of the analysis on a conceptual level. This is a challenge for any researcher, but especially for those new to the process of qualitative analysis. If you are new to qualitative research, you may opt to focus on thematic rather than theoretical interpretation.

Thoughts About Writing

Choices about analyzing and organizing coded data for the purpose of sharing research findings with the field should reflect the theoretical base that guided the work. Foremost among such decisions is not only your philosophical bent and research tradition, but also a description of how you came to know your participants, view your role as investigator, and understand the phenomenon under study from many points of view. That you established a trusted and trusting relationship with research participants is particularly important in qualitative research where the boundaries between personal privacy and public benefit can be quite fluid. When you write up and share your interpretations with the field, the spiral of qualitative research joins the spiral of inquiry with which the book began.

The written report weaves data analysis and interpretation together, bringing the many layers of meaning uncovered by the research into a cohesive whole. Inspired by Dawe (2011), think of writing up the research metaphorically as creating a fugue, a musical structure in which different voices are connected by a theme (or two) and still continue to be their own lines. Listen to and take in the way Dawe uses the words from Aldous Huxley's (1928/1996) *Point Counter Point* to describe a flute and string ensemble playing a Bach fugue:

> The parts live their separate lives; they touch, their paths cross, they combine for a moment to create a seemingly final and perfected harmony, only to break apart again. Each is always alone and separate and individual. "I am I," asserts the violin; "the world revolves round me." "Round me," calls the cello. "Round me," the flute insists. And all are equally right and equally wrong; and none of them will listen to the others. (Huxley, 1928/1996, p. 23)

We know as musicians the challenge of performing a fugue in an ensemble: Each performer must at once assert her independence as a soloist and attend to the voices of fellow performers—more inter-dependent than independent. Otherwise the composition loses its effect. A qualitative research study is written in a similarly contrapuntal style: All voices heard in the fieldwork must be present and communicated in the analysis and interpretation. Even unresolved dissonances may become important parts of the composition, making the piece in its entirety more intriguing and unique.

Chapter Summary

1. Ethical considerations require (a) care to avoid "dangerous knowledge," (b) approval from an Institutional Review Board, (c) written consent from participants for interview, observe and/or document review, (d) care regarding requirements for anonymity and confidentiality, (e) special consideration of vulnerable populations, and (f) concerns about reciprocity.

2. The phases of qualitative research are connected by the recognition that all research is interpretation.

3. Planning a qualitative study involves making choices about the unit of analysis, participant selection, details of engagement, and ways to gain access to the chosen sample. Grounded theory procedures are helpful for new researchers. A pilot study is a good way to find out whether your sample, as well as chosen methods and procedures, will address your research purpose.

4. In qualitative research, gathering, analyzing, and interpreting data overlap to varying degrees. Three primary methods comprise qualitative data collection: observation, interview, and document or artifact review. Combining these and having multiple data sources are important for making sure your data are credible and rigorous.

5. Qualitative observations exist on a continuum from direct observation (little interaction with participants) to participant observation (much interaction with participants). An observation guide is needed for keeping records.

6. The purpose of qualitative interviews is to understand an experience from a variety of perspectives. To ensure consistency among interviewees, it may be helpful to develop an interview guide.

7. Documents and/or artifacts produced by participants can be a rich source of data. Because they are open to interpretation, however, they should be used in conjunction with other data gathering procedures.

8. Data analysis and interpretation begin with preliminary coding in conjunction with data collection. Once preliminary codes are stable, categories help to organize and further reduce the data.

9. The process for analyzing data may be inductive or deductive. When you write up and share your work with the field, the spiral of qualitative research joins the spiral of inquiry.

Topics for Discussion

1. Perceptions of the benefits and drawbacks of qualitative methods for research.

2. You are studying music education across several communities, and one of your music-teacher participants shares in an interview that she is concerned about the way a certain group of students is treated in his school. What are the ethical issues raised by this experience? How might you resolve them?

Suggested Assignments

1. Imagine how you might explore your current research interest using qualitative methods. What procedures do you think would be most useful? What location and what participants would you choose? Explain.

2. Create your own observational study using video from YouTube or a similar resource. For example, enter "Music in Times Square" into the YouTube search engine. Choose three to five videos to observe, taking field notes, and making observer comments. Create codes to analyze your data. What do your selected videos suggest about music in Times Square? How well do you think your observation represents the totality of music in Times Square? Why?

3. Interview one or more of your colleagues about their experience in graduate school, or one or more of your students about their experience studying music. Review your notes and make observer comments. If possible, combine your data with others from your class and analyze using codes you develop together.

4. Visit the website for NAfME: The National Association for Music Education (http://www.nafme.org/). Take notes as if this site was a collection of documents that you were reviewing for research purposes. Create codes to analyze your data. What do your notes suggest about NAfME's vision of music education? How well do you think your notes represent NAfME's views? Why? (This is a large site; consider splitting this assignment between students.)

5. Combine the results of your NAfME observation from Assignment 4 with those of colleagues from your class. Analyze and interpret them collectively. How similar and different are your individual and collective impressions?

Recommended Reading

On Qualitative Observations:

Emerson, R. M., Fretz, R. I., & Shaw, L. L. (1995). *Writing ethnographic fieldnotes*. Chicago: The University of Chicago Press.

Emerson, R. M., Fretz, R. I., & Shaw, L. L. (2001). Participant observation and fieldnotes. In P. Atkinson, A. Coffey, S. Delamont, J. Lofland, & L. Lofland (Eds.), *Handbook of ethnography* (pp. 352–368). London: Sage.

Heath, C., Hindmarsh, J., & Luff, P. (2010). *Video in qualitative research: Analysing social interaction in everyday life*. Los Angeles, London, New Delhi, Singapore, Washington, DC: Sage.

Spradley, J. P. (1980). *Participant observation*. New York: Holt, Rinehart & Winston.

On Interviewing:

Brenner, M. E. (2006). Interviewing in educational research. In J. L. Green, G. Camilli, & P. B. Elmore (Eds.), *Handbook of complementary methods in educational research* (pp. 357–370). Washington, DC: American Educational Research Association.

King, N., & Horrocks, C. (2010). *Interviews in qualitative research*. London: Sage.

Norkunas, M. (2011). Teaching to listen: Listening exercises and self-reflexive journals. *The Oral History Review, 38*(1), 63–108.

On Qualitative Research Templates:

Mack, N., Woodsong, C., MacQueen, K. M., Guest G., & Namey, E. (2005). *Qualitative research methods: A data collector's field guide*. Research Triangle Park, NC: Family Health International. Retrieved November 23, 2011 from http://www.fhi.org/en/rh/pubs/booksreports/qrm_datacoll.htm

On Qualitative Data Analysis:

Erickson, F. (2006). Definition and analysis of data from videotape: Some research procedures and their rationales. In J. L. Green, G. Camilli, & P. B. Elmore (Eds.), *Handbook of complementary methods in educational research* (pp. 177–191). Washington, DC: American Educational Research Association.

Koenig, T. (2009). CAQDAS Comparison website. In Economic and Social Research Council, *ReStore: A sustainable web resources repository* [website]. Swindon, U.K.: Author. Retrieved November 2, 2011 from http://www.restore.ac.uk/lboro/research/software/caqdas_comparison.php

Meyer, D. Z., & Avery, L. M. (2009). Excel as a qualitative data analysis tool. *Field Methods,* 21, 91–112. Retrieved November 22, 2011 from www.sagepub.com

Poland, B. D. (2002). Transcription quality. In J. Gubrium & J. A. Holstein (Eds.), *Handbook of interview research: Context and method* (pp. 629–650). Thousand Oaks, CA: Sage.

Romppel, M. (2011). Qualitative analysis. In M. Romppel, *Resources related to content analysis and text analysis* [webpage]. Retrieved November 2, 2011 from http://www.content-analysis.de/software/qualitative-analysis

nine

Quantitative Research in Music Education

Letting Numbers Speak

Setting the stage for the next three chapters on understanding descriptive statistics, interpreting correlations, and designing selected quantitative projects, this chapter:

- Introduces basic concepts of measurement theory that impact on how questions are asked and hypotheses formulated;
- Briefly describes quantitative research in the study of musical development, learning, cognition, the improvement of performance skills, and other issues of relevance to music educators.

Quantitative research is about differences and commonalities (physical, biological, and/or socio-psychological traits) across larger numbers of individuals. The ultimate goal is the testing of theory by means of reliable and valid evidence that results in the ability to generalize findings as accepted fact, predict performance outcomes, and provide empirical guidelines for making informed conceptual and practical decisions.

Introduction

Imagine two choir teachers: one experienced (Teacher 1) and one quite new (Teacher 2). They have been paired to work together for professional development. In the course of observing, it seems that Teacher 2 says "okay" very frequently, while Teacher 1 says it hardly at all. What additional information is needed to determine whether this word is over-used? Certainly both teachers could count the number of "okays" uttered in a given class; perhaps Teacher 1 says "okay" three times while Teacher 2 says "okay" 12 times. But counting is done over unequal intervals. What else is needed to determine whether Teacher 2 is over-using the word?

In teaching and research contexts, counts are given meaning when they are used with measurements of equal intervals. A measure common to this kind of question is time. During what period of time did the counts above occur? If both teachers were observed for the same amount of time, then Teacher 2 uses "okay" four times as often as Teacher 1. If Teacher 1 was observed for 10 minutes and Teacher 2 was observed for 40 minutes, however, there may be no difference in the frequency of their use of the word. If the tables are turned, and Teacher 1 was observed for 40 minutes while Teacher 2 was observed for 10 minutes, Teacher 2's use of "okay" would be seen as very extreme when compared to Teacher 1.

The example above uses labels, counts, and measurements to describe and compare the issue under study; that is, the use of a specific mannerism in the choral rehearsal. The labels simply replaced the teachers' names, the counts recorded the occurrences of the undesired mannerism, and the measure—time—offered an agreed-upon standard—minutes, against which to consider the counts. Without measurement, the counts alone would have been somewhat meaningless.

To continue with the illustration, let's say Teachers 1 and 2 took their combined choral ensemble to a choral festival and received a rating of "1." The number by itself says little unless you know that rating of "1" means "excellent." In fact, in many countries higher numbers suggest a better performance level than do lower numbers, so the rating could be misinterpreted if its meaning was not explained. Other types of misinterpretations have to do with percentages. If a school reported 60 students in its choral program, you have no point of comparison. Your reaction would be different for a school that had 800 students versus one that had 4,000. Clearly, context knowledge is important in the interpretation of numbers.

Professional musicians know the meaning of numbers when it comes to tuning their instruments or when they contract for a gig, budget for a concert, or estimate audience size for a grant. Music educators use numbers to document the success of their programs by reporting counts of students in their ensembles and concert attendance or by comparing their music students' test scores or grades with those of non-music students.

Now imagine you are told that Johnny received a test score of 120 or that Teacher X has spent 45 minutes rehearsing the same piece. Both observations report measurements: Time for rehearsal length and a score for a test that reflects certain measured values for given answers. To you as an uninitiated bystander, the test score by itself means little if you do not know the test that provided the score. Once the content of the test and the overall range of scores become known, then Johnny's score takes on meaning because you can place his score within the range of all possible scores. The story behind the data becomes concrete to you.

Similarly, saying only that Teacher X spent 45 minutes of rehearsal time on the same composition relays little information. Far more details need to be known before the statement becomes meaningful. Those details, when studied by a researcher, might include the content of the rehearsal or the actions/behaviors exhibited by the director and/or the students, the type of ensemble, the students' age, the school setting, the time of year (e.g., "crunch" time before the winter concert), or other contextual information important to tell the story.

What story it is, of course, depends on your research purpose, which can be derived from many different angles, rehearsal strategies just one of them. The more details you have identified, the more likely it is that your study accounts fully what you want to know. However, more details also provide more challenges.

One solution, often critiqued by those who question quantitative methods as being useful in music education research, is to narrow your questions in such a way that they clearly connect to extant studies in the field (a topic extensively dealt with in Chapters 2 to 4). When you read quantitative studies, look for—rather than skipping over—statistical symbols and tables that represent the answers to a given question. Tables and graphs represent the story each investigation has to tell. Make its meaning come to life so that it becomes the basis for your own research questions. One investigation builds on the other; each part by itself means much less than all of them together. As Phillips and Burbules (2000) state:

> Science does not attempt to describe the *total reality* (i.e., *all* the truths) about, say, a classroom; rather, it seeks to develop *relevant* true statements—ones that can serve to explain the situation that is of concern or that describe the causal relationships that are the focus of interest. (p. 39; emphasis in original)

Seen in this light, even questions that initially may seem inconsequential can yield meaningful information when viewed as a smaller piece in the much larger mosaic of knowledge to which all research questions, quantitative and qualitative, contribute. In all cases, however, knowledge about the function of numbers as labeling, counting, or measuring determines whether and how to ascertain that your observations were more than chance occurrences.

Basic Assumptions Underlying Empirical Measurements

Measurement is a matter of making a decision about what value is best attached to an observed phenomenon, be it in the realm of human ability, interest, and/or personality (Thorndike, 1997, p. 9; see also Thorndike & Thorndike-Christ, 2010, Chapter 2). Lefrançois (1999) calls such decision making *evaluation*, setting it apart from measurement. Either way, whether you quantitatively evaluate or measure something, choosing what value works best for any given observation requires repeated efforts of defining, clarifying and testing what you have selected as your particular traits of interest. These traits, once operationalized as mutually exclusive classes, rubrics, or categories, are called *variables*.

After an appropriate and meaningful numerical value has been attached to a variable, its presence can be documented, compared across individuals or groups of individuals, and tested for any possible effects it may have on other variables. For the results of such purposes to be valid, some background knowledge about statistical assumptions underlying quantitative research designs is necessary. Here, the following four issues are singled out:

- The nature of a normal curve;
- The difference between population and sample;
- The concept of probability;
- Hypothesis testing.

These concepts are important for planning and visualizing how a stated research purpose and planned methods fit a particular design. The next three chapters give you selected hands-on procedures necessary to reach that goal. The brief discussion of the above bullets introduces you to some of the underlying principles guiding those procedures.

The Normal Curve

According to the German mathematician Carl Friedrich Gauss (1777–1855), repeated independent measurements of an infinite number of human characteristics, objects, and/or behaviors are distributed over a continuum in a predictable way. That continuum is called the normal curve (also known as the bell curve, see Figure 9.1). Its main characteristic lies in the relationship between all measured individual scores and how they are distributed around the mean (the mathematical average of all scores).

The following assumption guides the model of a normal curve: If a population of properties, such as all female children born in 2011, were measured on a specific characteristic—for example, weight—and if these measurements were plotted as a histogram (a type of two-dimensional chart) with the weight on the horizontal base line in ounces

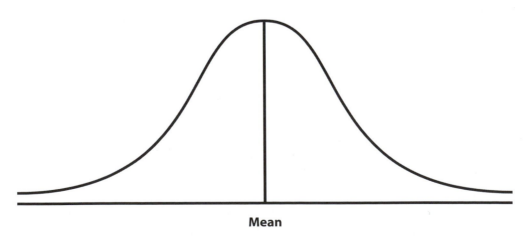

Mean

FIGURE 9.1   The Normal or Bell-Shaped Curve

and the frequency (number of humans) on the vertical line, the distribution of these various measurements would resemble a standard normal curve model. It represents individual measurements of an infinite number of people in relationship to the average of those measurements.

It would be nearly impossible to measure all individuals on the globe in order to test the accuracy of the model. This is why researchers have selected large groups of people, closely resembling and representative of the characteristics of all people, to obtain evidence in support of the theoretical model. Many independent measures of large samples of observations of individuals have supported the normal curve model with regard to most physical traits, such as height, weight, suit size, blood pressure, and length of life.

A controversial book by Herrnstein and Murray (1994), titled *The Bell Curve: Intelligence and Class Structure in American Life*, is the—possibly misguided—application of the normal curve in understanding human action/behavior as situated in a large distribution of individuals and groups of individuals. A humorous example of the fictitious misuse of the bell curve in human life is Garrison Keillor's radio show *A Prairie Home Companion*. In it, the town Lake Wobegon is described as a place "where all the women are strong, all the men are good looking, and all the children are above average."

The concept of averages, or *measures of central tendencies*, is an important aspect of the normal curve. It is described further in the next chapter, with visual examples and explanations of when, how, and why to use different types of averages with different types of observations. Here it suffices to say that an average calculated from the sum of all measures, divided by the total number of measurements, is called a *mean*. The mean tells you where to find the center-point of all scores. Knowing the location of the mean does not, however, tell you how all scores are dispersed, or spread around the mean score.

Research questions that suggest the use of quantitative methods ask where, how, and why a particular measurement may fall along the normal curve: Does it come close to the average of all measures or does it deviate greatly from that average? If an individual score falls repeatedly far away from the average, why does it do so? If someone measures consistently close to the average, is there some reason for that? Are there discernible and consistent patterns among all scores? A few of them? Answers to these and similar questions rely on and require repeated measures of the same observations to be certain that the measured values were not obtained by chance.

To make sure that more than one researcher can yield comparable results for a particular investigation, the research design and all methodological decisions in the published report must be painstakingly detailed. Full disclosure of all data is essential for any replication. However, acknowledging that "real world" experiences can never be fully repeated, two experiences may be very much alike, but they cannot be exactly the same. The passing of time causes all experiences to be unique even if they closely resemble each other. In addition, new knowledge gained by an individual during an interim period of time, as well as changes caused by natural or man-made events, are likely to produce conditions that affect all moments of life and, therefore, all experiences. Even under the best of circumstances, therefore, knowledge obtained through measured observations can never be fully verified but only *corroborated* against repeated, similar observations.

The construct of corroboration of evidence clearly affects the nature of measurement in quantitative research. As symbolic representations of observed experiences, even repeatedly obtained measures of similar actions or events can only be in support of prior observations, not verify them. The accuracy of appropriately designed quantitative findings is probable, but never certain.

The Relationship of a Population to Its Sample

In the technical language of measurement theory, the words *population* and *sample* carry precise meaning. In 1985, Moore defined population as "the entire group of objects about which information is desired" (p. 3). In current terminology, the definition would likely be modified to reflect what specifically is being studied: Persons, individuals, inhabitants, items, objects, or whatever other entities may be the subject of an investigation.

A sample is defined as a subset of that population. "Used to gain information about the whole" (p. 3), researchers employ various techniques of *sampling* to achieve this goal: From a defined population, a smaller group is selected and examined. The results of that examination are then used to generalize similar results for the total population from which the sample was drawn according to very specific *rules of randomization*. Note that any generalizations of results never exceed the population that generated the sample.

Imagine a box with a total of 10 disks. That total represents a population of disks because each disk is present. Now assume that in the box with 10 disks, there was a subset of five disks to be drawn from the total of the population of disks. That subset represents a sample of the population. How you draw the sample from the population is critical for coming up with findings that could be reported as being beyond chance. For instance, if you drew five disks from the population of 10 disks in such a manner that each disk had an equal chance of being selected, you could assume that the sample was representative of the population. Stated differently, when each object, individuals, or item in a population has an equal opportunity of being selected as part of the sample, that sample is considered to be a randomized sample.

Randomization procedures used to be tedious and somewhat prone to researcher mistakes. Computerized randomization procedures are much easier and more convenient. For example, "a free service offered to students and researchers" (Urbaniak & Plous, 2011), *Research Randomizer* allows you "to generate random numbers or assign participants to experimental conditions" (para. 2) (see Recommended Reading).

Randomization in survey research is crucial for obtaining valid results that are not generalized beyond the population from which the sample was drawn. Given the frequency of survey research in music education, it is advisable to become familiar with simple randomization procedures. You might even consider using a lengthy reference list (like the one in this book, for instance) and select at random a set of references for critical examination. Whatever you find for the subset—whether all spellings are correct, page numbers accurate, and content described in the text itself matches with what you find in the randomized sources—may be an indicator for what you could expect in all remaining references.

The Concept of Probability

Probability is a concern of all research but is expressed differently in the various modes of inquiry. Philosophers account for it with the process of inductive argumentation, in which arguments only corroborate the validity of a conclusion (see Chapter 5). In historical research (Chapter 6), the probable truth of evidence is established by procedures of verification. Confirmation of the data is sought by consulting public records, documents, or manuscripts. Such evidence allows the reader to trust the researcher that such consultations were carried out. In other words, the reader's own knowledge of the subject and the reader's perception of the researcher's integrity—together with documented evidence—are factors that lead to confidence in data accuracy.

In quantitative research, the confidence a researcher has in the accuracy of data is expressed in mathematical terms as *probabilities of chance*. There is a chance of error; that is, the data may not accurately represent what the researcher intended them to represent. Of course, there is also a chance that the data may accurately describe what was being observed. In neither case can you be certain that your research design fulfilled the assumption of normality. You therefore should make considerable efforts for all possible observations to have an equal chance of occurring. This effort is called *controlling for bias*.

The more your observations are what researchers call free of bias, the better the chance of your findings to be beyond chance. Since it is nearly impossible (other than in a laboratory situation) to eliminate all unwanted bias, be aware that the chances for findings to be in error may be rather great. Strong quantitative research designs reflect that possibility from the moment the research purpose is articulated. Statistical tests tell you how successful you were in that regard.

In the following chapters, you are introduced to a few of the many statistical tests available to determine the strength of your data. You can obtain additional (and more advanced) information when you take at least one additional course in quantitative research design and analysis, if not statistics in the social sciences or education. A researcher interested in questions requiring quantitative analyses should do no less.

Hypothesis Testing

A *hypothesis* is an educated guess about the outcome of each of the research problems or their specific sub-questions/problems. Whether or not it is feasible to make such an educated guess depends on the purpose of your investigation as being descriptive, relational, or experimental in nature. Hypothesis testing is called for only if you have reason to assume causality between two or more variables.

To illustrate, take the following fictitious research purpose (which you will re-visit in Chapter 12): "to investigate the relative effectiveness of two procedures for teaching sixth grade students to sing written music at sight." Two samples, Group A and Group B, are each selected at random from the larger population of sixth graders in a metropolitan school district. (Remember: In research language, "at random" means that all sixth graders in the school district had an equal chance of being selected.)

Each group contains 65 students. In statistical language, this is expressed as $N_A = 65$, $N_B = 65$. Group A is taught using Method Y; Group B is taught Method Z. The lesson content and the teacher are the same for both methods. Prior to instruction (in technical terms: the *treatment*), the students in both groups are tested for their ability in sight singing. Both groups have similar scores. It is hypothesized that differences in sight singing scores obtained after the completion of the treatment will make the relative effectiveness of the two methods evident. Those differences are tested by comparing the means of the two sets of scores. Following an equal time of instruction, each group is administered the same sight singing test again to assess any additional amount of learning that may have taken place under each teaching method.

The sub-purposes are: (1) to determine the learning outcomes for each of the methods; and (2) to compare their relative effectiveness. Statistical tests are to be utilized to estimate the effect of the two treatments. Three outcomes (or hypotheses) are possible: (a) there will be no difference in the relative effectiveness of the two methods; (b) Method Z will be more effective than Method Y; and (c) Method Y will be more effective than Method Z. Each of the three options is an assertion of a possible outcome of the study. The researcher hopes to find support for one of the three possibilities. Note that the study had one purpose, two sub-problem/questions, and three (statistical) hypotheses.

Statistical hypotheses may be stated in terms of direction of outcome or in terms of no direction. For example, the statement that Method Y will be more effective than Method Z reflects a direction of an expected outcome; the statement that there will be no difference between Method Y and Z does not anticipate a particular direction. The latter is called a *null hypothesis.* It assumes that the treatments will not have a significant effect on the performance of the groups. Any differences measured would be within the range of chance.

Empiricists and statisticians tend to be cautious people, and their language, while precise, is often couched in double negatives. Rather than assume differences between treatments, statisticians prefer to state at the outset that there are no significant differences between the treatment groups. The null hypothesis states that position. If the null hypothesis *cannot* be rejected, statistical tests are not warranted and any further statistical testing becomes unnecessary. Further testing takes place only when the null hypothesis *is rejected.*

In general, a researcher rejects a statistical hypothesis if the probability of its occurrence is so low that it may be considered to have occurred due to chance. Thus, the result of testing a statistical hypothesis does not offer irreversible proof for the acceptance or rejection of the hypothesis; it merely provides a probability of acceptance or rejection within set and restricted limits. The researcher has control over these limits of accepted probability levels.

In news media reports about research results of popular interest, it seems to have become customary to refer to any form of quantitatively gathered research data as experiment; a misnomer by standards of measurement theory. The term "experimental" is reserved for those designs that purposefully allow testing for causality. A purpose statement that carries the word "effect" in it would signal to readers that the researcher intended to establish such clear and strong connection between two or more variables.

Unless you work in a research lab where you can control the environment, true causation is difficult to establish in music education. Naturalistic settings like a classroom or rehearsal hall do not lend themselves well to controlling for unwanted bias in the many intervening variables that make instruction enjoyable on the one hand and unpredictable on the other. This is why research in the behavioral sciences relies heavily on what is known as *ex post facto* (Latin for "after the fact") and so-called *quasi-experimental* designs.

Projects whose variables are related but do not necessarily cause each other might be called relational. Their language should imply nothing more than that connections between variables might be possible. Investigations that focus on the detailed enumeration and description of specific variables in particular contexts should be referred to as descriptive-quantitative. Language to articulate the research purpose should be restricted to such terms as "describe," "observe," or "survey."

Statistical Assumptions and Design Decisions

Statisticians draw a distinction between tests in which assumptions can or cannot be made about a population or sample being "normally" distributed. In research language, you need to know whether the individuals you selected as your participants are representative of a clearly defined universe of people in which everyone had an equal chance of becoming part of the group under study. In cases where you can make that assumption, you select what are called *parametric* statistics. "Para" is Greek for "at or to one side of, beside, side by side" ("Para," 2011); "metric" comes from "meter" and means measured (as opposed to counted). "Parametric" statistics are based on the assumption that there is a sameness of certain characteristics in the various samples/populations that your data are based on. That sameness of sample characteristics is also called *homogeneity of variance*.

The information provided in the next three chapters remains largely in the realm of parametric statistics because these are more powerful and more commonly selected than what are known as distribution-free, or *non-parametric*, statistics. The latter are applicable when you know next to nothing about the shape of the curve under which a sample of people or a set of observations may fall, or when you know for a fact that the your data do not meet the required assumptions. This is largely the case when a sample has not been drawn according to accepted randomization procedures; when the sample is very small; or when you have reason to assume that its distribution might be biased beyond chance toward one side of the normal curve. The following chapters show how to determine whether normality for the frequency distribution of your data may be assumed.

There is an ongoing debate among statisticians about whether parametric statistics are sufficiently robust to analyze data that may not be normally distributed. The liberal view holds that basic parametric tests are generally preferable over non-parametric measurements. More conservatively inclined statisticians might counter, however, that non-parametric statistics should be considered more suitable for research in music classroom settings where sample sizes are too small to allow any accurate assumptions about their score distribution. Appendix K contains examples for both parametric and non-parametric statistical tests. They are excerpted from Motulsky (1995), corroborated by similarly comprehensive compilations in Asmus and Radocy (1992), Field (2005, back cover), and Pallant (2007, pp. 116–117). Each of those sources are highly recommended for learning further details about quantitative research methods spoken about in this book.

Most researchers prefer to use parametric tests whenever possible because of the greater variety of tests available and because the tests are better able to discern small differences between samples of subjects. The ability to assess small differences within a sample or between several samples mandates parametric statistical tests because they are more likely to lead the researcher to reject the null hypothesis when, indeed, it *should* be rejected. Parametric tests are also able to assess larger samples and to "squeeze" more information out of the data.

Quantitative Research in Music Education

In the early 20th century, many social scientists, among them psychologists and educators, adopted Gauss' theoretical model of the normal curve to answer questions about the nature of human behavior in its many forms. Psychologist Carl Seashore (1866–1949) was one of the first American researchers to quantify the nature of musical ability (also called talent or aptitude) in the form of identifiable and measurable traits, such as pitch discrimination and rhythmic acuity. Known as the *Seashore Test of Musical Ability* (1919), it attracted the interest of many music educators and began what continues to be a formidable history of quantitative research traditions in music education.

Later efforts building on the early "tests and measurements movement in music" (Mark, 1992, p. 50) resulted in the application of test theory to research on instructional effectiveness in classrooms and rehearsal halls. Such applications included the development of observation forms of many kinds by which to examine the effectiveness of specific instructional strategies according to numerous sets of different variables. Many of those efforts have been described, among others, by Froehlich (1984, 1995), Madsen, Greer and Madsen (1975), Madsen and Prickett (1987) and in numerous chapters of the 1992 *Handbook of Research on Music Teaching and Learning*.

Behavioristic models in particular seemed well suited to the observation of extant teaching and learning patterns and their relationship to effectiveness measures. Criticism about such behavioristic models, however, grew as qualitative research methods (see Chapters 7 and 8) gained in popularity and importance. Nonetheless, quantitative research in music education, vastly expanded since the middle of the 20th century, is ongoing and increasingly sophisticated (e.g., Colwell, 2002, 2006, 2011; Demorest, 2011; Duke, 2005; Duke, Simmons, & Cash, 2009; Hodges & Sebald, 2011; Juslin & Sloboda, 2010; Sloboda, 2005). Descriptive as well as experimental designs have been applied to the study of human cognition and musical perception and the development of theories related to motivation and learning. Quantitative methods have been used to test aesthetic theories and contribute to the observation of performance physiological and psychological constructs. Such fields as neuroscience and performing arts medicine have become more prominent in music education as well, strengthening efforts to connect the arts with the sciences in systematic ways.

The doors for further and more rigorous testing of many theories are wide open. This, at least, would be the position of those quantitatively inclined empiricists who believe in the power of scientifically gathered and tested knowledge for advancing instructional practices. Their belief in "the objective application of the senses or of reason" (Reimer, 1992, p. 27) subscribe to what philosophically may be called positivistic empiricism. It holds that only observed and measured data, tested and replicated for their reliability and validity, should become the basis of reasoning, making inferences, and drawing conclusions about specific events, human behavior, emotions, and affects.

A desire to separate scientifically tested knowledge from "other" forms of knowing led Heller and O'Connor (2002) to suggest that only historical and empirical–quantitative studies should be called research (p. 1089). In their view, philosophy and qualitative work would fall under the broader term of "scholarship." Arguing the validity of Heller and O'Connor's position is not the subject of this book or even these chapter(s). You may, however, choose to debate it after you have familiarized yourself with the step-by-step descriptions in the following chapters of turning observations into variables, variables into measures, and measures into analyzed research results.

Unlike Heller and O'Connor and other positivistic researchers like them, so-called postmodernists (and some post–positivists) agree with those researchers that all knowledge is "conjectural" at best. Measurements about what humans know and act on are "supported by the strongest (if imperfect) warrants we can muster at the time . . . always subject to reconsideration" (Phillips & Burbules, 2000, pp. 29–30). Quantitative research methods contribute to those warrants in a way different from qualitative methods. Because "knowledge claims are always *circumstantial*" (p. 31; emphasis in the original), the debate on "whose knowledge" to accept as the best and most trustworthy or reliable and valid, is ongoing.

Chapter Summary

1. Quantitative models in the empirical mode of inquiry are based on underlying statistical assumptions about the distribution of individual measures to their average (mean).
2. Numbers convey meaning when their characteristics as labels, counts, or measurements are understood.

3. Several assumptions must be fulfilled before the application of statistics to the analysis of quantified data can be considered meaningful. They derive from knowledge about the nature of a normal curve, the difference between population and sample, the concepts of probability and hypothesis testing, and the parametric or non-parametric distribution of scores.

4. Quantitative designs should take into consideration those very principles.

Topics for Further Exploration

1. Reasons for and against the argument that only quantitative or historical methods constitute research.

2. Use of the terms "objective" and "subjective" in research.

3. Grading as a form of measurement: What construct(s) are being measured? What does the score mean?

Suggested Assignments

1. Go back to the observations you made early in the research class about what you saw happening in NY Times Square. Select five such observations and break them down into *measurable* variables. From those variables select five and determine how you could best define each variable. Decide on a way by which to express the essence of that definition numerically in such a way that you can record each of the five variables in a systematic way.

2. Find a recent, accessible quantitative research article in *Update: Applications of Research in Music Education* and, to the best of your understanding of the numbers used in the entire text, write out a summary of the descriptions and/or relationships between the persons and variables studied.

3. Compile a list of rationales for and against grading as a valid measurement of student achievement. Sort out for yourself which purposes of grading seem valid to your goals as a teacher.

4. Make a list of ratings other than grading that you use in your professional life. What do they mean to you? In what context would you consider them well used or, in contrast, abusive?

Recommended Reading

Allen, M. J., & Yen, W. M. (2002). *Introduction to measurement theory.* Long Grove, IL: Waveland Press.

Demorest, S. (2001). *Teaching sight-singing in the choral rehearsal.* New York: Oxford University Press.

George, D., & Mallery, P. (2003). *SPSS for Windows step by step: A simple guide and reference. 11.0 update* (4th ed.). Boston: Allyn & Bacon.

Kenny, A. (2006), *Evaluation: Emergence, mode of inquiry, theory & practice (November 10, 2006).* Available at SSRN: http://ssrn.com/abstract=946402 or doi:10.2139/ssrn.946402. Retrieved January 16, 2012.

Moore, D. S., & Notz, W. J. (2008). *Statistics: Concepts and controversies* (7th ed.). New York: W. H. Freeman.

Motulsky, H. J. (2010). *Intuitive biostatistics* (2nd ed., completely revised). New York: Oxford University Press.

Shultz, K. S., & Whitney, D. J. (2005). *Measurement theory in action: Case studies and exercises.* Thousand Oaks, CA: Sage Publications, Inc.

ten

Understanding Descriptive Statistics

Debbie Rohwer

This chapter highlights the following concepts:

- Numbers in descriptive research:
  - level of measurement;
  - central tendency and variability;
- Types of descriptive studies:
  - survey research;
  - frequency count studies;
- Inputting data into a statistical program;
- Descriptive statistics in the classroom.

Descriptive statistics are used to summarize quantitative data. This chapter will discuss the basics of descriptive statistic choices for research, as well as how descriptive statistics can be used to improve classroom tests.

Introduction

While there are many types of research studies that describe phenomena, they can be simplified into those that describe what exists through an in-depth, contextual, "picture-in-words" of the phenomena (i.e., qualitative research, see Chapters 7–8) and those that describe what exists through numbers (i.e., quantitative research). In addition to descriptive studies, there are also other types of quantitative studies. Correlational studies look at the relationship of one observed phenomenon to another (see Chapter 11), and ex post facto and experimental studies look at differences between groups (see Chapter 12). All quantitative studies, however, use descriptive statistics to provide context to the overall picture of the data before using relationship or difference statistics.

Teachers commonly use numbers as a part of their classroom activities: whether it be to rate or rank students based on a playing test, or to report to the administration the number of students attending all-state band, or to ask the students to respond to questions about their own understanding of classroom content. Researchers who use numbers do so for some of the same basic reasons as teachers: To come up with information on such matters as skill level, or knowledge level, or frequency of an activity, or perceptions of musical learners. All of these data gathering and reporting scenarios start with a large data set that is then distilled into a descriptive, concise, manageable, and comparable format: a number.

The most important concept is that the purpose of the research must guide: (1) the way that the answers are obtained; and (2) the form of those answers. If your goal is to get at a contextual understanding of a setting, then numbers may not be appropriate to the purposes of that study. If, however, you have 1,000 responses to a specific question, and want to find one answer that can summarize the 1,000 responses best, then a number and specifically, a descriptive statistic may be very appropriate.

Numbers in Descriptive Research

Descriptive, quantitative studies gather data to answer questions such as "how often," or "how much." Understanding how to obtain answers to these types of questions, as well as relationship and difference questions in other types of research, necessitates a basic understanding of numerical concepts and the limitations that exist when choosing certain question formats. This chapter focuses on two such basic numerical concepts: (1) level of measurement and (2) central tendency and variability.

Level of Measurement

As a Ph.D. student who specializes in studio violin, *Christy* was weighing how she could ask elementary students about their instrument preference before they made the decision to join an ensemble in middle school. Did they want to play a string instrument? She discussed some of her question options with *Prof. E.*, such as her first question: What kind of instrument do you want to play next year? (With the possible responses being orchestra instrument or band instrument.) Or, she might want to provide more response options for the students, with possibilities being string, wind, brass, percussion. Or, she could list every instrument in orchestras and bands and ask the students to mark the one they preferred the most. Christy also considered that she may want the students to give an order to their preference for the instruments. For instance, she could ask them to rank a list of instruments in the order that would document their preference for playing the instruments. That way, she would know more than just the one they preferred most. Or, she could ask the students to specifically rate each instrument based on how much they would prefer to play each one.

Prof. E. told Christy that all of these options were viable, and she would have to weigh which format would address the research question best, as well as issues such as the students' ability to comprehend the question format and how she wanted to analyze the data. In order to understand data analysis choices, Prof. E. had to describe to Christy the basic number-related issues that might aid her in any item format decision.

When choosing a question format, begin by looking at the many possible ways a question can be constructed (as an example, see Figure 13.1 on page 252). Christy's first questions have response options that are called *nominal* (and later, in Chapter 12, we will also use the synonymous term, "categorical"). The first question has two response options: orchestra or band. Both options are "names" that have no inherent order, and the students would mark one answer and leave the other answer blank. Christy's next questions, with possible response options of "string, wind, brass, percussion" or "listing all instruments for the students to choose one" are also at the nominal level of measurement.

Christy moves to a different level of measurement when she ponders an ordered response format. In having respondents *rank* a list of instruments, Christy is using a format with an *ordinal* level of measurement. The ordered responses have a hierarchy to them, but the distance between the numbers is not equidistant; that is, someone who ranks cello first and bass second is only documenting order, not how much more they prefer cello over bass. And lastly, Christy weighs a third level of measurement format when she states that the students could *rate* each instrument based on how much they would prefer to play each one. With ratings, the specific distance between response options is considered to be equal; that is, for a 1–10 rating on preference for playing viola, if one respondent documents a 5 and another respondent documents a 10, Christy can note that the second respondent favors viola five equal spaced points more than the first respondent does. A rating would constitute an *interval* level of measurement.

Each of these *level of measurement* options leads to a choice about how the data can be analyzed. While the purpose of the study and the pragmatics of the respondents' ability to answer the questions have to be the primary guiding principles in question choice and design, it can be useful to weigh the amount of information you can obtain through the format of your question. Just as Christy demonstrates in her pondering, all of these questions may address the same topic, but the level of detail in the responses will differ.

Central Tendency and Variability

Taking an average of the responses in order to represent the complete data set with one representative number is a common way researchers analyze data. These "averages" are called *central tendencies*, and while they all provide a representative number, they do so in different ways. The *mode* is calculated for a nominal question by finding the most common response from the complete data set. The *median* is calculated for an ordinal question by ordering the responses from smallest to largest and taking the "middle" response. The *mean* is calculated for an interval question by using a traditional average: adding all responses together and dividing by the number of responses in the data set.

For Christy's nominal question of orchestra or band, then, if 47 people answer orchestra and 32 answer band, then the mode would be orchestra, the most common response. The median documents the middle response of the data set, so for Christy's instrument ranking question, she may get a subset of responses that documents the ranking of violin in the following way: 1, 3, 4, 4, 5. The middle response for these data would be 4. The mean could be used to document the answers for Christy's rating question. If, for instance, students had given responses on a 1–10 scale for how much they wanted to play violin, and a subset of the responses was 1, 2, 5, 8, 9, then by adding these responses (25) and dividing by the number of responses (5), the mean would be 5.

The strength of the mean is that it represents all numbers in the data set through the averaging procedure. That being said, there are cases where there may be extreme scores in the data set that can artificially skew the central tendency. This can happen, for instance, if you are asking salary information of respondents and almost all respondents are middle-class level, but you have one multi-millionaire. The multi-millionaire will artificially raise the salary average for the group. Instead of the mean, the median might be the more appropriate central tendency to use in this case, since it documents the middle number instead of averaging all the numbers. If your question is asked at the interval level of measurement, you always have the choice of using a central tendency other than the mean (i.e., the median or mode), if it provides the most representative number for the data. If your question is at the ordinal level, you can choose the median or mode. If your question is at the nominal level, your only central tendency option is the mode.

In addition to central tendency measures, *variability* statistics are calculated to represent the extent to which responses vary across the participants. For nominal level questions no variability statistic is documented, because the number that is used for the computer analysis of nominal level data is only a coding mechanism. For instance, orchestra might be coded 1 and band might be coded 0 for Christy's study, but the number itself is meaningless. For questions with ordinal level response formats, *percentiles* can be added that show the point where 25% of the ordinal responses lie, and the point where 75% of the ordinal responses lie so as to give more detail as to how the responses spread.

For questions with interval level response formats, *range* is added to document the distance between the highest and lowest scores, and *standard deviation* is added to give context as to how much the scores vary around the mean. A large standard deviation relative to the mean says that there is more spread to the scores, while a small standard deviation relative to the mean says that the scores tend to group together around the mean; a standard deviation of 0 means that all the scores are the same as the mean (see Figure 10.1).

A large standard deviation, then, means more variability and less agreement in responses. So, for instance, with Christy's subset of scores as listed above (1, 2, 5, 8, 9) the standard deviation is 3.5, while a different subset of scores (4, 5, 5, 5, 6) has the exact same mean of 5, but the standard deviation is much smaller at .7; Christy's scores show a much greater spread than the second set of scores.

The following descriptive research example from Dale's master's thesis demonstrates the use of descriptive statistics.

Dale was interested in surveying students and parents about instructional choices in the school district's music programs. He had found that parents and students alike were positive about scheduling (M = 4.98, SD = .10), trips (M = 4.82, SD = .23), and uniforms (M = 4.79, SD = .19), but the students (M = 2.10, SD = .86) perceived the classroom technology less favorably than did the parents (M = 4.01, SD = .35).

In these findings, the means provide a strength order to the responses, with the most positive responses on average being reported for scheduling (mean of 4.98) and the least positive responses on average being reported by the students for technology (mean of 2.10). In this scenario, the smallest standard deviation (i.e., the most agreement in responses) was found for scheduling (standard deviation of .10) and the largest standard deviation (i.e., the least agreement in responses) was found for student technology responses (standard deviation of .86).

Researchers have to consider level of measurement as an issue related to the clarity and purpose of questionnaire items. *Likert-type scales* provide a question format that is easy to construct and easily answered by respondents. While the level of measurement for Likert-type scales has been debated (see discussions in Ghiselli, Campbell, & Zedeck, 1981; Kline, 2005; Lubke & Muthen, 2004; Spector, 1976, 1980), textbooks tend to document affective response options (such as strongly agree, agree, neutral, disagree, strongly disagree) as being ordinal in nature. If used with behavioral response categories (such as always, frequently, sometimes, rarely, and never) there may be greater justification

Level of Measurement	Central Tendency	Variability
Interval	Mean	Range & Standard Deviation
Ordinal	Median	Percentile
Nominal	Mode	--

FIGURE 10.1 Summary: Level of Measurement, Central Tendency, and Variability

to accept Likert-type questions as interval level data, and with interval level questions a mean, range, and standard deviation can be calculated. As a side note to add to the debate, universities across the country provide individual item means for teacher evaluation items using affective Likert-type scales. Suffice it to say that you may see studies in the field of music education that analyze Likert-type questions as ordinal or interval level data (see Figure 10.2).

Types of Descriptive Studies

Survey research and frequency count investigations are two common types of descriptive studies found in the field of music education. Both types of studies aim to describe, with survey research describing by obtaining responses from individuals, and frequency count investigations describing by coding behaviors of individuals.

Survey Research

Survey research often follows the procedure of sampling a feasible number of participants to whom a researcher gives a questionnaire in the hope of generalizing the results to a larger group of individuals who are much like the sampled individuals. This procedure works well when you have a complete list of all people in the group to which you as a researcher would like to generalize (called the *target population*), and then you can choose a sampling procedure that allows everyone on the list to have a chance of being in the sample (called *probability sampling*).

Choosing the Sample

Examples of probability sampling procedures are *simple random sampling* where individuals are chosen from a list at random, or *stratified sampling* where individuals are randomly sampled from subgroups that need to be represented (such as voice part or gender). Sometimes probability sampling is not feasible because of pragmatic issues such as a population list not existing, and if that is the case, then alternative procedures

Behavioral Likert:

I practice using a metronome.

Always   Frequently   Sometimes   Rarely   Never

Affective Likert:

I feel that the ensemble uniforms in our school are attractive.

Strongly Agree   Agree   Neutral   Disagree   Strongly Disagree

FIGURE 10.2   Behavioral and Affective Likert-Type Questions

may need to be considered, such as *purposive sampling*, where you make a professional judgment concerning which individuals should be in the sample, or *convenience sampling*, where you take those participants who are readily available to you. Both of these non-probability sampling procedures, however, greatly impact readers' ability to generalize to a larger population beyond those in the study itself. Whether you choose to conduct a study through mailed questionnaire or online survey software systems such as SurveyMonkey or Zoomerang, the sampling procedures should be carefully weighed so that generalizability to the target population of interest is feasible.

Validity and Reliability

Before the questionnaire is sent out to the sample, you follow procedures to ensure that the items on the questionnaire are appropriate, clear, and cover the content well (i.e., valid), and that respondents answer the questions without excessive error (i.e., consistently/reliably). Types of validity found in music education studies are: *content validity*, *criterion validity*, and *construct validity*, and types of reliability are *internal consistency*, *test-retest*, and *interjudge reliability*.

Designing a Questionnaire

In designing a viable survey research instrument, it is important that the purposes of the study align specifically with the questions being asked. One way to learn to do this is to pay close attention to how survey items are worded in published studies inside and outside of the field of music education. Ensuring the comfort, anonymity, and confidentiality of the participants is also important in the process of planning how questions will be asked of the participants and how results will be reported. The Institutional Review Board (IRB) serves as an external set of eyes to ensure that procedures are ethical and that the protocols inform research participants of their rights in the study. Researchers who plan their studies with clarity and ethics in mind will be far ahead in their efforts to make a quality measurement tool.

Once the questions are written, the most common procedure for ensuring that a questionnaire (or other "test") will be useable and appropriate is to send it to a panel of experts for feedback on its content. You might include feedback prompts asking something like "Which questions on the questionnaire are superfluous to the topic that is being measured: teacher perceptions of technology?" and "Which questions should be added so as to address more completely the topic that is being measured: teacher perceptions of technology?" The panel then gives subjective feedback that is used to improve the content validity of the questionnaire.

Field Testing

Following the content validity procedure, it is common to ensure the clarity of the items on the questionnaire by asking a small group of individuals to discuss the item content with the researcher. This process is called a *field test*. It is best if the participants in the field test are of the same basic age and demographic as the respondents planned for the main study. This ensures the greatest potential for generalizability to the main study sample. The discussion with the field test participants often centers on issues such as the clarity of the instructions or whether certain acronyms or terms might be understood by the respondents. After the questionnaire has been adjusted based on content validity and field test input, the next step is to estimate the reliability of the questionnaire through a *pilot test*.

Pilot Testing

For reliability, you chose a group of individuals who are of the same basic age and demographic as the respondents who will be in the main study, and these individuals answer the questions on the questionnaire. A researcher may choose to give the questionnaire to the same pilot group of individuals twice to check for consistency of individual responses over time (called *test-retest reliability*). This procedure would be valuable if the questionnaire results were going to document responses on individual items. For instance, on a questionnaire of perceptions of technology, a researcher may want to provide means for individual questions, such as perceived value of smart-board, or Finale, or other technological devices or applications.

On a questionnaire where the items are summed to get one number as an overall score of, for instance, perception of technology, the summed number could be used to describe the extent of support for a general topic. In this case, a higher summed score would mean that the respondent valued technology more than someone who had a lower summed score; this type of reliability check is called *internal consistency*, with the most common type of internal consistency being *Cronbach's alpha*.

Administering the Questionnaire

After a researcher has "tested the test" (in this case, a questionnaire) thoroughly to ensure that it is as valid and reliable as possible, the next step is the administration of the questionnaire to the main study sample. Once responses to the questionnaire have been obtained, you as the researcher would need to determine the coverage of the information that was received: From those to whom the questionnaire was sent, how many responded? Unless an extremely high response is garnered, some form of *follow-up* should be considered in order to be able to describe the complete picture. If, for instance, only half of those who are sent a questionnaire respond, how do you know that their responses represent the full sample? What if those who do not respond are actually very much against the topic and those who do respond are in favor of the topic? In such a case, the incomplete information that is obtained from the initial half of the participants will not accurately represent the opinion of the whole.

Dillman (2007) advocates a series of follow-up reminders, further followed by a sampling of the non-respondents. This sub-group can be used to compare the non-respondent answers to the respondent answers. If the responses do not differ across the non-respondents and the respondents, then you have a more defensible stance that the results can be defended as representing the complete sample.

Frequency Count Studies

In addition to survey research studies, there are also descriptive studies that describe how often behaviors occur. These studies use *frequency counts* to document the extent of behavior.

As an experienced teacher interested in effective teaching, *Michelle* decided to investigate the amount and type of feedback that expert teachers provided to their students. She observed 10 expert teachers and found that the teachers most commonly gave many short, specific feedback statements that were directive for improvement, and then notified the students when they had achieved the goal that was set. Over the rehearsals Michelle viewed, the expert teachers demonstrated an average of 15 of these directive-followed-by-notification cycles in each rehearsal (range of 9–23, SD = 4.88).

In this example, Michelle noted that the expert teachers in her sample had a common trend in completing directive-followed-by-notification teaching cycles. The data from this study were tallies of the number of times that each teacher completed a cycle in a class period. The number of cycles documented in this study ranged from 9 to 23, with two teachers demonstrating 12 cycles. Table 10.1 shows the data for the frequency of complete teaching cycles from the 10 expert teachers.

Before the study was conducted, Michelle checked whether her measurement tool (in this case a coding sheet that documented how often a certain behavior occurred) corresponded to the teaching cycles reported in the relevant literature. She also had a panel of experts evaluate her coding sheet for its representativeness of teaching cycles. Checking against relevant literature and obtaining expert evaluations were steps to ensure that her understanding of the concept she was coding was accurate and complete; in short, that the tool had content validity. Next, she did a pilot test of the measurement tool

TABLE 10.1   Frequency Count of Complete Teaching Cycles

Cycles	Frequency	Percent
9.00	1	10.0
1.00	1	10.0
12.00	2	20.0
13.00	1	10.0
14.00	1	10.0
19.00	1	10.0
20.00	1	10.0
21.00	1	10.0
23.00	1	10.0
Total	10	100.0

by observing and coding a set of teacher behaviors using two observers: herself and a second qualified observer. The pilot showed her if there was agreement across the two sets of observations. This procedure assessed *interjudge reliability*, a measure that documents the consistency of a measurement tool across observers.

Studies using frequency counts can be conducted easily in any classroom by videotaping rehearsals/activities and then using a coding rubric to determine frequency of the specific behaviors of interest. For instance, you could document your students' amount of off-task behavior, or you could document your own eye contact frequency when conducting through video analysis. Formal or informal investigations such as these can be completed to guide instructional choices and improve teaching.

Inputting Data into a Statistical Program

Once data have been obtained from a sample, you need to input the data into a statistical program to calculate the appropriate statistics. One of the most commonly used statistical programs in the field of music education is SPSS (Statistical Package for the Social Sciences, version 19, as found at SPSS.com). SPSS is only one option from the many statistical programs that are available, but by seeing the input process for one example program, you will be able to envision the numerical and format issues that may transfer to any program. The example below takes a small sample of questionnaire data and describes the input process for illustration purposes.

Question 1, Demographic: What is your gender?
Answers: Male, Male, Female, Female, Female

Because the data for this question are nominal level, you assign a number to male (0 for instance) and a number to female (1 for instance), even though the number itself is for grouping only, and has no numerical meaning in itself. Do not be alarmed if your program adds decimals to the numbers; the coding of male and female remains the same. The inputted data for these five responses would look like the following, with each person's response to the gender question being a row (so Bob may be first across and Fred may be second across, etc.):

Gender

1. 0.00
2. 0.00
3. 1.00
4. 1.00
5. 1.00

The next step with this nominal level question would be to choose a central tendency and variability statistic from the descriptive choices. To do this, go to the "Analyze" drop-down and then choose Descriptive Statistics and Frequencies. Place the variable "gender" in the "Variable(s)" box by clicking on "Gender" and the curved arrow in the middle of

TABLE 10.2 SPSS Results for Nominal Data Input of Five Responses

	Statistics	
Gender		
Number	Valid Responses	5
	Missing Data	0
Mode		1.00
Range		1.00
Minimum		.00
Maximum		1.00

the box. From there click on "Statistics." Under "Central Tendency" choose Mode. Under "Dispersion" choose "Range," "Minimum," and "Maximum" as the statistic choices. Then click "Continue," and "OK." The resulting graphic will look similar to Table 10.2.

From this readout, then, you can ascertain that there were five valid responses and no missing data. The most common response was female (1). While the table documents that the responses ranged from the minimum numeric response of 0 (male) to the maximum response of 1 (female), range is not listed for nominal level data since the number is simply a place marker for grouping purposes.

Question 2, Behavioral Likert-type: I use a metronome when I practice my band music.
Possible Answers: Always, Frequently, Sometimes, Rarely, Never

Because the data for this question may be considered interval level, a number represents the strength of the responses from positive to negative: always (5), frequently (4), sometimes (3), rarely (2), never (1). The input data for these five responses would look like the following, with each person's response to the question being a row (so Sally's "Always" response would be first across, and Fred's "Frequently" response would be second across, etc.):

Practice

1. 5.00
2. 4.00
3. 5.00
4. 3.00
5. 2.00

The next step with this interval level question would be to choose a central tendency and variability statistic from the descriptive choices. To do this, go to the "analyze"

TABLE 10.3 SPSS Results for Interval Data: Central Tendency and Variability

	N	Range	Minimum	Maximum	Mean	Std. Deviation
			Descriptive Statistics			
Practice	5	3.00	2.00	5.00	3.8000	1.30384

drop-down and then choose "descriptive" with mean, standard deviation, minimum, maximum, and range as the statistic choices (see Table 10.3).

From this readout, you can ascertain that there were five valid responses. The central response was 3.8 with the most negative response being 2 (Rarely) and the most positive response being 5 (Always), and a spread around the mean of 1.3.

Descriptive Statistics in the Classroom

An understanding of how data can be obtained, structured, and analyzed is useful when publishing a research study, but it can also help teachers in the analysis of their own teaching behaviors. A descriptive quantitative study can measure time use in music classes, such as how experienced and novice teachers use instructional time. Informal questions can be asked, such as, "Am I spending too much time talking?" and "Is the content of my teacher talk serving an instructional purpose?" Descriptive inquiries can serve as important research-based questions that every teacher can ask and investigate in their own classroom.

Teachers can also use descriptive statistics to analyze and improve teacher-constructed tests, not necessarily for research study publication, but for improvement of their teaching and their understanding of student progress. This analysis can help them in knowing whether certain test items are successful in determining who knows the content and who does not. If, for instance, a test question is missed by the high scoring people on the test, but the low scorers on the test happen to get that test question correct, then the test item may not be serving the test well, and may not be giving the teacher accurate information about what the students know; that is, the low scorers may have guessed extremely well on that item, and/or the high scorers could have been distracted by one of the other possible responses.

You can investigate how easy or how difficult an item on a test is by using the formula as shown in Figure 10.3.

The closer to 1 the difficulty value is, the easier the item is and the closer to 0 that the difficulty value is, the more difficult the item is. So if 100 students took a test and all 100 of them got the first question correct, then the difficulty value for that item would be 1 (easy), whereas if only 10 out of the 100 got the second item correct, the difficulty value would be .10 (difficult). The variability of test scores is maximized when the difficulty values of a test average .5. In other words, mid-level difficulty items usually have the highest power to *discriminate* between those who know and those who do not know the content.

How well an item discriminates between high and low scorers on the test can be checked by analyzing the responses to individual questions for the high test scorers and

$$\text{Difficulty value for an item} \quad = \quad \frac{\text{\# of persons answering item correctly}}{\text{Total \# of persons taking the test}}$$

FIGURE 10.3 Formula for Determining Item Difficulty

for the low test scorers. You put the tests in order from highest to lowest score and then choose one item to analyze. Then, you tally the number of test takers who answered the item correctly. Lastly, you subtract the number of correct responses for the lower half tests from the number of correct responses for the upper half tests, and divide by the number of test takers in one of the groups (i.e., half of the class). This analysis is completed for each item on the test. The formula for this procedure for each item is shown in Figure 10.4.

If there are many more high-scoring test takers who get the item correct than lower scoring test takers, then the item will discriminate well (ideally with a discrimination value above .4). If, however, more lower scoring test takers get the item correct than the high scoring test takers, then the item will not distinguish well between the knowledgeable and the less knowledgeable (with the poorest items in need of elimination having values below .2).

If the test items are, for instance, multiple-choice items on a music theory test, you can further analyze how the students responded to each possible option out of the four choices provided. An ideal question would have those who knew the answer choosing the correct response and those who did not know the answer choosing randomly between the possible responses. When looking at the spread of how enticing the wrong answers were to test takers, you can divide the number of *distractor* (wrong) item choices by the total number of those answering the item incorrectly. For instance, if 30 people got number 1 wrong and there were three incorrect options, then ideally the 30 would be equally spread, with 10 on each incorrect response. If that is not the case, you can analyze which response options are, perhaps, distracting too many test takers, and conversely, which response options are not distracting enough test takers for the response options to be useful.

The most important next step would be to see how many upper-half, high-scoring test takers and how many lower-half, low-scoring test takers were torn away from the correct answer by each incorrect choice. If only lower-half test takers were drawn to the incorrect responses, and those lower-half test takers were drawn equally across the three wrong answers, then that is ideal. If, however, a large number of upper-half test takers were drawn to a wrong choice item, then that incorrect response may be too close to the correct response, thereby distracting, too well, the test takers who knew the material.

A close analysis of teacher-designed test items can lead to an improved understanding of the classroom content that needs more explanation, as well as a more complete understanding of the quality of the test itself. The task of making a useful test, and refining it so that it does the best possible job of helping teachers help those who are struggling with the course content should be a primary goal for all teachers.

$$\text{Discrimination value for an item} = \frac{\text{\# correct from upper half - \# correct from lower half}}{\text{\# of half of the respondents}}$$

FIGURE 10.4   Formula for Determining Item Discrimination

Chapter Summary

1. Designing and analyzing questions for research purposes requires an under-standing of the numerical concepts of level of measurement (nominal, ordinal, and interval), central tendency (mode, median, mean) and variability (percen-tile, range, standard deviation).
2. Survey research and frequency count studies are common descriptive studies in the field of music education.
3. Sampling is an important consideration when choosing subjects for a study.
4. All research measurement tools should be assessed for issues of validity and reliability.
5. Teachers and students can benefit from having classroom tests analyzed for dif-ficulty and discrimination.

Topics for Further Exploration

1. Consider how you might use descriptive statistics to summarize the home prac-tice behaviors of your students.
2. Discuss how real-world scenarios sometimes make ideal research studies diffi-cult. For instance, how in the real world can issues of ideal sample size, sampling choices, and test design be weighed?

Suggested Assignments

1. Individually and as a class, design a questionnaire on the topic of study skills. What types of questions seem to suggest nominal, ordinal, or interval data? If possible, administer and analyze your questionnaire using the statistics in this chapter.
2. Analyze a test you have given to your own students using difficulty and item analysis concepts, as appropriate to the type of test.

Recommended Reading

Cohen, R. J., & Swerdlik, M. E. (2005). *Psychological testing and assessment: An introduction to tests and measurement* (6th ed.). Boston, MA: McGraw-Hill.

Dillman, D. A. (2007). *Mail and Internet surveys: The tailored design method* (2nd ed.). Hoboken, NJ: Wiley.

eleven
Interpreting Correlations

Debbie Rohwer

This chapter highlights the following concepts:

- Components of a correlation coefficient:

  - direction and strength of a correlation;
  - measurement assumptions that can impact correlations;
  - significance of the correlation coefficient;

- Validity and reliability coefficients:

  - assessing validity and reliability with correlations;

- Inputting data into a statistical program.

Correlations look at relationships between variables. This chapter focuses on the parametric statistic called Pearson "r," appropriate when both sets of data are from interval level tests.

Introduction

Teachers commonly ask correlational questions concerning their students, such as "I wonder if students who score well in music also tend to be the smartest kids?" or "I wonder if those who practice the most also tend to receive the highest music scores?"

or "I wonder if those who have difficulty in music reading also tend to have difficulty in language arts/reading?" Research studies document similar questions in the form of correlational investigations.

For example, you may have two sets of scores for one group of individuals and notice that those individuals scoring well on one of the tests also tend to score well on the other. To determine exactly how closely both test results correlate with each other in a linear way, you calculate what is called a *correlation coefficient*. Many such correlation coefficients can be computed dependent on the level of measurement of the variables, but the statistic most commonly used to investigate the relationship between two tests for a group of people is called the *Pearson product moment correlation coefficient*. For a description of other possible types of correlations, consult Siegel and Castellan's (1988) *Nonparametric Statistics for the Behavioral Sciences*.

Components of a Correlation Coefficient

A first step in investigating a correlation is to view the data on a graph called a *scatterplot*. You could start with a single student's music score and reading score and plot both scores on a graph as illustrated in Figure 11.1. The horizontal axis shows the music test scores, the vertical axis the reading scores. Joe received a score of 80 on both the music and the reading test. With this knowledge, you find Joe's reading score on the vertical axis and the music score on the horizontal axis. Going up from the music score and over to the right from the reading score, the dots meet as shown in Figure 11.1.

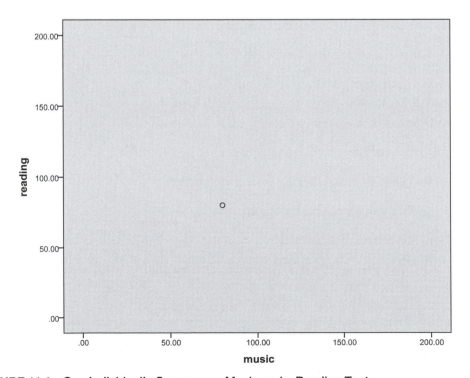

FIGURE 11.1   One Individual's Scores on a Music and a Reading Test

A single point on a graph does not provide much information, but if you followed this same procedure for an entire class, you might get a picture that would visualize the relationship between two tests for one group of individuals. Figure 11.2 represents a perfect positive correlation between two tests (music and reading tests). You can look for particular characteristics on the graph, such as the *direction* of the relationship and its *strength*.

Direction and Strength of a Correlation

A *perfect positive correlation* means that if you knew a student's score on one test, you could accurately predict the score on the other test. Thus, even if you did not know the student's score on the reading test, you could still know the student's reading score based on your knowledge of the music score. Those students who scored low on the music test also scored low on the reading test, and if you follow a straight path on the scatterplot, you would come to the other extreme that would document that those who scored high on the music test also scored high on the reading test. This linear path shows a positive direction to the line (bottom left to upper right). The opposite situation might occur as well when an *inverse* relationship exists between music and reading test scores for a group of students. Figure 11.3 illustrates the case of a *perfect negative correlation*.

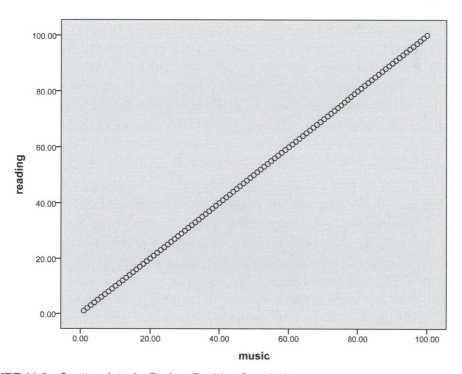

FIGURE 11.2 Scatterplot of a Perfect Positive Correlation

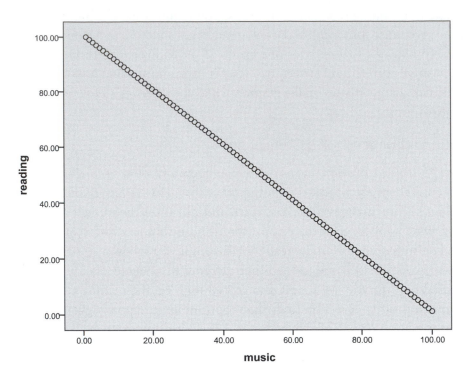

FIGURE 11.3   Scatterplot of Perfect Negative Correlation

In the case of a perfect negative correlation, knowing a student's score on the music test would make it possible to predict the student's reading score; those who scored high on the reading test scored low on the music test and if you follow a straight path on the scatterplot, you would come to the other extreme that would document that those who scored low on the reading test scored high on the music test. This linear path shows a negative direction to the line (upper left to bottom right). It must be noted here that the term "negative" in this case does not imply "bad." Researchers as well as teachers might expect and want negative relationships. For instance, a negative relationship could document that those who practice *more* also tend to make *fewer* errors. That would clearly be a positive educational outcome, even though it is a negative relationship between scores.

Results of correlations fall somewhere between a perfect positive relationship (r = +1.00) and a perfect negative relationship (r = –1.00). As the relationship becomes less strong, then the look of the relationship fattens. Consequently, you would be less accurate in predicting scores on the reading test based on your knowledge of the music test: there is more *static* (a less clear line) in the picture. For instance, a less strong correlation of r = .80 or r = –.80 might look like Figure 11.4.

When looking at *strength* of the correlation, the absolute value of the correlation coefficient is used; that is, r = .80 and r = –.80 are equally *strong*; these two correlations simply have a different *direction*, with one correlation being positive and the other correlation being negative. A still less strong correlation of r = .40 or r = –.40, with even more static is shown in Figure 11.5.

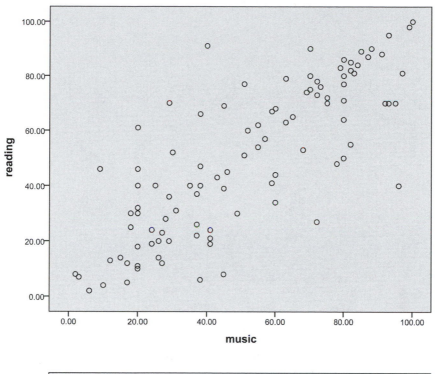

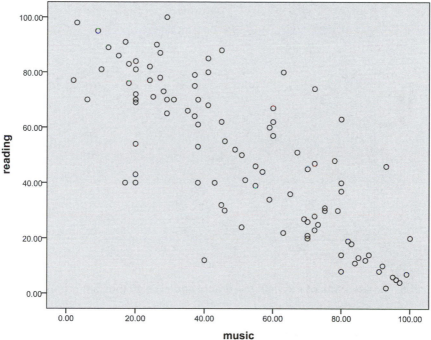

FIGURE 11.4   Scatterplots of r = +.80 (top graph) and r = −.80 (bottom graph)

A complete lack of a linear trend, a correlation of r = .00 might look like Figure 11.6. Note that when a correlation equals zero, you have no ability to predict a student's reading score based on the music score.

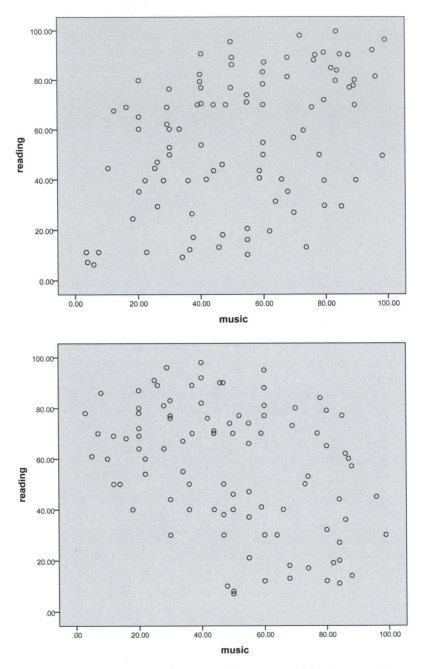

FIGURE 11.5 Scatterplots of r = +.40 (top graph) and r = −.40 (bottom graph)

Correlation and Causation

Establishing that a relationship between variables exists does not mean that one variable *causes* the other. For instance, a finding that those who score high on a music perform-ance exam also tend to have high reading scores documents that these two phenomena may be related. It does not imply that being in music *causes* students' reading scores to be higher. Perhaps students in music who get high reading scores *also* have support-

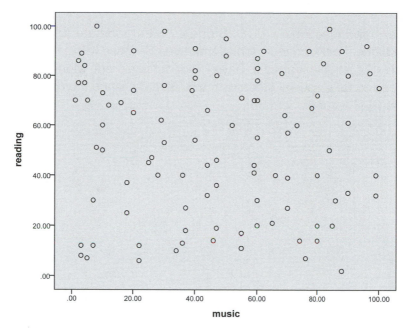

FIGURE 11.6 Scatterplot of r = .00

ive parents, have strong work ethics, eat well-balanced diets, etc. Any of these issues could have been the third-party variable that is embedded within a positive relationship between performance scores and reading scores. Correlation, then, does not imply causation; it only documents trends between variables.

Measurement Assumptions That Can Impact Parametric Correlations

In addition to making sure that your two data sets use interval-level data (see Chapter 10), the Pearson product moment correlation requires investigation of three other assumptions, or rules: linearity, outliers, and restriction of scores. Before deciding to calculate a correlation, a scatterplot (as shown earlier) can tell you whether the assumptions are met. One of the assumptions of the Pearson product moment correlation coefficient is that the two interval level data sets must form a linear distribution.

Linear and Non-linear Score Distributions

When data follow a straight path, they are considered to be linear distributions. The data gathered to investigate one of Muna's research questions, however, resulted in a distribution that was non-linear.

As a master's performance student, *Muna* was surrounded by friends who experienced performance anxiety. Curious about possible relationships between music performance and anxiety, she asked her friends if she could measure their anxiety and correlate those scores to their jury scores. When she plotted the correlation data, though, she noted its shape: it documented a non-linear trend (see Figure 11.7). Students with moderate anxiety tended to have the highest performance achievement, while those with a small amount or a great deal of anxiety tended to have lower achievement. Muna knew that she would need to take special steps with this data set since the data points were in the shape of a curve.

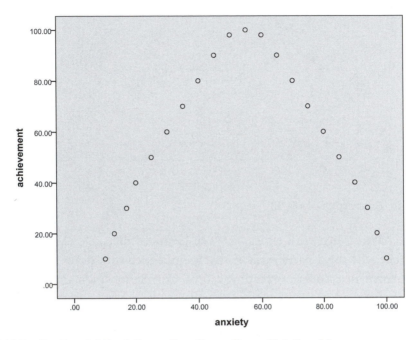

FIGURE 11.7 Scatterplot Depicting a Curvilinear Score Relationship

A different statistic is needed to represent relationships that have a curvilinear shape. If Muna had not looked at the scatterplot, she would not have known that this situation existed. She then would most likely have calculated the wrong statistic and come up with an inaccurate, very small linear correlation instead of the very strong curvilinear relationship that should be documented (r = .00 if Pearson is used, whereas if a correlation coefficient for curvilinear distributions was used such as eta, the correlation would result in r = .74). Muna took the correct step by viewing the scatterplot so that she could avoid the problem of using an inappropriate statistic.

Outliers

A scatterplot can also advise you of an *outlier* that may be present in the data. Figure 11.8 shows two correlations, one without and the other with an outlier. The second plot has an additional data point that is distant from the rest of the distribution.

In the top picture, the relationship between music and reading is r = .80, but the relationship documented in the bottom picture, with the addition of the outlier in the upper left-hand corner, lowers the correlation between music and reading to r = .53. In the case of an outlier, it is important to document its presence and provide the reader with

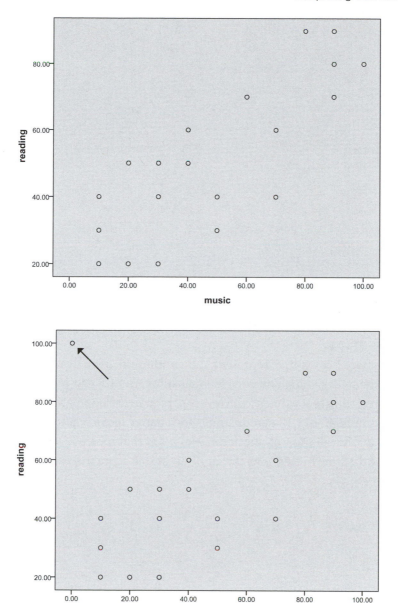

FIGURE 11.8   Scatterplots Without an Outlier (top graph) and With an Outlier (bottom graph)

the calculated correlation coefficient with and without the outlier in the data set. If you include this information in your report, the reader will better understand why decisions were made the way they were for the results of the study.

Restriction/Range of Scores

Lastly, you should look at the range of scores that are obtained before a correlation is calculated. Too narrow a range of scores can lead to an inaccurate, attenuated (lowered) correlation coefficient, such as the one shown in Figure 11.9, because there may be no high scores in the chosen sample that lead to a clearly discernible line.

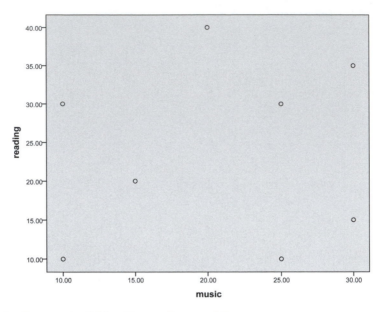

FIGURE 11.9   Scatterplot With a Narrow Range of Scores

Trying to obtain scores that represent the continuum of high to low scores is an important factor in designing any correlational study, in order to represent the overall population correlation that would exist if every person in the population were measured. The scatterplot in Figure 11.10 demonstrates the change of correlation coefficients that occurs simply by the addition of one additional point that increases the range of scores and the look of the line. In this case, the addition of one score increased the correlation from r = .12 to r = .90.

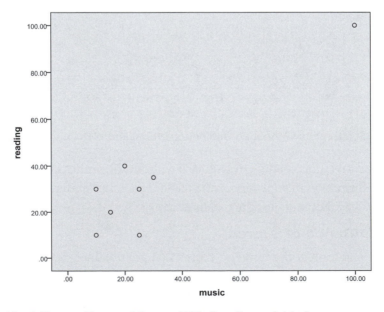

FIGURE 11.10   A Narrow Range of Scores With One Score Added

In this example, the one extreme score would most likely be documented as an outlier and taken out, but the basic issue is still important: A great variability of scores is necessary in order to document a linear trend. If you did a pilot test and found a restriction of scores to be apparent in the data, it would be advisable to find a greater spread of individuals so as to give as complete of a picture of the linear possibilities of the variables as possible. You might consider re-thinking your purpose or expanding the sample. Insufficient sample size has been the downfall of many quantitatively conceptualized projects.

Significance of the Correlation Coefficient

As demonstrated earlier, the correlation coefficient describes basic issues of strength and direction. In addition, most researchers report the statistical significance of the correlation. In layman's terms, statistical significance means the level of risk of the result happening by chance. This is expressed by the *p-value*. Music education researchers tend to choose a *p* value, or *significance* cutoff of .05, meaning that they are willing to take a 5% risk of the result happening by chance; or conversely, being 95% sure that the result is not occurring by chance.

In the case of a correlation, you are specifically testing whether the correlation is different from .00 (or no relationship). When setting the significance threshold at .05, you are documenting that a p value *below* .05 is within your chance/risk comfort zone. A calculated significance (p) value of .03 says that you are 97% sure that the calculated correlation is different from r = .00 (or no relationship) and not by chance. Conversely, a calculated significance (p) value of .99 says that you are only 1% sure that the calculated correlation is different from r = .00. This is not a bet that most people would be willing to make.

Type I and II Errors

It must be cautioned that there is always a risk of making a wrong decision when accepting a result as occurring or not occurring by chance. If you find a significant result in a study, there is a chance that the result should actually be a non-significant finding; your result, then, would be inaccurate to what the population would document if you had access to everyone. This is called a *Type I error*. Conversely, if you do not find a significant result even though the result should actually be significant, you have made a *Type II error*.

Practical Significance

A concern with significance testing is that statistical significance is relatively easy to obtain in a correlational study if the sample size is big enough. A sample of approximately 100 people will produce a significant result for a correlation coefficient of only r = .19, which is relatively close to r = .00. For a correlation that may be statistically significant but not practically meaningful, it may be necessary to state that the statistically significant correlation found in a study may be related to the large sample size, but is not practically meaningful. In such a case, it may be important to go beyond significance testing as the only determining factor to gauge the "importance" of a finding.

The *coefficient of determination* (r^2) can be used to obtain a percent of variance explained between the two tests in order to estimate practical significance. This information can be added to significance testing to get beyond the statistical issues associated with significance testing in isolation. For instance, if you take a correlation of $r = .19$ and square it, you can then discuss this number as the percent of information that is understood from this correlation; in this case, the correlation represents a 4% ($r^2 = .04$) overlap of information across the two tests. You understand 4% of the variance in one test based on information from the other test. (For an extensive discussion of coefficient of determination, see Grissom and Kim's [2005] *Effect Sizes for Research*.) A visual example of "information in common" that could be represented by r^2 can be seen in the darkest, middle part of the Venn diagram as depicted in Figure 11.11.

The coefficient of determination has been called a conservative estimate of practical significance (Cohen, 1988). An alternate form of documenting practical significance can be found in Cohen's more liberal effect size estimate for correlations, where the calculated correlation itself is used to determine practicality; Cohen (1988) documented a .1 correlation to be *small*, a .3 correlation to be *medium*, and a .5 or larger correlation coefficient to be *large*. Which decision (conservative or liberal) to favor has been the subject of debate among statisticians for many years. Your own choice is ideally a matter of informed judgment about that debate.

Statistical Inference

Another related caution with significance testing of correlations is the assumption that if a correlation is significant, then the result from the sample can automatically be generalized to the population. Known as *inference*, this complicated concept requires that many statistical issues such as probability sampling procedures and reliability of tests need to be considered carefully. For a thorough discussion of inferences and inferential statistics, please see Huck's (2012) *Reading Statistics and Research*.

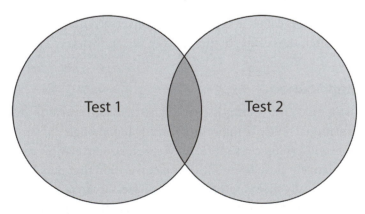

FIGURE 11.11   Venn Diagram for r^2

The following example highlights how Greg used some of the concepts addressed in this chapter to investigate a correlational question. By reviewing the Greg's procedures, you can check your understanding of these concepts.

Greg, an orchestra director, has noted informally that students who are highly skilled performers in his class also tend to have more years of piano lessons. He has decided to measure this trend formally. At the first round of all state orchestra auditions in one state region, he asked the organizers if they could have auditioning students answer one question as part of their application materials: How many years have you taken piano lessons? Before running the correlation, Greg checked the scatterplot to assess the viability of the correlation in terms of linearity, outliers, and restriction of scores. He found all assumptions to be tenable (acceptable) for using the Pearson product moment correlation coefficient. The result of the correlation between years of piano lessons and audition score was positive and strong ($N = 178$, $r = .84$, $p = .001$, $r^2 = .71$), with higher audition scores tending to align with those with more years of piano background, and lower scores tending to align with fewer (or no) years of piano instruction.

Greg documented that he checked the data for the assumptions of the statistic (linearity, outliers, and restriction of scores) before calculating the correlation. He used a Pearson product moment correlation, which is justifiable with two sets of interval level data. The correlation coefficient of .84 documents the positive trend toward the data with relatively little static. Prior to doing the calculation he determined that a significant *p* value would be set at below .05. Greg's findings actually had a *p* value of .001, which means that he could be 99.9% sure that the correlation was different from 0 and that the finding was not by chance. While the sample size was large, the correlation coefficient itself was also large, documenting less concern that a large sample size was the sole cause for the significance in this case. To document practical significance, Greg added coefficient of determination information ($r^2 = 71$) to the description. Based on this correlation, therefore, 71% of the variance across the two tests is understood.

Validity and Reliability Coefficients

In addition to being used to document the results of a research question, sometimes the correlation coefficients found in a method section of a study describe how one or more tests were assessed for appropriateness (*validity*) and consistency (*reliability*). Many of the statistical possibilities for checking appropriateness and consistency of a test use validity or reliability coefficients (which are correlation coefficients).

Assessing Validity and Reliability with Correlations

Checking for validity and reliability is especially important when constructing tests. If, for example, you were designing a test that measured music aptitude, but your test was shorter than many of the music aptitude tests on the market, you could check to see whether students' scores on your own test lined up (or were correlated to) scores on the longer, standardized test. If the scores on the shorter version documented a strong, positive correlation to the scores on the longer, standardized test, and the standardized test was considered to be valid, you could say that your test had strong *criterion-related validity*. The coefficient that would be obtained by correlating the two tests would then be called a *validity coefficient*.

If you were constructing a test that measured not just one small concept, like rhythmic accuracy, but a large construct like musicianship, you would first define the subcomponents of the construct, and then use advanced correlation statistics and other statistical procedures to document that while the subcomponents are not related to each other, the subcomponents do relate to the overall construct of musicianship. So for instance, you might use factor analysis to see whether items on a performance rubric, an ability to improvise test, and a theory test all link to the topic of musicianship, but do not overlap excessively with each other. This would be one way that you might document *construct validity*. Procedures related to construct validity are complicated, and beyond the scope of this text, but if you would like more information concerning this topic, please see Mitchell and Jolley's (2009) *Research Design Explained*.

On the reliability side, if items on a rubric (such as rhythmic accuracy, tonal accuracy, etc.) were added together to obtain one performance achievement score, you would want to estimate whether these items "grouped together" well. You could assess this by correlating each item to every other item to make sure that people who are the best performers tend to score high on these items, and people who are the lowest skilled performers tend to score low on these items, consistently. This type of reliability is called *internal consistency*. (The statistic used for this calculation is often Cronbach's alpha.) You would also want to make sure that judges using this rubric were consistent in their own scoring and across the other judges; this type of reliability is called *interjudge reliability*. (The statistic used for this calculation is often a Pearson product moment correlation coefficient, but it does depend on the level of measurement of the tests.)

As a teacher or researcher, you may want to improve common errors in musicians' performances through a treatment. But in order to measure the skill level of the students, you would need to know that the etude used to test them lends itself to consistent performances, and that the errors are not random. For instance, if Sally plays the etude twice and each time she plays a certain rhythm incorrectly, but she plays it the same way both times, then that etude is estimated to have high *test-retest reliability* for people of the same skill level as Sally. You can then determine if a type of treatment causes improved scores on Sally's performance, knowing that if the scores at the end show improvement, then the improvement is not from variability in the performance of the etude but due to the treatment itself. All of these types of reliability checks are done by calculating correlation coefficients, called *reliability coefficients*.

Inputting Data into a Statistical Program

As in Chapter 10, the following SPSS input process is provided as a way for you to envision the numerical and format issues that may transfer to any program. The example below provides a small set of data for a correlation study between the variables "Practice time" and "Audition score" and describes the input process for illustration purposes.

Test 1: total practice time as documented on a practice card the week before auditions

Test 2: audition performance score

Because the data for this question are both at the interval level of measurement, the Pearson product moment correlation will be used. The data shown below represent two data sets for five individuals, with each row being an individual's score on the two tests (so Sally may be first across and Fred may be second across, etc.), and with the amount of time in hours in the first column and the audition performance score in the second column. The variable names are therefore *practice* and *audition* (see Table 11.1).

The next step would be to check basic assumptions for correlation statistics: linearity, outliers, and restriction of scores. These issues can be weighed by looking at a scatterplot. To do this, go to the "Graphs" dropdown and then choose "Legacy dialogs," "Scatter/dot," and "Simple Scatter." By entering practice for the Y axis and audition for the X axis, you will get what is shown in Figure 11.12.

From the picture you can see the general positive, linear trend of the data (not curvilinear), no clear outlier cases, and a lack of restriction of scores (especially for this example of five data points; any real study would have a far larger sample size).

Next, a correlation coefficient can be calculated by going to the "Analyze" dropdown and choosing "Correlate," and "Bivariate" (for two sets of scores), and checking "Pearson" (provided your data are interval level). The readout, shown in Table 11.2, documents the sample size of five respondents, the correlation coefficient of $r = .663$ and the calculated significance of .223 (not significant—less than .05, but would be significant if the sample size were larger).

TABLE 11.1   Practice and Audition Scores (N = 5)

	Practice	**Audition**
1.	10.00	88
2.	4.00	87
3.	8.00	72
4.	3.00	35
5.	2.00	52

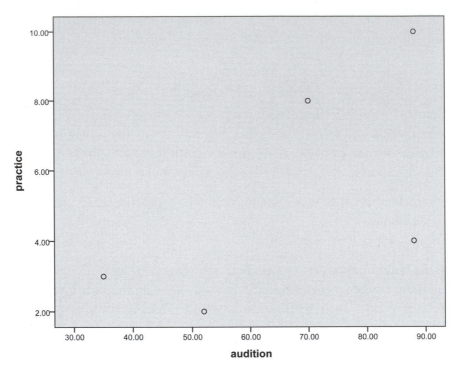

FIGURE 11.12 Scatterplot of Practice and Audition Correlation (N = 5)

TABLE 11.2 Readout Example: Practice and Audition Correlation
(N = 5)

	Correlations		
		Practice	**Audition**
Practice	Pearson Correlation	1	.663
	Sig. (2-tailed)		.223
	N	5	5
Audition	Pearson Correlation	.663	1
	Sig. (2-tailed)	.223	
	N	5	5

Do not be confused by the duplication inherent in the table. Any test will be perfectly correlated to itself with a score of 1, and the .663 is presented in mirror image for the correlation between the two tests. Even though there are many numbers in the table, if you were including this result in a research study, the numerical part of the result statement would look like this: ($N = 5$, $r = .66$, $p = .22$).

To conclude, correlations serve the purpose of establishing relationships between observed phenomena that can lead researchers and teachers alike to ask further questions about the strength of such relationships. For instance, music teachers can weigh trends, even informally, with their own students by considering correlation questions of interest, such as "Do students who tap their toes also tend to play more steadily?" These questions can lead to an analysis of the possible reasons that might exist for a seeming relationship: Is it the tapping or is there a third-party variable that may be causing students to play more steadily? Did the steady performers also have an extensive amount of musical experiences when they were young; or are the steady performers all highly coordinated? Learning how to weigh situations may help teachers make instructional decisions in a more carefully considered and informed manner. Clearly, a basic understanding of correlations can make real the possibility that answers will come from teachers in the field who have important, pragmatic questions that can advance the profession of music education as a whole.

Chapter Summary

1. Important components of interpreting correlation coefficients are (a) direction and strength, and (b) statistical significance.
2. In order to use correlations appropriately, it is important to check for the underlying measurement assumptions of linearity, outliers, and restriction of scores.
3. Scatterplots are valuable in assessing whether assumptions for parametric correlations have been met.
4. Correlations are useful in estimating the validity and reliability of measurement tools.

Topics for Further Exploration

1. Examples reinforcing why correlation does not imply causation.
2. The difference between the terms significant and important.
3. Choosing useful tests for research purposes.
4. Choosing well-balanced, representative samples for correlational studies.

Suggested Assignments

1. Choose two easily gathered variables such as height and undergraduate GPA and calculate the correlation for these two variables for the class. Discuss.
2. Correlate scores on a classroom test to the age of the class participants. Discuss.
3. Gather chair placement performance test score data or other test data on their own students and correlate that data to the students' practice or study time.

Recommended Reading

Cohen, J. (1988). *Statistical power analysis for the behavioral sciences* (2nd ed.). Hillsdale, NJ: Lawrence Erlbaum.
Ghiselli, E. E., Campbell, J. P., & Zedeck, S. (1981). *Measurement theory for the behavioral sciences*. San Francisco, CA: W. H. Freeman.

twelve

Designing Ex Post Facto and Experimental Studies

Debbie Rohwer

This chapter highlights the following concepts:

- Types of difference studies;
- Internal and external validity:

  - design options;

- Analysis of Variance:

  - the F statistic;
  - statistical issues with the ANOVA;

- Inputting data into a statistical program;
- Difference studies in the classroom.

Ex post facto (sometimes called causal-comparative) and experimental research investigates differences between two or more groups. This chapter describes and distinguishes between these two types of research design.

Introduction

As a high school music teacher, *Juan* noted a trend in his band classes over the last two years. Of the current students, male percussionists seemed to play at a higher level than female percussionists. He wondered if this was just an issue with this group of students or whether the issue was more widespread. To answer this question, he arranged for all high school percussionists in his district to take a performance test. He found that the difference between males and females was statistically significant, favoring males (M = 87.6, SD = .65) over females (M = 73.1, SD = .80). He pondered the clarity of this result. Maybe it wasn't gender in isolation, but something else that caused the result. Perhaps the male percussionists began instruction earlier or took more private lessons. Or some other variable was causing this finding altogether. It was challenging to know for sure.

Juan's dilemma—trying to understand differences between groups—is familiar to music education researchers. Research that investigates differences uses *ex post facto* (sometimes called causal-comparative), and/or *experimental* designs. The distinction between ex post facto and experimental research is determined by the *independent variable,* which is a nominal level grouping variable.

The independent variable in Juan's study is gender (with the distinct levels of male and female). In this case, the independent variable (gender) is pre-existing; the design of the study is therefore called *ex post facto* (Latin for "after the fact"). Studies in which the researcher is in control of the independent variable are called *experimental* (as, for example, in an experiment where you can determine who gets what treatment). The dependent variable in both ex post facto and experimental studies is a test. In Juan's case, the dependent variable was an interval level test of performance ability. The following section details considerations for both types of studies.

Types of Difference Studies

In ex post facto studies the independent variable is pre-existing (as in Juan's study). Such variables can also be called self-selected or non-manipulated. Examples relevant to music teachers may include gender (male, female), instrument family (woodwinds, brass, percussion), voice part (soprano, alto, tenor, bass), aptitude groupings (high, medium, low scorers), or grade level (middle school, high school).

As an example, take the following article titled "The effect of grade level on motivation scores." Here, the independent variable (the nominal level group variable) is grade level (middle school and high school), and the dependent variable (the interval level test) is motivation scores. Because the nominal-level independent variable is pre-existing—that is, the participants are already in middle school or high school—the study is ex post facto.

In an experimental design, the independent variable can be manipulated (or controlled) by the researcher. Examples might include treatment groups (block chord accompaniment versus arpeggiated accompaniment) or conditions (sight singing a song with Curwen hand signs, and also without hand signs). A researcher can also design a study that combines the two: one independent variable being manipulated (in the treatment groups) and one independent variable being pre-existing (e.g., gender).

> As an elementary music teacher, *Keisha* was interested in measuring the difference between those students who receive large movement training and small movement training. She had learned that large movements may help flow and feel related to rhythm, while small movements may be more transferrable to the Orff instrument techniques she used. She wondered if small movements would also help rhythmic feel. She designed an experiment where she tested the rhythmic steadiness of all four of her classes of third graders. Then she took two of the classes and taught them rhythms using small motor movements specific to Orff mallet technique. The other two classes learned the same rhythms but used large motor movements. She then measured all students at the end and found no significant differences in steadiness across the two treatment groups (large motor: M = 36.1, SD = .20; small motor: M = 35.8, SD = .39).

In contrast to Juan, Keisha designed a study with two different treatment groups (large motor training in one group and small motor training in the other group). Her study was experimental because as the researcher, she was in control of the independent variable.

Notice that in both of these examples, the independent variable is a *grouping* or *categorical variable* (at the nominal level of measurement, as discussed in Chapter 10), which places subjects into families or subgroups of people. The independent variable is able to differentiate better between scores on the test (the dependent variable) if the groupings maximize variance. This concept is the first component of Kerlinger's (1986) MAXMINCON principle, wherein studies ideally MAXimize variance, MINimize error, and CONtrol extraneous variables.

Maximizing variance (MAX) can be done by choosing independent variable groupings that allow for differences to be apparent. For instance, if you were trying to give clear examples to a young child of what the words "short" and "tall" meant, you probably would not pick as the examples one person who was 5 ft. 3 inches and another who measured 5 ft. 4 inches. You would most likely choose people who could maximize the difference, thereby clarifying the terms: Someone 4 ft. tall might represent "short" and someone 7 ft. tall would represent "tall." In the case of an experiment, then, you would not choose test score groupings (high and low groups, for instance) as an independent variable and then choose groupings that vary only by one point on the test (low: scoring 99, and high: scoring 100). Instead, it would be important to have a spread of representative scores that would maximize the groupings, such as lows having scores between 1 and 50, and highs having scores between 51 and 100.

Minimizing error variance (MIN) can be done by doing a validity check to make sure: (1) the testing instrument is appropriate for the age level of the test takers; (2) the items represent the concept being measured; and (3) the test does not have superfluous content or items that are missing but are necessary to represent the content appropriately. After a validity check and a field test to check for clarity, a pilot test can be done to assess the reliability of the instrument (see Chapter 10), with the goal of this three-step process being to lessen the impact of error variance.

The CON (CONtrol extraneous variables) in Kerlinger's principle can be accomplished by designing and implementing a study that allows confidence that factors other than the independent variable were not the cause of the results. In order to control for extraneous variables as possible causes, researchers must analyze, redesign, and discuss any research-related issues that could question the claim of the independent variable having been the most likely cause of the results of a study. Integral to such confidence is investigating the internal validity of research designs and procedures.

Internal and External Validity

Campbell and Stanley (1963) published a seminal list of what they called *threats to internal validity*. Such threats, detailed further below, are factors that could weaken a study by causing readers to question whether the independent variable or some other extraneous variable caused the results to happen the way they did. Since 1963, there have been further expansions of the initial list of threats to internal validity (Cook & Campbell, 1979; Shadish, Cook, & Campbell, 2001), but the issue is the same: Studies should be designed and conducted in such a way that the likelihood of any extraneous variables being the cause of the findings can be ruled out to the greatest extent possible.

Design Options

Threats to internal validity are partly based on the choices you make when planning a study as well as the choices made in the midst of carrying the study out. For instance, when designing an experimental study, you may choose: (1) whether to have a comparison group or not; (2) whether to use a pretest or not; and (3) whether to use random assignment or not. *Pre-experimental* (or less controlled) designs use fewer control options than true experimental designs.

A common middle-ground design, called a *quasi-experimental design*, uses a realistic combination of the three issues mentioned; it has a treatment and comparison group, each of which was intact (already formed) before the study began. Individuals in each group are given a pretest at the beginning of the study to see if the groups score equally on the test. Then each group receives "a level of the independent variable," technical language for saying that, for instance, one class receives guitar instruction on accompanying in block chords whereas the second class is instructed in arpeggiated chord accompaniment. After some period of training, members of both groups take a posttest. This design is called the *non-equivalent control group design* due to the use of non-randomly assigned, intact groups. Keisha's example earlier in this chapter was such a non-equivalent control group design because she used intact classes that were pretested, then "treated," and then post-tested. (For a detailed discussion of design issues, see Frankel and Wallen's (2009) *How to Design and Evaluate Research in Education*.)

Threats to Internal Validity

Designs that do not have a pretest or that do not use randomization have a potential *selection* threat. This means that the groups could be different from the start without the researcher knowing it. Consider the challenge faced in the following scenario: A researcher has two groups, one receiving "hand/sign and solfege" training and the other receiving "solfege alone" training. At the end of the treatment, all students take a sight singing performance exam. The "hand/sign and solfege" group had a mean score of 47.3 on the posttest and the "solfege alone" group had a mean score of 71.4 on the posttest. No pretest was given before the treatment. The results are shown in Table 12.1.

The posttest information alone may lead you to conclude that the training caused the "solfege alone" group to score higher than the "hand/sign and solfege" group. We don't know, however, whether the groups were equal at the beginning. It could have been that the "solfege alone" group actually might have *decreased* from an initial pre-treatment mean of 88.7 and the "hand/sign and solfege" group actually might have *increased* from an initial pre-treatment mean of 21.8.

Now think about the finding reported in Table 12.2.

Based on this example, you can see that a pretest is pivotal to understanding whether groups differ at the start of a study. If they do differ, you would then need to undertake further statistical solutions to analyzing the data, or change the design of the study. A statistical solution would be to use an advanced statistic to control for initial differences between groups. A design-based solution would be to take the initial groups and reorganize them by placing them into equal groups based on the pretest scores. Either way, interpretation of results without pretest information may be incorrect. Therefore, researchers need to weigh the pretest variable carefully in order to avoid a selection threat.

The selection threat is only one of a number of possible challenges that researchers face when trying to determine cause and effect. Other examples are:

TABLE 12.1 Scores on a Posttest-Only Design

Pretest Score	Treatment	Posttest Score
?	hand/sign and solfege	47.3
?	solfege alone	71.4

TABLE 12.2 Pre- and Posttest Scores on Sight Singing With and Without Solfege

Pretest Score	Treatment	Posttest Score
21.8	hand/sign and solfege	47.3
88.7	solfege alone	71.4

- *Implementation threat:* The researcher who gives positive feedback to one treatment group and less positive feedback to the other group, when feedback is not the measured independent variable (i.e., the treatments are not being implemented consistently across the groups).
- *Instrumentation threat*: The individuals in the performance judging panel who tire as the day goes on and become more lenient in their scoring (i.e., the scoring is not being conducted consistently across the participants).
- *Location threat*: The one treatment group is in a well-lit room and the other that is in the broom closet (i.e., the environment/setting is not consistent across groups).
- *History threat*: The students in one of the treatment groups get together outside of the treatment sessions to do extra study/work, while the other treatment group participants do not meet (i.e., students' study/work activities outside of the treatment are not consistent across groups).

Especially in ex post facto studies, almost anything in addition to or in place of the independent variable may have caused the results of the study.

In *Juan*'s study of male and female percussionists, the independent variable was out of his hands, and anything may have worked in conjunction with the independent variable to confound the clarity of the findings. As he wondered aloud, "Maybe the male percussionists are beginning instruction earlier or taking more private lessons, or some other variable is causing this finding altogether." Juan clearly had good reason to ponder additional causes for the result he found.

Threats to External Validity

While possible threats to internal validity make you consider the clarity of the independent variable as a cause for the study's results, *threats to external validity* lead to questions about whether a given study's design or methodological choices may be generalized to other settings. Whether an expert provides instruction for the treatment groups in a study may not be problematic for determining cause and effect (i.e., the internal validity), but it could make the results ungeneralizable to settings where the instructor is not an expert on the treatments. Or, a study that compares two treatments with a group of students who have participated in many different experiments may not call into question the internal validity of the study, but due to the students' experimental savvy, the results may not be generalizable to other, less savvy student samples. In fact, simply having students know that they are part of an investigation may make its results less generalizable to settings where the treatment is being implemented in an ordinary, non-research classroom setting. Both internal and external validity issues need to be weighed so that the best choice for determination of cause, issues of generalizability, and considerations of feasibility can be considered.

Analysis of Variance

The most common statistical method for analyzing data in difference studies (i.e., ex post facto studies or experimental studies) is the *analysis of variance* or *ANOVA*. In this chapter, the principles of the ANOVA will be explained as the main statistic by which you compare means of subgroups to determine the extent of difference between them.

In an ANOVA, the number of independent variables determines the naming of the ANOVA: A study with one independent variable is called a one-way ANOVA; a study with two independent variables, such as "treatment" and "gender," is called a two-way ANOVA.

Both Juan's and Keisha's research efforts (described earlier in this chapter) were one-way ANOVAs with two levels or subgroups to the independent variable. Gender was the independent variable in Juan's case, with male and female as the levels. In Keisha's study, treatment was the independent variable, with large motor and small motor treatment groups as the levels.

A two-way ANOVA with two levels to each independent variables (such as having both of the variables "treatment and gender" in the same study) can also be called a 2 × 2 ANOVA ("2 by 2"). This term describes the number of levels or subgroups in each independent variable. In the case of a 2 × 2 ANOVA, then, the variable "treatment groups" has two levels (such as moveable do training and fixed do training) and the variable "gender" also has two levels (male and female). This terminology changes according to the number of levels of each independent variable. For instance, you would call the statistic a 3 × 2 ANOVA for the following scenario: An ANOVA had two independent variables, but the first independent variable (treatment group) had three levels (such as Eastman counting system training, Gordon counting system training, and Kodaly counting system training) while the second independent variable had two levels (high and low). This design is illustrated in Figure 12.1.

The F Statistic

The result of an ANOVA is documented as an *F statistic*. The larger the F, the greater the calculated difference between groups. Also, the larger the F, the smaller the calculated significance value will be, documenting the smaller likelihood that differences were due to error or chance. Results of an ANOVA are listed together with a test of significance in which a p value (significance) below .05 indicates that the sets of means for the subgroups are significantly different from each other, with less than a 5% risk of the result being due to error or chance.

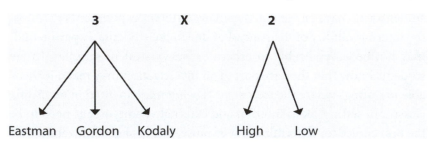

FIGURE 12.1   Illustration of a 3 × 2 ANOVA Design

For example, if a group of females and males was assessed for differences on a theory test, the ANOVA would be used to assess if the theory scores for the males (as seen in the first graph of Figure 12.2) differed from the theory scores for the females (as seen in the second graph of Figure 12.2). The height of the bars on the graphs in Figure 12.2 displays the number of people with that score; for instance, there were 12 females who scored 80 on the second graph, which makes up the tallest bar on the graph. Just by looking at the middle of each graph (a mean of 40 for the males and a mean of 80 for the females) you can envision that the means are probably going to be different enough not to be attributable to error or chance.

When the ANOVA is calculated for this data set, it documents a significant difference for the variable gender, $F(1, 62) = 220.44$, $p < .001$, favoring females ($M = 80.00$, $SD = 1.91$) over males ($M = 40.00$, $SD = 1.91$). The p value being smaller than .001 in the result sentence tells us that we are at least 99.9% sure that the groups differ, and not by error or chance. The large F value aligns with the small p value. The numbers in the parenthesis after the F are part of the calculation of the F; you would see these numbers in the ANOVA table if you looked at the degree of freedom column.

Whether you are looking at an ANOVA table or reading the results embedded in an article's results section, such as $F(1, 62) = 220.44$, $p < .001$, it is important to know what the numbers mean so that you can be an educated reader. The numbers in the parentheses are called the *degrees of freedom* (abbreviated as *df*). They serve as part of the calculation of the F statistic, but also tell you important information about the choices the researcher made. In the case of the gender study listed above, the parenthetical content reads "(1, 62)."

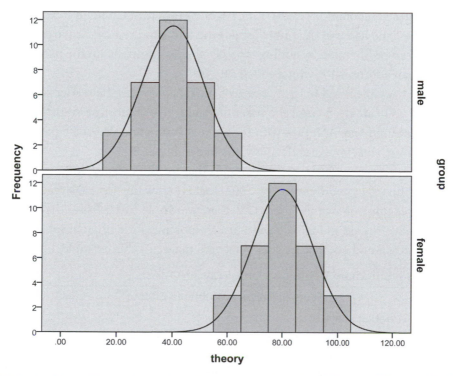

FIGURE 12.2   Music Theory Score Distributions for a Sample of Male and Female Students

The first number is the df for the independent variable, gender. If you add 1 to this number, it tells you the number of levels of the independent variable (note that this only works for independent variables). In this example, then, there are two levels to the variable gender (male and female). The second number in the parenthesis is the degree of freedom for error, and if you add this number (62) to the degree of freedom for the independent variable (1+62) and add 1 more, you will get the sample size for this one-way ANOVA. This study, therefore, had 64 people in it and the result that would be stated in the article would be that there was a significant main effect for gender, favoring females. You know that females outperformed males by looking at the original means for both subgroups. The term "main effect" is commonly used when discussing the results of independent variable findings.

Both Juan and Keisha could provide degree of freedom information for the results of their studies. Such information would remind the reader of the number of levels of the independent variable in each study as well as the sample size. In the case of Juan, comparing male and female percussionists on a performance test resulted in the following: $F(1, 92) = 27.3, p = .02$. He found a statistically significant difference between male and female percussionists, favoring males.

To determine sample size as well as number of subgroups (or levels) in this study, look at the first number in the parenthesis, the degree of freedom for the independent variable (1). The 1 (plus 1) states that there are two levels to the variable gender (males and females). Add the degree of freedom for gender number (1) to 92 and add 1 additional and you get the sample size of 94 students.

In Keisha's experiment with two treatment groups, no significant differences across the two groups were found: $F(1, 78) = .03, p = .92$. From the degrees of freedom, you can determine that she had two treatment levels (you add 1 to the 1 in the parenthesis). Her sample size can be obtained by adding together the two numbers in the parenthesis and then adding an additional 1, which equals 80.

The ANOVA table listed in many research articles provides the reader with the same information you can glean from the parenthetical way of reporting statistical findings. The table for a one-way ANOVA with the ex post facto variable "voice part" being the independent variable, for example, may look like Table 12.3.

The finding shown in Table 12.3 documents that for the variable voice part, there is a significant main effect or difference ($p = .003$) that is below the normal significance cutoff of .05. In the example shown in Figure 12.2, there were only two levels to the independent variable "gender" (male and female), and just by looking at the original subgroup means (80 and 40) you could say that females outscored males. In this example, however, there

TABLE 12.3   Summary Table of a One-Way ANOVA

Tests of Between-Subjects Effects

Dependent Variable: score

Source	Type III Sum of Squares	Df	Mean Square	F	Sig.
Voice part	1403.750	3	467.917	4.984	.003
Error	7135	76	93.882		

are four levels to the independent variable "voice part." You can discern this information by looking at the degree of freedom for the variable "voice part" (3) and then adding 1, which equals 4. You can also tell from this table that the degree of freedom for error is 76 and if you add 76 to 3 and add 1 more you will get the sample size for this study, which is 80. (For a discussion of how degree of freedom information works in all forms of ANOVAs and other statistics, see Huck's (2012) *Reading Statistics and Research*.)

Because the example deals with four levels to the variable "voice part" (soprano, alto, tenor, and bass), the basic ANOVA cannot describe the specifics of "where" the difference(s) lie; it only documents that there is a difference. After obtaining a significant ANOVA finding for a study that uses a variable with more than two levels, you could calculate a post hoc (Latin for "after this") test to determine information on the specific subgroup differences. Another option would be to calculate planned comparisons based on suggestions in the literature. Conducting further statistical tests like post hocs can sometimes be like data mining. The debate of data mining versus specified comparisons is a topic that needs to be purposefully and philosophically weighed.

Returning to the data set represented in Table 12.3: Descriptively, the sopranos had the lowest overall mean (49.00), with the altos (51.00), tenors (58.00), and basses (58.50) having higher mean scores. If a post hoc statistic were calculated, you could document that the lowest mean from the sopranos (49.00) was not significantly different from that of the altos (51.00), but the sopranos (49.00) were significantly different from both the tenors and the basses (58.00 and 58.50). The alto, tenor, and bass means did not significantly differ from each other (51.00, 58.00, and 58.50).

If a study has more than one independent variable, then it will document results for each independent variable, and will also document an *interaction* result, which highlights whether the findings need to be qualified or not. If there is a significant interaction between the independent variables, then the results are in some way hazy and need to be clarified. For instance, a researcher might find a significant main effect for gender, favoring females, but females in one of the treatment groups actually scored lower than the males in both of the treatment groups. It would then be misleading and incomplete to say that there was a significant main effect for gender, favoring females. The significant *interaction* helps clear up that misinterpretation by qualifying the main effect result. An interaction qualification statement may read:

> While there is a significant main effect for gender favoring females, the main effect was caused by females in treatment group one who outscored all other subgroups. Females in treatment group two, however, scored lower than both male treatment subgroups, so it may be wise to consider carefully the interaction of gender and treatment groups when making instructional decisions.

Table 12.4 displays findings from a study with two independent variables (treatment and age) and one interaction result. The table has degree of freedom (df) information, the F statistic, and the p values (Sig.). The other table information (i.e., Sum of Squares and Mean Square) is used as part of the calculation of the F statistic.

TABLE 12.4   Summary Table of a Two-Way ANOVA

Tests of Between-Subjects Effects

Dependent Variable: score

Source	Type III Sum of Squares	Df	Mean Square	F	Sig.
Treatment	4.000	1	4.000	.038	.846
Age	23104.000	1	23104.000	217.791	.000
Treatment*age	23104.000	1	23104.000	217.791	.000
Error	10184.000	96	106.083		

Once Table 12.4 has been analyzed to determine significance or non-significance, the original descriptive means of each subgroup could be looked up, a graph could be made, and then the following description could be written as results of the study:

1. There is no significant main effect for the variable treatment groups [F (1, 96) = .038, p = .85], with the visual group scoring: M= 50.0, SD = 11.43, and the auditory group scoring: M = 50.0, SD = 21.55.
2. There is a significant main effect for age [F (1, 96) = 217.79, p<.001], favoring younger students (M = 65.0, SD = 18.65) over older students (M = 35.0, SD = 17.34).
3. There is a significant interaction between treatment and age [F (1, 96) = 217.79, p<.001], showing the need to qualify the significant main effect for age. While younger students in the auditory group scored higher than all other subgroups (M = 80), younger students in the visual group achieved lower scores (M = 50), with those scores being equal to the scores of the older students in the visual group (M = 50). Also, older students in the auditory group scored the lowest of all subgroups (M = 20). This interaction can be seen in visual form in Figure 12.3.

Any time a significant interaction exists, you need to examine the subgroup means to determine where the non-parallel lines are occurring so that an explanation can be made of the qualifying information.

Statistical Issues with the ANOVA

The Analysis of Variance (ANOVA) is a *parametric* statistic (see Chapter 9) that has certain rules, or assumptions, governing its use. Most importantly, you need to be concerned with issues of *normality* (normal distribution of all scores) and *homogeneity of variance* (equal spread of scores). If these assumptions are not met, then non-parametric statistics (see Appendix K) or some other choice (such as transforming the data) must be used.

In order to calculate the results of a study by using an ANOVA, you first must establish that the distribution of the scores resembles the bell-shaped curve (see Figure 12.4). Distributions that are asymmetrically skewed (as shown in Figure 12.5) or too peaked (Figure 12.6), do not meet the assumption of normality and would not be appropriate for an ANOVA.

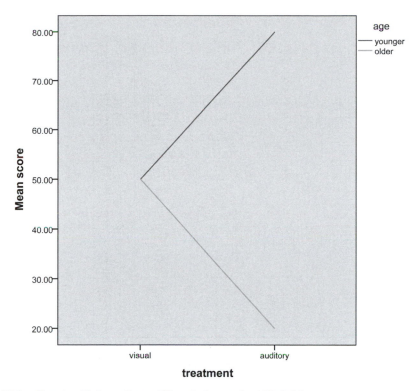

FIGURE 12.3   Graph of Interaction of Two Independent Variables

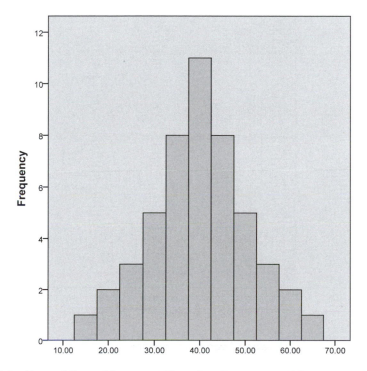

FIGURE 12.4   Normal Curve Histogram Based on Frequency of Scores in a Range from 0 to 70

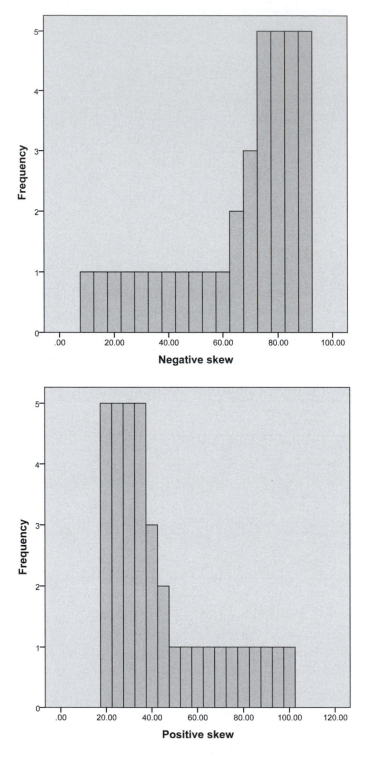

FIGURE 12.5 Asymmetrically Skewed Score Distributions

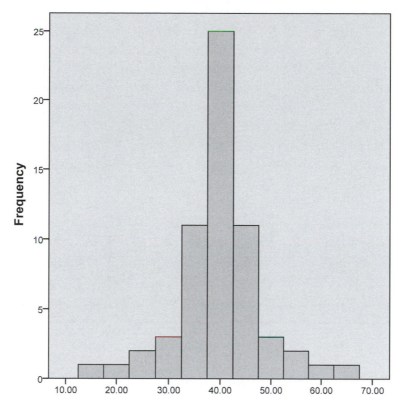

FIGURE 12.6   A Highly Peaked Score Distribution

It is also important that the spread of scores across each subgroup is similar, documenting "*homogeneity of variance.*" Figure 12.7 displays a pair of *box and whiskers* plots wherein the medians (represented by the horizontal line in the center of each box) are equal at 80. The equal picture sizes show an equality of variability.

The medians represented by the pictures shown in Figure 12.8 are similar, but the size of the box and whiskers shows a difference of spread (or variability). This discrepancy documents a problem with homogeneity of variance that would need to be solved in some way before an ANOVA could be calculated.

In general, it helps to have group sizes that are large in order to achieve a normal curve and to have enough *power* (see Cohen, 1988) so that the statistic can detect differences if they exist. A basic rule of thumb of 30 people in a group is an appropriate place to start for the purpose of meeting assumptions. Also important, however, is looking at past research to analyze sample size and significance results to determine how large your sample size might need to be to find differences if they exist.

As in other types of research, doing one or more pilot studies can help you estimate the power of a test to detect differences as well as the magnitude of the differences (called *effect size*). Since sample size can have an impact on statistical significance, adding effect size estimates can help the reader of an article gauge whether the stated statistical

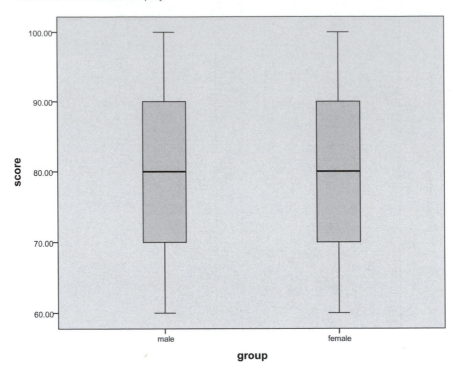

FIGURE 12.7   Box and Whisker Plots Suggesting Equality in Variability Between the Scores of Two Independent Variables

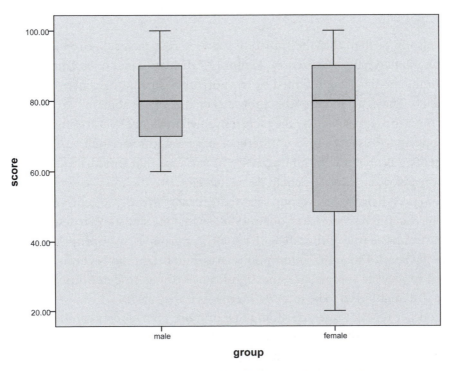

FIGURE 12.8   Box and Whisker Plots Suggesting Difference in Variability

significance was positively or negatively impacted by the sample size. This scenario can be seen when a result is statistically significant but has a small effect size (Type I error: can happen with a large sample size), or when a result is not statistically significant but has a large effect size (Type II error: can happen with a small sample size. For further discussion of Type I and II Error, see Chapter 10). Hence, it is important to plan a study's sample size carefully. Online sample size calculators are available to determine sample size estimates for a main study, using power and effect size data that can be gathered from a pilot study.

One other statistical issue to consider is a basic reminder that the .05 significance is used to calculate one statistic only. If you plan to run multiple ANOVAs, then you need to correct the .05 cutoff so that there is not an overuse of the data set. Statisticians sometimes describe studies that calculate multiple statistics with the same grouping variable but different dependent variables as "fishing" to find results, because there is a possibility that by just casting a line a great number of times (running statistics), you might catch a fish (find something significant). The fishing scenario might be seen in studies that use an independent variable such as gender to determine the effect on individual questions in a questionnaire (30 questions). In this case, there are 30 ANOVAs calculated. To counter this concern, the researcher can sum questions on a questionnaire and calculate one ANOVA instead of 30, or divide the .05 cutoff by the number of statistics to be calculated (in this case 30), thereby providing a more conservative cutoff that takes into account the multiple statistics being calculated (.05/30 = .002).

As a final note, there are many types of ANOVAs, such as an ANCOVA where you need to control for initial differences in group scores by weighting them on the posttest scores, or a repeated measures ANOVA where the same subjects are measured multiple times. Huck's (2012) text, *Reading Statistics and Research*, is a valuable resource that covers each of these advanced ANOVA options.

Inputting Data into a Statistical Program

The example below explains how to use SPSS (Statistical Package for the Social Sciences, available from www.spss.com) to examine data from an ex post facto study. It provides a small set of data with the independent variable being instrument family (woodwinds and brass) and the dependent variable being scores on a performance anxiety measure.

An ANOVA will be used to compare the scores of the woodwind and brass instrumentalists on a performance anxiety test. The inputted data for the example set of four woodwind and four brass instrumentalists shown in Table 12.5 would have two columns: one to demonstrate the independent variable groups and another to demonstrate the dependent variable scores. The independent variable column will have nominal level data: a number to represent those in the woodwind group (labeled 0 in this case) and a number to represent those in the brass group (labeled 1 in this case). Each row shows

TABLE 12.5   Example Data for One Independent and One Dependent Variable (N = 8)

	Group	Score
1.	0	91
2.	1	51
3.	0	83
4.	0	71
5.	1	70
6.	1	60
7.	1	61
8.	0	82

one person's group affiliation label and that same person's score on the performance anxiety test (so Sally the bassoonist may be first across, scoring 91 on the test, and Fred the trombonist may be second across, scoring 51, etc.).

The next step would be to check basic issues for calculating an ANOVA. These issues can be weighed by looking at histogram and box and whiskers graphs. To do this in SPSS, go to the "Analyze" drop-down and then choose "Descriptive Statistics" and "Explore." Place the variable "score" in the Dependent List and the variable "group" in the Factor list and then click on the "Plots" button. From there mark "Factor levels together" under "Boxplots" and" and "Histogram" under "Descriptive." Then click "Continue."

Viewing the box and whiskers graph, as shown in Figure 12.9, the spread, or *homogeneity of variance* across both groups appears consistent.

The histogram graph as shown in Figure 12.10 indicates that the distributions of the subgroup samples look like normal curves (display normality), especially for this example of eight data points. (Note that any real study would have a far larger sample size.)

You next calculate an ANOVA by going to the "Analyze" drop-down and choosing "General Linear Model" and "Univariate." Place the variable "score" in the Dependent Variable box and the variable "group" in the Fixed Factor(s) box. Then click "OK."

The readout will look like what is shown in Table 12.6, documenting that the difference between groups was statistically significant [$F(1, 6) = 13.12, p = .01$]. The original means can be obtained from the options button, showing that group 0 (woodwinds: mean of 81.75) had a higher overall mean score than 1 (brass: mean of 60.75).

Testing for differences among variables is at the core of many quantitative research designs. However, music teachers, too, can benefit from the procedures outlined in this chapter. For instance, when measuring differences in performance among students, a teacher might consider such ex post facto difference questions as "Do my students perform at different skill levels based on what instrument they have chosen to play, or their reading grades (high/low), or the amount of practice they reported last week (none/some/much)?" Music teachers can also weigh experimental difference questions of interest, such as "If I tried one method book format to introduce sight singing with

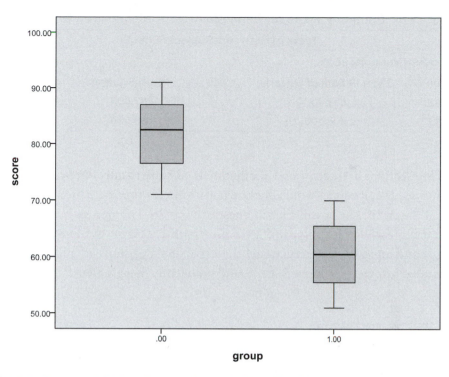

FIGURE 12.9   Box and Whisker Plots for Example Data (N = 8)

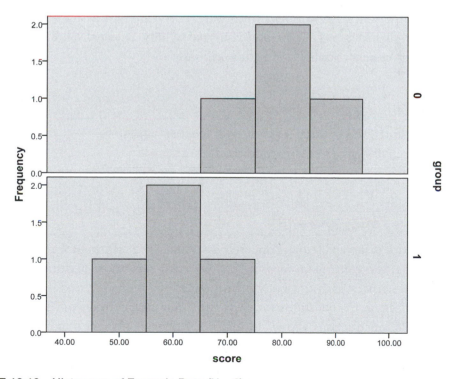

FIGURE 12.10   Histogram of Example Data (N = 8)

TABLE 12.6   Summary Table for Example ANOVA Results (N = 8)

Tests of Between-Subjects Effects

Dependent Variable: score

Source	Type III Sum of Squares	Df	Mean Square	F	Sig.
Group	882.000	1	882.000	13.115	.011
Error	403.500	6	67.250		

one of my sections of students and another method book to introduce sight singing with the other section, I wonder which method book format would help the students perform better at the end?" The possible list of questions is indeed numerous but always contextual to each teacher's interests and areas of expertise. It is always important to weigh, carefully and logically, all instructional choices so that decisions are not arbitrary or are not clouded by external, unpredictable, and potentially meaningless factors.

Chapter Summary

1. Ex post facto and experimental designs are types of difference studies found in quantitative music education research.
2. Analysis of variance measures differences between groups. Researchers need to check whether the assumptions of the ANOVA are met before using this statistic.
3. It is important for researchers to consider how a study is designed and implemented in order to avoid threats to internal validity. External validity issues can impact the generalizability of a study's finding.

Topics for Further Exploration

1. Types and levels of variables of interest to music educators.
2. Research designs and corresponding statistics.
3. How power, effect size, and sample size work together.

Suggested Assignments

1. Compare males and females on a self-assessment of performance anxiety. Then the class can construct a measure documenting severity of performance anxiety experiences, such as sweaty palms, quickened pulse, etc. and sum together responses on the questions for each individual to get an overall score. Using the SPSS instructions above, an instructor or students can then calculate an ANOVA, with gender being the independent variable, and performance anxiety being the dependent variable.

2. Design an experiment, such as jumping large/small, heavy/light origami frogs as described in "Activity-Based Statistics" (Schaeffer, Gnanadesikan, Watkins, & Witmer, 1996). Using the SPSS instructions above, an instructor or students can then calculate an ANOVA with the student-gathered data.

3. Descriptively or through the use of an ANOVA, use a demographic grouping variable of your choosing (such as grade, instrument, or gender) to compare the achievement of your students on an achievement or classroom test.

Recommended Reading

Frankel, J. R., & Wallen, N. E. (2009). *How to design and evaluate research in education* (7th ed.). Boston, MA: McGraw-Hill.

Huck, S. W. (2012). *Reading statistics and research* (6th ed.). Boston, MA: Pearson. Prentice Hall.

thirteen

Tools for Data Gathering

Basics of Content and Construction

This chapter:

- Describes essential characteristics of commonly used data gathering devices suitable in various modes of inquiry;
- Discusses methodological details involved in planning and designing specific tools—namely, interview schedules and questionnaires, tests for doing research, systematic observation protocols, and content analysis.

The purpose is to supplement information provided in previous chapters by describing a few of the tools that are useful for gathering data of various kinds. Additional "how to" sources, recommended at the end of the chapter, offer further guidance.

Introduction

This book began with what we call the spiral of inquiry—a process characterized by thinking, reading, observing, and sharing newly found information with others. In subsequent chapters, we often used the term "observe" broadly, referring to many forms of data gathering and analysis. You have learned in this textbook that different forms of observation—leading to the gathering of data and, at times, their simultaneous analysis—require devices, or tools, of varying kinds. Such tools can become useful in nearly any mode of inquiry.

Because of the diversity of available choices and the importance of carefully crafting data gathering devices, introductory research courses are often accompanied either by a lab or an additional class dedicated to the specifics of tool development. In places where that is not an option, this chapter is intended to help out. It describes a few of the methodological procedures that cross or straddle qualitative and quantitative research platforms, sometimes even bridging conceptual differences between the two.

Guidelines for planning and constructing tests, observation forms, surveys, and other devices useful for the collection and analysis of both quantitative and qualitative evidence may be found in various textbooks in the fields of education, psychology, and sociology (see Recommended Reading at the end of the chapter). *Rating scales* and *tests* are used to make thoughts and behaviors visible, to assess how well someone performs musically or academically in comparison to others, or to set performance standards of varying kinds. They can also ascertain how participants feel about specific issues you present to them. *Questionnaires* and *interviews* can provide similar information but might focus on how an individual or groups of individuals express their opinions. *Observation forms* of various kinds help to catalogue overtly visible actions and behaviors of individuals in groups or of entire groups.

The choices are, indeed, many, which may make it difficult to decide what kind of information is most suited for your own research purpose. Consider the progress of Jeannette, Carlos, and Juan in that regard.

Jeannette had begun working on a questionnaire concerning the perceptions of minority students about their own sense of singing voice as well as their beliefs about vocal production. She wanted to relate that information to a measure of cultural mistrust that had been used by Chinn (1997). While drafting items for the questionnaire, she realized that she perhaps should first talk informally with some classmates about the topic to give the questionnaire a contemporary "feel" by using language used "today" rather than nearly 20 years ago.

Having planned to model his research after Dale's thesis on high school teachers' perceived value of music technology (i.e., Smartboard, Finale, etc.) in their work with students, *Carlos* had come to the conclusion that his plans required adjustments for several reasons: (1) Dale's school district was large whereas Carlos's school district was small—in-depth interviews with the few music teachers in the school district might therefore be better than a formal questionnaire; (2) since the time Dale's study had been done, technological advances in self-guided music making had grown exponentially and Carlos was curious whether students might know more about such advances than their teachers.

In the course of reading several researchers' writings on operationalizing skills according to observable and measureable variables, *Juan* focused on a tool called the Continuous Response Digital Interface (e.g., Geringer & Madsen, 2004; Gregory, 1995, 2009; Schmidt, 1996). A website (http://www.music.fsu.edu/Music-Research-Centers/Center-for-Music-Research/CRDI/Research-Articles/2009) piqued his interest because of broad-based applications the CRDI seems to make possible. Juan planned on contacting the Center for Music Research at Florida State University for further details.

As may become clear from these examples, developing the kind of data gathering and analysis devices that Jeannette, Carlos, and Juan were thinking about for their respective projects requires foresight and good planning. This is so because the tools (or instruments) to be used in a study should be given careful thought with regard to the items to be included, the instructions (if applicable) to be given to the research participants, and the extent to which a tool yields reliable, valid, or trustworthy data.

Although statistical criteria of reliability and validity may be applicable only to quantitative research designs, comparable standards of excellence in research should be the goal of any qualitative researcher employing such designs. When the researcher is "the instrument," the level of preparation should be expected to be as stringent as it is for tools commonly serving the purpose of obtaining quantified information.

Essential Characteristics of Commonly Used Data Gathering Tools

The litmus test for the construction of any data gathering device is that the data you seek should accurately represent the research question that inspired them. By accurately, here is meant reliably and with validity in the case of quantitative data; in the case of qualitative work, coherent, credible, reflexive, resonant, rigorous, and worthy (Tracy, 2010; Malterud, 2001; Elliott, Fischer, & Rennie, 1999; see also Chapter 7). The terms should not be considered mutually exclusive but, instead, as being complementary.

The Constructs of Reliability and Validity Revisited

Establishing indicators for measurement reliability and validity has been discussed at length in prior chapters. It might be helpful, however, to recall the following: A requisite to the validity of a tool is its reliability, although a tool can be reliable without being valid. You could use a pencil to repeatedly measure your own body length and get close to the same number of pencil counts with repeated measures. But, such would be a foolish undertaking because there are better (more valid) ways to accurately obtain your body size.

Information can be considered reliable when repeated measurements yield the same results—whether obtained by two or more persons at the same moment or by one person over a specified period of time. Validity is a broader term with a wider array of definitions, all of which relate to the purpose for which a study is undertaken. This means that the validity of a data gathering tool is intrinsically linked to the data analysis itself, that part of research in which "what is out there" is either explained according to the particular theory within which the research purpose originated, or leads to the formulation of a theory.

At times, the best way to obtain valid data is with a battery of tools, that is, more than one. Jeannette's plans, for example, involved combining several data gathering devices that spanned from the measure of cultural mistrust used in Chinn's 1997 study (i.e., Terrell & Terrell, 1981, 1993) to measurements of vocal range and singing voice, to students' self-perceptions of the importance of singing in their lives. The development of rating scales of any kind always benefits from prior conversations (both informal and formal, that is, unstructured and structured) with potential study participants. Qualitatively obtained information would then lead to quantitative data gathering devices and any subsequent analysis.

It may appear that having only one tool to think about and to prepare for in a study is desirable over having to plan for several different ways by which to obtain your data. Such thinking is not necessarily accurate because "putting all your eggs in one basket" can be risky when it comes to determining a tool's validity or trustworthiness. If you try to use observation, interview, and performance ratings in a single study, you may face challenges of a different kind: Quantitatively, you need to make sure that the numbers in each tool are comparable to each other; qualitatively, you will have a huge amount of verbal data to analyze—a time-consuming and demanding process. This means that reliability, validity, and trustworthiness of data are more closely connected to each other than terminologies in quantitative and qualitative research approaches might suggest.

Working with Trustworthy and Useful Information

For data to be useful, they must be trustworthy. This is the case whether they are expressed numerically, verbally, or in images, and whether the research is about the past or the present. Empiricists, philosophers, and historians alike look for trustworthy and useful data when talking to informants, analyzing documents, systematically examining worldviews and belief systems, or seeking to obtain deep insights into ways of living and being in a particular sub-culture. Through transparency of procedures and interjudge consensus (see Chapters 10 and 11), they seek to establish, respectively, internal and external validity, also occasionally referred to as testimonial validity (e.g., Stephenson, Wagner, & Brandstatter, 1983). Skills of analytic reflexivity are judged by their degree of "credibility, dependability, and confirmability" (Elliott, Fischer, & Rennie, 1999, p. 218).

Many more terms than those documented here have been used to describe what in quantitative research has become known as reliability and validity. Always at stake is the extent to which one can believe in the accuracy of the data collected and in the likelihood that the data analysis is honest and true. Ethical conduct as a researcher therefore does not only mean that you show respect to your research participants and that you honor institutional guidelines but also that you act according to expected research conventions in your efforts to produce creditable data and results. At the heart of that expectation should not only be that you progressed in that regard but that you also described that progression in your original research report. The next section of this chapter therefore speaks to a few of the steps integral to that progression. We single out those tools that have not been explicitly addressed in previous chapters.

Planning Selected Data Gathering and Analysis Devices

This section describes aspects of constructing interview schedules and questionnaires, rating scales, tests specifically designed for research purposes, observation forms of various kinds, and procedures for content analysis. Like the tools spoken of in previous chapters, many of them may be used across quantitative and qualitative research traditions.

Interview Schedules and Questionnaires

In Chapter 8 you learned about the importance of interviews (both formal and informal) in qualitative research. Informal interviews (also called unstructured) are open-ended conversations between you (the researcher) and your participant(s). You have an overall purpose, but ideas are allowed to develop freely in a chat-like atmosphere in which no topic is off limits. Such interviews often are the first step in the development of a formal or structured interview.

Structured interviews are organized ahead of a conversation and follow a particular train of thought conceptualized for the purpose of your study. To prepare for such an interview, you develop an *interview schedule*; that is, an outline of leading questions you want to ask each of your participants. Interview schedules ease data analysis later because hardly any unexpected topics come up—they are built into the schedule from the beginning.

Structured interviews keep you and your participants "on-task" but also may stifle the conversational atmosphere. Unstructured interviews, on the other hand, allow you to "feel out" how each participant thinks about a particular issue. Most useful during the early, exploratory stages of a project—be it qualitative or quantitative—unstructured interviews can be beneficial in the planning stages of writing items for questionnaires and can help when examining your thoughts on research projects and ideas for future work. Their advantage lies in their openness—you can explore topics as the need arises. The disadvantage lies in not knowing when to end the conversation and making sure that all important aspects of your research purpose are equally addressed by all participants. It can be easy to get off track and hard to get back on.

Drafting a Questionnaire

Planning for and working out a questionnaire (or other survey instrument) requires detailed steps, many of which are addressed by Dillman (2007), already referenced in Chapter 10. Note that this textbook does not distinguish between *survey* and *questionnaire*. In daily life, the term survey is more commonly used than questionnaire, although the tool used for a survey is the questionnaire—a collection of written questions to which, in most cases, specific answers are expected. In either case, think of a questionnaire as a well-crafted, concise inventory of questions about either personal opinions or factual information.

The questionnaire should be a communicative tool between you (the researcher) and the population/sample in the study. The respondents should be at ease with the issues addressed and be able to understand the questions without having to guess their meaning. Unstructured interviews may be helpful for this aspect of questionnaire development because they can help you discover the language used by your target respondents. Simplicity (Doherty, 2006) and short sentences in which to couch the questions should be your goal—whether you develop a paper and pencil or a web-based format. This means that some technical terms might have to be "translated" into words that make sense to the respondents.

If an item cannot be readily justified in the context of a given purpose statement, eliminate the question from the draft. Your motto should always be to "keep it short" and to avoid questions that are ambiguous, rhetorical, or negative. Also, watch out for any leading questions that have "loaded" words or double meanings.

The first pilot draft of any questionnaire should contain open-ended answers that give the respondents an opportunity to point out issues you may have missed or stated unclearly. The next draft should be distributed to a group of respondents who resemble or are a sub-sample of the targeted population/sample you have in mind. Discussing their views on specific issues and learning about the perceptions they harbor regarding your topic may bring new aspects of importance, and even unanticipated variables to light.

When building the sequence of the survey, group questions according to response type; for instance, open-ended, multiple-choice, census-type and checklist items. Census-type questions usually center on participants' demographics, but be careful to avoid questions whose answers you could have found on your own by checking public records or other publicly available documents. In Figure 13.1 you see an example for each of the other three question types worded for a survey about job satisfaction among music teachers.

Whichever formats you choose, order the items in each group from broadest to most specific. That process is called *filtering* because it allows the respondent to move from one section to the next without having to read all items that are not applicable to his or her situation. An example might be:

Have you purchased a musical instrument within the last 12 months?

The researcher-provided answers should be:

Yes _, No_. If yes, please continue with the following questions. If no, go to Section B, page 3.

Of course, computerized surveys, such as those available from www.surveymonkey.com allow for possibly better and more expedient ways of moving from one item to the next.

The Issue: Job Satisfaction of Music Teachers

Type of question   *Possible wording*

Open-ended: What do you find most satisfying about your
chosen profession?

Yes-No: Do you feel that reason(s) for enjoying your work
outweigh your reason(s) for not enjoying it?

Multiple Choice   Yes—Most of the time—Not sure—Seldom—Not at all

Checklist: Of the 10 reasons given here, please check
[or rank by importance] up to five:
      __ I love to perform with the children
      __ The pay is adequate
      __ I love working with children
      __ I feel valued in my work
      __ I like being off in the summer
      __ I like my weekly schedule
      __ My non-music colleagues and I work well
         together
      __ I always strive for improving the quality of
         my work
      __ My work gives me opportunities to be creative
      __ I can adequately manage my professional
         and family duties

FIGURE 13.1   Various Response Formats to One Questionnaire Item

Pilot-testing not only your complete survey but also the cover letter is paramount. Leedy and Ormrod (2001) advise researchers to inform responders how they came to be selected and why their information is essential to the research project. They also suggest that candidates should not reveal that an investigation is in fulfillment of a degree. Some sample drafts of IRB-created form letters, however, require just that. Check with your advisor about expected policy. The letter should include detailed instructions about how to answer the survey and where to send it after completion, as well as an offer to share the results with respondents. Make sure to remember that promise once your project has been completed.

Rating Scales

Muna developed a self-rating scale for her students' practicing habits (similar to a Likert scale, see Chapter 10) by chatting with them about practice. She talked to each student individually and summarized the nature of their conversation after each session in her research log book, planning to incorporate those reported habits in the self-rating tool later. For consistency, she talked to each student during at least two lessons, scheduled approximately a week apart, so that she could note inconsistencies or differences in comments by the students. She would have preferred more than two conversational sessions per student but was afraid of student burn-out or boredom.

Muna had two reasons for multiple, time-spaced conversations: (1) she wanted to be certain that she improved on her own way of conversing with her students; and (2) she wanted the students to become comfortable with talking about practicing. She had not previously discussed practicing in a systematic way.

Likert-type scales are used in questionnaires to enable respondents to numerically value specific tasks. You might, for instance, ask music teachers to rate their level of job satisfaction. Another kind of rating scale is the criterion-referenced scale, in which each ranking is defined according to specific, pre-set criteria. Such a scale is used for judging how close a performance comes to an established standard. Those standards should be based on evidence from the literature if possible; if not, setting and testing them would be one of your tasks as both a researcher and a teacher who wants to improve performance rating or adjudication scales for classroom use only.

Begin by ranking a large number of recorded student performances from highest to lowest by category (i.e., pitch, rhythm, style, technique, tone quality). Listen for the spread of performance levels and qualities and come up with clearly stated *descriptors* (words or phrases) that detail performance criteria within each category from highest to lowest. Check your descriptors by selecting several of the recorded student performances by chance and rate them according to the scales you developed. Establish a rating consistency score for yourself (see interjudge reliability, Chapter 11).

A low score indicates that your criteria are not very clear. Continue to adjust the criteria until you reach a satisfactorily high consistency score with yourself. Then create a recording of "anchors" that represent performances at each of the levels described in your scale. Use this to teach any additional reviewers about the criteria for each performance level. Make sure, however, that the examples you use as anchors are not drawn from the sample you intend to use, particularly if your purpose is research-oriented.

The reliability of the ranking scores in your study is dependent upon how well your judges consistently apply the defined performance criteria to a given performance. It is preferable that you as the researcher not be involved as a judge. This means that your judges need to learn to consistently and in agreement with each other apply the criterion rankings as you set them. Plan on a sufficient number of training sessions and prepare enough examples so that a judge's own ratings become consistent over time (internal consistency) and generally agree with other judges' ratings. (One application of these procedures may be found in Gordon, 1967.)

Tests Designed for Use in Research

At least two types of written tests are commonly used as research tools: (1) essays and/or test items that require short answers; and (2) multiple-choice options. Essay tests, best in small classes or for small groups, allow research participants to respond to a question freely and in their own words. This form of assessment can be either qualitatively or quantitatively analyzed but favors those respondents who like to write and are at ease with expressing themselves verbally. It also has several drawbacks: (1) there seldom is time allotted for proper contemplation and for organizing the content into a well-structured essay; and (2) applying a score to essays tends to be more a matter of personal preferences than adherence to a priori established criteria. You could minimize the subjectivity of scoring by providing the respondents with a list of anticipated topics that should be covered in the essay and describing how those would be weighted within the overall essay.

Readily quantifiable tests include true–false answers, multiple-choice answers, completion of sentences, matching items of information, and appropriately rank-ordering response choices provided by the researcher. As you are likely aware, multiple-choice test items are the most commonly used and suitable for large group testing. The items are relatively easy to score and the presence of several alternative answers reduces the chance of guessing. For the purpose of this book, we describe below how you may plan the items in a quantifiable music achievement test for the purpose of assessing music students' entry level of music knowledge and skills in an introductory college music class.

Planning the Test

A teaching fellow (call her Carla) in a large music department of a university in the midwestern United States instructs an introductory music education course for elementary education majors. The actual purpose of the course is to prepare pre-service teachers in basic classroom music skills, a requirement for teacher certification. A prerequisite for developing these skills is the development of basic musicianship skills as defined by the music education faculty of the department.

Musicianship as defined by the faculty involves the successful execution of tasks in specific content areas at various levels of comprehension and conceptualization. The music content areas are:

Pitch: Notation, melodic patterns, intervals
Rhythm: Note values, rhythmic quality, rhythmic patterns
Timbre: Instruments, voices, tone color
Harmony: Polyphony, homophony

The four levels of comprehension and conceptualization are that the student:

■ Knows basic terms;
■ Identifies same-different;
■ Compares concepts;
■ Applies concepts to improvisation and the analysis of student compositions.

Carla wants to find out how much and at what level of conceptualization her students exhibit this type of musicianship when beginning the class. She believes they would more easily demonstrate many of the prerequisite musicianship skills demanded by the music faculty if the music examples were drawn from popular songs they were already familiar with.

To examine her assumption, Carla designed a musicianship test to be given to the students early in the semester. She began by determining how many test items she needed in light of the definition of musicianship as provided by the faculty. A so-called specification table allowed her to do that (Table 13.1). It tallies the objectives for a specific group of learning tasks in such a way that you can determine how many tasks you would need per rubric to cover the objectives.

Across the top of the table are the categories of instructional objectives or types of learning to be tested. In the left-hand column is a listing of the content areas to be covered. The numbers in the cells state the projected quantity of questions for each area, if the test is not to exceed 60 items. Carla decided on that number in light of the time she had available for each student and considering that she wanted half of the tasks to be paper-and-pencil items and the other half performance items.

Note that the relative number of questions in each category relates to the importance of each rubric as weighted by Carla. A blank cell means no testing task. How to weigh particular items in the overall scheme of class content depends on the purpose of the research. If this was an achievement test to be given at the end of a semester, for instance, you would need to tell your students where you placed your instructional emphasis throughout the semester.

TABLE 13.1   Two-Way Specification Table (Adapted from Anastasi, 1988, p. 431)

Instructional Objectives

Content Areas	Knows basic terms	Identifies same-different	Compares concepts	Applies concepts to the analysis of compositions	Total
Pitch					
Notation	3		3		**6**
Melodic patterns		3	3	3	**9**
Intervals		3			**3**
Rhythm					
Rhythmic quality			3	2	**5**
Rhythmic patterns		3		2	**5**
Note Values	3				**3**
Tone color					
Instruments	3	2	2	2	**9**
Voices	2		2	2	**6**
Harmony					
Polyphony	2	2	2	2	**8**
Homophony		2	2	2	**6**
Total	**13**	**15**	**17**	**15**	**60**

The totals of each column represent the relative importance of each conceptual task as weighted by Carla, and the total on the right-hand side of the table represents the relative weight attached by her to each of the content areas. While this is not the only way to plan the development of an examination or a test, it is a good way to lay out the tasks before you begin designing them.

Judging from the table, Carla tried to be even-handed about which tasks to focus on but perhaps favored instrument knowledge and the issue of polyphony a bit more than she should have if she wanted to use familiar examples from popular music for the tasks. This point was raised by two of her teaching fellow colleagues when Carla asked for critical feedback about the table prior to designing and item analyzing the tasks themselves.

Designing Tasks and/or Writing Items

Many general sources on the writing of test items are available. Among many others, see Nunnally and Bernstein (1994), Gronlund and Waugh (2009), and Johnson, Nadas, and Green (2010), as well as additional sources recommended at the end of this chapter. Principally, sources on test development and other achievement measures stress that a test should be constructed as efficiently as possible so as to minimize error and bias. At the same time, for each learning task to be tested you should have a minimum of two items so as to establish a measure of response consistency.

When designing test items for conducting research, bear in mind the following points:

1. Because items must be brief, the intention of questions can be easily misunderstood. To avoid that problem, strive for clarity in your statements and avoid ambiguous or double-meaning phrases.
2. Eliminate all "Either-Or" questions because any one answer can only respond to one of the two choices.
3. Use correct grammar. In the case of a multiple-choice format, all response possibilities must not only be grammatically correct but also grammatically consistent and of approximately the same length. Test constructors tend to spend more time in phrasing the correct answer than in phrasing the wrong options. This leads to guessing an answer by appearance rather than by knowledge of its content.
4. Similarly, take care with the wording of incorrect responses because poor grammar may serve as a clue for incorrect answers.
5. Performance-based items should draw on musical tasks with which your participants are familiar—unless, of course, your objective is to find out how a respondent handles unfamiliar musical tasks. But even those must be within the range of skills that can be reasonably expected from your study participants.
6. Dependent on the purpose of your study and connected to the previous point, you should provide your respondents with enough time to practice what you expect them to do. You also should make sure that your instructions are clear and that the respondents can ask for clarification before commencing the task.

7. Accept criticism for as long as possible. When you revise a drafted test, have it examined again by another group of individuals you trust. Once the test is used for research, corrections cannot be made anymore. Include calculations of the revision of drafts when setting your time schedule.

Tools for Observations of Many Kinds

There are many possible purposes for classroom observation; of those, Waxman, Tharp, and Hilberg (2004, p. 3) emphasize four: (1) describing instructional practices; (2) investigating instructional inequities for different groups of students; (3) improving teacher education programs; and (4) improving teachers' classroom instruction based on feedback from individual classroom profiles. Each of those purposes impacts your questions as well as choices of methods by which to observe.

Purposes that lead to quantifying the data require coding and tallying procedures on pre-designed observation forms. Researchers who favor qualitative methods might question such controlling process for reasons described in Chapters 7 and 8. Either choice, a priori codes or a posteriori interpretative analysis, takes time and diligence when you want to assure that your data are valid and reliable or trustworthy and honest.

In the realm of quantitative education research throughout the 1960s and early 1970s, so-called *systematic observation techniques* seemed to mandate the presence of non-participant observers either in the actual classroom setting or when viewing videotaped lessons. In either situation, instructional actions theorized as important contributors to effective teaching were "coded" and tallied when observed (see, among others, Flanders, 1970; Gage, 1963; Medley & Mitzel, 1963; Rosenshine & Furst, 1973; and Travers, 1973). More recent applications in music education include, among others, Duke, 1994, 1999/2000; Froehlich, 1995; Madsen, Prickett, Gates, and Alabama Project, 1987; Sink, 2002. Contemporary observation techniques have become technologically as well as philosophically more diversified (e.g., Gumm, 2003; Henry & Weber, 2010; Waxman, Tharp, & Hilberg, 2004). Participant and non-participant observational approaches are employed side by side and may utilize pre-formulated, non-judgmental categorical systems; evaluation forms for effective instruction; and intuitive, holistic-narrative descriptions of formal and informal learning situations.

Systematically gathered observational tools are useful for keeping track of specific actions and behaviors you see and hear in the presence of others as well as for interpreting complex relationships. You already know about narratives, portfolios, checklists, tallies, and ratings scales and their use in research (see above and Chapters 7–12). Additional possibilities include so-called running records, anecdotal records, checklists, rating scales, narrative event sampling, portfolios and third-party testimonies, tally event sampling, and time sampling description, among others. (This terminology is freely adapted from Nicolson and Shipstead's distinction of eight different forms of record keeping in early childhood research [2002, pp. xv–xviii]). The approaches can stand on their own or, in some cases, in combination—be it in qualitative or quantitative research designs.

Running records are those in which you write in the present tense and for a specified length of time or designated activity what specific persons say, do (Nicolson & Shipstead, 2002, p. 114), or even omit to do. Anecdotal records are "more than something interesting, emotional, or amusing to share." Rather, they are "directly observed incident[s] written in a short, concise, non-judgmental narrative" (p. 136). The terms narrative and tally as applied to event- as well as time-sampling refer to choices of situations created by particular individuals with consequences for behaviors and actions by other individuals. From all behaviors and actions possible you select those that directly speak to the topic of your research.

In narrative sampling, for instance, you isolate incidents in which one action causes subsequent ones to occur and describe verbally those situations in which you see causally related actions or behaviors (Nicolson & Shipstead, 2002, p. 203). Tally event sampling is similar. For example, you might choose to observe only those students who have been identified by a teacher as "difficult to handle" and tally such observed incidents. In that case, you are interested in their frequency of occurrence, rather than their specific characteristics. In time sampling, real-time durations become the measure for sampled incidents. It is done either by notating observed actions according to equal time intervals or by recording the time lapse between the action that caused subsequent ones to occur and the action that concluded the incident.

Any of the sampling techniques described in the previous paragraph require the skill and/or experience of drawing inferences from one observed action or event to another. For instance, when you observe a choir singing solfège and see the singers' eyes uniformly directed to the front, you may infer that the director is using hand signs even if you yourself cannot see them (Standley & Madsen, 1991, p. 7). This is an inference that differs from judgments in which you summarize observations by describing a teacher as "excellent" or a student as "lazy." In both cases, the actions from which an observer might have drawn such evaluative judgments would need to be documented to allow for the rendered interpretive "summary." Without such documentation, the judgment would not meet standards of systematic observation as a research tool.

Forms for reporting specific observations—"live" or recorded—are referred to as *systems*, *instruments*, *schedules*, *protocols*, or *inventories*. Documenting observed activities on such forms is referred to as *coding* and requires knowledge of the purpose for which the observations take place. The coding is done either by the researcher or by designated observers who have been trained by the researcher. Ways of coding differ depending on whether your methods are qualitative or quantitative. Qualitative codes, as described in Chapter 8, emerge inductively from the data. Quantitative codes are usually determined ahead of time based on information from the scholarly literature.

"Live" and Recorded Observations

"Live" observations occur in real time while classroom activities are proceeding; if an event is not noticed at the moment that it occurs, it is lost for all time. That is problematic for any kind of research, but especially so for quantitative analysis, which requires observer reliability. To establish reliability, either more than one observer is needed in the classroom or one trained observer conducts all observations over a specified length of time. When recording equipment is used, there generally is no other person in the classroom than the one who handles the equipment. But even that need may be eliminated if the camera is stationary and on remote control. Recorded observations have the advantage that events can be reviewed and studied repeatedly. Coding reliability may therefore be higher for video- or audio-based observation than when observers are stationed in the classroom. The disadvantage of observing recorded lessons is that the positioning of the camera in the classroom (whether hand-held or stationary) dictates to some degree what you may study. This is especially the case in large classes or performance group settings.

Both types of direct observation, "live" and recorded, carry with them a certain degree of intrusion into what otherwise would be assumed to be a normal setting. This makes it highly advisable for any researcher interested in the use of systematic observation techniques to minimize the appearance of intrusion by allowing those under observation to get accustomed to the recording equipment and/or the observer(s). That process, however, takes time and should be considered carefully. It might be just as important to conduct carefully planned observations that focus on the actions and behavior of students who are directly engaged with music making and listening outside of school.

Observer Training

Often, specific research plans and designs require you to serve as the observer as well as the researcher. But if you plan to observe teachers and/or students in different schools, you might consider recruiting some additional helpers for your project. Whichever option you choose, practicing observation skills is important. Known as observer training, its purpose is to become comfortable with the setting(s), the individuals with whom you will be together over a specified period of time, and the issues you have elected to focus on. Most importantly, however, practice becomes necessary to get fully "in tune" with the purpose of your project: Are you interested in observing student actions outside or inside the classroom? Do you address questions concerning classroom management and expectations of "good" classroom conduct? Does your focus lie on issues concerning your own actions as the teacher? Or, are you looking for causality between teacher actions and learning gains? Is your research directed at behavioral issues, teacher self-improvement, effectiveness, or non-guided/tutored learning?

Know the Purpose

In *behavioral research*, specific beliefs about the relationship between motivation and action have resulted in many studies on so-called "on-task" and "off-task" behavior, how students react to specific teacher actions, and what instructional (motivational) strategies might yield the most consistently positive pupil behavior (as operationalized by the researcher). Research on teacher self-improvement can also be situated in behaviorist theories but does not have to be. Methodologically, such research may include tallying the frequency and quality of cueing, phrasing, and modeling in conducting situations as well as the giving of cutoffs, the beating of time, inflection of voice, and facial expressions throughout rehearsals. Such functional effectiveness research is based on the assumption that it is possible to define, observe, and measure those variables or actions that make one teacher more "effective" than another.

Possibly in response to behavioral and effectiveness research traditions in music education, observational research on informal learning in music has been purposefully open-ended and contextually flexible (see Chapters 7 and 8). It clearly has steadily grown since the middle of the 20th century (see, among others, Abrahams & Head, 2005; Clements, 2010; deNora, 2000; Green, 2001, 2011; Shehan-Campbell, 2010). Whatever your project's focus, be prepared to spend a good deal of time to internalize its purpose and rationale in very tangible terms.

For instance, in the psychological theory of *behaviorism*, going back to psychologists I. Pavlov (1849–1936) and B. F. Skinner (1904–1990), causality is central. What is or is not appropriate in a particular context can be "corrected" by giving immediate rewards and/or "disincentives" (known as "reinforcement") as deemed appropriate in the situation at hand. As an observer, you therefore would need to take into consideration the teacher's interpretation of pupil conduct. Quantitatively spoken, the criterion measure for, respectively, on-task or off-task or positive or negative behavior depends on the teacher's expectations toward "good behavior" in the classroom. You therefore would need to make contextually valid judgments about teacher and student actions (both verbal and non-verbal) as they are observed either "live" or as tape-recorded lessons.

As a spin-off from effectiveness research and due to increased emphasis on school accountability across districts, states, and even nations, the last 20 years have seen a trend to morph direct observation forms into evaluation forms. Many such forms exist, usually specific to a particular state and/or school district. With the help of checklists, rating scales, and open-ended commentary about desirable and undesirable teaching strategies (according to the interpretations of school officials who serve as observers), the forms make evaluative and inferential judgments for the purpose of creating individual profiles of teacher effectiveness over time.

Teacher self-improvement studies (discussed above) use similar techniques to those common in behavioral research but often for a different purpose. Checkmarks, observational categories, and rating scales assess clarity of communication along with patterns of verbal versus non-verbal interaction in the classroom, sequencing of instruction, and other pedagogically important constructs (Gumm, 2003; Price, 1992, 1998; Price & Yarbrough, 1993/1994; Sink, 2002). Negative and positive reinforcement, the degree of eye contact with the performers, and the relationship of individual coaching to sectional work vis-à-vis the entire ensemble are also frequently included. Focus, however, is less on testing theory than gaining insights into the superiority of one teaching method and/or style over another. The research is practice-oriented, as a result of which observation protocol and observer training may differ from case to case. In some instances, descriptive qualitative narratives are added to explain, illuminate, and otherwise enhance any quantitatively analyzed data, an approach that is sometimes called "mixed methods."

From whichever perspective you approach observational tasks, you can use preexisting forms and templates or develop new ones. If you make use of available forms, be sure the content matches your project purpose fully. Re-examine reported reliability scores and establish new ones for your own project. Plan on doing at least one pilot study in which you take a tape-recorded lesson or segment thereof and watch what you see with the help of the form in front of you. If you find that the items on the form consistently match what you see and hear, your initial judgment may be proven valid. If for some reason you find that you have to write into the form many additional observations and comments or that you or other observers have serious disagreements, you should either adjust the existing form or develop new observational guidelines, in the form of a tally sheet or checklist, categorical roster, or any other means by which you can systematically document and analyze observational data. Whether or not you lean toward qualitative or quantitative methods of data gathering and analysis, you might apply what Ponterotto and Grieger (1999) suggested for all research; namely, "merging qualitative and quantitative perspectives in a researcher identity" (p. 49). As an example of a divergent viewpoint, see Sciarra, 1999.

Content Analysis

After *Michelle* had collected and critically analyzed sources from various disciplines and perspectives related to music education and school reform, she realized her data set had become quite large. She would need some guidance in analyzing them according to her research questions. *Prof. E.* directed her to look up "content analysis" as an additional research tool. In doing so, Michelle discovered that the term tends to be used rather loosely by one group of researchers and very stringently by another.

Content analysis stands for various analytic techniques by which documents, artifacts, and even transcribed conversations can be examined. Evidence may be drawn from the content of newspaper and journal articles, books, speeches, conference reports, and minutes of professional associations, letters, and diaries. Methods range from informal and intuitively guided text analyses to technical, quantitative methods of word counts within various printed documents, including transcriptions of interviews, diaries, and observational narratives.

Much literature exists on the subject of content analysis. It comes to us from such disciplines as library science, journalism research, and other "soft" sciences. In music education, content analysis has been used as a qualitative rather than quantitative means of data analysis, but both should be considered equally useful in examining written texts, the spoken word, and pictorial performance venues. In its broadest sense, content analysis asks: "Who says what to whom, why, and with what effect?"

Many recent sources reiterate what Holsti (1969) stated when he defined content analysis as "any technique for making inferences by objectively and systematically identifying specified characteristics of messages" (p. 14). True to current thinking about the place of so-called objectivity and subjectivity in all research, more recent sources (e.g., Krippendorff, 2004; Krippendorff & Bock, 2009) stress the value of multiple perspectives by which to examine who the author behind a given text is (that is, the person behind the name); or, what meanings, associations, values, motives, or intentions might be inferred from a particular communication, be it written or spoken.

Procedures for addressing such questions are not unlike other coding mechanisms described earlier: Complex interactive and communicative structures are categorized within *units of analysis* so that the researcher can gain insights into the "architecture" of a given text, how its structure might have been developed, and/or why it is what it is. Content analysis may also be applied to the analysis of creative writing, be it poetry or words put to music. In other words, any written signs and symbols employed by a sender (Source A) for the purpose of communicating a meaning to the recipient (Source B) can be examined.

Because content analytic procedures may be applied to the investigation of any documentary evidence, units of analysis vary greatly. In literary research, they can be one sentence or a paragraph, one page or an entire chapter. In social science research, a unit of analysis may be the individual or the group of individuals under study.

The Technique

Many software programs exist in a variety of disciplines that facilitate content analytic techniques (e.g., Gottschalk & Bechtel, 2008; Hansen, 2009; Neuendorf, 2002, 2006; Thelwall, 2009). Neuendorf's (2006) comprehensive online source about content analysis provides web page resources, bibliographies, archives, reliability and coding procedures that allow readers, for a fee, to review such programs online. Perusing those sources will remind you once again that the criteria according to which documentary evidence is gathered and analyzed depend entirely on the purpose of a project. Traditionally, however, three investigative areas seem to have emerged that may specifically prove useful for research in music education: (1) values, attitudes, and beliefs of specific individuals or groups of individuals as they reflect developments in society, in a profession, or in a field of study; (2) linguistic styles in relationship to communicative patterns among various groups of people; and (3) documents as reflections of prevailing trends of thought among different generations of people.

The coding procedures can be highly formalized (as in available computer programs) or individually structured by the researcher. As with the use of standardized and researcher-constructed tests, self-designed content analysis procedures require a greater degree of scrutiny concerning their reliability, validity, and/or trustworthiness than "tried-and-proven" procedures. Methodologically, however, all approaches should take into consideration the following questions: How is the research problem defined in terms of analytic *categories*? What *unit of analysis* becomes the basis for classification (a word, sentence, paragraph, or statement per person or group)? What system of *enumeration* will be used if the study lies in the realm of quantitative analysis? And, in the case of qualitative methods, how will you establish the trustworthiness of your interpretative efforts?

The smaller and more specific a unit of analysis, the easier it tends to be to establish its observer reliability; the broader the unit, the harder (even possibly unsuitable) such an undertaking becomes. Systems of enumeration may be frequency counts of documented units (in quantitative analysis), space attributed to such units in a transcript, intensity of terms used to make a point, or a combination of all of the above. In the case of measuring the intensity with which something was or is said, Likert-type rating scales might be useful.

For all procedures, describe the processes you chose clearly and do not hesitate to point out where you encountered difficulties with establishing clear analytic categories or rubrics. No research methodology is without its challenges and acknowledging where they occurred may be one important indicator of trustworthiness.

In summary, each content analytic tool sets its own demands and, as is the case with all other devices described earlier, requires careful preparation. Whatever your purpose, be prepared for the fact that nothing is as easy as at first it appears. Anticipate the unexpected and know that whenever you work with people or machines, complications can arise. A good researcher knows this and plans accordingly, assuming always that everything takes longer than anticipated. If things do not work out as planned, stay calm and do the best you can by acknowledging in your written report why you were not able to execute all of the planned steps as conceptualized.

Awareness of flaws or mistakes does not necessarily weaken a project as long as either gives you the motivation to think of new and possibly better ways to address such weaknesses in the future. Think back to the spiral of inquiry mentioned at the beginning of this book: The ongoingness of the process itself is the driving force that allows you to make mistakes and learn from them. Furthermore, not everything that seemingly "goes wrong" in a study is your fault. Rather, it is the inevitable fact that life has its own rules. We may be able to anticipate and even work around them, but we cannot always control them, no matter how hard we try to expect the unexpected.

Chapter Summary

1. The purpose of your study guides all decisions concerning any particular data-gathering tool suitable for your study.
2. Knowledge about details involved in the development of data-gathering tools can impact decisions about the kind of questions you choose to answer.
3. Among the many tools commonly found in music education research, surveys, tests, rating scales, observation forms, and content analysis are used most frequently. Although computer programs may ease the step-by-step procedures of documenting all reliability and validity scores, continue to focus on trustworthiness and usefulness as additional quality indicators.

4. The development of any one of the tools mentioned above takes time and should be repeatedly pilot tested. Even pre-existing tools require the re-examination of previously reported scores of reliability and validity.
5. Expect the unexpected.

Topics for Further Exploration

1. Connect each of the tools described above with students in RC 533: Which students might be interested in which tools, and why?
2. Connect each of the tools described above to the research interests of students in your research class.

Suggested Assignments

1. Find a recent research study that details the development of a specific research tool. Summarize and evaluate the author's description of that process.
2. Find a published research article that is expressly derived from a dissertation and that deals with the development of a research tool. Compare how the author described the process in the dissertation and, subsequently, in the published article.
3. Design a short (approximately 25-item) achievement test on factual knowledge suitable in a music appreciation class as you might envision it.
4. Compose three essay questions to assess some conceptual knowledge in music education and list criteria for scoring them.
5. Develop a criterion-related rating scale to evaluate a music-teaching situation of your choice.
6. Draft a questionnaire to obtain information on how non-music students view music students':

    a. Attitudes toward the rest of the university.
    b. Attitudes toward social position within the university.
    c. Abilities in non-music subject matters.

7. Examine up to five available computer software programs for the use in direct observation and content analysis. Rank them according to their ease of usability and compare the rankings among your peers.
8. Assess and evaluate existing published tests for use in:

    a. Music education:

        i. Music aptitude;
        ii. Music achievement;
        iii. Music teaching style.

b. Possibilities in general education and social science:

i. Learning style;

ii. Ethnic identity.

9. Of the studies listed in Appendix K, select two methodologically different articles on a comparable topic (gender, improvisation, outreach/partnerships, policy/school reform, recruitment/retention, and student learning). Abstract both studies and determine the relative strength of each of the data-gathering tool(s) used.

10. Discuss validity and reliability issues concerning measures in existing music education studies.

Recommended Reading

Barman, B. S. (2009). *Tools and techniques of data or information collection and its analysis* (Version 6). Available from http://knol.google.com/k/methods-and-analysis-techniques-for-information-collection

Bernard, H. R., & Ryan, G. W. (2010). *Analyzing qualitative data: Systematic approaches.* Los Angeles, CA: Sage.

Braverman, M. T., & Slater, J. K. (Eds.). (1996). *Advances in survey research.* San Francisco, CA: Jossey-Bass.

Campbell, J. D. (1990). Self-esteem and clarity of the self-concept. *Journal of Personality and Social Psychology, 59*(3), 538–549.

Divakaran, A. (Ed.). (2009). *Multimedia content analysis: Theory and applications.* New York: Springer.

Everitt, B. (2010). *Multivariable modeling and multivariate analysis for the behavioral* sciences. Boca Raton: CRC Press.

Fetterman, D. (2010). *Ethnography: Step-by-step* (3rd ed.). Los Angeles: Sage.

Francosi, R. (2010). *Quantitative narrative analysis.* Los Angeles, CA: Sage.

Guerra-López, I. (2008). *Performance evaluation: Proven approaches for improving program and organizational performance.* San Francisco, CA: Jossey-Bass.

Gumm, A. (2003). *Music teaching style: Moving beyond tradition.* Galesville, MD: Meredith Music Publications, a division of G.W. Music, Inc.

Izard, J. (2005). Overview of test construction. In K. N. Ross (Series Ed.), *Quantitative research methods in educational planning.* Module 6. UNESCO: International Institute for Educational Planning. Retrieved July 22, 2011 from http://www.sacmeq.org and http://www.unesco.org/iiep.

Kopala, M., & Suzuki, L. A. (Eds.). (1999). *Using qualitative methods in psychology.* Thousand Oaks, CA: Sage.

Kubiszyn, T., & Borich, G. (2000). *Educational testing and measurement: Classroom application and practice* (6th ed.). New York: John Wiley & Sons, Inc.

Loader, B. R., Park, M., & Abington, O. (Eds.). (2007). *Young citizens in the digital age: Political engagement, young people, and new media.* New York: Routledge.

Roblyer, M. D. (2006). *Integrating educational technology into teaching* (4th ed.). Upper Saddle River, NJ: Pearson/Merrill Prentice Hall.

Thorndike, R. M., & Thorndike-Christ, T. (2010). *Measurement and evaluation in psychology and education* (8th ed.). Boston: Pearson.

Wiesner, W. H., & Cronshaw, S. F. (1988). A meta-analytic investigation of the impact of interview format and degree of structure on the validity of the employment interview. *Journal of Occupational Psychology, 61,* 275–290. Retrieved July 7, 2011 from http://commonsenseatheism.com/wp-content/uploads/2011/01/Wiesner-Cronshaw-A-meta-analytic-investigation-of-the-impact-of-interview-format-and-degree-of-structure-on-the-validity-of-the-employment-interview.pdf

Yanow, D., & Schwartz-Shea, P. (Eds.). (2006). *Interpretation and method: Empirical research methods and the interpretive turn.* Armonk, NY: Sharpe.

fourteen

"So What?"

Interpreting and Sharing Your Findings

This chapter addresses how to:

- Interpret your findings with the help of the "so what" question;
- Make the original research accessible to different audiences;
- Continue the spiral of inquiry by thinking about further research in light of the work accomplished.

Although different modes of inquiry bring with them a variety of formats and expectations toward how a completed research document might look, this chapter focuses on common elements among them as the springboard for future projects.

Introduction

Conducting an investigation—for the purpose of writing a dissertation or to carry out a long-standing research agenda—can take much of your time. In either case, though, consider the process as being incomplete as long as you have not publicly shared the results of the investigation with the profession at large. The spiral of inquiry requires no less. In fact, some universities, as an integral part of accepting a dissertation for the doctoral degree, expect the submission of a scholarly article to a peer-reviewed journal. Such a requirement might even include the acceptance of the manuscript for publication.

If your university does not have a publishing requirement for graduation, explaining to others what you did and why, in your view, it matters, is an essential step in the spiral of inquiry for several reasons. One, you interpret your findings in light of the literature you reviewed for the study. Two, you help the reader understand how your findings fit into the body of knowledge you found when you asked your research question(s). And, three, you articulate in your own mind and for the readers where the spiral of inquiry will take you in your next project(s).

Unless, as might be the case in phenomenological studies, data gathering and interpretation fall together, consider accompanying the interpretation of your work with the rendition of Miles Davis's popular tune "So What?" as recorded live in 1958 for the famous *Kind of Blue* album. (You can watch it by entering "Miles Davis So What" into the search engine at www.youtube.com.) A two-note motive that hints at the title ("So What?") drives this tune, moving between instruments and frequent key changes. The motive should play like a tape loop in your brain, reminding you to think about your readership as broader than the members of your thesis or dissertation committee.

The "So What" Factor in Interpreting Your Findings

As the only student in RC 533 who had written a master's thesis, *Dale* was asked by his classmates more than once about his experiences with the entire process of writing the research document and submitting it for approval to his thesis committee. According to his recollections, Dale had found interpreting his findings tougher than expected. Only repeated rewrites of what in his case was the last chapter in his thesis eventually satisfied his committee members.

His thesis, a quantitative study, had followed the layout typical of most such studies: Chapter 1 contained rationale, purpose, questions, delimitations, and definition of terms. Chapter 2, the literature review, reported the content of studies pivotal to Dale's rationale and planned methodology already referred to in Chapter 1. Chapter 3 detailed those methods and related procedures, and Chapter 4 presented all results in the order of the research questions. Chapter 5—called Summary, Discussion, Conclusions, and Recommendations for Future Research—was just what it said: A brief version of the entire work with additional interpretations and comments about the findings. Dale also remembered how he had dragged his feet when it came to drawing conclusions that went beyond a repeat of the findings. But he had the most trouble in articulating what the findings meant in light of his related literature chapter, in terms of practical significance for music teachers, and in application to future research.

Not all thesis or dissertation layouts resemble what Dale experienced as a master's student, but all studies should have a "so what" component to them. Although expectations and requirements for the actual organization of theses and dissertations may vary from institution to institution, the following elements should be present in some form and be repeated prior to interpreting the findings: (a) the rationale for having conducted the investigation; (b) the purpose and any specifications of the purpose; (c) a reiteration of the most relevant research studies that led to your rationale and purpose; (d) a description of how you actually carried out your own work and analyzed the data; and (e) all results and conclusions relative to your stated purpose. Subsequent speculation about the subject may prove appropriate in the context of developing new questions that deserve further study.

You may recognize this list as the scholarly process in its broadest form. While the order in which the elements appear is negotiable and somewhat flexible, their presence should not be. In most quantitative research, the dissertation chapters tend to follow the arrangement as exercised by Dale above; deviations are possible but seldom occur. In philosophical, historical, and qualitative research, a greater degree of flexibility and organizational liberties are the norm. For instance, you may find all five elements dealt with in the first chapter even if it was written last.

From Summary to Discussion/Interpretation to Conclusion

Most music education theses and dissertations include the interpretation of findings in a final "summary and conclusions" chapter (sometimes so titled). Writing that chapter feels like the end of your research, and in many ways it is. But this activity—not just writing the final chapter, but also interpreting your findings within that chapter—is actually the beginning of your communications with the field about your research. Subsequent publications will likely stem more from this chapter than from the others, because it is here that you go from summary to interpretation to conclusion.

Begin with a summary of your project that includes purpose, questions, sub-purposes or hypotheses, and the theoretical context within which you placed them. Make this summary substantive yet succinct—more than an outline, but much less than is included in earlier chapters. Following your summary, describe your data gathering and analysis methods and summarize your findings. List them in the order in which you asked your research questions and bring into the discussion the references that most helped you articulate the questions. Highlight similarities and differences between your and previous findings and conclude from such highlights how your research may have impacted the body of knowledge about music learning and teaching. Worded differently, share with the reader how you believe your work contributes to what at least some colleagues in the field are thinking and writing about.

Finally, remind the reader about the functions of your research in the overall scheme of the learning and teaching of music. For instance, talk about whether you consider your findings to contribute primarily to basic research or whether you see them more in the "applied" category (see Chapters 1 and 3). Do you understand them as contributing a solution to a practical problem or to establishing "better" approaches than those generally practiced? Did you contribute to improving pedagogical "engineering," that is, suggested tangible methodological or technological changes in instructional tools? Did you intend to illuminate further what happens in the field, namely, particular classrooms? Or, did your findings aim at re-defining music instructional contexts and point to the importance of investigating such contexts systematically?

When you address the application of your findings to extant knowledge, further distinguish between direct, practical applications and possible questions for future research. Do not overreach in such speculations; instead, couch them in question format to avoid making claims you cannot support. At the same time, do not shy away from speculating about the consequences of future investigations on the subject but include suggestions how you might be able to improve even your own research design and method. Nearly all studies, like most performances, leave room for improvement, and to recognize that fact should be the trademark of any good researcher.

Titling Your Thesis or Dissertation

Whenever someone asks you what your research is about, you probably wish for a short, catchy answer. That, unfortunately, does not work too well with original research projects because their purposes are expected to be precise and to the point. That point, however, lies in the intricacies of available research literature and usually takes some explaining before your question or problematic becomes clear to anyone less familiar with the topic than you are.

The best solution is perhaps the least creative one; that is, to let the title reflect the purpose statement as closely as possible. A common practice in dissertations and theses, it can make the title cumbersome and sometimes questionably long. If you digress from that practice, avoid claiming more in the title than what you actually addressed in the study; beware of exaggerations and promises your findings cannot keep.

An already spoken to challenge for some novice researchers is inaccurate wording. For instance, titling a study "The effect of [variable A] on [variable B]" is inappropriate when you only observed both variables together rather than investigating the causality of one on the other. The issue of accurate wording is also important in historical as well as descriptive (qualitative and quantitative), correlational and grounded theory studies. Make sure, therefore, that the data (facts, figures, dates, and/or verbatim quotations) in your text fully support the wording of your title.

Paying Attention to Details

By their very nature, theses and dissertations are lengthy documents; in the case of dissertations, sometimes even lengthier than many books. This means that most readers would be less knowledgeable about your particular subject area than you are. Keep this fact in mind when you work on your final chapter (whether it appears first or last in your work). Tell your readers exactly what you did when, and also give reasons for the conclusions you drew; otherwise, the reader may form different deductions and interpretations. That, however, might lead to unwarranted criticism, misunderstandings, and confusion.

In Chapter 3 you read about connecting arguments in such a way that the reader can follow your reasoning for any claims you make. We used as example two sentences:

Sentence 1	*Sentence 2*
"It is raining" (p)	"The street is wet" (q)

According to common-sense experiences, the street gets wet (q) when it is raining (p). The logic is easy to follow once both sentences show up together. Now assume you present the reader only with the second sentence (q) because you stated on page 30 of a 200-page document that it was a rainy day (p). Because you wrote the sentence, you remember it; but your readers likely do not. For them, q would seemingly stand by itself, leading to possibly other reasons for the wet pavement.

We also remind you that the same number of sentences, placed in different order, can lead to more than one conclusion. Keep this fact in mind for any writing task but, particularly, when you work on your final chapter. You may think you have said it all and that everyone follows your way of thinking. Remember that in the course of your research, you have come to know your topic very well. Do not assume that your readers are equally as informed. Help them to connect the dots in the way you see them connected.

To avoid the possibility of miscommunication, lead the reader through your own thought processes from the beginning to the end of your work—even at the risk of being a bit repetitive. Only if you tell your readers what they are to take away from your work can you be sure that it is understood in the way you intended it. In doing so, keep your problem statement or articulated problematic intact so that you do not claim more in the final chapter than you addressed in the body of the research. The same applies to any key definitions you used.

In several chapters throughout this book, we have referred to other elements of clear writing, reiterating them here. First, be cautious about making causal inferences when you should only talk about relational connections. A second wording you should be careful about is the term "significant." As you have learned, statisticians have very precise definitions for when to refer to significant and not-significant differences in linking measurements to each other, be it causally or relationally. If you use the term in a quantitative study, be sure to draw clear distinctions between practical and statistical significance, interpreting any numbers in the context of sample size and numbers of variables. In qualitative research, avoid the term "significant" unless you have provided a definition (stipulated or operational) before making use of it. Better and more descriptive words can be easily found in any thesaurus.

When you have attended to summary, interpretation, and title as suggested, you then have room to think of and share with your readers the possibilities that lie ahead. This is why we urge you to think of your final chapter of your thesis or dissertation as a springboard for further activities, such as those described in the next section. In all cases, the "so what" factor earlier highlighted should now become the driving force for such projects.

Making Your Work Accessible to Different Audiences

A ready-made tool kit for reaching different audiences within the large field of music education, consider the summary chapter in an officially accepted dissertation or thesis as the informational "raw data" that can serve future publication purposes and functions. Adjustments to title and modifications in layout are necessary, however, if you want to bring your work to the attention of audiences other than your thesis or dissertation committee.

Editorial boards, professional organizations, publishing houses, and/or funding agencies each have specific policies and guidelines for length of publication. Such guidelines tend to explicate details about writing style, the content of the report, and the description of all methodological–technical aspects of the project, such as the target audience and other relevant information. You also need to re-examine the title and determine whether it captures the spirit of your work without misrepresenting it.

What follows are suggestions for preparing the content of your first research report and turning its content into material for public dissemination. Consider certain key issues when, for instance:

- Preparing either a scholarly or a general-interest article for submission to peer-reviewed scholarly, professional, or trade journals;
- Submitting a paper proposal for a conference;
- Writing a proposal to university-wide or external funding agencies;
- Preparing a chapter to be published in books or monographs;
- Structuring a workshop or clinic on or around your topic.

We present the choices in the order in which they may most likely occur in the career of a novice researcher. It should be noted also that the procedures described here refer to high normative standards; deviations from the norm are possible.

Proposing a Conference Paper

Presenting papers at professional conferences is an important activity for any scholar, but is especially useful for novice researchers. You get to know fellow researchers from different parts of the country (and/or world) and can discuss matters of mutual concern. Observing scholarly discourse in action can be exciting and a lot of fun, especially if you go to the same conferences on a regular basis. Most professional societies sponsor paper reading sessions whenever the society has a formal meeting, notices of which (in the form of calls for papers) are generally announced in professional journals and on the Internet.

Organizers of large conferences also include so-called poster sessions as an alternative to paper reading sessions. Not publicly read, you visually present key aspects of your study on a large-scale poster. The more attractive the poster, the more likely viewers will stop and want to talk about your work. Your poster may be constructed by hand, but increasing numbers of researchers create and then enlarge a slide from PowerPoint or a similar program. You may then distribute a longer and more complete paper to interested colleagues if they so request.

Poster sessions and paper reading session are equally important for making your work known to the profession at large. In music education, poster sessions tend not to have specified topics while "calls for papers" generally have a set theme, albeit broadly worded. The calls include the conference language(s) if it is an international meeting, maximum length of the paper, number of copies to be submitted, number of accepted tables or graphs, curriculum vitae of the author, and due date for submitting the paper(s).

Most of the time, proposals in the form of abstracts (on average between 200–500 words) are forwarded to the chairperson of the organization, who then distributes the applicant's paper on an anonymous basis for review to researchers in the field. As is the practice in most peer reviews, the referees recommend to the chairperson those proposals most appropriate because of overall purpose, specificity of questions, and methodological excellence.

The researchers whose abstracts or actual papers are deemed most worthy of presentation are invited to read the paper to the attending membership. In some instances, papers are distributed ahead of time to all participants so that more time is available for discussion. Most paper reading sessions do provide some Question and Answer (Q&A) time. The papers are often published—either in revised form or as presented—in proceedings of the sponsoring organization or in its journal and provide you, the novice researcher, with an excellent (possibly first) opportunity of becoming a published author.

Even the longest research paper is shorter than an entire dissertation, but not necessarily shorter than a dissertation's summary chapter. Thus, after just having completed a one hundred to two hundred page document, the challenge of reducing the information to approximately 15 to 20 typewritten pages is formidable. It is a process, however, that teaches you to economize your writing style and organization.

Make use of your summary chapter by shortening its original research rationale but highlighting its pivotal references. Follow that section with the purpose/sub-purposes/questions of the study. If it is a quantitative study, next describe your methods and procedures. In a historical study, the bulk of the report should be devoted to a description of the process of data collection and verification. Reports of philosophical studies should focus on the presentation of the sequence of arguments in the complete line of argumentation. Generalizations and speculations about findings might be reserved for the Q&A session that typically follows a paper presentation.

Preparing an Article for Submission in a Peer-Reviewed Journal

From the beginning of the book, we have asked you to direct your critical reading of related literature to scholarly rather than general-interest articles. As you may recall, the request was motivated by the fact that scholarly journals are refereed by a panel of experts whereas general-interest articles may not be. Furthermore, we wanted you to pay attention to methodological details that allow researchers to separate documented evidence from personal opinion and speculation. Even if they are refereed, however, such is not necessarily the case in general-interest articles because they are usually too short to contain bibliographic and procedural information; the "so what" factor tends to matter more to the readers of general interest articles than how you got there.

Most refereed journals, both scholarly and general-interest directed, have a page on which contributions are solicited. On that page, you commonly find a brief section outlining the steps you, a prospective contributor, should follow in preparing an article for publication. The instructions normally include the suggested maximum length of the article, specific manuscript style, placement of bibliography, graphs, tables, and figures, and the number of copies and format (i.e., paper or electronic) of the manuscript that should be forwarded to the editor. On the same page, you also find the name and address of the person to whom the manuscript should be sent.

Although the advent of e-journals has made page limitations less important, always consult the publishing guidelines for any particular journal—whether it is an e-journal or in hard copy. Also pay attention to a journal's or publishing house's code of ethics; it spells out the prevailing policy about: (1) submitting an article to several journals; (2) publishing an article that has already appeared elsewhere; (3) identifying the authorship of a publication; (4) making several articles out of one primary document; (5) considering copyrights; and (6) presenting papers at professional conferences.

Once you have completed your manuscript and forwarded it to the editorial office, the manuscript enters a rather methodical review process that can vary from journal to journal in terms of time, rigor of review, and suggestions for improvement. On receipt of the manuscript, the journal editor reviews the article and decides if it meets the overall specifications as stated on the journal solicitation page. If the editor decides the manuscript does not meet the minimum criteria for publication, the article may not even enter the peer-review process but, instead, is immediately returned to the sender.

Manuscripts that pass the initial screening are submitted to members of the editorial board for evaluation. Normally, three, sometimes four, members of the board review each manuscript. The reviewers are generally instructed to return their evaluations to the editor within a reasonable amount of time and to recommend whether the manuscript should be: (a) accepted and published as received; (b) returned to the author for revision and corrections, with the opportunity to resubmit the manuscript to the review board; or (c) rejected as not suitable within the accepted journal standards, and perhaps recommended for submission to a more appropriate publication organ.

Most journals have a standard rating form for the referees to use in evaluating a manuscript. The form includes such items as quality of writing style (use of appropriate grammar, correct spelling, punctuation, etc.) and clarity of writing. It is common procedure that reviewers also offer anonymous suggestions for improving the manuscript. The editor generally reserves the right to serve as the final arbiter in any dispute over a manuscript, and is ultimately responsible for the final decision to publish or reject a submitted research report.

Even if your manuscript is accepted without revision, you may have to wait a while before you actually see it in print. Most journals publish on a regular basis, in intervals of one to four times a year, and usually have two or more future issues in a ready state for distribution. This means that even a manuscript without any revisions can experience a time lag of nine months or more from submission to publication. Although the entire review process is time consuming, the peer evaluation process is, in a way, like the democratic process: It perhaps is slow and cumbersome, but preferred by many scholars over the alternative—a non-refereed process in which the editor makes all decisions single-handedly.

Scholarly Articles

In scholarly articles, reviewers evaluate items other than quality and clarity of writing style (i.e., use of appropriate grammar, correct spelling, punctuation, etc.). They also look for a logically argued rationale and research purpose; defined research specifications (questions, sub-purposes, or hypotheses); appropriate methods for the mode of inquiry chosen; and conclusions based on the findings of the inquiry. If these points are judged by the referees to be clearly described, the manuscript is usually accepted without change or with minor revisions. But not all referees see eye to eye on certain issues. Be prepared, therefore, to receive a variety of opinions on your work. Respond to any suggestions for revisions as best as you can and stay in close touch with the editor about any questions or unresolved concerns.

Regardless of the mode of inquiry employed and space limitations imposed, include your rationale for the study and discuss those references that helped you in articulating your theoretical perspective and purpose. From there on, the formats of articles in the various modes of inquiry may differ. In quantitative research, the methods and procedures for gathering data must be described in detail and the results of the analysis should be presented in tabular form, followed by a section titled "Conclusions." Similar approaches may be true in qualitative research articles, but depending on the particular type of study you conducted, you have some latitude in determining how to combine methods of data gathering with analysis and discussions of findings. Consult a variety of journals before you settle on any one form of organizing your material.

If the study is historical in nature, the major primary sources for the investigation of all questions need to be listed; when and where applicable, procedures for their verification should also be described. Because of the restricted space available in a journal, it is likely that the findings will have to be limited to some key questions, with a second article possibly following later. The process used to answer your research questions should be described in detail with reference to all primary evidence collected.

In philosophical inquiry, a description of your primary beliefs should precede a discussion of the form of argumentation the discourse follows. Subsequently, the most important points in the argumentation should be summarized and adequately documented. As is the case with all other research articles, philosophical writings should make room for a conclusion section in which the points made are consistent with the purpose and specific problematic addressed in the study.

General-Interest Articles

Think back to the scientific elements in your research: The rationale, the questions, the related literature, the methods, and the findings/interpretations. Some of these sections contain useful and rich material that your colleagues in the field should know. Ask yourself whether any of these would be useful for practitioners in the field.

Consider beginning with the findings/interpretations: What have you learned from your work that you think should be shared with the profession at large? Have you come to question certain, previously taken-for-granted principles of instruction? Could you envision doing things differently in the future? Might you be able to ask your colleagues for feedback on your insights and see how they think about what you bring up as possibilities for the future?

Or, take a look at your related literature section. Are there specific studies that you feel are worth talking about other than in scholarly circles? Have you encountered particular investigations that a larger audience of readers might find interesting and/or beneficial for their own work? Could you make such information relevant by simplifying what in the studies sounded complicated and technical?

To answer those questions, put on your "teacher hat" and think back to how you started the research process: What intimidated you? What intrigued you? How would you take the intimidation factor out of research? How could you motivate others to think about research as "thinking again" or "looking again?" What, specifically, do you propose others think about or should look at again? Can you come up with interesting ways to describe situations where you did that and, as a result, improved your teaching skills? If so, how did you know that they had improved? Such questions and stories around them make excellent material for general-interest articles suitable for publication in a variety of refereed and non-refereed journals. They are needed in our profession for the purpose of ongoing communication and clarification of practice.

Seeking Internal or External Funding

Even small amounts of funding can make a big difference for a research agenda. For this reason, many colleges and universities, and even some school districts offer competitive opportunities for research funding. Funding by outside agencies and institutions, when available, occurs on a competitive basis. This means that grants awarded by foundations and the federal government not only apply very strict standards of evaluation but often also have a predetermined funding priority. To apply for any type of funding, you must learn to respond to the funding agencies on their terms.

Research proposals for foundations, companies, or other funding agencies that are external to the university can be as complete and detailed as a dissertation proposal (see Chapter 4) or as short as a single, bulleted page. To expedite the reviewers' speed of reading, however, funding proposals re-order the particular elements common to the scientific process. Typically, this includes: (1) a one-page summary of the benefits of the research for the funding agencies as well as for specific target groups precedes any methodological or budgetary details; (2) a summary of the proposed budget often follows next, sometimes coupled with a record of your previous research; (3) a narrative description of method and design, again with budgetary specifics, goes before any detailed narrative description of the proposal itself. Generally downplayed is a detailed discussion of the related research;

instead, you are expected to say in a few sentences or paragraphs how your research is or is not different from what is already available and known, and provide parenthetical or footnoted references that indicate your familiarity with related research.

A caveat: There are perhaps as many different application formats as there are funding agencies. This means you need to obtain the forms early in the process, just as you were urged by your teacher to obtain the IRB forms from your university early in your first research project. The forms tell you what to do; follow them painstakingly, using their language and terminology.

At times, grant funding can limit your freedom in presenting your own research. It is severely limited because both private and public agencies call for research studies whose findings support a result they favor. Usually, only experienced researchers obtain those grants because it takes advanced research skills and a track record of completed projects not only to design and carry out other people's agendas but also to compete nationally and/or internationally with other researchers.

Preparing a Chapter for Publication

One of the mainstays of scholarly productivity is participating in projects that lead to the publication of a book chapter. Such a chapter may appear in a collection of essays with different topics written by multiple authors and published in one handbook, or in a monograph, a chapter-based book around a single theme. There are many avenues that lead to an invitation to participate in either of such books.

Frequently, papers that are presented at symposia are published in a collection of symposium proceedings, most often in the form of a book. At times, presenters know ahead of time that their work is being considered for publication and can take that into consideration as they prepare. If you make a presentation at a conference where such a decision is made after the event has taken place, you will likely need to re-write portions of the paper to account for a broader readership. This gives you the opportunity to consider and include questions and comments raised by conference attendees during your presentation. Because the chapter will reach readers who did not attend the conference, it is important to clearly explain any terms that might have been commonly understood and used by attendees (for instance, insider talk).

A second avenue for contributing a chapter to a book occurs as the result of being invited due to expertise and a certain level of professional accomplishment. Even then, you should inform yourself about the overall purpose of the book or monograph and make sure that you fully understand the editor's overall intent for the publication. You are expected to comply with those expectations, even if you feel that you would prefer different style and presentation formats.

Especially when contributing to multiple-author projects (such as symposium documents, professional handbooks, or monographs), peer criticism may be an important component in the publishing process. It may therefore require a great deal of time and energy before the final version of your manuscript fully meets the expectations of the editor(s) and anonymous editorial readers.

Planning Workshops and Seminars

Like foundations and funding agencies, professional organizations of which you are already a member accept applications for presenting clinics, workshops, and seminars at national or regional conferences. To present during a conference you have attended in the past, obtain the forms and get a sense of what you need to do to organize and apply as a presenter. This information is usually available on an organization's website or in the professional journal. You might also consider teaming up with one or two colleagues to plan a panel discussion with input from the public, take research findings and turn them into general-interest material as described earlier, or present topics you encountered in your critical reading as challenging but interesting at the same time. Always thinking of yourself as the teacher you are, engage the attending public in exercises, discussion, and activities that are pertinent to the issues you examined in your original research (see above). You may or may not refer to that research explicitly. Instead, have handouts ready for distribution in which you list some very selected sources that are easy to get and easy to read. Comprehensive bibliographies should be reserved for more scholarly meetings.

Continuing the Research Journey

True to the spiral of inquiry, reaching different audiences with the results of your first research project gets you deeper into the "ongoingness" of research than you probably ever expected. The same is true when—after thinking about the "so what" factor imbedded in the results of your first study—you begin to imagine new projects to follow up on your findings. Begin the journey by replicating your initial investigation. It is an important step in establishing yourself as a researcher, a role you may never have envisioned before but may find quite "doable" and even intriguing after you have learned about the new challenges inherent in becoming a music teacher–scholar.

Replicating a Study

To replicate a study is an important scientific practice, even requirement, in many fields, especially those disciplines that rely on experimental designs in lab settings. While such studies exist in music education, they are not as numerous as studies in natural settings but just as important. Conducting a second investigation based on an existing model, such as your thesis or dissertation, has great benefits and also a few, albeit smaller drawbacks.

The benefits are that you have organized, written out, and described all required methods and procedures, know what to do when questions arise, and have a template for the text you need to write—even if in a much more limited number of pages. The drawbacks include the following: It may be necessary to change design and procedures either because circumstances have changed or because they did not work very well in the first place. Any criticisms of design or methodology that were expressed by you in the conclusion of the original project or voiced by others should be responded to in the new study. Without the guidance of a mentor, you need to learn to become your own best critic, a role you already should know well as a performer. You might also consider co-authoring your work together with your former mentor or other trusted colleagues. Who knows, some new projects as well as lifelong friendships may spring up from such collaborations.

The most serious drawback of replicating a study may be that the term "replication" itself can present conceptual as well as methodological challenges. Historical and philosophical questions cannot be fully replicated but, instead, need to be modified to allow for new angles to be examined. If you carry out new historical or philosophical data analyses, however, you do not replicate but produce a new study because new data lead to new questions. In both qualitative and most quantitative research, it also is quite possible that institutional contexts change too much for findings to be comparable across different school, socio-cultural, or geographic settings. Once you incorporate that knowledge into your new study, you may not want to call it replication but simply indicate that you stayed close to the original study design.

Professional Aspirations as a Researcher

Whether you plan on continuing in the spiral of inquiry as suggested depends on your professional and life goals, a topic with which we began this book. Several factors generally motivate a person to engage in research: (1) seeking a terminal graduate degree; (2) hoping to obtain financial support from institutional grants; (3) satisfying job requirements, especially if employed by institutions of higher education (the so-called "publish-or-perish" syndrome); (4) taking pleasure in being professionally visible and recognized by one's peers; and (5) simply enjoying the research process itself.

A word about the "publish-or-perish" syndrome: If you are motivated to do research for any of the other reasons mentioned above, chances are that you do not feel pushed to publish, but that you want to publish because you would like for your voice to be heard. The study of the learning and teaching of music reaches into so many research avenues that finding a niche in the vastness of the field should not be too difficult.

Rainbow and Froehlich (1987) stated in their *Coda* to the 1987 edition:

> There is some hidden benefit for all who undertake the study of music. Likewise, there is hidden benefit for all who study the research process. This benefit begins with the discovery of skepticism as a positive force in the search for truth. That skepticism, if applied to one's own work, leads to self-criticism, an important ingredient in the search for quality. Finally, skepticism and self-criticism can also cause one to seek solutions to some of the problems [and challenges] observed in one's work and environment. Although such an attitude is the essence of research, it must not be confined to those who actually conduct research. Instead, that attitude should be applied to musical performance, the writing of music, or the teaching of music to learners of any age group. To conclude, and at the risk of being repetitive: Being inquisitive, self-critical, and seeking solutions to perceived problems are traits needed in all

music educators who search for quality in their work as musician-performers, teachers, and researchers. (p. 282)

Scholarship should be foremost an attitude rather than an obligation, a process rather than a product. Once you have taken to that process, ongoing curiosity and a spirit of critically examining accepted truths will become second nature. Sharing the results of those attitudinal characteristics will then guide you in all further steps that lie ahead.

Chapter Summary

1. Sharing your research findings and gained insights with the profession should be considered integral to the research process itself.
2. In theses and dissertations, that sharing happens in the form of an interpretative summary and conclusion chapter that, dependent on the mode and methods used in your work, is likely to appear first or last in your original research document.
3. Interpreting your findings means presenting them in the light of the literature that helped you formulate your research question and rationale.
4. Be careful about the use of terminology that suggests causality between observed events and/or actions when your study was not about causality but description only.
5. Let the summary and conclusion chapter become the "raw material" for subsequent work: Replications and extensions of the original research, poster and paper presentations, scholarly and general interest articles, grant proposals, general workshops, and conference sessions.
6. Let an attitude of ongoing curiosity and a spirit of critically examining accepted truths become second nature in everything you undertake as a musician, teacher, and/or researcher.

Recommended Reading

Locke, L. F., Spirduso, W. W., & Silverman, S. J. (2007). *Proposals that work. A guide for planning dissertations and grant proposals* (5th ed.). Thousand Oaks, CA: Sage.
Ogden, T. E., & Goldberg, I. A. (2002). *Research proposals: A guide to success* (3rd ed.). San Diego, CA: Academic Press.

Recapitulation
Placing Your Research Experience in the Bigger Picture

As you read previously, the final chapter in a research report is intended to tell the whole story—the story of the project, if you will—that points the way to future research. Information taken from earlier chapters typically leads to conclusions that contain thoughts about implications for what may lie ahead. It is in that vein that we offer these closing thoughts: a summary and an outlook for the future.

Summary

Think about the journey so far: You began the research journey as a virtual visitor to Times Square. Illustrated in part by what peers in a fictitious research class experienced, the steps involved in your inquiry then spiraled into reading, observations of many kinds, and ongoing reflection upon specific projects, which most likely continue at varying levels of specificity. Regardless of where you stand right now in terms of completing your envisioned project, you already know much more about what it takes to use available information as a springboard for future actions. You also may have learned that it is not always easy to ask questions or, more importantly, to address them comprehensively. In fact, your journey most likely generated more questions than it answered.

You also encountered situations in which answers were not always right/wrong, yes/ no, either/or; instead, they lay in the gray area of "maybe." They emphasized uncertainty over certainty and ambiguity over a sense of clarity. What started as a "fact," became instead a "construct" subject to revision based on newly found evidence. As such, you discovered that experts do not know everything and that even the best-informed person can be wrong.

In the Preface to this edition we stated our task for this book to be fourfold: (1) expand on the meaning of music education and research; (2) help you find your niche in that definition; (3) teach tangible research skills that are useful for music educators with diverse instructional goals and career aspirations; and (4) minimize possible apprehensions about "research" as something foreign and unfamiliar to most, if not all music students. You alone can determine the extent to which those goals fulfilled your own expectations. Whatever your response, we hope that as a result of using this textbook, you have begun to place your own personal experiences with research into the larger frame of music education as a field of study.

It was our intention that this book would take you from your own research project to the larger picture of inquisitiveness as a state of mind, asking you to think about, engage in, and work with:

- Modes of inquiry and worldviews as important contributors to how you generate and evaluate knowledge;
- Means by which to find evidence in the support of producing new knowledge or examining old truths.

We see these two bullets related to each other as illustrated in Figure 15.1.

RESEARCH FORMS

Experimental	Descriptive	Interpretive	Speculative
Cause-Effect Studies			
Quasi-Experimental			
Non-Experimental	Case Studies	Grounded Theory	
Relational Studies	Clinical Research	Life History	Narratives
Causal-comparative &		Ethnobiography	Critical-Ethnobiography
Descriptive-comparative Studies		Oral History	
			Text & Document Analysis
			(Hermeneutics)
			Interpretivism
			Phenomenology
	Action Research		
			Artifact Analysis
			Conversational Analysis

WORLDVIEWS
(Belief Systems)

From ABSOLUTISM	TO	RELATIVISM
EMPIRICISM		EXISTENTIALISM
MODERNISM		
FORMALISM		
		POSTMODERNISM
IDEALISM	PRAGMATISM	
MATERIALISM		
NATURALISM		
RATIONALISM		

FIGURE 15.1   Connections Between Research Forms and Worldviews

As you select your research methods in response to your research purpose, you inevitably place yourself somewhere within that illustration. Be sure it is where you want to be philosophically as well as methodologically. The choices you make have ramifications for what is to follow; that is, how your research agenda weaves through your life's work. You may compare this process to taking up a particular instrument early in life and staying with that choice throughout your life, thereby perfecting the art and craft of performing on that one instrument. There are also those among us who have learned to play many different instruments (hardly any music educator can do without those experiences).

You may similarly opt to test the research waters by asking questions that are philosophically far apart from each other, situated in different modes of inquiry, and require a variety of methods and research tools. Whichever choices you make, avoid favoring one approach over any other simply because one method seems easier than another. Do not let methodologies be the "tail that wags the [research] dog."

If you choose not to generate new research but wish to continue to evaluate current literature pertinent to your own area of interest, it is similarly important to make a connection between modes of inquiry and belief systems. Such insights provide you with an important tool for critically examining the choices made by researchers as well as teachers. Understanding the reasons behind such choices make it easier to determine how a particular study actually contributes to the body of knowledge as a whole.

Modes of Inquiry and Worldviews as Forces for Generating Knowledge

In the course of reading this text, you learned that physical observations alone do not create knowledge. Instead, the power of reasoning puts into context that which has been observed. With your ability to differentiate between reasoned logic and common sense, avoid relying on just one source of knowledge. Rather, examine as many sources as possible, weighing one against another.

Why and how we search for knowledge through different forms of evidence depends on our beliefs about what constitutes perceived and factual reality. If you believe, for instance, that right and wrong are relative to context and therefore not necessarily absolute values even in classroom management issues, you are not likely to begin a study with an inflexible set of observational variables. Conversely, if you believe that the purpose of education is to instill in all young people absolute values of socially accepted "rights and wrongs," you might wish to study the extent to which one set of rules was observable in many classrooms across several school districts. The two beliefs might yield very different research questions and, thus, modes and methods of inquiry concerning classroom management.

Clearly, it is not easy to pinpoint exactly how or what one thinks. Understanding theoretical definitions of different worldviews tends to be easier than figuring out where one stands on particular issues and how consistent one is in applying them—to everyday living, to professional life, or to research. An absolutist in ethical questions of right and wrong may be a relativist when it comes to choosing repertoire for a particular group of students. Professing the unalienable right of students for self-expression does not fit easily with formalism and functionalism when it comes to the disciplinary authority of the teacher. The difficulty lies in navigating between who you are in your private role as person and who you are in your public role as teacher.

A similar duality of roles might occur when you make research decisions. From the viewpoint of the practitioner–teacher you are or wish to become, you might want to generate knowledge that is immediately applicable to your own instructional actions. From the vantage point of commencing a research career, however, following a sequential path of planning for a battery of studies within the descriptive–relational–causal loop may be a more promising option. Or, as the practically minded person you are, you may want to be seen as an educational "engineer" who devises technological improvements for sight-reading software rather than testing hypotheses about musical taste.

The above examples suggest that decisions about what questions to ask, which methods to employ, and how to design a study can generate markedly different pieces of information in the puzzle called the body of knowledge of music education. Which pieces you contribute as a researcher may also lead to different career paths. Questions, methods, and designs within the purview of funding agencies and institutional research agendas lead to different opportunities from the active pursuit of research interests outside those typically funded or supported by interested agencies.

Knowledge, Truth, and Evidence in the Research Process

Ongoing and systematic inquisitiveness leads to what one group of scholars calls truth, another group knowledge, and yet another evidence. The term "evidence" as used in this book distinguishes between overtly discernible patterns of actions, behaviors and thought and covert, intuitive feelings and sensations. Whatever word you use, any evidence is always time-bound, thus requiring renewed examination.

Both overt actions and covert sensations are subject to change because the knowledge base that triggers those actions and sensations gets altered. Rapid advances in science and technology affirm, question, or advance accepted laws, paradigms, and theories on an ongoing basis. Research in the humanities, music education included, may be slower, because results are not readily agreed and acted upon by a profession. Especially in arts-related fields, change advocated by research does not come easily due to time-tested and long accepted and expected practices.

However, thanks to advances in the fields of psychology, education, sociology, anthropology, and many other social and applied sciences, improvements in music pedagogies of many kinds continue to be researched and recommended by scholars in music, education, and music education. Although such improvements might make you feel confident about the validity of current instructional approaches, an inquiring and critical mind remains vigilant about new thoughts, ideas, discoveries, and insights. What seems true and agreed-upon practice today might change tomorrow.

The best way to determine which laws, paradigms, and theories require scrutiny by means of testing and ongoing examination is to remain engaged as a researcher.

Continuously probing deeper by means of the spiral of inquiry allows you to stay abreast not only of the ever changing (if not growing) body of knowledge about music, education, and music education but also of latest research methods, procedures, and designs that generate new insights into what music education practices are or should be.

This book, then, can be summed up as follows:

1. Through inquisitiveness an area of interest develops. Efforts at finding answers to specific questions result in a field of study in which knowledge is accumulated. Through the process of challenging and testing the answers to any given question, knowledge in the form of facts and beliefs are obtained. The more observations confirm either one of the forms of knowledge, the greater the certainty of its validity. Although both may, over time, undergo change, they are the working body of knowledge in the field of study on which all its operations are based.

2. Any one answer to a question serves not so much the purpose of "knowing something once and for all" but of stimulating additional questioning. No single answer gives the full truth. Rather, what matters is to be engaged in continuously searching for more complete answers to the questions that are already out there or wait to be asked.

3. There is no guarantee that either accepted facts or beliefs remain the same over time. New technologies and investigative methodologies, different perspectives and new information from external fields may contribute to a reevaluation of once-held convictions. One task of a researcher is to determine what evidence is outdated and which continues to stand scholarly scrutiny.

4. Methods of seeking evidence by means of logic, observation, and/or experimentation are all valid approaches in the search for answers to specific questions. However, the very method employed in seeking to establish facts as truth carries with it inherent limitations that must be acknowledged in the evaluation of such facts.

5. Because sole reliance on any one source of evidence may put blinders on one's inquiry, the most convincing research projects may be those that use multiple sources of evidence, thereby examining a question from many angles.

6. An obstacle to the spirit of any form of inquiry may be one's own limitations, not only in terms of time and other resources, but also in separating what one would like to be true from what well-researched evidence suggests as being true.

Outlook for the Future

The above six points may serve you well not only in your research endeavors but also in whatever else you may choose to do professionally. Assuming that a music educator is almost always a teacher in some capacity, we distill the following guidelines for future action under: (1) the teacher as skeptic; (2) the teacher as technology expert; (3) the teacher as experimenter/entrepreneur; and (4) the teacher as hands-on researcher. The order follows what we believe to be the most likely sequence within which you can take on any or all of those roles.

The Teacher as Skeptic

To be a skeptic means to be informed and to understand the nature of the sources from which you get your information. Accessing professional publications (both scholarly and trade-orientated) via the Internet or in hard copy, therefore, would be an important first step. Make a point of not only reading what is of immediate interest to you but also looking at information about specializations outside your own area of expertise. Even if you cannot read a journal from cover to cover, get a sense of the issue as a whole. This applies also to articles you may at first find too difficult to understand; do not reject them right away. The more you read, the easier it is to understand even seemingly convoluted sentences. On the basis of such reading, you may wish to engage your colleagues in conversations about pedagogical issues that concern you, and to participate in conversations similarly instigated by others.

Examine what you read and hear about from as many angles as you can. Weigh common sense against possible counter-arguments and be open to the gray areas of "maybe." Accept that there are always two sides to an issue and that any seeming solution to a problem has another side to it—the side effect not always counted on. Keep track of such observations: Put them into words, write them down, and share them.

Invite colleagues to observe you, preferably suggesting specifics you want them to focus on. Ask them whether you may learn from them by observing their work. Spend time talking about issues of concern and do not be afraid of constructive criticism. It is hard to receive at first, but you will soon discover the benefits of being open to peer comments that are not intended to judge, but to expand professional knowledge.

The Teacher as (Technology) Expert

You alone know what type of technologies and teaching methodologies your workplace sanctions, has available, endorses and encourages. Keep abreast of what is "out there," ready to use by those who can afford it. Consider writing research grants that require the use of such new developments.

If you believe you are technologically challenged, find someone who can teach you or guide you in finding out where to go or whom to contact. Begin small by asking for inexpensive items first, similar to how you may have gone to your local music merchants to obtain instruments for rent or discounted sheet music. But this time, do the asking in writing, adhering as much as possible to the guidelines for grant proposal as previously described (Chapter 14). Keep the proposal short but be sure it contains all necessary, scientific components.

Find a way to turn what you now have started in partial fulfillment of your research class into a project that benefits your long-term work. Reflect on long-held beliefs and practiced methods or look for tools (electronic or mechanical) that would make your ideas concrete. Find ways by which to share your ideas with colleagues that might be receptive to your ideas. Ask for feedback and constructive criticism. Consider preparing a general-interest article for a state or national journal that describes your ideas, especially when you have begun examining them historically, empirically, or philosophically.

The Teacher as Experimenter/Entrepreneur

Without worrying too much about upholding proper research protocols, engage in some action research by which you assess pros and cons of particular instructional methods you favor, technological learning devices you use, or both. Video record and take notes about what you observe about yourself and your students, and identify questions that you think are worth pursuing further. Begin looking at pertinent literature as described earlier as the starting point of the research spiral. Consider what you might be able to do to identify specific research topics and questions.

Ponder the possibility of turning the action research into a well-designed study by engaging a colleague to help you collect data. Plan a visit to your local university to discuss your thoughts with the music education faculty there. They very likely stand ready to help you with the overall approach, appropriate research protocol, and—possibly—with locating grant opportunities. The faculty might refer you to design experts or even get personally involved. Cooperation between universities and schools continues to be a much-needed component in nearly all research agendas typical of music education as a field of study.

The Teacher as Hands-On Researcher

It certainly is difficult to combine the many duties of a full-time music educator with those of a bona fide researcher. But it can and has been done and that is why it is included here. Admittedly, however, it seems there should be little to say at this point because one purpose of the book was to lead you down this very path. We therefore hope that following the steps described in the book will guide you from here on, always keeping in mind the context of your own realities, and we wish you well in your efforts.

When all is said and done, a research mind in music education should be more than a grant-producing fact seeker or technological expert. Instead, the research mindset should be seen as an attitude that applies to living life in general. As this recapitulation was written, an article written by Isaacson, biographer of the late Steve Jobs appeared in the *New York Times Sunday Review* (October 30, 2011). In it, Isaacson stated succinctly what seems to be at stake also for music education scholars: "the world of invention and innovation . . . means combining an appreciation of the humanities with an understanding of science—connecting artistry to technology, poetry to processors" (Isaacson, 2011, pp. 1 and 8).

Being at home with both scientific and imaginative thinking, feeling comfortable with the language of the humanities and the language spoken in the sciences may be a requisite for understanding what lies ahead not only for music education but also for music and education as discrete fields. Such understanding requires what Isaacson called "experiential wisdom" coupled with analytic rigor (p. 8).

The field of music education demands both qualities of us—whether we teach small children, older adults, facilitate learning in unconventional settings, or conduct band, choirs, orchestras, or folk and other popular music ensembles. A well-developed research mind adjusts to change, understands the need to do so, and looks at the world with a sense of curiosity, imagination, and excitement. Much is to be discovered, much remains to be done.

Questions With Which Students in RC 533 Began Their Inquiries

	Teacher	Learner	Music	All Combinations
Carlos	*HOW* can technology aid me in the teaching of general musicianship skills, such as composing and music analysis/theory? *HOW* can I measure the benefits of technology in the learning of musicianship skills?	*WHAT* technological knowledge do my students bring to the classroom that I can use to their benefit? *WHAT* can they teach me?	*WHAT* type of music is best suited for students to pay attention to technology as a compositional tool? *WHAT* aspects could they find intriguing enough that they want to learn the requisite performance or compositional skills?	*HOW* can I generate a learning environment that is self-guided and allows the students to explore new approaches to mastering required musicianship skills?
Chi-Hui	*HOW* do music teachers get trained in Taiwan and the U.S.? *WHO* is involved in determining what teachers learn in both countries?	*WHAT* are the students like in both places?	*HOW* does the school music repertoire differ from each other? *HOW* alike is it across one country? *WHAT* is music literacy and *HOW* does its definition compare across countries?	*HOW* does the teacher–student ratio compare in both countries for grade school, high school, and college? *WHY* is the approach to teaching Western art music so different when the music is the same?
Christy	*HOW* do I teach differently from what others say or do? *WHAT* and *HOW* do others teach? *HOW* (and *WHY*) do I know that I am effective?	*WHO* are my students? *HOW* do my students compare to those of other studio teachers?	*HOW* does the repertoire I select for the students compare to what my colleagues choose? *WHAT* repertoire was taught in the past?	*WHAT* do I mean by "effective?" *WHAT* do others mean?

	Teacher	Learner	Music	All Combinations
Dale	*HOW* have teachers taught in the past? *WHAT* are the work conditions of my band director colleagues in my home district? *HOW* do they compare to my own? *WHY* do I want to know this? *HOW* can this knowledge benefit me?	*WHAT* is the teacher–student ratio in each school?	*HOW* alike is the repertoire among my colleagues? *WHO* comes to the concerts?	*HOW* aware are administrators and parents of the work conditions as perceived by my colleagues?
Greg	*WHAT* do different teachers mean by motivation and are they in agreement with each other?	*WHY* are my students not motivated? *WHEN* do I know that a student is motivated?	*HOW* does the type of music we play impact motivation?	*WHAT* is the difference between the occupational socialization of teachers who are known as "good" motivators and those who are not?
Jeannette	*WHAT* do teachers know about "cultural mistrust"?	*HOW* do minority choral students differ in behavior from non-minority students?	*WHERE* does music repertoire choice fit in?	*WHAT* is "cultural mistrust"? *HOW* is it assessed/measured?
Juan	*HOW* can I become a better applied teacher? *WHAT* is good teaching? *HOW* can it be measured? *HOW* much do I know about	*HOW* does my students' parent(s)' musical and/or educational background(s) contribute to my students' attitude toward the	*WHAT* is good music? Can taste be measured? If so, *HOW*?	*HOW* similar/different is my musical and educational upbringing from that of my students, and their parents?

	my students' musical preferences?	instrument they play? The practicing they do? The music they like or dislike?		
Keisha	HOW have early childhood teachers been taught?	HOW do different specialized methods propose to teach children's (K–2) learning of rhythmic and pitch patterns? WHY are rhythm and pitch patterns important for young children to learn?	WHAT songs are useful for reinforcing rhythmic and pitch patterns?	WHAT are efficient methods of early childhood teaching? WHAT are the rationales for those methods? WHERE and HOW were they studied?
Liam	WHEN studying different conductors' conducting behavior, how prominent is eye contact as a communication skill in each of them?	Within any one ensemble, HOW many performers look at the conductor in a noticeable pattern across different scores?	HOW consistent are observable eye contact patterns across different compositions. Are they impacted by difficulty levels or length?	HOW important is eye contact between conductor and ensemble members in professional groups? WHAT is accepted conductor research knowledge in the professional field of performance and in music education?
Marguerite	WHAT do teachers know about informal learning? WHO has experienced it? WHERE are the teachers who have experienced it?	WHAT is informal learning? HOW can it be observed in students? HOW do students describe their own practicing at home?	HOW different is the music students select in informal learning settings? WHO takes the leadership in informal learning settings in which several students are involved?	HOW do attitudes toward formal and informal learning compare across different teachers and students?

	Teacher	Learner	Music	All Combinations
Michelle	*HOW* can teachers become major decision makers in matters concerning the arts? *WHO* is involved in making decisions about the arts in the curriculum?	*WHAT* do students say they want to learn? *HOW* can one best involve students and their parents in advocacy projects that reach the larger community?	Is there agreement among decision makers about *WHAT* kind of music is to be performed and *WHY*?	*WHAT* do schools across the nation do for arts advocacy and political action promoting the arts in schools and society? *WHY, WHEN,* and *HOW* should something declared good for society also be included in the school curriculum?
Muna	Of my experiences as a college student, *WHAT* were the best memories? The worst? *HOW* could the latter have been avoided? *HOW* often did they occur? *HOW* accurate is my memory?	*WHAT* do other students say about those experiences? *WHEN* did they occur most often? *WHAT* do I know about teaching?	*WHAT* is music appreciation? *WHAT* aspects are most important? *WHAT* musical works do I know well enough that I could teach about them? *WHAT* do I know about those works? *WHAT* is good music?	*HOW* do I take into consideration what is important to different people?

Appendix B
Subject-Specific Indices for Music Education Research

Music Specific Indices—Free

- CAIRSS for Music: http://ucairss.utsa.edu/
- Music Education Search System: http://129.171.228.57/fmi/xsl/MESS/index.xsl

General Education or Social Science Indices—Free

- Education Resources Information Center (ERIC): http://www.eric.ed.gov/
- World Cat: http://www.worldcat.org
- Google Scholar: http://scholar.google.com/

Music Specific Indices—Subscription

- International Index of Music Periodicals (IIMP)
- International Index to the Performing Arts (IIPA)
- Music and Performing Arts Online: Combines IIMP and IIPA
- Music Index
- Répertoire International de Littérature Musicale (RILM Abstracts of Music Literature)
- Retrospective Index to Music Periodicals (RIPM) 1800–1950
- RISM: Le Répertoire International des Sources Musicales (RISM)

General Education and Social Science Indices—Subscription

- Academic Search Premier: Indexing and abstracting 8,450 journals, with full text for 4,600 of those.
- Arts and Humanities Search: Corresponds to the Arts & Humanities Citation Index, covering 1,300 arts and humanities journals, plus relevant social and natural science journals, with additional records from the Current Contents series of publications.
- ProQuest Digital Dissertations & Theses Database: Provides various levels of access to dissertations and theses depending on the type of subscription held by your university (full text or abstract only).
- PQDT Open "provides full text of open access dissertations and theses free of charge."
- Education Index: "Index of leading publications in the field of education." Now a First Search product, part of OCLC. 1983–present.
- PsycINFO: "An abstract database that provides systematic coverage of the psychological literature from the 1800s to the present."

Sources for full text journal articles—Subscription

- Academic Search Complete: Indexing and abstracting for 8,450 journals, with full text for 4,600 of those.
- Sage Journals Online: Offers access to American Educational Research Journal, Educational Policy, Educational Researcher, General Music Today, Music Educators Journal, Journal of Music Teacher Education, Journal of Research in Music Education, Update: applications of research in music education among others.

Publication Indices: Sources for Search Terms

- Using the PsychINFO Index Terms and Keywords: http://www.youtube.com/watch?v=dFeyRb73yZM
- Using EBSCO search limiters: http://www.youtube.com/watch?v=KzaLwPYSF5E
- Boolean keyword searching: http://www.youtube.com/watch?v=1kYhfz8YseY
- Academic Search Premier has "Subject Terms" on the search page, operating like a thesaurus. Academic Search Complete is another EBSCO service. This link offers a comparison of the two: http://www.ebscohost.com/uploads/imported/thisTopic-dbTopic-1168.pdf

Appendix C
Preliminary Sources for Music Education Research

Overview Sources: Review Publications

Certain scholarly periodicals specialize in review articles. For music educators, review articles can be found most frequently in these periodicals:

- *Update: Applications of Research in Music Education*
- *Bulletin of the Council for Research in Music Education*

Within the field of education are a few other well-known periodicals for review articles:

- *Review of Educational Research*
- *Review of Research in Education*

Lexica (Encyclopedias and Dictionaries)

If your topic is historical or philosophical, you may find relevant information in a music lexicon; however, most of these are not useful for music education research except to confirm music terminology or historical facts. Still, music scholars are expected to be familiar with the following notable music lexicons:

- *Baker's Biographical Dictionary of Musicians*
- *Die Musik in Geschichte und Gegenwart* (MGG)

- *The Harvard Dictionary of Music*
- *The New Grove Dictionary of Music and Musicians* (after 2008 published electronically as part of Oxford Music Online)
- *Oxford Music Online* (formerly *The New Grove Dictionary of Music and Musicians*)

Notable encyclopedias in the field of education include:

- *The Encyclopedia of Educational Research*
- *The International Encyclopedia of Education*

Appendix D

Scholarly Periodicals for Music Education Research

Arts Education Policy Review
Black Music Research Journal
Black Perspective in Music
British Journal of Music Education
Bulletin of the Council for Research in Music Education
Choral Journal
Dialog in Instrumental Music
International Journal of Choral Research
International Journal of Music Education
Jazz Educators Journal
Journal of Historical Research in Music Education
Journal of Music Teacher Education
Journal of Music Therapy
Journal of Research in Music Education
Journal of Research in Singing
Journal of Voice
Missouri Journal of Research in Music Education
Philosophy of Music Education Review

Quarterly Journal of Music Teaching and Learning
Research Studies in Music Education
Southeastern Journal of Music Education
Southern Music Education Journal
Update: Applications of Research in Music Education
Visions of Research in Music Education

Appendix E

Working Out a Course or Project Timeline

Research as coursework

- Find out what the instructor's goals are for you in the context of the course.
- Consider commitments during the semester that might keep you from making progress; discuss with instructor early in term.
- Look over the syllabus for assignments. These are your tasks. Plot them on a calendar. These may include:

  - Proposal requirements and due date;
  - IRB submission, if separate;
  - Other permissions (i.e., school district, etc.) if required;
  - Comprehensive exam, if related to final project;
  - First and subsequent drafts;
  - Copyright permissions, if applicable;

Research for thesis or dissertation

- Take into consideration that everything takes longer than expected. For everything, allow yourself extra time.
- Begin with the endpoint: Find out the requirements set by your institution for the submission of final project materials according to a realistic graduation date. These requirements may include:

  - Proposal requirements and due date;
  - IRB submission, if separate;
  - Other permissions (i.e., school district, etc.) if required;
  - Comprehensive exam, if related to final project;
  - First and subsequent drafts;
  - Copyright permissions, if applicable;

- "Fair copy" (the copy you defend);
- Scheduling of defense;
- Final copy.

■ A term project for a research course takes the full term. Consider the project to begin with the first assignment you do. Keep track of your work. Consider keeping a journal.

■ Stay in touch with your instructor about steps you are taking and thoughts that move you forward.

■ Work ahead with reading and drafts.

- Schedule for final defense;
- "Fair copy" (the copy you defend);
- Article submission, if required;
- Defend thesis or dissertation;
- Prepare and submit final copy.

■ Look into obligations you have outside of thesis/dissertation work.

■ Build in time for your advisor and committee to respond to drafts.

■ Communicate with your advisor and committee about their availability during the process of completing the work.

■ Truly look at the calendar. Consider monthly, weekly, and daily installments for your work, including at least two to three hours' writing time every day. If you do not have that kind of time, lengthen the time allotted to the project.

■ Schedule ongoing (i.e., weekly) consultation with your advisor.

■ Plot these things on a calendar and hang it by your desk. Checking off what is done will give you a sense of accomplishment!

Appendix F

Selected "-isms" as Found by Rainbow & Froehlich, 1987

Sources

AHDEL: *The American Heritage Dictionary of the English Language.* (1970)
Angeles: Angeles, P. A. (1981). *Dictionary of Philosophy.*
Flew: Flew, A. (1984). *A Dictionary of Philosophy* (rev. 2nd ed.).

Absolutism

AHDEL

1. A political form of state in which all power is vested in the monarch and his advisers.
2. The political theory reflecting this form.

Angeles:

1. Truth (value, reality) is viewed to be objectively real, final, and eternal.
2. Only one unchanging and correct explanation of reality exists.

Relativism

AHDEL

Truth is viewed to be relative to the individual and to the time or place in which he or she acts.

Angeles:

Re: value theory. Values differ from society to society, person to person, are not universally applicable at all times or in all places, are correct or incorrect only relative to their conformity with accepted norms or values; opposite to *absolutism*. (Re:

3. Political theory: Unquestionable allegiance to a ruler or ruling class in a political system.

Flew:
1. Politically, exercise of unrestricted power.
2. Philosophically, juxtaposed to *relativism*.

protagorean). Relativity of knowledge and the *relativity of sense perception...*

Flew:
Variety of meanings: 1. The social environment is considered important in the determination of beliefs of what is and what ought to be. 2. Because of the diversity of social environments, there are no universal standards of good and bad, right and wrong. 3. Relativism regarding factual knowledge: the belief that there is objective knowledge of realities independent of the knower.

Existentialism
AHDEL:
A body of ethical thought, current in the 19th and 20th centuries, centering around the uniqueness and isolation of individual experience in a universe indifferent or even hostile to man, regarding human existence as unexplainable, and emphasizing man's freedom of choice and responsibility for the consequences of his acts.

Angeles:
As a modern philosophical view incepted by Søren Kirkegaard and Friedrich Nietzsche (historical roots of the view go back to the Greeks and medieval philosophy). Selected points: *existence* precedes *essence*. ... Truth is subjectivity. The reality of individual existence cannot be communicated by abstractions. Individuals have complete freedom of the will and can become completely other than what they are. "The universe has no direction or scheme. It is meaningless and absurd."

Flew:
Not a dogma or system of thought but a

Rationalism
AHDEL:
The exercise of reason, rather than the acceptance of empiricism, authority, or spiritual revelation, provides the basis for action or belief. Reason is the prime source of knowledge and of spiritual truth.

Angeles:
Reason is the primary source of knowledge and independent of sense perception. Some points: 1. By abstract reasoning (thinking), fundamental truths can be obtained. 2. Reality is knowable and knowledge is independent of observation and experience (empirical methods). 3. Some truths about reality are known prior to any experience. 4. The principal origin of knowledge is reason, and science is basically a result of that reasoning. 5. "Truth is not tested by sense-verification procedures, but by such criteria as logical consistency." 6. Rational method can be applied to any subject matter whatsoever and can provide adequate explanations. 7. "Absolute certainty about things is the ideal of knowledge." ...

philosophical attitude. Its origins: Attributed to Kierkegaard, . . . View opposite to rationalism and empiricism. There are no natural laws that govern all beings. Reason is not necessarily the power that guides human activity . . .

Empiricism

AHDEL:

Experience, especially of the senses, is the only source of knowledge.

2. (a) The employment of empirical methods, as in an art or science, (b) An empirical conclusion.
3. The practice of medicine without scientific knowledge.

Angeles:

1. Ideas are abstractions formed by "compounding (combining, recombining) what is experienced (observed, immediately given in sensation)." 2. Experience is the sole source of knowledge. 3. Knowledge is dependent on sense data and directly derived or indirectly inferred from the sense data. . . . 4. Reason cannot be the sole source of knowledge of reality. Reference to sense experience and the use of the sense organs are necessary in the use of reason. . . .

Flew:

All knowledge or "at least all knowledge of matters of fact as distinct from that of purely logical relations between concepts

Flew:

1. The doctrines of philosophers like Descartes, Spinoza, and Leibniz. Some characteristics: (a) Reason alone can provide knowledge of what exists; (b) knowledge forms a single (deductive) system; and (c) everything can be brought under a single system of knowledge. 2. Term refers to those philosophers who accept only (b) and (c). 3. Religious belief is rejected as being without rational foundation. A commitment to reason means opposition to faith, prejudice, habit or any other source of conviction that is considered irrational.

Idealism

AHDEL:

1. The action of envisioning things in an ideal form. 2. Pursuit of one's ideals. 3. An idealizing treatment of subject in literature or art. 4. The theory that the object of external perception, in itself or as perceived, consists of ideas. . . .

Angeles:

Also referred to . . . *immaterialism*. 1. "The universe is an embodiment of a mind. 2. Reality is dependent for its existence upon a mind and its activities." 3. Reality is mental (spiritual, psychical) matter. . . . 4. Knowledge exists only in the form of mental states and processes. Reality expresses itself as ideas and thoughts. . . . The external world is not physical. (Angeles continues with a discussion of idealism in various forms.)

Flew:

A group of philosophical theories with the common view that "the external world" is created by the mind. "Idealism does not quarrel with the plain man's view that

is based on experience." . . . Empiricism has taken several forms, "but one common feature has been the tendency to start from experimental sciences, as a kind of prototype or paradigm case of human knowledge." Should be contrasted to rationalism which assigned a similar role to mathematics. . . .

material things exist; rather, it disagrees with the analysis of a material thing that many philosophers have offered, according to which the material world is wholly independent of minds." Three principal types of idealism are acknowledged: *Berkeleian idealism, transcendental idealism,* and *objective idealism* (may also be called *absolute idealism*) . . . .

Formalism

AHDEL:

"Rigorous or excessive adherence to recognized forms. The mathematical or logical structure of a scientific argument, especially as distinguished from its content."

Angeles:

"Any system that stresses form (principles, rules, laws) as the significant or ultimate ground of explanation or evaluation."

Flew:

1. (mathematics). A view pioneered by D. Hilbert: the only foundation necessary for mathematics is its formalization and the proof that the system produced is consistent.

Pragmatism

AHDEL:

1. *Philosophy.* "The theory, developed by Charles S. Peirce and William James, that the meaning of a proposition or course of action lies in its observable consequences, and that the sum of these consequences constitutes its meaning. 2. A method or tendency in the conduct of political affairs characterized by the rejection of theory and precedent, and by the use of practical means and expedients."

Angeles:

1. "Knowledge is derived from experience, experimental methods, and practical efforts." . . . 2. "Knowledge must be used to solve the problems of everyday, practical affairs . . . and thinking must relate to practice and action." 3. The truth and meaning of ideas are asserted by their consequences. . . . 4. "Truth is that which has practical value in our experience of life." . . . 5. Truth changes and is tentative. . . .

Flew:

"A label for a doctrine about meaning first made a philosophical term in 1878 by C. S. Peirce. . . ."

Naturalism

AHDEL:

1. Conformity to nature; factual or realistic representation, especially in art and literature. 2. *Philosophy.* The system of thought holding that all phenomena can be explained in terms of natural causes and laws, without attributing moral, spiritual, or supernatural significance to them. 3. *Theology.* The doctrine that all religious truths are derived from nature and natural causes and not from revelation. 4. Conduct or thought prompted by natural desires or instincts.

Angeles:
1. *Monistic*: Nature is the only reality.
2. *Antisupernaturalistic*: "All phenomena can be explained in terms of the inherent interrelationships of natural events . . ."
3. *Proscientific*: (a) Natural phenomena can be explained by the methodology of the sciences, assuming the methodologies improve.
4. *Humanistic*: "Humans are one of the many (natural) manifestations of the universe . . ." [It follows naturalism (critical, ethical).]

Flew:
1. What is studied by the non-human and human sciences is all there is. There is no need for finding explanations for things outside the Universe. . . . 2. (in philosophical ethics), since G. E. Moore, the view . . . "that value words are definable in terms of neutral statements of fact. . . ."

Materialism

AHDEL:

1. The opinion "that physical matter in its movements and modifications is the only reality." Thought, feeling, mind, and will is explainable by physical law. . . . 2. Physical well-being and worldly possessions constitute the greatest good and highest value in life. 3. Undue regard for worldly concerns . . . .

Angeles:
1. Nothing but matter in motion exists. "Mind is caused by material changes . . . and is completely dependent upon matter" . . . . 2. Purpose, awareness, intention, goals, meaning, direction, intelligence, willing, and striving are not characteristic of matter and the universe. 3. Nonmaterial entities such as spirits, ghosts, demons, angels do not exist. Consequently, there is no God or nothing supernatural in the universe. . . . 7. "Matter can be neither created nor destroyed. 8. No life, no mind, is immortal. . . . 11. Values do not exist in the universe independently of the activities of humans." [This definition is followed by definitions for: materialism (dialectical—Marx, Engels, mechanistic, reductive)]

Flew:
What exists is "either matter or entirely dependent on matter for its existence. The precise meaning and status of this doctrine are, however, far from clear."

Philosophical Definitions of Selected "-isms" from the Internet, 2012

Reminder: The definitions in this Appendix accurately represented the sites below when they were submitted for publication. However, because they are only partially refereed and are subject to change, do not be surprised if they change over time. Caution and further work are needed prior to accepting them as scholarly and trustworthy.

Sources

IEP: Fieser, J., & Dowden, B. (1995). *The Internet encyclopedia of philosophy*. Retrieved July 5, 2012 from http://www.iep.utm.edu/

WIKI: Glossary of philosophy. In *Wikipedia: The free encyclopedia*. Retrieved July 5, 2012 from http://en.wikipedia.org/wiki/Glossary_of_philosophy

The ISM Book: Saint-Andre, P. (1996). *The Ism book*. Retrieved July 5, 2012 from http://www.ismbook.com/ismlist.html

PHR: Chrisomalis, S. (2007). *The phrontistery. Philosphical 'isms.'* Retrieved July 5, 2012 from http://phrontistery.info/isms.html

Absolutism

IEP:—

WIKI: The position that in a particular domain of thought all statements in that domain are either absolutely true or absolutely false: none is true for some cultures or eras while false for other cultures or eras. [See also moral, enlightened and political a.]

The ISM Book: 1. (religion) Within some forms of Christianity (esp. Calvinism), the doctrine that one's salvation is predestined and determined solely by the will of God, uninfluenced by reasons such as one's deeds or intentions; more commonly called the doctrine of predestination. 2. (politics) The doctrine that a sovereign or government ought to possess absolute power over individuals and society; an older and less common term for totalitarianism. 3. (metaphysics) Rarely, a thoroughgoing idealism.

PHR: Doctrine of government by a single absolute ruler; autocracy.

Relativism

IEP: Relativism is sometimes identified (usually by its critics) as the thesis that all points of view are equally valid. In ethics, this amounts to saying that all moralities are equally good; in epistemology it implies that all beliefs, or belief systems, are equally true. Critics of relativism typically dismiss such views as incoherent since they imply the validity even of the view that relativism is false. They also charge that such views are pernicious since they undermine the enterprise of trying to improve our ways of thinking.

. . .

Although there are many different kinds of relativism, they all have two features in common:

1) They all assert that one thing (e.g. moral values, beauty, knowledge, taste, or meaning) is relative to some particular framework or standpoint (e.g., the individual subject, a culture, an era, a language, or a conceptual scheme); and

2) They all deny that any standpoint is uniquely privileged over all others.

WIKI: The view that the meaning and value of human beliefs and behaviors have no absolute reference. Relativists claim that humans understand and evaluate beliefs and behaviors only in terms of, for example, their historical and cultural context. Philosophers identify many different kinds of relativism depending upon what allegedly depends on something and what something depends on.

The ISM Book: 1. (epistemology) The view (opposed to objectivism and realism) that truth and value are relative to an observer or group of observers. One example is cultural relativism, which claims that different cultures have different but perfectly legitimate and equally valid standards of truth and value (see polylogism and postmodernism). Relativism is often another word for subjectivism, although the latter term is more personal and does not generally refer to social forms of relativism.

PHR:—

Rationalism

IEP:—

WIKI: A theory or method based on the thesis that human reason can in principle be the source of all knowledge. In the modern period, rationalism was initially championed by René Descartes and spread during the 17th and 18th centuries, primarily in continental Europe.

The ISM Book: A tradition of philosophy in the 17th and 18th centuries that emphasized deductive reasoning and focused on the "hard" branches of philosophy (e.g., epistemology) instead of the value branches (e.g., ethics, politics, and aesthetics); the most prominent rationalists were Descartes (1596–1650), Leibniz (1646–1716), and Spinoza (1632–1677). . . .

PHR: Belief that reason is the fundamental source of knowledge.

Existentialism

IEP: A catch-all term for those philosophers who consider the nature of the human condition as a key philosophical problem and who share the view that this problem is best addressed through ontology. . . .

WIKI: The philosophical movement that views human existence as having a set of underlying themes and characteristics, such as anxiety, dread, freedom, awareness of death, and consciousness of existing, that are primary. That is, they cannot be reduced to or explained by a natural-scientific approach or any approach that attempts to detach itself from or rise above these themes.

The ISM Book: An influential movement in 20th-century ethics holding that values are not universal but instead that each person must create his own values as a result of living life. Its guiding phrase, formulated by, Jean-Paul Sartre (1905–1980), was "existence precedes essence." Although existentialism was a form of individualism, it was also very much a kind of pessimism and opposed to any attempt at ethical naturalism since it held that there is no stable human nature and therefore that there are no common human values. . . .

PHR: Doctrine of individual human responsibility in an unfathomable universe.

Empiricism

IEP:—

WIKI: The doctrine that all knowledge ultimately comes from experience, denying the notion of innate ideas or a priori knowledge about the world.

The ISM Book: 1. (epistemology) A theory of knowledge holding that experience is the most reliable source of knowledge. In general, empiricism emphasizes induction over deduction and reality over theory. . . . More specifically, the school of empiricism in the 17th and 18th centuries reacted against the excesses of medieval scholasticism and rationalism by formulating a more systematic grounding for empirical knowledge. The founder of that school was John Locke (1632–1704), whose epistemology tended towards representationalism rather than realism, leading eventually to the skepticism of David Hume (1711–1776). By empiricism is sometimes meant more narrowly a focus on scientific experiment; however, a more appropriate term for that view is scientism or experimentalism.

PHR: Doctrine that the experience of the senses is the only source of knowledge.

Idealism

IEP: A movement in German philosophy that began in the 1780s and lasted until the 1840s. . . . Kant's transcendental idealism was a modest philosophical doctrine about the difference between appearances and things in themselves, which claimed that the objects of human cognition are appearances and not things in themselves. Fichte, Schelling, and Hegel radicalized this view, transforming Kant's transcendental idealism into absolute idealism, which holds that things in themselves are a contradiction in terms, because a thing must be an object of our consciousness if it is to be an object at all. . . .

WIKI: The doctrine that reality or knowledge is founded on ideas (mental experience). Depending on the specific ideal, idealism is usually juxtaposed with materialism or realism. [See also objective, German, subjective, and transcendental i.]

The ISM Book 1. (metaphysics) In the original, Platonic sense, a theory claiming that the primary reality consists of eternal, unchanging, non-physical archetypes, of which the particular entities perceived by the senses are imperfect copies. The most significant forms of idealism after Platonism are the monadology of Leibniz (a kind of panpsychism) and Hegelianism. Although spiritualism is similar to idealism, it usually refers more to religious, supernatural conceptions of reality than to philosophical theories. The opposite of idealism is materialism. 2. (epistemology) Any theory holding that valid human knowledge is a matter of mentally grasping non-physical archetypes rather than in perceiving (or abstracting concepts from) physical entities.

The PHR: Belief that our experiences of the world consist of ideas.

Modernism

IEP:—

WIKI: Describes a series of reforming cultural movements in art and architecture, music, literature and the applied arts which emerged roughly in the period 1884–1914. The term covers many political, cultural and artistic movements rooted in the changes in Western society at the end of the 19th and beginning of the 20th century. It is a trend of thought that affirms the power of human beings to create, improve, and reshape their environment, with the aid of scientific knowledge, technology and practical experimentation.

The ISM Book:—

PHR:—

Postmodernism

IEP:—

WIKI: Philosophical movement characterized by the postmodern criticism and analysis of Western philosophy. Beginning as a critique of Continental philosophy, it was heavily influenced by phenomenology, structuralism and existentialism, and by the philosophers Friedrich Nietzsche and Martin Heidegger. It was also influenced to some degree by Ludwig Wittgenstein's later criticisms of analytic philosophy. Within postmodern philosophy, there are numerous interrelated fields, including deconstruction and several fields beginning with the prefix "post-", such as post-structuralism, post-Marxism, and post-feminism. In particular postmodern philosophy has spawned a huge literature of critical theory.

The Ism Book 1. (epistemology) A radical form of relativism (similar to polylogism and opposed to scientism and objectivism) holding that there are no privileged viewpoints and that objective knowledge is effectively unattainable. 2. (aesthetics) A late 20th-century theory and practice of art that devalued representationalism and formalism in favor of a kind of eclecticism and experimentalism.

PHR:—

Materialism

IEP:— [See Materialism, Indian]

WIKI: The philosophical view that the only thing that can truly be said to 'exist' is matter; that fundamentally, all things are composed of 'material' and all phenomena are the result of material interactions. [See also Christian, historical, dialectic, eliminative, emergent, evolutionary, French, and reductive m.]

The ISM Book: 1. (metaphysics) The view that fundamentally only matter exists. Materialism is opposed to idealism and considers any talk of the soul to be a throwback to the bad old days of spiritualism and vitalism. Because matter can be known completely in terms of physical laws (see reductionism), materialism often lends heavy support to determinism.

PHR: Belief that matter is the only extant substance.

Naturalism

IEP: Naturalism is an approach to philosophical problems that interprets them as tractable through the methods of the empirical sciences or at least, without a distinctively a priori project of theorizing. . . .

Naturalism often assigns a key role to the methods and results of the empirical sciences, and sometimes aspires to reductionism and physicalism. However, there are many versions of naturalism and some are explicitly non-scientistic. What they share is a repudiation of the view of philosophy as exclusively a priori theorizing concerned with a distinctively philosophical set of questions.

WIKI: Any of several philosophical stances, typically those descended from materialism and pragmatism, that do not distinguish the supernatural (including strange entities like non-natural values, and universals as they are commonly conceived) from nature. Naturalism does not necessarily claim that phenomena or hypotheses commonly labeled as supernatural do not exist or are wrong, but insists that all phenomena and hypotheses can be studied by the same methods and therefore anything considered supernatural is either non-existent, unknowable, or not inherently different from natural phenomena or hypotheses. [See also humanistic, legal, metaphysical, and methodological n.]

The ISM Book: 1. (metaphysics) The idea that the universe operates according to its own laws, without intervention by any gods (opposed to theism and spiritualism, but compatible with deism). 2. (ethics) The view that some or all human values (food, water, shelter, safety, psychological closeness, knowledge, etc.) are based on the characteristics of the human organism. For example, existentialism could be considered a humanistic form of individualism, but it differs from many other forms of humanism in denying ethical naturalism. 3. (aesthetics) The theory that the purpose of art (especially literature) is to present human experience "as is" without evaluation or the projection of ethical ideals (historically, naturalism developed in reaction to romanticism).

PHR: Belief that the world can be explained in terms of natural forces.

Formalism

IEP:—

WIKI: Means a number of different things.

In the study of the arts and literature, formalism refers to the style of criticism that focuses on artistic or literary techniques in themselves, in separation from the work's social and historical context. See formalism (art), formalism (literature]. [See also mathematical, legal f. and f. in economic anthropology.]

The ISM Book: 1. (ethics) A theory that emphasizes adherence to formal rules, usually in preference to the benefits or consequences of human action; an example is deontologism. 2. (aesthetics) A theory that emphasizes the importance of artistic form, often in preference to artistic content; examples include some varieties of classicism and modernism.

PHR:—

Pragmatism

IEP: Pragmatism is a philosophical movement that includes those who claim that an ideology or proposition is true if it works satisfactorily, that the meaning of a proposition is to be found in the practical consequences of accepting it, and that unpractical ideas are to be rejected. Pragmatism originated in the United States during the latter quarter of the 19th century.

WIKI: Philosophy which originated in the United States in the late 19th century. Pragmatism is characterized by the insistence on consequences, utility and practicality as vital components of meaning and truth. Pragmatism objects to the view that human concepts and intellect represent reality, and therefore stands in opposition to both formalist and rationalist schools of philosophy. Rather, pragmatism holds that it is only in the struggle of intelligent organisms with the surrounding environment that theories acquire significance, and only with a theory's success in this struggle that it becomes true.

The ISM Book 1. (epistemology) The view, originated by C. S. Peirce (1839–1914) and made famous by William James (1842–1910) and James Dewey (1859–1952), that the truth of a concept is to be evaluated by its practical consequences for human affairs. 2. (ethics) A form of consequentialism that differs from utilitarianism by emphasizing practical action instead of usefulness to others. While pragmatism is thus a kind of humanism, it rejects naturalism and often tends to be a kind of relativism.

PHR: Doctrine emphasizing practical value of philosophy.

Appendix H

Qualitative and Quantitative Studies for Comparison of Selected Issues

Gender

Abeles, H. (2009, Jul.) Are musical instrument gender associations changing? *Journal of Research in Music Education*, *57*(2), 127–139.

Abramo, J. (2011, Apr.). Gender differences of popular music production in secondary schools. *Journal of Research in Music Education*, *59*(1), 21–43.

Hoffman, A. R. (2008). Gender, identity and the sixth grade band classroom. *Gender, Education, Music & Society*, *4*, 1–12. Retrieved April 25, 2009 from www.queensu.ca/music/links/gems/hoffman5.pdf

Legg, R. (2010, Jun.). "One equal music": An exploration of gender perceptions and the fair assessment by beginning music teachers of musical compositions. *Music Education Research*, *12*(2), 141–149.

Roulston, K., & Misawa, M. (2011, Mar.). Music teachers' constructions of gender in elementary education. *Music Education Research*, *13*(1), 3–28.

Improvisation

Azzara, C. D. (1993, Winter). Audiation-based improvisation techniques and elementary instrumental music students' music achievement. *Journal of Research in Music Education*, *41*(4), 328–342.

Beegle, A. C. (2010, October). A classroom-based study of small-group planned improvisation with fifth-grade children. *Journal of Research in Music Education*, *58*(3), 219–239.

Reese, J. W. (2006). Definitions of improvisation: Perspectives of three elementary general music teachers. Master's thesis (M.M.). University of Michigan. AAT 1440086.

Seddon, F., & Biasutti, M. (2010, July) Strategies students adopted when learning to play an improvised blues in an e-learning environment. *Journal of Research in Music Education*, *58*(2), 147–167.

Watson, Kevin E. (2020, Oct.). The effects of aural versus notated instructional materials on achievement and self-efficacy in jazz improvisation. *Journal of Research in Music Education*, *58*(3), 240–259.

Outreach/Partnerships

Abeles, H. F. (2004). The effect of three orchestra/school partnerships on students' interest in instrumental music instruction. *Journal of Research in Music Education, 57*(2), 127–139.

Bose, J. H. (2008). *Aesthetic education: Philosophy and teaching artist practice at Lincoln Center Institute* (Doctoral dissertation). Available from ProQuest Digital Dissertations (AAT 3310664).

Frierson-Campbell, C. (2003). Professional need and the contexts of in-service music teacher identity. In H. Froehlich, D. Coan, & R. R. Rideout, *Sociology of music education symposium III: Social dimensions of music, music teaching and learning* (pp. 199–216). Amherst, MA: Department of Music & Dance, University of Massachusetts.

Hearn, E. A. (2006). *Collaborative partnerships for experiential education in music: A case study of a higher education school of music educational outreach program and its K–8 partners* (Doctoral dissertation). Available from ProQuest Digital Dissertations (AAT 3208464).

Rives, J. A. (2006). *Coordinated organizations, activities, and personnel: An ethnographic study of organizational behavior in the Wichita, Kansas String Education Plan (WSEP). An educational program for the development of symphony orchestra musicians and audiences* (Doctoral dissertation). Available from ProQuest Digital Dissertations (AAT 3215159).

Soto, A. C., Lum, C., & Campbell, P. S. (2009, January). A university-school music partnership for music education majors in a culturally distinctive community. *Journal of Research in Music Education, 56*(4), 388–356.

Policy/School Reform

Gerrity, K. W. (2007) *No Child Left Behind: Determining the impact of policy on music education* (Doctoral dissertation). Retrieved from ProQuest Digital Dissertations database. (UMI No. 3262133).

Kinney, D. W. (2010). Selected nonmusic predictors of urban students' decisions to enroll and persist in middle school band programs. *Journal of Research in Music Education, 57*(4), 334–350.

Kos, R. P. (2007) *Incidental change: The influence of educational policy implementation on music education programs and practice* (Doctoral dissertation). Retrieved November 25, 2007 from ProQuest Digital Dissertations database. (UMI No. 3261425).

Recruitment/Retention

Costa-Giomi, E., Flowers, P. J., & Sasaki, W. (2005). Piano lessons of beginning students who persist or drop out: Teacher behavior, student behavior, and lesson progress. *Journal of Research in Music Education, 53*(3), 234–47.

Gouzouasis, P., Henrey, J., & Belliveau, G. (2008, March.). Turning points: A transitional story of grade seven music students' participation in high school band programmes. *Music Education Research, 10*(1), 75–90.

Student Learning

Hewitt, M. P. (2011, Apr.). The impact of self-evaluation instruction on student self-evaluation, music performance, and self-evaluation accuracy. *Journal of Research in Music Education, 59*(1), 6–20.

Latukefu, L. (2010). Peer assessment in tertiary level singing: Changing and shaping culture through social interaction. *Research Studies in Music Education,* June, *32*, 61–73

Silvey, P. E. (2005, Summer). Learning to perform Benjamin Britten's "Rejoice in the Lamb": The perspectives of three high school choral singers. *Journal of Research in Music Education, 53*(2), 102–119.

Woody, R. H., & Lehmann, A. C. (2010). Student musicians' ear-playing ability as a function of vernacular music experiences. *Journal of Research in Music Education, 58*(2), 101–115.

Appendix I
John Curwen

Note. In Dickinson, P. (Ed.). (2010). *Bernarr Rainbow on music: Memoirs and selected writings*, pp. 134–136. Woodbridge, Suffolk, UK, and Rochester, NY: The Boydell Press. Re-printed with permission by the Chair of the Trustees of the Bernarr Rainbow Trust.

A Visit to Miss Glover's School

John Curwen's own account published in the *Independent Magazine*, 1842, p. 240

This is an infant school at Norwich. It does not differ in its general aspect and arrangements from other infant schools. The daily employments of the children, their average age, and their appearance, correspond with what may be seen in most schools of a similar kind. But in one thing they are remarkably distinguished from all other schools that we have ever seen. These little children conduct their singing exercises with so much facility and delight, and, at the same time, with such accuracy both of time and tune, as to fill with astonishment all who hear them. Our readers will readily believe that this must be the case, when we tell them that, in the course of our visit, we heard the children sing canons in four, six and even in the eight parts, with great precision and beauty of execution. This was done from notes, without any instrument to lead them, and only in one case did the voices flatten, and in that case only by half-a-tone. To those who have been accustomed to the singing of young children, this will appear indeed astonishing, but we shall astonish them still more when we say, that the training which has produced such results does not occupy more than two hours in the week!—a length of time not greater than is given to singing exercises in every infant school in the land! Whence, then, arises the difference? From this cause—that, while in other schools, the time is loosely spent without plan or design, in Miss Glover's school the time is husbanded by a carefully arranged method. But this is not sufficient to explain all: it is necessary to add, that the method itself contains *more of true science*; and *less of technicality*; than any other method taught in England.

We will first describe the system as we saw it in operation, and then examine briefly its principles.

As we entered the room, the soft and regulated tone, and the sweet blending of the voices, such as to take not the ear by force, but steal on the senses as by some magic spell, assured us that music, real music, with all its subduing power, dwelt there.

On the gallery were seated all the younger children, with heads erect and shoulders back, singing (with the Sol-fa syllables), and as they sung, eagerly looking towards an upright board which stood at a little distance from the letters foot of the gallery. On this board were printed one above the other the initial letters of the Sol-fa syllables, show-ing much shorter distances between *Me* and *Fah* and between *Te* and *Do* (the third and fourth, and seventh and eighth *of the scale*; for in this method *Do* is always the key-tone) than between the other notes. This *Musical Ladder*, as it is styled, corresponds with what we call the Modulator. By the side of the 'Ladder' stood a little monitor with a wand in her hand. She was pointing to the notes as the children sang them. The very movement of her wand was musical. She also held in charge with her other hand, a little infant, the youngest in the school, who could scarcely stand, but who nevertheless could sing. The children are taught to sing in this way, looking at the exact intervals as depicted on the Musical Ladder, until they enter the higher class of the school. This may be in the course of the six months, or in a much shorter time. We did not observe any distinct classifica-tion for the singing lessons; they are taken as part of the ordinary routine of the school. The children are thus rendered perfectly familiar with *an accurate pictorial representa-tion of interval*; indeed they must carry a musical ladder in their mind's eye wherever they go; and by the correct association of mind thus established, they are well prepared for the next stage in their advancement.

This we had an opportunity of examining in another part of the room, where stood a class of twenty—the elder children in the school—having in their left hand the 'Sol-fa Tune Book', and in their right, short wands for the purpose of beating time.

The tune books were supported on a small instrument in the shape of a cross, with the longest bar extending beyond the book to the right-hand. Upon this projecting part of the "book-holder", as soon as the tune began, the loud beats of the measure were pretty sharply struck, while the soft beats were indicated by gentle touches of the wand on their left arm.

Miss Glover, the lady from whose invention and zealous patronage all these results have sprung, and whose Christian solicitude for the better interests of the children thus taught we have been thankful to witness, with a courtesy which we cannot too grate-fully acknowledge, kindly exhibited to us every part of the method. The plan of procedure was in this wise: Supposing them about to sing the 14th canon, which is in eight parts, the teacher steps into the middle of the circle and announces 'fourteenth canon.' Immediately eight children hold up their wands, dividing the class into equal portions, so that each child may know which leader she is to follow. The chord of the keytone is then struck on a glass harmonicon, which is placed in the room for the purpose, and the canon begins. When the first division has sung the first measure, the monitor of the next division, giving a glance at those under her, which means 'follow me,' takes up the strain, beating time upon the book-holder and her arm. The rest of the division marked the time by *touching* with their wands the accent marks in their books. Thus round the class the growing harmony proceeds, until it swells out in the fullest chorus. Turning round we observed that the children on the gallery, by the help of a monitor and the musical ladder, were joining in the melody. Several pieces with words were also sung very beauti-fully, and on the following day Miss Glover very kindly exhibited to us, with a select class, her method of teaching the minor scale, and the manner in which the more advanced children were introduced, by easy steps, to the correct use of the old notation.

Coded Qualitative Data Stored in a Spreadsheet or Word Processor Table

Data are from Frierson-Campbell (2003).

File/Date	Line	Spkr	Role	Code	Cat	Transcribed Data
Glenwood 4.4.01	50–54	OC	Bldg Adm	5	PMTE	Anthony believes his current art and music teachers are "pretty neat people," especially his art teacher who does after school activities in the hallways and has a lot of student art work posted all over the school.
Glenwood 4.4.01	55–57	Anthony	Mus Tch	4	PMTE	I like to, you know, go into the class when Tom is playing his guitar and join in, to give a positive feeling. I'm happy to see kids enjoying music.

Mike 10.16.01	31–32	OC	Dist Adm	2	PMTE	The music supervisor mentioned that "academic teachers" [his term] were "coverage teachers" (by grade and/or subject) and that their building administrators would pay for substitute teachers when they went out for inservice training.
Rob 5.31.01	2–8	Rob	Mus Tch	1	PMTE	Sometimes they have grade level meetings um I'm not included in them. And—I get along with everybody around here. But—so I don't take it personally. It's just that we tend not to be included. And whenever we have been included . . . see, what they do, in here, is that they put together the music teachers, the art teachers, and the gym teachers, and we all sit together and say "what are we doing here" and we write down some issues that nobody reads. You know . . . and that's not right.
Gary 5.3.02	122–123	Gary	Mus Tch	3	PMTE	We get a lot of respect from the principal because we know how to have success with problem kids. Everything they ask us to do we come through with.

Appendix K

Choices in Statistical Tests for Parametric and Non-parametric Data

Comparisons are drawn from http://www.graphpad.com/www/book/choose.htm, taken from Chapter 37 of: Motulsky, H. (1995). *Intuitive biostatistics*. New York: Oxford University Press. See also Asmus and Radocy (1992, pp. 179–180), Field (2005, back-cover), and Pallant (2007, pp. 116–117).

Note: The boldfaced concepts and tests are discussed in Chapters 10–12.

What your study is about	PARAMETRIC Measurement (from Gaussian Population)	NONPARAMETRIC Rank, Score, or Measurement (from Non-Gaussian Population)
Describe one group	**Mean, SD**	**Median**
Compare one group to a hypothetical value	One-sample *t* test	Wilcoxon test
Compare two unpaired groups	Unpaired *t* test	Mann-Whitney test
Compare two paired groups	Paired *t* test	Wilcoxon test
Compare three or more unmatched groups	One-way **ANOVA**	Kruskal-Wallis test

Compare three or more matched groups	Repeated-measures ANOVA	Friedman test
Quantify association between two variables	**Pearson correlation (r)**	Spearman correlation
Predict value from another measured variable	Simple linear regression or Non-linear regression	Non-parametric regression
Predict value from several measured or binomial variables	Multiple linear regression or Multiple non-linear regression	

References

Abrahams, F., & Head, P. D. (2005). *Case studies in music education* (2nd ed.). Chicago: GIA Publications, Inc.

Abramo, J. (2011). Gender differences of popular music production in secondary schools. *Journal of Research in Music Education, 59*(1), 21–43.

Allen, M. (2004). *Smart thinking: Skills for critical understanding and writing* (2nd ed.). New York: Oxford University Press.

Allsup, R. (2003). Mutual learning and democratic action in instrumental music education. *Journal of Research in Music Education, 51*(1), 24–37.

Altheide, D., Coyle, M., DeVriese, K., & Schneider, C. (2008). Emergent qualitative document analysis. In S. N. Hesse-Biber, & P. Leavy (Eds.), *Handbook of emergent methods* (pp. 127–151). New York: The Guilford Press.

The American Heritage Dictionary of the English Language (1970). (2nd ed.). New York: American Heritage Publishing Company.

The American Heritage Dictionary of the English Language. (2011). (5th ed.). Boston: Houghton Mifflin Harcourt.

American Psychological Association. (2009). *Publication manual of the American Psychological Association* (6th ed.). Washington, DC: American Psychological Association.

Anastasi, A. (1988). *Psychological testing* (6th ed.). Englewood Cliffs, NJ: Macmillan Publishing Company.

Angeles, P. A. (1981). *A dictionary of philosophy.* New York: Barnes and Noble Books.

Arnold, D. (Ed.). (2004). *Cultural identities and the aesthetics of Britishness.* Manchester & New York: Manchester University Press. New York: Palgrave.

Asmus, E. P., & Radocy, R. E. (1992). Quantitative analysis. In R. Colwell, & C. Richardson (Eds.), *The new handbook of research on music teaching and learning* (pp. 141–183). New York: Oxford University Press.

Bachwani-Paritosh, R. (2007, January 5). On using mind-maps in qualitative research [web log post]. Retrieved February 7, 2012 from http://onqualitativeresearch.blogspot.com/2007/01/on-using-mind-maps-in-qualitative.html

Baker, V. D. (2003). Inclusion of women composers in college music history textbooks. *Journal of Historical Research in Music Education, 25*(1), 5–19.

Baldwin, J. A. (1955). *Notes of a native son.* Boston, MA: Beacon Press.

Barone, T. E. (1989). Ways of being at risk: The case of Billy Charles Barnett. *Phi Delta Kappan, 71*(2), 147–151. Retrieved January 21, 2012 from http://www.jstor.org/stable/20404091

Barone, T. E. (1992). Beyond theory and method: A case of critical storytelling. *Theory into Practice, 31*(2), 142–147. Retrieved February 25, 2010 from www.wilsonweb.com

Barone, T., & Eisner, E. (1997). Arts-based educational research. In R. M. Jaeger (Ed.), *Complementary methods for research in education* (2nd ed.). Washington, DC: American Educational Research Association.

Barone, T., & Eisner, E. (2006). Arts-based educational research. In J. L. Green, G. Camilli, & P. B. Elmore (Eds.), *Handbook of complementary methods in educational research* (pp. 95–109). Washington, DC: American Educational Research Association.

Barone, T., & Eisner, E. (2012). *Arts-based research.* Los Angeles: Sage Publications.

Barrett, J. (2007). The researcher as instrument: Learning to conduct qualitative research through analyzing and interpreting a choral rehearsal. *Music Education Research, 9*(3), 417–433. Retrieved August 6, 2008 from http://rsm.sagepub.com

Barrett, M. S., & Stauffer, S. L. (2009). *Narrative inquiry in music education: Troubling certainty.* New York: Springer Science + Business Media.

Barzun, J., & Graff, H. F. (2004). *The modern researcher* (6th ed.). Belmont, CA: Wadsworth/Thomson Learning.

Bassett, J. (2010). A philosophical inquiry on the valuation and selection of musical materials for culturally diverse learners in global environments (Doctoral dissertation). Graduate School Theses and Dissertations. Paper 1571. Retrieved November 10, 2011 from http://scholarcommons.usf.edu/etd/1571

Battisti, F., & Garofalo, R. (1990). *Guide to score study for the wind band conductor.* Ft. Lauderdale: Meredith Music Publications.

Becker, H. S. (1973). *Outsiders: Studies in the sociology of deviance.* New York: The Free Press of Glencoe.

Becker, H. S. (1997). *Tricks of the trade.* Chicago: University of Chicago Press.

Beegle, A. (2004). American music education 1941–1946: Meeting needs and making adjustments during World War II. *Journal of Historical Research in Music Education, 26*(1), 54–67.

Beegle, A. C. (2010). A classroom-based study of small-group planned improvisation with fifth-grade children. *Journal of Research in Music Education, 58*(3), 219–239.

Benton, C. W. (2002). A study of the effects of metacognition on sight-singing achievement and attitudes among students in a middle school choral music program (Doctoral dissertation). Retrieved from ProQuest Dissertations & Theses: Full Text (AAT 3077263).

Birge, E. B. (1928/1966). *History of public school music in the United States.* (New and augmented ed.). Reston, VA: Music Educators National Conference.

Bleiker, R. (2009). *Aesthetics and world politics.* Houndmills, Basingstoke, & New York: Palgrave Macmillan.

Bogdan, R. C., & Biklen, S. K. (2003). *Qualitative research for education: An introduction to theories and methods* (4th ed.). New York: Pearson Education Group.

Borenstein, M. (2009). *Introduction to meta-analysis.* Chichester, U.K: John Wiley & Sons.

Bose, J. H. (2008). *Aesthetic education: Philosophy and teaching artist practice at Lincoln Center Institute* (Doctoral dissertation). Available from ProQuest Digital Dissertations (AAT 3310664).

Bouij, C. (1998). Swedish music teachers in training and professional life. *International Journal of Music Education, 32*, 24–32.

Bowers, J. K. (1991). Effect of vocal models, curriculum, and grade level on the pitch matching accuracy of adolescent male singers in various stages of vocal development. *The Missouri Journal of Research in Music Education, 28*, 1–15.

Bowman, W. D. (1980). *Tacit knowing, musical experience, and music instruction: The significance of Michael Polanyi's thought for music education* (Doctoral dissertation, University of Illinois at Urbana-Champaign). Retrieved from ProQuest Dissertations & Theses: Full Text. (Publication No. AAT 8108454).

Bowman, W. D. (1992). Philosophy, criticism, and music education: Some tentative steps down a less-traveled road. *Bulletin of the Council for Research in Music Education, 114*, 1–19.

Bowman, W. D. (1998). *Philosophical perspectives on music.* New York: Oxford University Press.

Bowman, W. (2002). Educating musically. In R. Colwell, & C. Richardson (Eds.), *The new handbook of research on music teaching and learning* (pp. 63–84). New York: Oxford University Press.

Bowman, W. D. (2006). Why narrative? Why now? *Research Studies in Music Education, 27*, 5–20.

Bowman, W. D. & Frega, A. L. (Eds.). (2012). *The Oxford handbook of philosophy in music education.* New York: Oxford.

Bradley, D. (2007). The sounds of silence: Talking race in music education. *Action, Criticism, and Theory for Music Education, 6*(4), 132–162. Retrieved October 16, 2011 from http://act.maydaygroup.org/articles/Bradley6_4.pdf

Brenner, M. E. (2006). Interviewing in educational research. In J. L. Green, G. Camilli, & P. B. Elmore (Eds.), *Handbook of complementary methods in educational research* (pp. 357–370). Washington, DC: American Educational Research Association.

Bresler, L. (2005). What musicianship can teach educational research. *Music Education Research, 7*(2), 169–183.

Brink-Budgen, R., van den (2010). *Critical thinking for students. Learn the skills of analyzing, evaluating and producing arguments* (4th ed.). Oxford: How To Books.

Britton, A. P. (1969). Research in the United States. *Journal of Research in Music Education, 17*(1), 108–111.

Bruner, J. (1986). *Actual minds, possible worlds*. Cambridge, MA: Harvard University Press.

Cahnmann-Taylor, M., & Siegesmund, R. (2008). *Arts-based research in education: Foundations for practice.* New York: Routledge.

Campbell, D. T., & Stanley, J. C. (1963). *Experimental and quasi-experimental designs for research*. Boston, MA: Houghton Mifflin.

Campbell, P. S. (1998). *Songs in their heads: Music and its meaning in children's lives*. New York: Oxford University Press.

Campbell, P. S. (2003). Ethnomusicology and music education: Crossroads for knowing music, education, and culture. *Research Studies in Music Education, 21*(16), 16–30.

Campbell, P. S. (2010). *Songs in their heads: Music and its meaning in children's lives* (2nd ed.). New York: Oxford University Press.

Cannavo, S. (1998). *Think to win: The power of logic in everyday life*. New York: Prometheus Books.

Chandler, D. L. (2004). *Colleen Jean Kirk (1918–2004): Her life, career and her influence on American choral music education* (Doctoral dissertation). Retrieved from ProQuest Dissertations & Theses: Full Text. (AAT 3160549).

Charmaz, K. (2006). *Constructing grounded theory: A practical guide through qualitative analysis* [Kindle edition]. London & Thousand Oaks, CA: Sage Publications. Retrieved from Amazon.com on November 17, 2011.

Charmaz, K. (2008a). Constructionism and the grounded theory method. In J. A. Holstein, & J. F. Gubrium (Eds.), *Handbook of constructionist research* (pp. 397–412). New York: Guilford Press.

Charmaz, K. (2008b). Grounded theory as an emergent method. In S. N. Hesse-Biber, & P. Leavy (Eds.), *Handbook of emergent methods* (pp. 155–170). New York: The Guilford Press.

Chavous, T. M. (2000). The relationships among racial identity, perceived ethnic fit, and organizational involvement for African American students at a predominantly White university. *Journal of Black Psychology, 26*(1), 79–100. Abstract retrieved December 8, 2010 from Google Scholar. http://jbp.sagepub.com/content/26/1/79.abstract

Chinn, B. J. (1997). Vocal self-identification, singing style, and singing range in relationship to a measure of cultural mistrust in African-American adolescent females. *Journal of Research in Music Education, 45*(4), 636–649.

Cho, G. J. (1975). *Some non-Chinese elements in the ancient Japanese music: An analytic-comparative study.* Unpublished doctoral dissertation, Northwestern University, Evanston, IL.

Cho, G. J. (2003). *The discovery of musical equal temperament in China and Europe in the sixteenth century.* Lewiston, NY: The Edwin Mellen Press.

Cho, K. (2010). *A constructivist approach to studio instruction: A case study of a flute class* (Doctoral dissertation). Retrieved from ProQuest Dissertations & Theses: Full Text (AAT 3424900).

Chrisomalis, S. (2007). *The phrontistery: Philosophical 'isms.'* Retrieved July 25, 2011 from http://phrontistery.info/isms.html.

Clandinin, D. J. (2006). Narrative inquiry: A methodology for studying lived experience. *Research Studies in Music Education, 27*, 44–54. Retrieved February 25, 2010 from www.sagepub.com

Clements, A. C. (Ed.). (2010). *Alternative approaches in music education: Cases in the field*. Published in partnership with MENC, The National Association of Music Education. Plymouth, UK: Rowman and Littlefield.

Clifford, J. (1983). On ethnographic authority. *Representations, 2*, 118–146. Retrieved January 21, 2012 from http://heavysideindustries.com/wp-content/uploads/2010/08/On-Ethnographic-Authority-James-Clifford.pdf.

Cohen, J. (1988). *Statistical power analysis for the behavioral sciences* (2nd ed.). Hillsdale, NJ: Lawrence Erlbaum.

Collingwood, R. G. (1946/1994). *The idea of history* (rev. ed.). Oxford: Oxford University Press.

Colwell, R. (Ed.). (1991). *Basic concepts of music education II*. Colorado: University of Colorado Press.

Colwell, R. (Ed.). (1992). *Handbook of research on music teaching and learning*. New York: Schirmer Books.

Colwell, R. (Ed.). (2006). *MENC handbook of research methodologies*. New York: Oxford University Press.

Colwell, R. (2011). Roles of direct instruction, critical thinking, and transfer in the design of curriculum for music learning. In R. Colwell, & P. R. Webster (Eds.), *MENC Handbook of research on music learning*: Vol. 1. Strategies (pp. 84–139). New York: Oxford University Press.

Colwell, R., & Richardson, C. (Eds.). (2002). *The new handbook of research on music teaching and learning*. New York: Oxford University Press.

Colwell, R., & Webster, P. R. (Eds.). (2011). *MENC handbook of research on music learning. Vols. 1–2*. New York: Oxford University Press.

Cook, T. D & Campbell, D. T. (1979). *Quasi-experimentation: Design and analysis for field settings*. Chicago, IL: Rand McNally College.

Cooksey, J. M. (1999). *Working with adolescent voices*. St. Louis, MO: Concordia Publishing House.

Connelly, F. M., & Clandinin, D. J. (2006). Narrative inquiry. In J. L. Green, G. Camilli, & P. Elmore (Eds.), *Handbook of complementary methods in education research* (3rd ed., pp. 477–487). Mahwah, NJ: Lawrence Erlbaum.

Cooper, H. M., Hedges, L. V., & Valentine, J. C. (2009). *The handbook of research synthesis and meta-analysis* (2nd ed.). New York: Russell Sage Foundation.

Copi, I., Cohen, C., & McMahon, K. (2011). *Introduction to logic* (14th ed.). Upper Saddle River, NJ: Pearson Prentice Hall. Retrieved June 24, 2011 from http://www.coursesmart.com/9780205820474/firstsection#X2ludGVybmFsX1BGUmVhZGVyP3htbGlkPTk3ODDAyMDU4MjA0NzQvOTE=

Corbin, J., & Strauss, A. (2008). *Basics of qualitative research* (3rd ed.). Los Angeles, CA: Sage.

Corey, E. C. (2006). *Michael Oakeshott on religion, aesthetics, and politics*. Columbia, MO: University of Missouri Press.

Cox, G. (2002). Transforming research in music education history. In R. Colwell, & C. Richardson, (eds.), *The new handbook of research on music teaching and learning* (pp. 695–706). New York: Oxford University Press.

Cox, G., & Stevens, R. (Eds.). (2010). *The origins and foundations of music education: Cross-cultural historical studies of music in compulsory schooling*. London & New York: Continuum.

Craig, S. (2003). *Narrative inquiries of school reform: Storied lives, storied landscapes, storied metaphors*. Greenwich, CT: Information Age Publisher.

Creswell, J. W. (2007). *Qualitative inquiry and research design: Choosing among five approaches*. Thousand Oaks, CA: Sage.

Creswell, J. W. (2009). *Research design: Qualitative, quantitative, and mixed methods approaches* (3rd ed.). London & New York: Sage.

Cyrier, A. (1981). A study of the vocal registers and transitional pitches of the adolescent female. *Missouri Journal of Research in Music Education, 4*(5), 84–86.

Danto, E. A. (2008). *Historical research*. New York: Oxford University Press.

Dawe, T. J. (2011) The fugue fugue. [weblog]. *Beams and struts: A magazine for hungry brains and thirsty souls*. Retrieved July 8, 2011 from http://beamsandstruts.com/essays/item/275-the-fugue-variations

Deasy, R. J. (Ed.). (2002). *Critical links: Learning in the arts and student academic and social development*. Washington, DC: Arts Education Partnership. Retrieved January 22, 2010 from http://www.aep-arts.org/files/research/CriticalLinks.pdf

DeCuir-Gunby, J. T. (2009). A review of the racial identity development of African American adolescents: The role of education. *Review of Educational Research, 79*, 103–124. Retrieved on November 15, 2010 from ProQuest Central (Legacy Platform).

Deemter, van, K. (2010). *Not exactly. In praise of vagueness*. New York: Oxford University Press.

Dees, M. I. (2005). *A review of eight university clarinet studios: An investigation of pedagogical style, content and philosophy through observations and interviews* (Doctoral dissertation). Retrieved from ProQuest Dissertations & Theses: Full Text. (AAT 3216587).

Demorest, S. M. (2011). Biological and environmental factors in music cognition and learning. In R. Colwell, & P. R. Webster (Eds.), *MENC Handbook of research on music learning*: Vol. 1. Strategies (pp. 173–215). New York: Oxford University Press.

deNora, T. (2000). *Music in everyday life*. Cambridge: Cambridge University Press.

Denzin, N. K., & Lincoln, Y.S . (2005). Introduction: the discipline and practice of qualitative research. In N. K. Denzin, & Y. S. Lincoln (Eds.), *The Sage handbook of qualitative research* (3rd ed.) (pp. 1–32). Thousand Oaks, CA: Sage Publications.

Department of Health and Human Services. (2009). *Code of Federal regulations: Title 45, public welfare. Title 46, protection of human subjects*. Washington, DC: Author. Retrieved October 7, 2011 from http://www.hhs.gov/ohrp/policy/ohrpregulations.pdf

Dickie, G. (1997). *Introduction to aesthetics: An analytic approach*. New York: Oxford University Press.

Dickinson, P. (Ed.). (2010). *Bernarr Rainbow on music: Memoirs and selected writings*. Woodbridge, Suffolk, UK, and Rochester, NY: The Boydell Press.

Dillman, D. A. (2007). *Mail and Internet surveys: The tailored design method* (2nd ed.). Hoboken, NJ: Wiley.

Doherty, P. B. (2006). The context and culture of the Web research environment. In D. Williams, M. Hricko, & S. Howell (Eds.), *Online assessment, measurement and evaluation: Emerging practices* (pp. 10–27). doi:10.4018/978-1-59140-747-8.ch002

Duke, R. A. (1994). Bringing the art of rehearsing into focus: The rehearsal frame as a model for prescriptive analysis of rehearsal conducting. *Journal of Band Research, 30*(1), 78–95.

Duke, R. A. (1999/2000). Measures of instructional effectiveness in music research. *Bulletin of the Council for Research in Music Education, 143*, 1–49.

Duke, R. A. (2005). *Intelligent music teaching: Essays on the core principles of effective instruction*. Austin, TX: Learning and Behavior Resources.

Duke, R. A., Simmons, A. L., & Cash, C. D. (2009, Spring). It's not how much, it's how: Characteristics of practice behavior and retention of performance skills. *Journal of Research in Music Education, 1*(56), 310–321.

Duvenage, P. (2003). *Habermas and aesthetics: The limits of communicative reason*. Cambridge, UK, & Malden, MA: Polity Press.

Eisner, E. (2008). Persistent tensions in arts-based research. In M. Cahnmann-Taylor, & R. Siegesmund (Eds.), *Arts-based research in education: Foundations for practice* (pp. 16–27). New York: Routledge.

Elliott, D. J. (1995). *Music matters: A new philosophy of music education*. New York: Oxford University Press.

Elliott, D. J. (2002). Philosophical perspectives on research. In R. Colwell, & C. Richardson (Eds.), *The new handbook of research on music teaching and learning* (pp. 85–102). A project of the Music Educators National Conference New York: Oxford University Press.

Elliott, D. J. (n/d). What does praxial mean? Retrieved January 18, 2012, from http://www.davidelliottmusic.com/music-matters/what-does-praxial-mean/

Elliott, R., Fischer, C. T., & Rennie, D. L. (1999). Evolving guidelines for publication of qualitative research studies in psychology and related fields. *British Journal of Clinical Psychology, 38*, 215–229. Retrieved July 6, 2011 from http://www.psy.au.dk/fileadmin/site_files/filer_psykologi/dokumenter/Forskerskolen/Kurser09/Fishman/No_7-Elliott__Fischer__Rennie__1999_Standards_Qual_Research.PDF.

Ellis, C., & Bochner, A. P. (2000). Autoethnography, personal narrative, reflexivity: Researcher as subject. In N. K. Denzin, & Y. S. Lincoln (Eds.), *Handbook of qualitative research* (pp. 733–768). Thousand Oaks, CA: Sage Publications.

Eshelman, D. A. (1995). *The instructional knowledge of exemplary elementary general music teachers: Commonalities based on David J. Elliott's Model of the Professional Music Educator* (Doctoral dissertation). Retrieved from ProQuest Dissertations & Theses: Full Text. (AAT 9532348).

Felt, T. E. (1976/1981). *Researching, writing, and publishing local history* (2nd ed.). Nashville, TN: American Association for State and Local History.

Field, A. (2005). *Discovering statistics using SPSS* (2nd ed.). London: Sage.

Field, S. T. (1997). Critical thinking skills and the secondary school choral music curriculum (Doctoral dissertation). Retrieved from ProQuest Dissertations & Theses: Full Text. (Publication No. AAT 9810958).

Fieser, J., & Dowden, B. (1995). *The Internet encyclopedia of philosophy*. Retrieved October 15, 2011 from http://www.iep.utm.edu/

Flanders, N. (1970). *Analyzing teaching behavior*. Menlo Park, CA: Addison-Wesley.

Flew, A. (1984). *A dictionary of philosophy* (rev. 2nd ed.). New York: St. Martin's Press.

Frankel, J. R., & Wallen, N. E. (2009). *How to design and evaluate research in education* (7th ed.). Boston, MA: McGraw-Hill.

French, S. E., Seidman, E., Allen, L., & Aber, J. L. (2006). The development of ethnic identity during adolescence. *Developmental Psychology, 42*(1), 1–10. Retrieved November 28, 2010 from http://www.uic.edu/depts/oce/OCEweb/06SU/Week1-TheDevelopmentofEthnicIdentity.pdf

Frierson-Campbell, C. (2003). Professional need and the contexts of in-service music teacher identity. In H. Froehlich, D. Coan, & R. R. Rideout (Eds.), *Sociology of music education symposium III: Social dimensions of music, music teaching and learning* (pp. 199–216). Amherst, MA: Department of Music & Dance, University of Massachusetts.

Frierson-Campbell, C., & Newman, T. (2008). Towards a rationale for a scholarly practicum for jazz performance majors: A collaborative autoethnography. *Proceedings of the 28th International Society for Music Education World Conference, Bologna, Italy, July, 2008* (pp. 97–101).

Froehlich-Rainbow, H. (1984). Systematische Beobachtung als Methode musikpädagogischer Unterrichtsforschung. Eine Darstellung anhand amerikanischer Materialien. Mit einem Nachwort von Sigrid Abel-Struth: Deutsche Ansätze musikpädagogischer Unterrichtsforschung. Mainz: Schott. [Systematic classroom observation as method of music education research. A presentation of American materials. With an afterword by Sigird Abel-Struth: German attempts at classroom observation as music education research.]

Froehlich, H. (1995). Measurement dependability in the systematic observation of music instruction: A review, some questions, and possibilities for a (new?) approach. *Psychomusicology, 14*, 182–196.

Froehlich, H., & Cattley, G. (1993). Language, metaphor, and analogy in the music education research process. In E. R. Jorgensen (Ed.), *Philosopher, teacher, musician: Perspectives on music education* (pp. 243–258). Urbana and Chicago: University of Illinois Press.

Gackle, M. L. (1991). The adolescent female voice, characteristics of change and stages of development. *Choral Journal, 31*(9), 17–25. Retrieved December 3, 2010 from http://faculty.washington.edu/demorest/gackle.pdf

Gackle, L. (2000a). Understanding voice transformation in female adolescents. In L. Thurman, & G. Welch (Eds.), *Bodymind and voice: Foundations of voice education* (rev. ed.) (pp. 739–744). Collegeville, MN: The VoiceCare Network & the National Center for Voice and Speech.

Gackle, L. (2000b). Female adolescent transforming voices: Voice classification, voice skill development, and music literature selection. In L. Thurman & G. Welch (Eds.), *Bodymind and voice: foundations of voice education* (rev. ed.) (pp. 814–820). Collegeville, MN: The VoiceCare Network & the National Center for Voice and Speech.

Gackle, L. (2010). *Finding Ophelia's voice, opening Ophelia's heart: Nurturing the adolescent female voice.* Dayton, OH: Heritage Music Press.

Gage, N. L. (1963). *Handbook of research on teaching.* Chicago: Rand McNally.

Gall, M. D., Gall, J. P., & Borg, W. R. (2007). *Educational research: An introduction* (8th ed.). New York: Allyn & Bacon/Merrill.

Garberich, M. (2008). The nature of inspiration in artistic creativity (Doctoral dissertation). Retrieved from ProQuest Dissertations & Theses: Full Text. (AAT 3348106).

Gates, T. (1999). Music education research at the dawn of the third mediamorphosis. *Desert Skies Symposium, Tucson, Arizona, February 15–18. The University of Arizona.*

Gearing, R. E. (2004). Bracketing in research: A typology. *Qualitative Health Research, 14*(10), 1429–1452.

Geertz, C. (1973). Thick description: Toward an interpretive theory of culture. In *The interpretation of cultures* (pp. 3–30). New York: Basic Books.

Geringer, J. M., & Madsen, C. K. (2004). A fifteen-year history of the *Continuous Response Digital Response*: Issues relating to validity and reliability. *Bulletin of the Council for Research in Music Education, 160*, 1–15. Retrieved from JSTOR.com

Ghiselli, E. E., Campbell, J. P., & Zedeck, S. (1981). *Measurement theory for the behavioral sciences.* San Francisco, CA: Freeman.

Glaser, B. G., & Strauss, A. L. (1967). *The discovery of grounded theory: Strategies for qualitative research* [fourth paperback printing, 2009]. Piscataway, NJ: Transaction publishers. Retrieved November 20, 2011 from www.books.google.com

Glesne, C. (2011). *Becoming qualitative researchers: An introduction* (4th ed.). White Plains, NY: Longman.

Glover, A. (2002). The unreasonable logic of western epistemologies: Rhetoric, writing and the affective domain (Doctoral dissertation). Retrieved from ProQuest Dissertations & Theses: Full Text. (AAT 3087114).

Goble, J. S. (2009). Nationalism in United States music education during World War II. *Journal of Historical Research in Music Education, 30*(2), 103–117.

Goldman, A. (2006). Social epistemology. In E. N. Zalta (Ed.), (2010), *The Stanford encyclopedia of philosophy* (Summer 2010 edition). Retrieved February 18, 2011 from http://plato.stanford.edu/archives/sum2010/entries/epistemology-social/

Gordon, E. (1980). *Learning sequences in music: Skill, content, and patterns.* Chicago: G.I.A. Publications.

Gottschalk, L. A., & Bechtel, R. J. (Eds.). (2008). *Computerized content analysis of speech and verbal texts and its many applications.* New York: Nova Science Publishers.

Gould, E. (2005). Nomadic turns: epistemology, experience, and women university band directors. *Philosophy of Music Education Review, 13*(2), 147–164.

Gould, E. (2007). Legible bodies in music education: Becoming-matter. *Action, Criticism, and Theory for Music Education, 6*(4), 201–223. Retrieved May 25, 2011 from http://act.maydaygroup.org/articles/Gould6_4.pdf

Gouzouasis, P., Henrey, J., & Belliveau, G. (2008). Turning points: A transitional story of grade seven music students' participation in high school band programmes. *Music Education Research, 10*(1), 75–90.

Green, G. A. (1990). Effect of vocal modeling on pitch-matching accuracy of elementary school children. *Journal of Research in Music Education, 38*(3), 225–232.

Green, L. (2001). *How popular musicians learn: A case for music education.* Aldershot, UK, & Burlington VT: Ashgate.

Green, L. (Ed.). (2011). *Learning, teaching and musical identities. Voices across cultures.* Bloomington, IN: Indiana University Press.

Gregory, D. (1995). The Continuous Response Digital Interface: An analysis of reliability measures. Research note. *Psychomusicology, 14,* 197–208.

Gregory, D. (2009). Using clinical video excerpts to prompt music therapy majors' recall of related experiences and self-attributions of comfort and skill. *Journal of Music Therapy, 46*(4), 287–208.

Grissom, R. J., & Kim, J. K. (2005). *Effect sizes for research: A broad practical approach.* Mahwah, NJ: Lawrence Erlbaum.

Gronlund, N. E., & Waugh, C. K. (2009). *Assessment of student achievement.* Upper Saddle River, NJ: Pearson.

Gruhn, W. (2001). European "methods" for American nineteenth-century singing instruction: A cross-cultural perspective on historical research. *Journal of Historical Research in Music Education, 23*(1), 3–18.

Gumm, A. (2003). *Music teaching style. Moving beyond tradition.* Galesville, MD: Meredith Music Publishing, Inc.

Handel, G. A., & Humphreys, J. T. (2005). The Phoenix Indian school band, 1894–1930. *Journal of Historical Research in Music Education, 26*(2), 144–161.

Hansen, A. (2009). *Mass communication research methods.* London & Thousand Oaks, CA: Sage.

Hargreaves, D. J., & North, A. C. (Eds.). (2001). *Musical development and learning: The international perspective.* London & New York: Continuum.

Hart, A. (2007). *Gabriel's horses.* Atlanta: Peachtree.

Hart, C. (1998). *Doing a literature review. Releasing the social science research imagination.* London: Sage.

Hart, C. (2007) *Doing a literature search: A comprehensive guide for the social sciences.* London: Sage.

Harwood, E. (1993). Content and context in children's playground songs. *Update: Applications of Research in Music Education, 12*(1), 4–8.

Hash, P. M. (2008). History of Illinois School Band Association: 1924–1941. *Journal of Historical Research in Music Education, 30*(1), 4–20.

Haskell, J. A. (1987). Vocal self-perception: The other side of the equation. *Journal of Voice, 1*(2), 172–179.

Haslanger, S., Tuana, N., & O'Connor, P. (2011). Topics in feminism. In E. N. Zalta (Ed.), *The Stanford encyclopedia of philosophy* (Fall 2011 ed.). Retrieved October 15, 2011 from http://plato.stanford.edu/archives/fall2011/entries/feminism-topics

Haywood, J. (2006). You can't be in my choir if you can't stand up: One journey toward inclusion. *Music Education Research, 8*(3), 407–416. Retrieved July 6, 2009 from Academic Search Premier.

Hearne, V. (1995). Can an ape tell a joke? In T. Kidder (Ed.), *Best American essays of 1994.* New York: Ticknor and Fields.

Hegel, G. W. F. (1929). *The science of logic.* (W. H. Johnston and L. G. Struthers, Trans.). London: George Allen and Unwin.

Helfer, J. A. (2003). *Susanne K. Langer's epistemology of mind as an interpretive resource for music education* (Doctoral dissertation). Retrieved from ProQuest Dissertations & Theses: Full Text. (AAT 3101858).

Heller, G. N. (1995). *Historical research in music education: A bibliography* (3rd ed.). Lawrence, KS: The University of Kansas.

Heller, J. J., & O'Connor, J. P. (2002). Maintaining quality in research and reporting. In R. Colwell, & C. Richardson (Eds.), *The new handbook of research on music teaching and learning* (pp. 1089–1107). New York: Oxford University Press.

Henry, M. A., & Weber, A. (2010). *Supervising student teachers: The professional way.* New York: R&L Education.

Henry, N. B. (Ed.). (1958). *Basic concepts in music education.* Chicago, IL: University of Chicago Press.

Herrnstein, R. J., & Murray, C. A. (1994). *The bell curve: Intelligence and class structure in American life.* New York: Free Press.

History. (n.d.). In *Wikipedia.* Retrieved June 8, 2011 from www.wikipedia.org

Ho, W.-Ch. (2000). Political influences on curriculum content and musical meaning: Hong Kong secondary music education, 1949–1997. *Journal of Historical Research in Music Education, 22*(1), 5–24.

Hodges, D., & Sebald, D. (2011). *Music in the human experience: An introduction to music psychology.* New York: Routledge.

Hoffman, A. R. (2008). Gender, identity and the sixth grade band classroom. *Gender, Education, Music & Society, 4,* 1–12. Retrieved April 25, 2009 from www.queensu.ca/music/links/gems/hoffman5.pdf

Holsti, O. R. (1969). *Content analysis for the social sciences and humanities.* Reading, MA: Addison-Wesley.

Howe, S. W. (2009). A historical view of women in music education careers. *Philosophy of Music Education Review, 17*(2), 162–183.

Huck, S. W. (2012). *Reading statistics and research* (6th ed.). Boston, MA: Pearson.

Hult, C. A. (1996). *Researching and writing in the humanities and arts.* Boston: Allyn and Bacon.

Huxley, A. (1928/1996). *Point counter point.* Normal, IL: Dalkey Archive Press.

Isaacson, W. (2011). The genius of Jobs: Steve Job's biographer reflects. *The New York Times Sunday Review* (October 30), 1 & 8.

Isbell, D. (2006). The Steamboat Springs High School Ski Band, 1935–2005. *Journal of Historical Research in Music Education, 28*(1), 21–37.

Jackson, Y. (Ed.). (2006). *Encyclopedia of multicultural psychology.* Thousand Oaks, CA: Sage.

Jensen-Hole, C. (2005). *Experiencing the interdependent nature of musicianship and educatorship as defined by David J. Elliott in the context of the collegiate level vocal jazz ensemble* (Doctoral dissertation, University of North Texas). Retrieved May 18, 2007 from http://www.unt.edu/etd/all/August2005/Open/Jensen-Hole_catherine_mary/index.htm

Jevic, L., & Springgay, S. (2008). A/r/tography as an ethics of embodiment. Visual Journals in Preservice Education. *Qualitative Inquiry, 14*(1), 67–89. Retrieved October 16, 2011 from Sage Journals online.

Johnson, M., Nadas, R., & Green, S. (2010). Marking essays on screen and on paper. *Education Journal, 121,* 39–41.

Johnston, H. (1993). The use of video self-assessment, peer-assessment, and instructor feedback in evaluating conducting skills in music student teachers. *British Journal of Music Education, 10*(1), 57–63. doi:10.1017/S0265051700001431 (published online: December 18, 2008).

Jorgensen, E. R. (1995). Editorial. *Philosophy of Music Education Review* (special issue on phenomenology and music education), *3*(1), 1–2.

Juslin, P. N., & Sloboda, J. (2010). *Handbook of music and emotion: Theory, research, applications.* New York: Oxford University Press.

Justice, A. (2008). Wired music education page. In *University of North Texas Libraries.* Denton, TX: University of North Texas. Retrieved February 10, 2011 from http://www.library.unt.edu/music/music-resources/wired-music-education

Karpf, J. (2002). "Would that it were so in America!": William Bradbury's observations of European music educators, 1847–1849. *Journal of Historical Research in Music Education, 24*(1), 5–38.

Kedem, Y. (2008). *Performance, conservation, and creativity: Mentoring for musicianship in four string music studios* (Doctoral dissertation). Retrieved from ProQuest Dissertations & Theses: Full Text. (AAT 3337816).

Keefe, R. (2000). *Theories of vagueness.* Cambridge: Cambridge University Press.

Kemp, A. E., & Lepherd, L. (1992) Research methods in international and comparative music education. In R. Colwell (Ed.), *Handbook of research on music teaching and learning* (pp. 102–114). New York: Schirmer Books.

Kennedy, M. A. (2000). Creative music making since the time of the singing schools: Fringe benefits. *Journal of Historical Research in Music Education, 21,* 132–148.

Kerlinger, F. N. (1986). *Foundations of behavioral research* (3rd ed.). New York: Holt, Rinehart and Winston.

Kertz-Welzel, A. (2008). Music education in the twenty-first century: A cross-cultural comparison of German and American music education towards a new concept of international dialogue. *Music Education Research, 10*(4), 439–449.

Killian, J. N. (1990). Effect of model characteristics on musical preference of junior high school students. *Journal of Research in Music Education, 38*(2), 115–123.

King, N., & Horrocks, C. (2010). *Interviews in qualitative research.* London: Sage.

Kline, T. (2005). *Psychological testing: A practical approach to design and evaluation.* Thousand Oaks, CA: Sage.

Koenig, T. (2009). CAQDAS Comparison. In Economic and Social Research Council, *ReStore: A sustainable web resources repository* [website]. Swindon, U.K.: Author. Retrieved November 2, 2011 from http://www.restore.ac.uk/lboro/research/software/caqdas_comparison.php

Kos, R. P. (2007). *Incidental change: The influence of educational policy implementation on music education programs and practice* (Doctoral dissertation). Retrieved from ProQuest Digital Dissertations database (AAT 3261425).

Kou, M.-L. L. (2001). Development of music education in Taiwan (1895–1995). *Journal of Historical Research in Music Education, 22*(2), 177–190.

Krippendorff, K. (2004). *Content analysis: An introduction to its methodology* (2nd ed.). Thousand Oaks, CA: Sage.

Krippendorff, K., & Bock, M. A. (Eds.). (2009). *The content analysis reader.* Thousand Oaks, CA: Sage.

Kuehmann, K. M. (1987). *A theoretical model for curriculum development in general music for fundamentalist Christian elementary schools* (Doctoral dissertation). Retrieved from ProQuest Dissertations & Theses: Full Text. (AAT 8805484).

Kuhn, T. S. (1962/1970). *The structure of scientific revolutions* (2nd ed.). Chicago: University of Chicago Press.

Ladson-Billings, G. (2009). *The dreamkeepers: Successful teachers of African American children* (2nd ed.). San Francisco: Jossey-Bass.

Lamb, R., Dolloff, L., & Wieland Howe, S. (2002). Feminism, feminist research, and gender research in music education: A selective review. In R. Colwell, & C. Richardson (Eds.), *The new handbook of research on music learning and teaching* (pp. 648–774). New York: Oxford University Press.

Lamkin, J. R., II (2003). *Beyond the podium: A phenomenological investigation of the lifeworlds of experienced high school band directors* (Doctoral dissertation). Retrieved from ProQuest Dissertations & Theses: Full Text. (AAT 3115690).

Lather, P. (1991). *Getting smart: Feminist research and pedagogy with/in the postmodern.* London: Routledge.

Lather, P. (2006). Paradigm proliferation as a good thing to think with: Teaching research in education as a wild profusion. *International Journal of Qualitative Studies in Education, 19(1),* 35–57. Retrieved January 12, 2012 from http://people.ehe.ohio-state.edu/plather/files/2008/11/qse-06-me.pdf

Latukefu, L. (2010). Peer assessment in tertiary level singing: Changing and shaping culture through social interaction. *Research Studies in Music Education, 32(2),* 61–73.

Lee, A. H.-C. (2002). The influence of Japanese music education in Taiwan during the Japanese protectorate. *Journal of Historical Research in Music Education, 23(2),* 106–118.

Lee, W. R. (1982). *Education through music: The life and work of Charles Hubert Farnsworth (1859–1947)* (Doctoral dissertation). Retrieved from ProQuest Dissertations & Theses: Full Text. (AAT 8307271).

Lee, W. R. (1997). Music education and rural reform: 1900–1925. *Journal of Research in Music Education, 45(2),* 306–326.

Lee, W. R. (2002). Charles H. Farnsworth's "Music in the secondary school". *Journal of Historical Research in Music Education, 24(1),* 39–61.

Leedy, P. D., & Ormrod, J. E. (2001). *Practical research: Planning and design* (7th ed.). Upper Saddle River, NJ: Merrill Prentice Hall.

Lefrançois, G. R. (2000). *Psychology for teaching* (10th ed.). Belmont, CA: Wadsworth.

Legg, R. (2010). "One equal music": An exploration of gender perceptions and the fair assessment by beginning music teachers of musical compositions. *Music Education Research, 12(2),* 141–149.

Leonard, H. S. (1957). *Principles of right reason.* New York: Henry Holt.

Lepherd, L. (Ed.). (1995). *Music education in international perspective: National systems.* Toowoomba, QD, Australia: University of Southern Queensland Press.

Lisk, E. S. (1991). *The creative director: Alternative rehearsal techniques* (3rd ed.). Ft. Lauderdale: Meredith Music Publications.

Livingston, C., & Smith, D. E. (Eds.). (2008). *Rhode Island's musical heritage: An exploration.* Sterling Heights, MI: Harmonie Park Press.

Loewenberg, P. (1983/1985/1996). *Decoding the past: The psychological approach.* New Brunswick, NJ: Transaction Publishers.

Louth, J. (2008). *Music, metaphor, and ideology: Toward a critical theory of forms in music education* (Doctoral dissertation). Retrieved from ProQuest Dissertations & Theses, Full Text. (ATT NR39299).

Lubke, G. H., & Muthen, B. O. (2004). Applying multigroup confirmatory factor models for continuous outcomes to Likert scale data complicates meaningful group comparisons. *Structural Equation Modeling, 11,* 514–534.

Macarthur, S. (2002). *Feminist aesthetics in music.* Westport, CT; London: Greenwood Press.

Madsen, C. K., Prickett, C. A., Gates, J. T., & Alabama Project (1987). *Applications of research in music behavior.* With a foreword by J. Terry Gates. Tuscaloosa, AL: University of Alabama Press.

Madsen, C. K., Greer, R. G., & Madsen, C. H. (Eds.). (1975). *Research in music behavior: Modifying music behavior in the classroom.* New York: Teachers College Press.

Malterud, K. (2001). Qualitative research: Standards, challenges, and guidelines. *The Lancet, 358* (August), 483–488. Retrieved July 6, 2011 from http://www.dmcgpal.dk/files/malterud_lancet2001

Manen, M., van (1990). *Researching lived experience: Human science for an action sensitive pedagogy.* Ontario, Canada: The Althouse Press.

Mang, E. H. S. (1997). The effects of training with male and female vocal modeling on the melodic singing achievement of grade one children. *Canadian Music Educator, 38(4),* 25–34.

Mark, M. L. (1980). The Music Educators National Conference and World War II home front programs. *Bulletin of Historical Research in Music Education, 1(1),* 1–16.

Mark, M. (1992). *A history of music education research*. In R. Colwell, *Handbook of research on music teaching and learning* (pp. 48–59). New York: Schirmer Books.

Mark, M. L. (Ed.). (2008). *Music education: Source readings from Ancient Greece to today* (3rd ed.). New York & London: Routledge.

Marsh, K. (2008). *The musical playground: Global tradition and change in children's songs and games*. New York: Oxford University Press.

Mautner, T. (2005). *The Penguin dictionary of philosophy*. New York: Penguin Books.

May, L. F. (2005). Early musical development of selected African American jazz musicians in Indianapolis in the 1930s and 1940s. *Journal of Historical Research in Music Education, 27*(1), 21–32.

McCarthy, M. (1993). The birth of internationalism in music education, 1899–1938. *International Journal of Music Education, 21*, 3–15.

McCarthy, M. (1995). *Canticle to hope:* Widening horizons in international music education, 1939–1953. *International Journal of Music Education, 25*, 38–49.

McCarthy, M. (1999). *The Bulletin of Historical Research in Music Education*: A content analysis of articles in the first twenty volumes. *Bulletin of Historical Research in Music Education, 20*(3), 181–202.

McCarthy, M. (2002). The past in the present: Revitalising history in music education. *British Journal of Music Education, 20*(2), 121–134.

McCarthy, M. (2004). *Toward a global community: The International Society for Music Education 1953–2003*. Nedlands, Perth: International Society for Music Education.

McCarthy, M. (2007). Narrative inquiry as a way of knowing in music education. *Research Studies in Music Education, 29*(3), 3–12.

McCarthy, M. (2011). A content analysis of articles published in volumes 21–30 of the *Journal of Historical Research in Music Education*: Assessing development and trends in historical research. Paper presented at the Chattanooga Symposium on the History of Music Education. Chattanooga, TN, June 2–4.

Medley, D. H., & Mitzel, H. E. (1963). Measuring classroom behavior by systematic observation. In N. L. Gage (Ed.), *Handbook of research on teaching* (pp. 247–328). New York: Teachers College Press.

Merriam, S. B. (2002). Qualitative research in practice: Examples for discussion and analysis. San Francisco, CA: Jossey-Bass.

Meyer, D. Z., & Avery, L. M. (2009). Excel as a qualitative data analysis tool. *Field Methods, 21*, 91–112. Retrieved November 22, 2011 from www.sagepub.com

Miksza, Peter. (2006). Relationships among impulsiveness, locus of control, sex, and music practice. *Journal of Research in Music Education, 54*(4), 308–323. Retrieved March 22, 2008 from the Academic Search Premier database.

Mitchell, M. L., & Jolley, J. M. (2009). *Research design explained* (7th ed.). Belmont, CA: Wadsworth.

Mithen, S. J. (2006). *The singing Neanderthals: The origins of music, language, mind, and body*. Cambridge, MA: Harvard University Press.

Modern Language Association. (2009). *MLA handbook for writers of research papers* (7th ed.). New York: Author.

Moga, E., Burger, K., Hetland, L., & Winner, E. (2000). Does studying the arts engender creative thinking? Evidence for near but not far transfer. *The Journal of Aesthetic Education, 34*(3–4), 91–104.

Montemayor, M., & Moss, E. A. (2009). Effects of recorded models on novice teachers' rehearsal verbalizations, evaluations, and conducting. *Journal of Research in Music Education, 57*(3), 236–251. Retrieved January 12, 2011 from EBSCOhost.

Moore, D. S. (1985). *Statistics: Concepts and controversies* (2nd ed.). New York: W. H. Freeman.

Moorhead, G. E., & Pond, D. (1978/1941, 1942, 1944, 1951). *Music of young children* (Reprinted from original, 4 v. in 1). Santa Barbara, CA: Pillsbury Foundation for the Advancement of Music Education.

Mortyakowa, J. (2011). *Existential piano teacher: The application of Jean-Paul Sartre's philosophy to piano instruction in a higher educational setting* (Doctoral dissertation). Retrieved from ProQuest Dissertations & Theses. Full Text (AAT 3358229).

Motulsky, H. J. (1995). *Intuitive biostatistics*. New York: Oxford University Press. Chapter 37 retrieved January 28, 2012 from http://www.graphpad.com/www/book/choose.htm

Moustakas, C. (1994). *Phenomenological research methods*. Thousand Oaks, CA: Sage.

Music as epistemology: from a letter to a Finnish theoretician. (n.d.). Retrieved February 18, 2011 from http://www.nachtschimmen.eu/_pdf/9802_NAN.pdf

Music Educators National Conference. (1988, February). Special Issue: The Sesquicentennial. *Music Educators Journal, 74*(6).

Music Educators National Conference. (2007). *MENC: A century of service to music education 1907–2007*. Reston, VA: MENC: The National Association for Music Education.

Nagao, I. (2000). A synchronous approach to two great music educators: Peter William Dykema and Koji Nagai. *Journal of Historical Research in Music Education, 21*(2), 149–161.

Nelson, S. L. (2004). The use of creativity in music textbook series, 1900–1950. *Journal of Historical Research in Music Education, 25,* 128–141.

Neuendorf, K. A. (2002). *The content analysis guidebook.* Thousand Oaks, CA: Sage.

Neuendorf, K. A. (2006). *The content analysis guidebook online.* Retrieved on July 9, 2011 from http://academic.csuohio.edu/kneuendorf/content/index.htm

Nichols, J. (2005). Music education in home schooling: A preliminary inquiry. *Bulletin of the Council for Research in Music Education, 166,* 27–42.

Nicolson, S., & Shipstead, S. G. (2002). *Through the looking glass: Observations in the early childhood classroom* (3rd ed.). Upper Saddle River, NJ: Merrill Prentice-Hall.

Niebur, L. L. (1997). *Standards, assessment, and stories of practice in general music* (Doctoral dissertation). Retrieved from ProQuest Digital Dissertations (AAT 9725323).

Norkunas, M. (2011). Teaching to listen: Listening exercises and self-reflexive journals. *The Oral History Review, 38*(1), 63–108. Retrieved September 10, 2011 from Oxford Journals Online.

North, A. C., & Hargreaves, D. J. (1999). Music and adolescent identity. *Music Education Research, 1*(1), 75–92.

Nunnally, J., & Bernstein, I. (1994). *Psychometric theory* (3rd ed.). New York: McGraw Hill.

Oral History Association. www.oralhistory.org. Accessed January 10, 2012.

Orrel, M. S. (1995). *The work of Grace C. Nash in music education in the United States, 1960–1990, and her influence upon members of the American Orff-Schulwerk Association in the states of Arizona and Colorado* (Doctoral dissertation). Retrieved from ProQuest Dissertations & Theses. Full Text. (ATT 9611456).

Pallant, J. (2007). *SPSS survival manual* (3rd ed.). New York: Open University Press, McGraw-Hill Education.

para-. (2011). *Collins English dictionary: Complete and unabridged* (10th ed.). Retrieved January 15, 2012 from http://dictionary.reference.com/browse/para-

Patton, M. Q. (2001). *Qualitative evaluation and research methods* (3rd ed.). Thousand Oaks, CA: Sage.

Pemberton, C. A. (1987). Revisionist historians: Writers reflected in their writings. *Journal of Research in Music Education, 35*(4), 213–220.

Pemberton, C. (1992). Research in music education: One historian's experiences, perspectives, and suggestions. *Contribution to Music Education, 19,* 87–100.

Pemberton, C. A. (1999). Unconventional wisdom: Observing how research, writing and editing fly in the face of clichés. *Bulletin of Historical Research in Music Education, 20*(2), 115–120.

Phelps, R. P., Sadoff, R. H., Warburton, E. C., & Ferrara, L. (2005). *A guide to research in music education* (5th ed.). Lanham, MD: Scarecrow Press.

Phillips, D. C., & Burbules, N. C. (2000). *Postpositivism and educational research.* Lanham, MD: Rowman and Littlefield.

Phillips, K. H. (2007). *Exploring research in music education and music therapy.* New York: Oxford University Press.

Phillips, K. H., & Doneski, S. M. (2011). Research on elementary and secondary school singing. In R. Colwell, & P. R. Webster (Eds.), *MENC handbook of research on music learning*: Vol. 2. Applications (pp. 176–232). New York: Oxford University Press.

Pidwirny, M., & Jones, S. (2010). *Fundamentals of physical geography: Chapter 3* (e-book), (2nd ed.). Okanagan, BC: University of British Columbia Okanagan. Retrieved February 9, 2011 from http://www.physicalgeography.net/fundamentals/contents.html

Pigliucci, M. (2009). *Ah, metaphysics! Do we need metaphysics anymore?* [Weblog post]. Retrieved February 23, 2011 from http://www.psychologytoday.com/blog/rationally-speaking/200909/ah-metaphysics

Ponterotto, J. G., & Grieger, I. (1999). Merging qualitative and quantitative perspectives in a research identity. In M. Kopala, & L. A. Suzuki (Eds.), *Using qualitative methods in psychology* (pp. 49–62). Thousand Oaks, CA: Sage.

Popper, K. R. (1945). *The open society and its enemies.* London: Routledge.

Popper, K. R. (1959). *The logic of scientific discovery.* New York: Basic Books.

Popper, K. R. (1968). *Conjectures and refutations: The growth of scientific knowledge.* New York: Harper & Row.

Preston, K. Y., & Humphreys, J. T. (2007). Historical research on music education and music therapy: Doctoral dissertations of the twentieth century. *Journal of Historical Research in Music Education, 29*(1), 55–73.

Price, H. (1992). Sequential patterns of music instruction and learning to use them. *Journal of Research in Music Education, 40*(1), 14–29.

Price, H. (Eds.). (1998). *Music education research: An anthology from the* Journal of Research in Music Education. Washington, DC: Music Educators National Conference.

Price, H. E., & Yarbrough, C. (1993/1994). Effect of scripted sequential patterns of instruction in music rehearsals on teaching evaluations by college nonmusic majors. *Bulletin of the Council for Research in Music Education, 119,* 170–178.

Prior, L. (2008). Researching documents: Emerging methods. In S. N. Hesse-Biber, & P. Leavy (Eds.), *Handbook of emergent methods* (pp. 111–126). New York: The Guilford Press.

Rainbow, E., & Froehlich, H. (1987). *Research in music education: An introduction to systematic inquiry.* New York: Schirmer Books.

Rao, Doreen (1988). *Craft, singing craft and musical experience: A philosophical study with implications for vocal music education as aesthetic education* (Doctoral dissertation). Retrieved from ProQuest Dissertations & Theses: Full Text. (AAT 8902692).

Rauscher, J. L. (1996). A comparison of vocal techniques, timbres, and ranges considered aesthetically pleasing in western and non-western cultures. *Missouri Journal of Research in Music Education, 33,* 55.

Rauscher, F. H., Shaw, G. L., & Ky, K.N. (1993). Music and spatial task performance. *Nature, 365*(6447), 611.

Redfield, M. (2003). *The politics of aesthetics: nationalism, gender, romanticism.* Stanford, CA: Stanford University Press.

Reese, J. W. (2006). Definitions of improvisation: Perspectives of three elementary general music teachers (Master's thesis). Retrieved from Proquest Digital Dissertations (AAT 1440086).

Regelski, T., & Gates, T. (Eds.). (2009). *Music education for changing times: Guiding visions for practice (landscapes: the arts, aesthetics, and education).* Dordrecht: Springer.

Reimer, B. (1992). Toward a philosophical foundation for music education research. In R. Colwell (Ed.), *Handbook of research on music teaching and learning* (pp. 21–37). New York: Schirmer Books.

Reimer, B. (2008). Research in music education: Personal and professional reflections in a time of perplexity: 2008 senior researcher award acceptance speech. *Journal of Research in Music Education, 56*(3), 190–204.

Revkin, L. K. (1984). *An historical and philosophical inquiry into the development of Dalcroze eurhythmics and its influence on music education in the French cantons of Switzerland* (Doctoral dissertation). Retrieved from ProQuest Dissertations & Theses: Full Text. (AAT 8411180).

Richardson, L., & St. Pierre, E. (2005). Writing: A method of inquiry. In N. Denzin, & Y. Lincoln (Eds.), *Handbook of qualitative research* (3rd ed.) (pp. 959–978). Thousand Oaks, CA: Sage.

Ritchie, D. A. (2003). *Doing oral history: A practical guide* (2nd ed.). Oxford & New York: Oxford University Press.

Rosenshine, B., & Furst, N. (1973). The use of direct observation to study teaching. In R. M. W. Travers (Ed.), *Second handbook of research on teaching* (pp. 122–183). Chicago: Rand McNally.

Rothchild, I. (2006). *Induction, deduction, and the scientific method: An eclectic overview of the practice of science.* Madison, WI: Society for the Study of Reproduction. Retrieved September 19, 2011 from http://www.ssr.org/Induction.shtml

Roulston, K. (2006). Mapping the possibilities of qualitative research in music education: A primer. *Music Education Research, 8*(2), 153–173.

Roulston, K., & Misawa, M. (2011). Music teachers' constructions of gender in elementary education. *Music Education Research, 13*(1), 3–28.

Runfola, M., & Swanwick, K. (2002). Developmental characteristics of music learners. In R. Colwell, & C. Richardson (Eds.), *The new handbook of research on music teaching and learning* (pp. 373–397). New York: Oxford University Press.

Ruppert, S. S. (2006). *Critical evidence: How the arts benefit student achievement.* Washington, DC: National Assembly of State Arts Agencies. Retrieved January 22, 2010 from http://www.nasaa-arts.org/publications/critical-evidence.pdf

Russell, B. (1959). *Wisdom of the West: A historical survey of Western philosophy in its social and political setting.* Garden City, NY: Doubleday.

Saint-Andre, P. (1996). *The ism book.* Retrieved July 25, 2011 from http://www.ismbook.com/ismlist.html

Saldaňa, J. (2008). Second chair: An ethnodrama. *Research Studies in Music Education, 30,* 177–191. Retrieved January 21, 2012 from http://rsm.sagepub.com/content/30/2/177

Savage, J. (2010). *A phenomenology of contemporary flute improvisation: Contextual explications of techniques, aesthetics, and performance practices* (Doctoral dissertation). Retrieved from ProQuest Dissertations & Theses: Full Text. (AAT 3426969).

Schaeffer, R. L., Gnanadesikan, M., Watkins, A., & Witmer, J. A. (1996). *Activity-based statistics.* New York: Springer.

Schmidt, C. P. (1996). Research with the Continuous Response Digital Interface: A review with implications for future research. *Philosophy of Music Education Review, 4*(1), 20–32. Retrieved November 6, 2011 from JSTOR.com

Schmidt, M., & Knowles, J. G. (1995). Four women's stories of "failure" as beginning teachers. *Teacher and Teacher Education, 11*(5), 429–444.

Schoenfeld, A. H. (1999). The core, the canon, and the development of research skills: Issues in the preparation of education researchers. In E. C., Lagemann, & L. S. Shulman (Eds.), *Issues in education research: Problems and possibilities* (pp. 166–202). San Francisco: Jossey-Bass.

Schwandt, T. A. (2003). Three epistemological stances for qualitative inquiry: Interpretivism, hermeneutics, and social constructionism. In N. K. Denzin, & Y. S. Lincoln (Eds.), *The landscape of qualitative research: Theories and issues* (2nd ed.) (pp. 292–331). Thousand Oaks, CA: Sage.

Sciarra, D. (1999). The role of the qualitative researcher. In M. Kopala, & L. A. Suzuki (Eds.), *Using qualitative methods in psychology* (pp. 37–48). Thousand Oaks, CA: Sage.

Scruton, R. (1997). *The aesthetics of music*. New York: Oxford University Press.

Seddon, F., & Biasutti, M. (2010) Strategies students adopted when learning to play an improvised blues in an e-learning environment. *Journal of Research in Music Education, 58*(2), 147–167.

Shadish, W. R., Cook, T. D., & Campbell, D. T. (2001). *Experimental and quasi-experimental designs for generalized causal inference*. Beverly, MA: Wadsworth.

Shehan-Campbell, P. (2010). *Songs in their heads. Music and its meaning in children's lives* (2nd ed.). New York: Oxford University Press.

Shopes, L. (2011). Oral history. In N. K. Denzin, & Y. S. Lincoln (Eds.), *The SAGE handbook of qualitative research* (4th ed.) (pp. 451–465). Thousand Oaks, CA: Sage.

Shulman, L. S. (1999). Professing educational scholarship. In E. C. Lagemann, & L. S. Shulman (Eds.), *Issues in education research: Problems and possibilities* (pp. 159–165). San Francisco: Jossey-Bass.

Siegel, S., & Castellan, N. J. (1988). *Nonparametric statistics for the behavioral sciences* (2nd ed.). Boston, MA: McGraw-Hill.

Silvey, P. E. (2005). Learning to perform Benjamin Britten's "Rejoice in the Lamb": The perspectives of three high school choral singers. *Journal of Research in Music Education, 53*(2), 102–119.

Sink, P. E. (2002). Behavioral research on direct music instruction. In R. Colwell, & C. Richardson (Eds.), *The new handbook of research on music teaching and learning* (pp. 327–347). New York: Oxford University Press.

Sloboda, J. (2005). *Exploring the musical mind*. New York: Oxford University Press.

Small, A., & McCachern, F. (1983). Effect of male and female vocal modeling on pitch-matching accuracy of first-grade children. *Journal of Research in Music Education, 31*(3), 227–234.

Small, C. (1977/1996). *Music-society-education: A radical examination of the prophetic function of music in Western, Eastern and African cultures with its impact on society and its use in education*. London: Calder. Re-print in 1996 as *Music, society, education*. With a new foreword by Robert Walser. Hanover, NH: University Press of New England/Wesleyan University Press.

Small, C. (1997). Musicking: A ritual in social space. In R. Rideout (Ed.), *On the Sociology of music education* (pp. 1–12). Proceedings of the Oklahoma Symposium for Music Education in April, 1995, Oklahoma University School of Music, Norman, Oklahoma.

Small, C. (1987/1998a). *Music of the common tongue: Survival and celebration in African American music*. London: J. Calder, New York: Riverrun Press. Re-printed in 1998 by Hanover, NH: University Press of New England/Wesleyan University Press.

Small, C. (1998b). *Musicking. The meanings of performing and listening*. Hanover, NH: University Press of New England/Wesleyan University Press.

Smith, D. W. (2011). Phenomenology. In E. N. Zalta (Ed.), *The Stanford encyclopedia of philosophy* (Fall 2011 ed.). Retrieved September 26, 2011 from http://plato.stanford.edu/archives/fall2011/entries/phenomenology

Sorensen, R. (2001). *Vagueness and contradiction*. Oxford: Clarendon Press.

Spector, P. E. (1976). Choosing response categories for summated rating scales. *Journal of Applied Psychology, 61*, 374–375.

Spector, P. E. (1980). Ratings of equal and unequal response choice intervals. *Journal of Social Psychology, 112*, 115–119.

Springgay, S., Irwin, R. L., Leggo, C., & Gouzouasis, P. (Eds.). (2007). A/R/Tography. Rotterdam, NL: Sense Publishers.

St. Pierre, E. A. (2008). Afterword: Decentering voice in qualitative inquiry. In A. Y. Jackson, & L. A. Mazzei (Eds.), *Voice in qualitative inquiry: Challenging conventional interpretive and critical conceptions in qualitative research* (pp. 221–236). New York: Routledge. Retrieved January 25, 2012 from www.books.Google.com

St. Pierre, E. A., & Roulston, K. (2006). The state of qualitative inquiry: A contested science. *International Journal of Qualitative Studies in Education, 19*(6), 673–684. Retrieved November 5, 2011 from http://www.petajwhite.net/Uni/910/Legit%20and%20Representation/Representation%20Precis/St%20Pierre%20and%20Roulston.pdf

Stake, R. (1995). *The art of case study research*. Thousand Oaks, CA: Sage.

Stake, R., Bresler, L., & Mabry, L. (1991). *Custom and cherishing: The arts in elementary schools.* Urbana-Champaign: Council for Research in Music Education, School of Music, University of Illinois.

Standley, J. M., & Madsen, C. K. (1991). An observation procedure to differentiate teaching experience and expertise in music education. *Journal of Research in Music Education, 39*(1), 5–11. Downloaded from jrm.sagepub.com at University of North Texas Library on July 20, 2011.

Steele, K. M., Dalla Bella, S., Peretz, I., Dunlop, T., Dawe, L. A., Humphrey, G. K., Shannon, R. A., Kirby Jr., J. L., & Olmstead, C. G. (1999). Prelude or requiem for the "Mozart effect"? *Nature, 400,* 827. Retrieved January 31, 2011 from http://www1.appstate.edu/~kms/research/Steele.htm

Stephenson, G. M., Wagner, W., & Brandstatter, H. (1983). An experimental study of social performance and delay on the testimonial validity of story recall. *European Journal of Social Psychology, 13*(2), 175–191. First published online: February 22, 2006, DOI: 10.1002/ejsp.2420130207. Retrieved July 20, 2011 from http://onlinelibrary.wiley.com/doi/10.1002/ejsp.2420130207/abstract

Stone, L. (1979). The revival of narrative: Reflections on a new old history. *Past and Present, 85,* 3–24.

Strauss, A., & Corbin, J. (1990). *Basics of qualitative research: Grounded theory procedures and techniques.* Newbury Park, CA: Sage.

Strauss, A. L., & Corbin, J. M. (1998). *Basics of qualitative research: Techniques and procedures for developing grounded theory.* Thousand Oaks, CA: Sage Publications.

Strike, K., & Posner, G. (1983). Types of synthesis and their criteria. In S. A. Ward, & L. J. Reed (Eds.), *Knowledge structure and use: Implications for synthesis and interpretation* (pp. 345–362). Philadelphia, PA: Temple University Press.

Swanwick, K. (2011). Musical development: Revisiting a generic theory. In R. Colwell, & P. R. Webster (Eds.), *MENC Handbook of research on music learning*: Vol. 1. Strategies (pp. 173–215). New York: Oxford University Press.

Terrell, F., & Terrell, S. (1981). An inventory to measure cultural mistrust among Blacks. *Western Journal of Black Studies, 5*(3), 180–185.

Terrell, F., & Terrell, S. (1993). African-American cultures. In W. D. Battle (Ed.), *Communication disorders in multicultural populations* (pp. 3–7). Boston: Andover Medical Publishers.

Thelwall, M. (2009). *Introduction to webometrics: Quantitative web research for the social sciences.* San Rafael, CA: Morgan & Claypool Publishers. [Digital file]

Thorndike, R. M. (1997). *Measurement and evaluation in psychology and education* (6th ed.). Upper Saddle River, NJ: Merrill, an imprint of Prentice-Hall.

Thorndike, R. M., & Thorndike-Christ, T. M. (2010). *Measurement and evaluation in psychology and education* (8th ed.). New York: Pearson.

Tracy, S. J. (2010). Qualitative quality: Eight "big-tent" criteria for excellent qualitative research. *Qualitative Inquiry, 16,* 837–851. Retrieved July 29, 2011 from Sage Journals Online.

Tragesser, R. S. (1977). *Phenomenology and logic.* Ithaca: Cornell University Press.

Travers, R. M. W. (Ed.). (1973). *Second handbook of research on teaching.* A project of the American Educational Research Association. Chicago: Rand McNally.

Tsai, J. L., Chentsova-Dutton, Y., & Wong, Y. (2002). Why and how researchers should study ethnic identity, acculturation, and cultural orientation. In G. C. N. Hall, & S. Okazaki (Eds.), *Asian American psychology: The science of lives in context.* Washington, DC: American Psychological Association. Retrieved November 28, 2010 from http://www-psych.stanford.edu/~tsailab/PDF/Why%20and %20How%20 Researchers%20Should%20Study%20Ethnic%20Identity.pdf

Turabian, K. L., Booth, W. C., Colomb, G. G., & Williams, J. M. (2008). *A manual for writers of term papers, theses, and dissertations* (7th ed.). Chicago: University of Chicago Press.

University of Chicago Press. (2010). *The Chicago manual of style* (16th ed.). Chicago: Author.

Urbaniak, G. C., & Plous, S. (2011). *Research randomizer (Version 3.0).* Retrieved on January 11, 2012 from http://www.randomizer.org/

VanWelden, K. (2004). Racially stereotyped music and conductor race: Perceptions of performance. *Bulletin of the Council for Research in Music Education, 160,* 38–48. Retrieved November 6, 2011 from JSTOR.com

Vaughn, K., & Winner, E. (2000). SAT scores of students who study the arts: What we can and cannot conclude about the association. *Journal of Aesthetic Education, 34*(3–4), 77–89.

Vogt, J. (2003). Philosophy–music education–curriculum: Some casual remarks on some basic concepts. *Action, Criticism, and Theory for Music Education, 2*(1, September 2003), 2–25. Retrieved November 4, 2011 from http://act.maydaygroup.org/articles/Vogt2_1.pdf

Volk, T. M. (2007). Anne Shaw Faulkner Oberndorfer (1877–1948): Music educator for the homemakers of America. *Journal of Historical Research in Music Education, 29*(1), 26–39.

Walker, L. N. (2009). Stories from the front. In M. Barrett, & S. Stauffer (Eds.), *Narrative inquiry in music education: Troubling certainty* (pp. 179–194). Dordrecht, NL: Springer Science + Media Business.

Ward-Steinman, P. M. (2003). Musical training and compensation in the Big Band era: A case study of Madura's Danceland from 1930–1950. *Journal of Historical Research in Music Education, 24*(2), 164–177.

Warnock, E. C. (2009). The anti-semitic origins of Henry Ford's arts education patronage. *Journal of Historical Research in Music Education, 30*(2), 79–102.

Wasiak, E. B. (2000). School bands in Saskatchewan, Canada: A history. *Journal of Historical Research in Music Education, 21*(2), 112–131.

Waxman, H. C., Tharp, R. G., & Hilberg, R. S. (Eds.). (2004). *Observational research in U.S. classrooms: New approaches for understanding cultural and linguistic diversity.* Cambridge, UK, & New York: Cambridge University Press.

Welch, G. F. (2000). The ontogenesis of musical behaviour: A sociological perspective. *Research Studies in Music Education, 14*(1), 1–13.

Welch, G. F., & White, P. (1994). The developing voice: Education and vocal efficiency, a physical perspective. *Bulletin of the Council for Research in Music Education, 119*, 146–156.

Weston, A. (2009). *A rulebook for arguments.* (4th ed.). Indianapolis & Cambridge: Hackett Publishing Company, Inc.

Whale, M. (2009). *Music as the between: The idea of meeting in existence, music and education* (Doctoral dissertation). Retrieved from ProQuest Dissertations & Theses: Full Text. (AAT NR60888).

Whalen, M. (2008). *Charles L. Gary: His contribution to and perspective on music education in the United States* (Doctoral dissertation). Retrieved from ProQuest Dissertations & Theses: Full Text. (AAT 3294711).

Whaley, A. L. (2001). Cultural mistrust and mental health services for African Americans: A review and meta-analysis. *The Counseling Psychologist, 29*, 513. Retrieved November 15, 2010 from tcp.sagepub.com

Wheelwright, P. (1962). *Valid thinking: An introduction to logic.* New York: Odyssey Press.

Wikipedia Free Dictionary/Glossary of Philosophical Isms. Retrieved July 25, 2011 from http://en.wiktionary.org/wiki/Appendix:Glossary.

Williams, B. B. (1990). *An investigation of selected female singing and speaking-voice characteristics through comparison of a group of pre-menarcheal girls to a group of post-menarcheal girls.* Doctoral Dissertation, University of North Texas.

Williams, B. J. (2010). *Music composition pedagogy: A history, philosophy and guide* (Doctoral dissertation). Retrieved from ProQuest Dissertations & Theses: Full Text. (AAT 3424619).

Williams, D. A., & Shannon, S. G. (Eds.). (2004). *August Wilson and Black aesthetics.* New York & Houndmills, Basingstoke, UK: Palgrave Macmillan.

Willingham, D. T. (2007, Summer). Critical thinking: Why is it so hard to teach? *American Educator, 31*(2), 8–19. Retrieved November 3, 2011 from http://www.aft.org/pdfs/americaneducator/summer2007/Crit_Thinking.pdf

Wood, G. S. (2008). *The purpose of the past: Reflections on the use of history.* New York: The Penguin Press.

Worrell, F. C., & Gardner-Kitt, D. L. (2006). The relationship between racial and ethnic identity in Black adolescents: The Cross Racial Identity Scale and the Multigroup Ethnic Identity Measure. *Identity: An International Journal of Theory and Research, 6*(4), 293–315.

Yarbrough, C. (1985). The relationship of behavioral self-assessment to the achievement of basic conducting skills. *Journal of Research in Music Education, 35*(3), 183–189.

Yarbrough, C. (1996). The future of scholarly inquiry in music education: 1996 senior researcher award acceptance address. *Journal of Research in Music Education, 44*(3), 190–203.

Yarbrough, C. (2008). *An introduction to scholarship in music.* San Diego, CA: University Readers.

Yin, R. K. (Ed.). (2003). *Case study research: Design and methods* (3rd ed.). Applied Social Research Methods Series, Vol. 5. Thousand Oaks, CA: Sage.

Zalanowski, A., & Stratton, V. (2000). Focus of attention to elements of culturally familiar and unfamiliar music. *ISME Yearbook, 24*, 452–455.

About the Authors

Hildegard Froehlich, Professor Emeritus, College of Music, University of North Texas, continues to be professionally active as a national and international consultant, teacher, and lecturer about the learning and teaching of music in higher education. Her most recent book (2007) is *Sociology for Music Teachers: Perspectives for Practice*. She has kept active musically by co-founding (in 1976), directing, and now singing with the Denton Bach Chorus of the Denton Bach Society in Denton, Texas.

Carol Frierson-Campbell, currently Chair and Associate Professor of Music at William Paterson University, teaches undergraduate and graduate courses in instrumental music education and research. Her primary research interests include music education in inner-city settings and the development of research skills for graduate-level music education students. Her two-volume book *Teaching Music in the Urban Classroom* is a result of one of those interests; this textbook is a result of the other.

Debbie Rohwer is Professor and Chair of Music Education at the University of North Texas. She also directs and facilitates the Denton New Horizons Senior Citizen Band, which she initially organized in 1997, and she serves as the Chair of the Adult and Community Music Education Special Research Interest Group through MENC. Dr. Rohwer's research on the topic of music learning with children and adults has been published extensively in national and international journals and books.

Marie McCarthy is Professor of Music Education at the University of Michigan where she teaches courses on general music and a range of graduate seminars in music education. Her research interests include the social, cultural, and historical foundations of music education, the processes of music transmission across cultures, and spiritual dimensions of music education. Her publications include two books: *Passing It On: The Transmission of Music in Irish Culture*, and *Toward a Global Community: A History of the International Society for Music Education, 1953–2003*.

Darryl A. Coan is Professor of Music Education at Southern Illinois University Edwardsville. He completed his doctoral work at University of Illinois Urbana-Champaign in 1992. He helped found and produce *Action, Criticism and Theory for Music Education* (http://act.maydaygroup.org), a peer-reviewed journal of the Mayday Group (http://www.maydaygroup.org).

Index